The Gothic Forms of Victorian Poetry

Edinburgh Critical Studies in Victorian Culture

Recent books in the series:

Reading Ideas in Victorian Literature: Literary Content as Artistic Experience
Patrick Fessenbecker

Home and Identity in Nineteenth-Century Literary London
Lisa C. Robertson

Writing the Sphinx: Literature, Culture and Egyptology
Eleanor Dobson

Oscar Wilde and the Radical Politics of the Fin de Siècle
Deaglán Ó Donghaile

The Sculptural Body in Victorian Literature: Encrypted Sexualities
Patricia Pulham

New Media and the Rise of the Popular Woman Writer, 1832–1860
Alexis Easley

Elizabeth Robins Pennell: Critical Essays
Dave Buchanan and Kimberly Morse-Jones

Reading Bodies in Victorian Fiction: Associationism, Empathy and Literary Authority
Peter Katz

The Alternative Modernity of the Bicycle in British and French Literature, 1880 – 1920
Una Brogan

The Gothic Forms of Victorian Poetry
Olivia Loksing Moy

For a complete list of titles published visit the Edinburgh Critical Studies in Victorian Culture web page at www.edinburghuniversitypress.com/series/ECVC

Also available:
Victoriographies – A Journal of Nineteenth-Century Writing, 1790–1914, edited by Diane Piccitto and Patricia Pulham
ISSN: 2044-2416
www.eupjournals.com/vic

The Gothic Forms of Victorian Poetry

Olivia Loksing Moy

EDINBURGH
University Press

*To Victoria, Olympia, Jubilant,
James, and Elma Moy*

Edinburgh University Press is one of the leading university presses in the UK. We publish academic books and journals in our selected subject areas across the humanities and social sciences, combining cutting-edge scholarship with high editorial and production values to produce academic works of lasting importance. For more information visit our website: edinburghuniversitypress.com

© Olivia Loksing Moy 2024

Edinburgh University Press Ltd
13 Infirmary Street
Edinburgh EH1 1LT

Typeset in 11/13 Adobe Sabon
by Manila Typesetting Company

A CIP record for this book is available from the British Library

ISBN 978 1 4744 8718 4 (paperback)
ISBN 978 1 4744 8717 7 (hardback)
ISBN 978 1 4744 8719 1 (webready PDF)
ISBN 978 1 4744 8720 7 (epub)

The right of Olivia Loksing Moy to be identified as the author of this work has been asserted in accordance with the Copyright, Designs and Patents Act 1988, and the Copyright and Related Rights Regulations 2003 (SI No. 2498).

Contents

List of Illustrations	vi
Acknowledgments	viii
Introduction: Framed, Imprisoned, Overheard	1
1. Gothic Overhearing: Inquisition, Confession, and Accusation in Browning's Dramatic Monologues	33
2. The Gothic Poetess: Self-Confinement in the Sonnet Cell	90
3. Gothic Shock and Swap: Suspended Bodies and Fluctuating Frames in D. G. Rossetti's Double Works	144
4. The Cloistered Cleric: Confessional, Confinement, and Hopkins's Poetics of Wavering	210
Conclusion: Emily Brontë's Udolphics: The Gondal and Non-Gondal Poems	258
Bibliography	281
Index	299

Illustrations

Figures

3.1   D. G. Rossetti, *Lilith, Sibylla Palmifera, Proserpine*, and *Astarte Syriaca*
Courtesy of Tate Gallery, London; Manchester City Art Gallery; Delaware Art Museum, Newark; and Lady Lever Art Gallery, National Museums Liverpool, Port Sunlight, United Kingdom   145

3.2   D. G. Rossetti, *The Blessed Damozel*, Fogg Museum, 1943.202 Harvard Art Museums collections online, <https://hvrd.art/o/299805> (last accessed 20 December 2021)   147

3.3   D. G. Rossetti, *Proserpine*, 7th Version, 1874, Tate Gallery, London   173

3.4   D. G. Rossetti, *Proserpine*, 7th Version, with frame, 1874, Tate Gallery, London   174

3.5   D. G. Rossetti, *Astarte Syriaca*, 1877, Manchester City Art Gallery, Manchester   178

3.6   D. G. Rossetti, *Astarte Syriaca*, with frame, 1877, Manchester City Art Gallery, Manchester   179

3.7   D. G. Rossetti, *Lady Lilith*, 1866–8 (altered 1872–3). Oil on canvas, 39x34 in., Delaware Art Museum, Samuel and Mary R. Bancroft Memorial, 1935   184

3.8	D. G. Rossetti, *Lady Lilith*, 1866–8 (altered 1872–3). Oil on canvas, 39x34 in., frame: 53 ¼ x 48 in., Delaware Art Museum, Samuel and Mary R. Bancroft Memorial, 1935	185
3.9	D. G. Rossetti, *Sibylla Palmifera*, 1870, Courtesy of Lady Lever Art Gallery, National Museums Liverpool, Port Sunlight, United Kingdom	190
3.10	D. G. Rossetti, *Sibylla Palmifera*, with frame, 1870, Courtesy of Lady Lever Art Gallery, National Museums Liverpool, Port Sunlight, United Kingdom	191

Table

1.1	Triangulation of speaker, overhearer, and audience in "Mr. Sludge, 'The Medium'"	75

Acknowledgments

This book would not exist without the gentle prodding of three stalwart friends: Simon Reader, Jang Wook Huh, and J. Bret Maney were my trusted companions down the path of assistant professorship. *The Gothic Forms of Poetry* is the product of hundreds of check-ins and their tireless, motivational cheerleading.

Many scholars contributed to the formation of this work. Jason Rudy and Christopher Rovee were seminal in turning the manuscript draft into a book, transforming my ugly feelings into intellectual zeal. They galvanized me to seriously start (Rudy) and finish (Rovee) the project. Christopher Rovee and Emily Harrington provided invaluable feedback on the complete manuscript. Chris's attentive edits and careful reading of the full work exemplified forms of care and generosity few and far between. Patrick O'Malley offered key recalibrations to my final chapter on Hopkins at the eleventh hour. Senior scholars who have long inspired me were beacons of encouragement in the field at large: Susan Wolfson, Orrin Wang, and Ammiel Alcalay. Consciously or not, they have served as mentors, just as their books have served as exemplars. These are the people who continually make me want to write.

Gothic Forms received its first audience as a dissertation at Columbia University, benefiting from the keen eyes of Erik Gray, Jenny Davidson, Jim Adams, Anahid Nersessian, and the late Gerhard Joseph, who is sorely missed. Lee Behlman, Karl Johnson, Sophia Hsu, and Juan Jesús Payán read and commented on individual chapters. While still in its proposal stages, this book benefited from the generosity of Talia Schaffer, Siraj Ahmed, Will Fisher, Jessica Yood, Paula Loscocco, Deirdre O'Boy, and Erik Gray. Romanticist scholars abroad, now close friends, supported my original "Ann Radcliffe project": Yun Pei, Tomoko Nakagawa, Li-ching Chen, and Nora and Keith Crook. I also thank Lin Fu, Eve Eure, Mary Mullen, Wendy Xin, Walter Blanco, Mario DiGangi, Robert Farrell, Gary Schwartz, David Hyman, and Chris Bonastia.

Acknowledgments ix

The Gothic Forms of Victorian Poetry was supported by various grants and fellowships: a 2019 Nancy Weiss Malkiel Scholars Award from the Institute for Citizens and Scholars, a CUNY Traditional A Grant, and the CUNY Faculty Fellowship Publication Program organized by Maryann McKenzie. Thanks go to Carrie Hintz and the FFPP cohort she crafted: Lisa Blankenship, Rosanne Carlos, Jennifer Malloy, Jorge Matos, and Simon Reader. Elizabeth Denlinger and Charles Carter at the New York Public Library graciously facilitated some of my Radcliffe research at the Pforzheimer Collection. The cover image was procured only through the kindness and help of Leslie Morris at the Houghton Library. I appreciate all these scholars and institutions for the imprints they have left on the shape of this work.

Sections of Chapter 2 were published as part of a special issue of *Women's Writing* on Ann Radcliffe; I thank Taylor and Francis for their permission to reprint. The Tate Gallery, London, National Museums Liverpool, Manchester Art Gallery, Delaware Art Museum, and Harvard Art Museum granted permissions to reproduce images by D. G. Rossetti. Parts of *The Gothic Forms of Victorian Poetry* were presented at the Dickens Universe, the University of Pennsylvania graduate colloquium, annual meetings of the British Association of Romantic Studies, as well as the CUNY Victorian Seminar. I thank Anne Humpherys and Gerhard Joseph for creating an intimate space for Victorian scholars of all ranks to share their work.

This book came to fruition under the careful guidance of the Edinburgh University Press editorial and design team, including Michelle Houston, Susannah Butler, Fiona Conn, Caitlin Murphy, and Christine Barton. I also thank the anonymous scholars who reviewed my manuscripts for the Press. I am grateful to Francis Paul Merencillo for his diligent and meticulous editing and indexing work, and for all my many talented students in the Bronx who naturally saw their professor as an author.

Three major pillars of friendship outlasted all challenges: Rosie Walia, Marco Ramírez Rojas, and Marcello Di Bello. Ken and Yuko Moy of Westport, CT opened their home to me, providing a blissful writing retreat—a welcome respite to one who had been long in city pent. My heartfelt thanks go out to them. The unwavering support of Karl Johnson and Mira Goral, two research and writing powerhouses, came complete with in-house editing. My Grolier friends, Arthur Schwarz, Eve Kahn, and Mark Samuels Lasner, very early on, helped me envision my manuscript as a material object and physical book. Finally, I cannot overstate the indelible impact on me from the incredible sisterhood of Rosie Walia, Evelyn Durán, Lise Esdaile, Sarah Ohmer, and Mary Phillips, who remind and teach me, always, to celebrate my own victories as I would champion theirs.

Introduction: Framed, Imprisoned, Overheard

A lonely damsel imprisoned within a castle or convent cell. The eavesdropping of a prisoner next door. The framed image of a woman with a sinister past. These are all familiar scenes from the 1790s Gothic novel, which exploded onto the English literary scene with wildly popular works like Ann Radcliffe's *The Mysteries of Udolpho* and Matthew Lewis's *The Monk*. They are also, however, key features of famous high Victorian poems, including Tennyson's "Mariana" and Browning's "My Last Duchess." *The Gothic Forms of Victorian Poetry* explores the ways in which themes and structures of the eighteenth-century Gothic novel became conventionalized in nineteenth-century poetry, reappearing as quintessential Victorian verse forms: dramatic monologues, women's sonnet sequences and metasonnets, and Pre-Raphaelite picture poems. Reading earlier fiction alongside later verse, I argue that Victorian poets adopted and transformed tropes central to the Gothic novel, leading to innovations in verse that naturalized and elevated content from a scandalous novel genre. These signature tropes—inquisitional confession and accusation, female confinement and the damsel in distress, supernatural switches between living and dead bodies—are transfigured into poetic forms that we recognize and teach today as canonically Victorian.

Characteristically, Gothic romances are populated by three stock figures: the egomaniacal, murderous husband; the sanctimonious monk figure whose lust outweighs his love for God; and the damsel in distress, imprisoned, framed, or already dead. Such counts, monks, and damsels are sprinkled throughout canonical Victorian poetry. Subsumed within a shared literary consciousness, and already familiar to a nineteenth-century reading audience, these figures found new afterlives in a succeeding generation of Victorian characters. We might consider, for instance, Robert Browning's Duke of Ferrara as a literary descendant of Radcliffe's tyrannical Italian Count Montoni. Tennyson's St. Simeon Stylites mirrors the blasphemous egotism of Matthew Lewis's villainous monk Ambrosio. And the women pictured in D. G. Rossetti's "double sonnets" are objectified and mystified like the infamous waxen image in *Mysteries of Udolpho*. The recurring figure of trapped women especially—from Mariana in the moated grange to the Lady of Shalott—represent Victorian reincarnations of Romantic Gothic's female victims. These women, frozen in art or banished to dungeons and convents, are certainly drawn from Shakespearean and Arthurian tales; but they are also variations of Radcliffe's dark, frustrated heroines. Forging such connections allows us to detect a distinct lineage: a Gothic cast of characters from 1790s sensation novels transformed into their poetic counterparts and reappearing in some of the most famous poems of the Victorian era.

That Victorian poets incorporated characters from 1790s Gothic novels is not entirely surprising. But the connection I trace reaches beyond thematic likenesses and expands to the realm of formal influence. It is this delicate dance from content to form, from characters to rhetorical structures, that constitutes the key contribution of this study. What happens when Victorian authors remix and remaster familiar characters from Gothic romance and present them in poetic form? What does it look like when a literary trope gets converted from a Romantic novel into a Victorian poem? Put plainly, what are Gothic forms and how do they travel? In this book, I identify and isolate novelistic tropes that migrate into poetic contexts—including Gothic overhearing, Gothic confinement, Gothic motherhood, and the "realist supernatural." They begin in sensation fiction of the 1790s and persist in dramatically altered forms within mainstream poetry of the long nineteenth century.

* * *

Historically, 1790s English Gothic has been cast as a sensational craze, mere hackwork that coincided with the French Revolution and quickly dwindled away before resurging a decade later. But where did all this Gothic energy go for the better part of the nineteenth century? The Gothic did not fade into the subconscious of Europe after a decade, only to erupt at the *fin de siècle* with works like Bram Stoker's *Dracula* and Robert Louis Stevenson's *The Strange Case of Dr. Jekyll and Mr. Hyde*. Nor was it a constitutive presence in only a small subset of authors, such as Wilkie Collins and the Brontë sisters. The notion that Gothic writing surged in the 1790s and 1890s—mirroring anxieties about the Reign of Terror and, much later, the turn of the century, but remaining latent and suppressed for decades in between—has always been a convenient narrative, but a problematic one. On the contrary, the immense popularity of Gothic romances and their cheap imitations, available through chapbooks, penny dreadfuls, women's periodicals, and circulating libraries, meant that Victorian poets, such as British Poet Laureate Alfred Tennyson, had few qualms crossing genre and class boundaries to take inspiration from the imaginations of commercial Grub Street writers. Mad monks, suffering nuns, murderous counts, and trapped heroines proliferate in major works of Victorian poetry, from Browning's *The Ring and the Book* to Hopkins's "The Wreck of the Deutschland."

The lineage connecting Romantic Gothic fiction with nineteenth-century poetry is not an obvious one. In his 1800 Preface to *Lyrical Ballads*, Wordsworth famously lambastes "frantic novels, sickly and stupid German Tragedies, and deluges of idle and extravagant stories in verse" for "blunt[ing] the discriminating powers of the mind," reducing them "to a state of almost savage torpor."[1] Here he alludes to recently published sensational works such as Lewis's *Monk* (1796) and Radcliffe's *The Mysteries of Udolpho* (1794), the latter of which had sold over 23,000 copies by 1816. Wordsworth and Coleridge professedly sought to cultivate a new readership, one that could learn to be excited without "gross and violent stimulants." Gothic novels, though popular, were almost universally maligned for their immoral content, their authors cast as members of "the terrorist School" and "the German school." These texts were also notorious for the "guilty" context of their production and reception: Gothic writing was condemned "because of the way that it was seen to 'circulate' so promiscuously among . . . an undisciplined yet ever-expanding reading public."[2] Wordsworth hoped that his poetry, in enlisting the "real language of men," might reduce some of the mental torpor of readers induced by such imitative repetition.[3] But William Lane's Minerva Press contracted a host of commercial authors to churn out titles at a prodigious rate, many of which were overt imitations of existing bestsellers. Readers of all types, the lower classes especially, devoured them. Still, the ubiquity and commercial success of the Gothic does not make it easy to define.

* * *

What is Gothic? Readers mostly recognize Gothic as a loose, baggy tradition defined by a "bag of tropes" from which authors repeatedly draw. Bats, ghosts, devils, trap doors, giant objects, mysterious noises, and Italian banditti—like the Gothic machinery in the mock recipe below—make for a rather clichéd laundry list.

> Take—An old castle, half of it ruinous.
> A long gallery, with a great many doors, some secret ones.
> Three murdered bodies, quite fresh.
> As many skeletons, in chests and presses.
> An old woman hanging by the neck; with her throat cut.
> Assassins and desperadoes, *quant. suff.*
> Noises, whispers, and groans, threescore at least.
> Mix them together, in the form of three volumes, to be taken at any of the watering places, before going to bed.[4]

This passage on "Terrorist Novel Writing" from *The Spirit of the Public Journals for 1797* is quoted in nearly every study of Gothic fiction. The elements enumerated here are the very same ticked off on Catherine Morland's Gothic-parodic checklist in Jane Austen's *Northanger Abbey* (1817). Those thematic markers, so formulaic as to have become satirized, are ubiquitous in the hundreds of titles published by the Minerva Press. But given the repetition and unoriginality of Gothic, how might we as twenty-first-century critics read these excesses of nineteenth-century Gothic production—and how might we make them meaningful? Rather than rely expressly on such tropes as identifiers, *The Gothic Forms of Victorian Poetry* also reconceives of Gothic through a new fundamental organizing principle: as a set of formal structures that configure the relationships between speakers and their imagined audiences. Gothic forms are hidden in plain sight as the structural building blocks to some of the best-loved poems of nineteenth-century Britain.

If the "bag of tropes" model and the recipe for Gothic thematic soup in the cauldron has worked thus far, then why redefine Gothic through a formal lens? For so long, the Gothic has been a notoriously capacious category in literature, alternately serving as a historical, aesthetic, or thematic label.[5] Critics have characterized the tradition as a psychological manifestation of anxieties—whether a suspicion of Enlightenment values; fears about backlash of the French Revolution; repressed Freudian fantasies; religious doubt resurfaced; or bourgeois fears about ancestry, inheritance, and property transfer in an age of rapid industrialization.[6] But as past scholarship can attest, the Gothic is elusive, difficult to define outright, and far easier to describe by example. From the telltale signs of skeletons, mysterious groans, and castle ruins, any one of these elements can merit a text as Gothic, even when these conventions do not cohere. This book redefines and complicates the category of Gothic by upgrading it from the model of a cauldron's stew. It identifies, as "Gothic," poems that do not only bear those phenotypical traits. For sure, Keats's poems of medieval romance (*Lamia, The Eve of St. Agnes; Isabella, or the Pot of Basil;* "La belle dame sans merci") and Byron's orientalist and feudal romances (*The Giaour; The Corsair; Childe Harold's Pilgrimage*) comprise this familiar tradition. Yet as I will show, focusing on a wholly separate category of texts than the usual suspects of nineteenth-century English literature, Gothic romance is still formally embedded in the genealogical or genetic make-up of even canonical Victorian poems.

Through the new readings posed here, Gothic becomes a continuous and ubiquitous aesthetic concern between 1780 and 1890, rather than an aberrational outpouring briefly bookending this interval. My literary examples span a wide range of historical literary movements, including the Romantic Sonnet Revival, rise of the Gothic novel, resurgence of the dramatic monologue, formation of the Pre-Raphaelite Brotherhood, and Oxford Movement. Focusing on fiction by Ann Radcliffe, Matthew Lewis, and Mary Wollstonecraft, alongside verses by major nineteenth-century poets, I offer a revisionist history that looks beyond the traditional subset of Victorian literature typically considered "Gothic." By extending the influence of these 1790s authors outside the typical purview of the Gothic romance, we can see that many Victorian poetic forms—dramatic monologues, metasonnets, and picture poems—are inherently Gothic in their formal construction.

Recognizing this subtle absorption of Gothic content revises our understanding of nineteenth-century poets not as strict tastemakers of high poetry, but adapters and innovators of popular forms, catering to a generation of Victorian readers fluent in the structures of Gothic literary machinery. *The Gothic Forms of Victorian Poetry* thus conceives of genre formation as a process that occurs dynamically not only across periods, but across genres and class lines, borrowed from Romantic novels and reappropriated in Victorian poetry. Anxieties surrounding constraints of middle-class domesticity, women's marriage and property rights, sexual expression, and the renewal of Catholic thought were manifest in a period of legal changes, seen in the 1829 Roman Catholic Relief Act, 1857 Matrimonial Causes

Act, 1870 Married Women's Property Act, and the 1885 Criminal Law Amendment Act outlawing all male homosexual acts. Against this historical backdrop, Radcliffean Gothic offered later poets a restrained, yet powerful means for expressing the perversity and shifting sense of social and political values with which they grappled.

Gothic Tropes, Poetic Forms

What is Gothic Form? While Gothic themes are easily identifiable—through live burial, infanticide, giant objects, or ancestral hauntings—Gothic forms have been more difficult to pinpoint.[7] Scholars have recognized the way in which, for example, Radcliffe's protracted novels absorb various subgenres, including sensation fiction, sentimental fiction, poetry, diary, and travel writing.[8] But beneath this capacious hybridity, what are the literary devices specific to the Gothic itself?

Gothic Tropes

Live burial
Infanticide
Giant helmets
Churchyard phantoms
Mysterious lights in the castle window
Mysterious sounds in the forest
Floating body parts
Locks, bolts, keys, chains
Banditti
Feudal restoration
Damsel in distress
Murderous Italian count
Criminal monk
Hermits
Prisons, dungeons, and graveyards
Supernatural artwork
Monasteries, nunneries, catacombs

Gothic Forms

Gothic overhearing: related to criminal eavesdropping, Catholic confessional, secrets, and spying
Gothic confinement: related to prison, female safety, or motherhood
Gothic motherhood: the womb as prison, the world a jail for women
Gothic framing: framed art, framed bodies, a picture or painting as sites of confusion between the two
Gothic swaps: switching of corpses, replacement of dead bodies with live ones, art and life, shock and surprise

Gothic forms are not simply idiosyncratic techniques manufacturing fear and suspense, relying on excess and instability. Throughout this book, I identify Gothic forms as structural positionings and patterns of confinement that function in concert with thematic content across genres. These include Gothic overhearing (related to secrets and spying), Gothic confinement (related to prisons, female safety, or motherhood), forced confessions (from the Catholic Inquisition), Gothic framing (of both art and bodies), and Gothic swaps (the switching of bodies, evoking shock and surprise). Due to the contortions embedded in and embodied by each of these forms, these moves are easy to miss. Furthermore, each of these contortions emphasizes restriction and restraint, contributing to a distinctive poetics of Gothic enclosure. As each chapter will show, Victorian poets repurposed popular Gothic conventions in formally innovative ways, through a subtle migration of tropes that elude attention and even obscure this line of inheritance. I locate this formal machinery throughout six foundational Gothic novels by Ann Radcliffe, William Godwin, and Mary Wollstonecraft, mapping the transformation of novelistic themes *into* poetic forms.

The transformation of tropes into forms that I trace in each chapter differs from a simple hybridization of poetry and prose. Within Victorian literature, the verse-novels of George Meredith and Arthur Clough show us what it looks like to stage a novel in verse, while the novels of George Eliot and Thomas Hardy demonstrate how poetic elements can be incorporated into prose. But how do novelistic Gothic tropes, even when separated from their thematic associations, become integrated into poetic forms? This cross-genre influence manifests in two different ways. First, I approach the Gothic romance as a space in which novelists could experiment with poetic forms by subjecting them to different contexts. In the first chapter, for example, I turn to various moments in Radcliffe's and Lewis's prose that contain identifiable seeds of the dramatic monologue. These scenarios teach us about the limitations of poetic lyric address and dramatic monologue. They show us, for instance, the conditions and permutations that can push a poem from one formal category to the next. They also reveal how such poetic ideals are explored and staged through prose. As we will see, the long Gothic romance can in fact serve as a testing lab or Petri dish for incubating poetic innovations within the ample space of its pages.

Second, when poetic forms subsume novelistic tropes, they compel the poem's speakers and readers to re-enact those Gothic themes they echo in expressly physical ways. Surprisingly, Gothic forms in Victorian poetry are not spectral and phantasmagoric, but modeled upon a realistic, corporeal poetics of the living body in movement. The passages I discuss from both Gothic fiction and Victorian poems rely upon a choreography that highlights the physicality of bodily movement. Each Gothic form I explore plays with the positioning of the speaker, reader, or author in ways that demand a particularly physical brand of formal analysis. In my discussion of the "Gothic sonnet," for instance, poets and speakers call out for violent imprisonment just as a character might in a Gothic novel, but they also embody this confinement formally themselves. Through this bodily poetics, authors consciously stage structures of overhearing, imprisonment, or fluctuation by engaging the full physicality of all parties involved. Characters, readers, and sometimes the form of the poem itself all participate in this physical poetics, creating structures and spaces that contort, imprison, or compromise the living body in Gothic ways, without necessarily relying on the imagery of ghosts or corpses.

All of these physicalized contortions are some embodiment of restriction and restraint, of imprisonment and containment. When tropes transmogrify into forms—when characters, setting, or predicaments of plot become formalized as poetic structures (sonnets or dramatic monologues)—we gain, by reflecting upon these contortions and experiencing them first-hand, fresh readings of familiar authors and texts. What might recognizing a poetics of Gothic enclosure afford us? By experiencing these poems as formal containers, these novelistic ideas as poetic shapes, we experience the constriction and restraint that so elegantly ties together Victorian Poetry and the Gothic—an unlikely marriage but a connection predicated upon the celebration of restriction in both theme and form.

To ask the question, "What is Gothic form?" requires us to confront still tougher questions: "What is form, and what does form explain?" This book engages ongoing debates regarding the future of New Formalism that dispute the utility of this slippery term "form" and its value as a unit of literary study altogether, among them the voices of Marjorie Levinson, Anahid Nersessian, and Jonathan Kramnick.[9] As Heather Dubrow has asked, "Is form merely another word for genre?"[10] Decidedly not, if to research the Gothic indicates a range of diverse generic investments, spanning Gothic ballads, Gothic romance, Gothic dramas, or Gothic tales and short stories. Some critics have sidestepped the question by replacing "form" with alternative, yet equally unclear terms, opting to discuss a "Gothic mode" or "Gothic sensibility" instead. For fear of abusing the word "form" or enlisting it as a convenient catch-all, I define literary form as an amalgamation of *textual shape, expectations*, and *rules* that render a text recognizable as an identifiable type.[11] It yields a useful set of family resemblances to be shared with other texts of its kind. Most distinctively, form carries in it a sense of physicality that I explore in each of my chapters. The visual or bodily characteristics imbedded in specific poetic, novelistic, or dramatic forms lend them their distinctive shapes: A dramatic monologue, for instance, has its "shape" rooted in a triangle—the triangulation of speaker, audience, and auditor. A sonnet bears some commitment to the number fourteen, with stanzas emulating the shape of a room, orbiting combinations of eight plus six or twelve plus two. Meanwhile, D. G. Rossetti's "picture poems" always appear as a "package deal" in the sister arts of poetry and painting, to be read in double or in parallel, often positioning living objects (the poet, us as readers or models), before a mirror.

From these near-tangible bodies of texts, we as readers experience form on the page in particular ways. The accompanying rules and expectations that adhere to such textual shapes dictate conventions for both author and reader. As Stephanie Sandler points out, "*meter, rhyme, alliteration, assonance*, and *repetition*—or *lyric, monologue*, and *sonnet*—all poetic devices and genres that mark the text as poetic and that have their own histories and associations ... are too specific to verbal utterance to do us much good" along the "border zones" of paintings and poems, novels and newspapers, collage and installation.[12] And Harold Bloom offers a useful directive when he locates the revelation of poetic form as dependent upon "The Breaking of Form."[13] Participating in the identification of forms and departures from them allows for a sense of physical play on behalf of both author and critic—of crafting and molding literary shapes, like sculpture or dough. The formal range from rigidity to flexibility becomes even more exciting, ever more fruitful, when we stretch our analyses to carry over conventions across genres, trading and borrowing ideas or terminology as needed. In this way, *The Gothic Forms of Victorian Poetry* accepts the invitation to visit new juxtapositions that critics may have previously shied away from: penny dreadfuls and Wordsworth poems, the "tale of the bleeding nuns" in Lewis's *The Monk* and "The Wreck of the Deutschland" by Hopkins; doppelgängers and fleshly bodies in the works of Radcliffe and Rossetti. Such bartering across genres presents a new, substantial border zone of overlapping influence between the Romantic novel and the Victorian poem.

From the Margins to the Mainstream

A study of the Gothic necessarily bears anxieties about its minorness, as well as its close associations to formal failure on many counts. Its aesthetic components of horror, supernaturalism, violence, and feudal barbarity often seem to undermine the genre's canonicity.[14] These elements, historically deprecated as unevenness of style, and marked by sameness or excess, make it easy to write off Gothic as aesthetically defective or immature. Even when recognized in the verse of major poets, the Gothic is invoked in highly biographical terms or treated as a symptom of inexperience in youthful works. These include juvenilia and early-career writing, such as Tennyson's *Maud*, Browning's *Pauline*, or Barrett Browning's "Legend of the Brown Rosarie."[15] And while Hulme famously posed the Gothic as the poor, "illegitimate child" of Romanticism, I present the Gothic as an integral, yet inconspicuous part of mainstream Victorian tradition.[16] *The Gothic Forms of Victorian Poetry* recenters Victorian Gothic in terms other than late nineteenth-century revival.

By so doing, I invite a greater convergence between the sometimes-disparate fields of Gothic Studies and Victorian poetry criticism, insisting upon its critical relevance to now canonical works of the nineteenth century. Whereas Sandra Gilbert and Sarah Gubar's *The Madwoman in the Attic* identified common Gothic themes among gynotexts by the Brontës, Eliot, Austen, and Dickinson, this book brings the influence of an author like Ann Radcliffe to bear on works by canonical poets, such as Robert Browning, Elizabeth Barrett Browning, Christina Rossetti, Gerard Manley Hopkins, Dante Gabriel Rossetti, William Wordsworth, and John Keats. In this way, I show that Victorian poetry also embodies this idea of the Radcliffean realist supernatural, both neutralizing and naturalizing potent Gothic content in "non-Gothic" texts by decidedly "non-Gothic" authors. *Gothic Forms* thus bridges the specialization of Gothic studies—the critical work of Fred Botting, Robert Miles, and David Punter—with scholarship on Victorian poetry by critics such as Isobel Armstrong, Herbert Tucker, Meredith Martin, and Cornelia Pearsall.[17]

Why pair 1790s Gothic with Victorian poetry? Explorations of Romantic Gothic are well-trodden territory in a rich line of criticism. Since Robert Platzner's early positioning of "Gothic versus Romantic" and Robert Hulme's rejoinder of 1971, criticism by Michael Gamer, Jerrold Hogle, Robert Miles, Fred Botting,

David Richter, Angela Wright, Emma Clery, and Diane Long Hoeveler have updated our understanding of the genre's far-reaching circulation, reception, and literary influence.[18] But while studies of Romantic Gothic abound, monographs on Victorian Gothic are far rarer, with a tendency to center around key examples of novels and short fiction.[19] *Jane Eyre*, *Wuthering Heights*, *Villette*, *The Woman in White*, *The Picture of Dorian Gray*, *The Strange Case of Dr. Jekyll and Mr. Hyde*, and *The Mysteries of London* are among the familiar suspects. Even within studies of Gothic poetry, criticism often relies on texts by the same recognizable authors, such as Poe, Swinburne, and Keats. And because Gothic studies is dominated by *Frankenstein* (1818; second edition: 1832), inarguably the most important Gothic text of the period, attention to Victorian Gothic authors has been eclipsed by Shelley's innovations and the inauguration of second-generation Female Gothic. In this sense, a mini-canon prioritizing *Frankenstein* and *fin de siècle* writers has dominated the scene of nineteenth-century criticism in Gothic. I look to the 1790s, a chronologically Romantic moment, in an effort to draw lines of influence that reach across a continuous, "long" nineteenth century, shaping Victorian poetry in particular.

Methodology: Of Loosely Wrought Urns and Lyric Buckets

How best to read Gothic, given its positioning just outside of the canon? In reading Gothic and non-Gothic works together, we must recognize, of course, the false distinction in labeling them canonical or non-canonical texts. Walpole, Radcliffe, and Lewis clearly represent the pinnacle of Gothic studies' own canon, with chapbooks and "downmarket" novels situated lower down on the scale. Moreover, a generally dismissive assumption prevails that one typically does not close read Gothic romances, simply because Gothic romances do not hold up to close reading. (Reading one is as good as reading them all.) For the New Critics, close reading yielded best results when applied to poems, due to the professed unity of their structure. But well-wrought urns were decidedly objects of high art, not low art. Whereas a curated canon of Victorian poetry has long enjoyed close readings by generations of students and critics, what is the practical role of close reading for a genre whose overwhelming quantity and the sheer length of its novels—many on average eight hundred pages long—render them "unreadable"?

Here, I do not champion the Radcliffean novel as a well-wrought urn. These texts, neither carefully tailored nor admired for concision, are the loose and baggy antitheses of Cleanth Brooks's urn and unity of structure, their content patently recycled, reused, and rendered trite. Yet this is what Gothic fiction, despite its repetition and stylistic excess, affords us: the opportunity to study loosely wrought vases, or even vast buckets, which contain the same tropes repeated over and again, ultimately presenting as a messy bag of tricks or "a formal muddle."[20] In romances of six hundred pages, where plot always works itself out (and often somewhat hastily, just within the final chapter), the many pages that lie in between afford writers an experimental space ripe for authorial experimentation. This is not a disparagement of the form of Gothic romance, but rather a way of reclaiming Gothic fiction from its assignation as a genre marked by instability and fragmentation. With compositions that seem to go on for far too long and flaunt their unoriginality, too often is Gothic romance considered a genre that does not merit rereading, nor any study beyond its own framework and subset of Gothic texts.[21] But those pages are also the source of techniques harvested and applied in a different literary space: the Victorian poem. While Marjorie Perloff reminds us that the study of lyric poetry has long privileged canonical poems, one of the many ways this book destabilizes otherwise uncontested ideals of lyric is by looking to sensational fiction as a place from whence key formal developments of lyric forms arose.[22] In this sense, the fact that a Gothic novel, unlike a lyric poem, is not compactly constructed becomes a practical asset, not an aesthetic failure. We might loosen the stranglehold of canonical poems on the study of lyric theory by inviting 1790s Gothic into the discussion.

My methodological approach combines an ear and eye trained by New Formalism, sharpened against the imperatives of historical poetics, to ask how and why forms develop when they do. How does a sprawling, overarching "aesthetic" like the Gothic inspire specific formal developments in the 1830s, 1840s, and 1850s? I contextualize my readings within genre and chronology but also challenge typical pairings, reading scenes of 1790s novels through a Victorian poetic lens. This cross-genre, cross-period approach answers Caroline Levine's call to transport forms from a space of comfort to unfamiliar ground, recognizing the "affordances" these forms (Radcliffean tropes) incur when placed in a new habitat (Victorian poetry). My study thus transcends traditionally bifurcated frameworks of genre (novel/poetry), period (Romantic/Victorian), class (low Gothic/high Victorian), and gender (Female Gothic/Male Gothic) to present a new literary history of Gothic that spans the nineteenth century and goes beyond its major texts.

Three studies of English and Irish Gothic serve as important precursors to this book by establishing the omnipresence of the Gothic throughout nineteenth-century literature. Susan Wolfson's *Romantic Shades and Shadows* elucidates the ubiquity of apparitional poetics in phantom-like instances of spectral language and haunted reading. In her study, the Gothic is not sidelined to the 1790s or 1890s but serves as a constitutive fabric of nineteenth-century language, from the Romantics to the Modernists, from Keats to Yeats. Riffing on Derrida's pun of hauntology/ontology, Wolfson uncovers literature through "the apparitional semblances in verbal textures: chance associations, ruptures of logic, figural recurrences, and overproductions."[23] Terry Castle's classic chapter on "The Spectralization of the Other" from *The Female Thermometer* refuses a "two-world reading" that starkly divides the Gothic/non-Gothic, rational/irrational, realist/supernatural, repressed/actualized. Insisting that we recognize in Radcliffe's novels "the supernaturalization of everyday life," Castle shows that it is not just the enchanted forest or cursed castle that may be haunted, but that "to be a Radcliffean hero or heroine in one sense means just this: to be 'haunted,' to find oneself obsessed by spectral images of those one loves."[24] In the same way, *Gothic Forms* refuses and resists the divide between a rational, Protestant English, Victorian realism and a superstitious, foreign, Romantic Gothic world of fictional romance. Instead, it insists upon reading the two together, recognizing the hybridity and interaction of their texts across genres. Finally, Patrick O'Malley's *Catholicism, Sexual Deviance, and Victorian Gothic Culture* locates the pervasive and enduring language of the Gothic throughout the nineteenth century in Catholic texts and tracts. As he argues, Gothic language was the site for harnessing fears of an English sense of threat from Catholicism and homosexuality. Parodic and villainized portrayals of Catholic ritualism colored not only Protestant views of Catholic life, but infiltrated the religious language of members of the Oxford Movement as well.[25] This argument recognizes that Catholic representations in fictional romance and in nineteenth-century life did not operate in separate spheres, but actively and mutually influenced one another, contributing to what it meant to be an English Catholic.

Constitutive of all three studies is the insistence that the Gothic is not predicated upon ghost-seeing. Rather, it is contingent upon specific forms of reading and exegesis. Wolfson describes this as "a register of *literary* reading: close, slow, careful and open to various, not necessarily reconcilable, energies in the movements of language."[26] The Gothic did not fade from daily discourse, but was suffused in writing throughout the middle of the century with "penumbral nuances" of language.[27] The Gothic is not marginal to mainstream nineteenth-century writing, but an essential part of it. These three studies model the fine-tuning of our readerly, Gothic critical lens in order to properly recognize such images and echoes—which do not resurface now and then as phantoms, but linger everywhere and always, from 1790 through 1890.

Moreover, this book continues the work of Eve Sedgwick's *The Coherence of Gothic Conventions,* a classic study of Gothic that "besides pointing to and naming thematic conventions," takes, as its main critical activity, "assimilating those conventions to each other."[28] Using live burial and the unspeakable as its two main examples, Sedgwick's work explores that "web of metaphor" in terms of a coherence that is generative and not reductive.[29] My emphasis on Gothic forms in lieu of Gothic themes follows her two levels of application, that at the level of argument (e.g. the thematics of live burial), and that at the level of formal reflexivity, namely the Gothic's insistent self-referentiality or "the presence of this continuous, reiterative stream of explicitly thematic language."[30] For Sedgwick, in Gothic, "the two levels seem especially close to each other." This book demonstrates how Gothic theme and form work in concert. Like Sedgwick's study, it engages productively with the repetitions and clichés constitutive of Gothic style, recognizing them as productive literary elements, rather than discounting them, for it is only by "pointing to the variety and resonance of the connections in the web of metaphor . . . that it becomes clear how distinct and usable the Gothic is [as] a literary tradition."[31] *Gothic Forms* takes up Sedgwick's charge in proving the distinctiveness and usability of the Gothic literary tradition, affirming its "usefulness" in non-Gothic or mainstream Victorian texts.

By identifying confinement and the poetics of enclosure as central Gothic form, this book further engages with Sedgwick's emphasis on spatial, "inside-outside relations."[32] Sedgwick's work "codif[ies] the spatial model[s]" previously neglected in criticism through

> three main elements: (what's inside, what's outside, and what separates them) . . . The self and whatever it is that is outside . . . [demands] a fundamental reorganization . . . The worst violence, the most potent magic, and the most paralyzing instances of the uncanny in these novels . . . are evoked in the very breach of the imprisoning wall.[33]

The readings and analyses in the chapters that follow likewise codify and map, in physical, spatial, and bodily terms, those very separations between inside and outside. They outline a variety of formal patterns and contortions central to the Gothic and to Victorian poetry: the dungeon gate, the cloister wall, the convent threshold, and the fourth wall between dramatic monologue speaker and auditor.

The movements and motions gestured to in the scholarship of Wolfson, Castle and Sedgwick—the playful dancing across pages of spectral hauntings, the literary sensibility of a spirited Gothic critic willing to chase down "shades that are nuances, shades that are apparitional," the "fundamental reorganization [of] . . . what's inside, what's outside, and what separates them . . . creating a doubleness where singleness should be"—are all touchstones for the bridging work proposed in *Gothic Forms*.[34] This book is not a conventional influence study (*The Italian* is an unrealized source text for "St. Simeon Stylites"), nor one that insists on "anticipation." Instead, I construct readings that test the portability of 1790s Gothic, exploring what these prose innovations can teach us about poetry outside the discrete world of Gothic studies. I show how Victorian poets and Gothic novelists could engage in the same projects of formal experimentation, despite their differences in genre, class, and historical period. Close readings of overhearing in Radcliffe can contribute to Browning studies, while carefully tracing Gothic representations of Catholicism yields new revelations for the poetry of Hopkins.

The Gothic Forms of Victorian Poetry thus tackles questions posed recently by scholars of new formalism and historical poetics, from Caroline Levine to Virginia Jackson and Yopie Prins. How do forms travel and transfer? How do we trace them in their movements across period and across genres? To whom do we attribute the popularity of particular forms? What does it mean for one author to borrow or appropriate a form championed by another? Scholars have credited the innovations of the Victorian dramatic monologue, for instance, to Browning and Tennyson, until historical correctives pointed also to Felicia Hemans, Amy Levy, and Augusta Weber as early users of the form. But these designations should not blind us to the idea that novelists could also participate in the formal experimentations being executed by poets, and vice versa. That the novel should influence poetic form is not a new concept, but it warrants careful critical attention when this occurs in the transitional period between 1790 and 1840, when the English novel had yet to triumph over poetry as the genre of first note. Such questions of genre formation challenge ideas of the purity and hybridity of poetic forms, inviting us to reconsider forms as essential building blocks or finished literary products. How do we talk responsibly about formal archetypes (such as Ina Beth Session's "perfect dramatic monologue") while recognizing all forms as hybrid developments? Readings that illuminate the hybridity of nineteenth-century poetic forms have been modeled by scholars such as David Shaw, Ulrich Knoepflmacher, and Herbert Tucker.[35] In this vein, *Gothic Forms* joins the conversation with recent cross-genre studies, such as Anne McCarthy's *Awful Parenthesis*, Monique Morgan's *Narrative Means, Lyric Ends*, and Dino Franco Felluga and Emily Allen's *Novel-Poetry*, which bridge cultural and critical gaps by using comparativist approaches to traverse a Romantic-Victorian divide.[36]

Radcliffe and Lewis, A Doubled Tradition

Though Horace Walpole, of Strawberry Hill fame, is credited to have initiated the English Gothic revival with *The Castle of Otranto* in 1764, Ann Radcliffe certainly solidified the tradition, creating a new standard of novelistic innovation. She elevated the genre through the unmitigated success of her novels, which took off by her third publication, *The Romance of the Forest*. Her oeuvre includes *The Castles of Athlin and Dunbayne* (1789), *A Sicilian Romance* (1790), *The Romance of the Forest* (1791), *The Mysteries of Udolpho* (1794), for The *Italian* (1797), and *Gaston de Blondeville* (1826).[37] The highest-paid novelist of the decade, Radcliffe was considered the "founder of a class or school," deemed "the Shakespeare of Romance Writers," and lavishly commended by Sir Walter Scott, Nathan Drake, Samuel T. Coleridge, and Lord Byron.[38] Her novels were so lucrative that for the copyright to *Udolpho*, publishers granted her 500 pounds and for *The Italian*, 800 pounds, up to eighty times the average of typical authors.[39]

Radcliffe was considered the dominant Gothic innovator of her time, her six major novels spawning countless imitations and chapbooks, influencing the Marquis de Sade, Sir Walter Scott, Edgar Allan Poe, and Sheridan Le Fanu. Her influence was so ubiquitous that in 1819, Keats boasted, somewhat derisively, of the fine "Mother Radcliff names" he used in his Gothic poems, *Isabella; or, the Pot of Basil* and *The Eve of St. Agnes*.[40] From its inception in 1790 until 1810, the Minerva Press generated over eight hundred works of fiction, a third of which had Gothic titles by professional writers who produced new titles at an astonishing pace.[41] Printed in inexpensive duodecimo format, their Gothic content inspired countless imitators who capitalized on the Radcliffe brand, including Isaac Crookenden, Catherine Cuthbertson, Mrs. Isaacs, Mary Meeke, Regina Maria Roche, Eleanor Sleath, and Mary Ann Radcliffe, whose *Manfroné; or, The one-handed monk* (1809) was often mistakenly attributed to "Udolpho's unrivalled Foundress."[42] Radcliffe was thus the progenitor of a vast industry of Gothic writing, setting off a vogue monetized by William Lane and his Minerva Press.[43] Spurious attributions and lookalikes flooded the market, with authors named Mary Ann Radcliffe and Eliza Ratcliffe, and titles such as *Mysteries of Abruzzo* (1802), *Mysteries of Ferney Castle* (1810), *The Monk of Udolpho* (1807), *Romance of the Appennines* (1808), *Romance of the Castle* (1800), *Romance of the Highlands* (1810), and *Romance of the Hebrides* (1809).[44] These titles reached wide audiences due to their ubiquity and low prices.[45] Poorer readers could opt for chapbooks or bluebooks, "thirty-six four-by-seven inch pages stitched into a flimsy paper cover and sold for six pence," or rely on the Minerva circulating library organized by Lane.

At this juncture, Radcliffe's novels need no recovery. Coinciding with feminist studies of the 1980s, serious critical scholarship on Radcliffe was solidified with major literary biographies by Robert Miles and Rictor Norton, along with seminal published dissertations on the Gothic by Arno Press that explore the "Great Enchantress" and the "mighty magician." These were accompanied by explorations of the Female Gothic tradition, which blossomed under Ellen Moers, Julian Fleenor, Diane Hoeveler, and Emma Clery, among others. Since Radcliffe's initial recovery in the 1990s, a new spate of criticism commemorating her 250th anniversary in 2014 has energized the field, with anniversary essays, conference celebrations, special journal issues, and new publications by Angela Wright, Dale Townshend, Andrew Smith, and Mark Bennett, among others. *The Mysteries of Udolpho* is no longer recognized as merely a passing reference in Jane Austen's *Emma* or the basis of *Northanger Abbey*'s Gothic satire.

Critics have typically used Radcliffe and Lewis as figures to mark the distinction between what is deemed Female Gothic and Male Gothic.[46] Female Gothic, recognized in the novels of Clara Reeve and Sophia Lee, emphasizes subtle, psychological terror, while Male Gothic relies on grotesque, physical horror. The former features heroines who restore power, property, and title through the matrilineal line, with plotlines often offering rationalizations that explain away superstitious fears by the novel's end. Male Gothic, in the vein of Horace Walpole, William Beckford, and Matthew Lewis, features morally ambivalent male antiheroes and fantastic plots that rely heavily on the supernatural.

Indeed, the single greatest contribution of Radcliffe to the Gothic tradition is her innovation of the "explained" or "realist supernatural."[47] In this technique, a long explanation is provided to disabuse her heroines of any mystical suspicions, especially at the very end of her novels. A flickering light in the window is not a ghost, but servants attending to late-night business around the castle; the haunting spirits of murdered ghosts actually turn out to be minor banditti; a moldering corpse is but a waxen figure; mysterious cries of an angry ghost are actually groans of a prisoner behind a trapdoor. Disavowing supernatural causes to tie up her plots, Radcliffe mixed Gothic machinery with the novel of sensibility, forging a new genre of romance that did not center on superstition. Her romances undercut the shock typical of supernatural endings.

Radcliffe and the Female Gothic tradition serve as the main touchstones for poetic comparison throughout *Gothic Forms* in several ways. Because Radcliffe's Gothic utilizes poetic realism rather than Lewis's overt superstition and supernaturalism, the Gothic elements of her novels could more easily be subsumed into the language of high Victorian poetry, avoiding the heavy-handed mechanisms of dead infants or satanic incantations. As Deborah Rogers has comically stated, "Ann Radcliffe was a great deal too enlightened ever to have anything to say to a ghost. In those days the ancient love of superstition had faded, and the new groping after spiritual presences had not begun."[48] In Female Gothic, the supernatural is always feared, but the possibility of its presence always explained away by the novel's end. The more shocking and mystical elements are veiled in Radcliffean novels, thus creating a more palatable mode of Gothic from which Victorian poets could draw. Victorian poems incorporate Gothic aspects without including Lewis's outlandish supernaturalism. Again, we can see Gothic form serving as an outlet for themes framed and molded into shapes of restraint, as it appears in Victorian literature, rather than exhibiting shocking content rife with extreme and excess.

Moreover, Radcliffe combined her Gothic prose with elements of poetry, landscape writing, and sentimental fiction, making her work riper terrain for Victorian poets to draw from. Her novels show a deep connection to aesthetic ideals of beauty, terror, obscurity, imagination, and the sublime.[49] But as much as Radcliffe's novels continually utilize Romantic conventions, they also satirize the repetition and ubiquity of these clichés, as the following chapters will show.[50] Embracing the humorous, parodic modes of Gothic makes these novels a site for Romantic critique, a significant point of commonality between the Gothic novel and the poetry of the Victorians.

Throughout *Gothic Forms*, the presence of female authors and characters plays an important role, and the looming figure of "Mother Radcliff" carries the feminist thread underlying this project. The divisive language of "Male" and "Female Gothic" reveals gendered tensions surrounding Gothic texts, in which the divergent treatment of male bodies versus female ones yields uneasy conclusions. Mary Wollstonecraft famously criticized Burke for his "Gothic notions of beauty" and his defense of sexist chivalric ideals amidst the context of the French Revolution: "Will her form have lost the smooth delicacy that inspires love, when stripped of its Gothic drapery? . . . Is there no beauteous proportion in virtue, when not clothed in a sensual garb?"[51] Gothic works are subversive and revolutionary, unleashing repressed violence and sexual desires; yet these liberating releases are often at the bodily cost of female characters. The Gothic can be infamously conservative in its portrayal of women, upholding patriarchal values especially in endings that belittle the adventures and agency of its female characters.[52] Women's bodies become expected sites of pain or disfiguration, at times depending on pornographic descriptions in passages to fuel plot struggles between "the beater and the beaten,"[53] the losers and the winners.[54] But how do Gothic forms continue to be subversive of gender norms as they travel into the nineteenth century? Does Victorian poetry simply reappropriate the Gothic heroine as an embodiment of the precept of "suffer and be still?" My readings of nineteenth-century poems attend especially to the representations of women's bodies—exploring portrayals of the poetess figure as a symbol at the turn of the century, considering the treatment of Pre-Raphaelite studio models, and recognizing the Minerva Press as a literary industry based on the productivity of professional women writers purportedly appealing to female readers. The readings that follow often employ a mode I call "physical close reading," which pays special attention to poetic forms in terms of bodily restraint, physical punishment, and thrall—attending to the gender dynamics of power and victimization among speaker, poet, and metaphorized figures. Gothic novels are certainly examples of sentimental fiction that rely on charged expectations of gendered suffering—but Radcliffe's repetitive constructions of sighing heroines and their dispelled fears also satirizes these stereotypes, as will be seen in Chapter 2.

* * *

For its Gothic texts, *The Gothic Forms of Victorian Poetry* focuses on novels published in the 1790s by Ann Radcliffe, Matthew Lewis, Mary Wollstonecraft, and William Godwin: Radcliffe's *The Romance of the Forest* (1791), *The Mysteries of Udolpho* (1794), and *The Italian* (1797); Lewis's *The Monk* (1796); William Godwin's *Caleb Williams* (1794), and Mary Wollstonecraft's *Maria* (1798). The first two authors represent two major poles of 1790s Gothic fiction, while the latter two penned landmark political and psychological novels. Working across the turn of the nineteenth century, I discuss five major Victorian poets who were writing from 1830 to 1890, drawing from their most celebrated poems to those that are rarely anthologized. I read poems by Robert Browning, Elizabeth Barrett Browning, Christina Rossetti, Dante Gabriel Rossetti, Gerard Manley Hopkins, and Emily Brontë.

Each of my chapters pairs a trope from the Gothic novel with the development of a specific poetic form, moving chronologically through the work of major British novelists and poets from the 1770s to 1870. Chapter 1 links the trope of Gothic overhearing as a structure essential to Robert Browning's early dramatic monologues. By entitling his first pair of dramatic monologues "Madhouse Cells" and featuring social outcasts as his poetic speakers, Browning calls attention to a Gothic genealogy that inherits a poetics of eavesdropping on the prisoner-next-door. I show that such examples of overheard prisoners are already ubiquitous in the semi-satirized figures of 1790s Gothic novels, where they pour forth their feelings and are overheard across castle walls, monastic cloisters, and jails of the Inquisition. In their novels, Radcliffe and Lewis plant the seeds of guilty overhearing and inquisitional confession that become fundamental structures to dramatic monologue form. Recognizing this Gothic indebtedness accounts for the flavor of criminality and collusion inherent not just in Browning's early works like *Pippa Passes* and "Soliloquy of the Spanish Cloister," but in his later oeuvre as well.

Radcliffe's heroines are often lyric poets themselves, and these damsels in distress, locked away in castles and dungeons, learn to make the most of limited space and freedom. Chapter 2, "The Gothic Poetess: Self-Confinement in the Sonnet Cell," reads Romantic and Victorian metasonnets against the trope of liberty-in-restraint, a familiar message used by Gothic patriarchs to reassure their imprisoned young women to rest easy in their cells—and to appreciate Gothic confinement as a space for productivity and protection. We see this message also rehearsed in nineteenth-century sonnets, where a poet defends the constrictions of sonnet form by likening the poem to a maiden, trapped or bound. The literal prison becomes a formal one. Women sonneteers in particular had to reckon with the burdens of this discourse. Yet rather than reject this figuration of the prison, Elizabeth Barrett Browning and Christina Rossetti actively exploit Gothic modes of confinement, exalting in what I label a poetics of Gothic enclosure. Construing the sonnet as a prison and a womb, they embody the tropes of Gothic motherhood from 1790s novels, intensifying the structural constrictions of sonnet form through innovative sonnet sequences and *bouts-rimés*.

Turning to the experience of the Gothic reader, Chapter 3 considers disorienting, "eleventh-hour" swaps at a novel's ending: a dead body turns out to be a waxen image, or a supernatural spirit turns out to be a sleepwalking servant. Here, I draw a connection between Radcliffe's "realist supernatural" and the "realist symbolism" of D. G. Rossetti's "double works," his sets of paired poems and paintings composed after the peak of the Pre-Raphaelite Brotherhood. It is no coincidence, I argue, that the vehement attacks against Rossetti and his "Fleshly School of Poetry" echo the same attacks launched by opponents of Gothic writing by "the terrorist school," whose works caused readers' hairs to stand on end. Rossetti exploits the same discomfiting, physical shock engendered in Gothic novel-readers, depicting women as alternately ethereal and physical. Conflating the mythological and religious with the corporeal and sexual, destabilizing the lines between sensually pleasing art and pornography, Rossetti's representations of women posed rebellious challenges to the "Woman Question" of the period, as it was mirrored through reforms in prostitution and the treatment of women's bodies with alterations to the 1864 Contagious Diseases Act.

Chapter 4 unifies the Gothic tropes of the preceding three chapters by considering the private writings of G. M. Hopkins. A Jesuit priest sequestered from the world of popular fiction, Hopkins serves as an unlikely connecting figure between the world of 1790s Gothic and canonical Victorian poetry. He is a poet whose sonnets, dramatic lyrics, and confessions have broad appeal and continue to be legible to a popular, non-Catholic readership. Yet in his monodramas with God, Hopkins explores the horrifying darkness of lapsed faith in his so-called "Terrible Sonnets," where the Gothic valences of fictional drama and romance reach psychological extremes on an autobiographical level. Hopkins lives out the experience of spiritual doubt not simply through religious meditation and composition but through shocking, bodily experiences of faith and revelation, through stress and instress. Read against the anti-Catholic subtext of English Gothic novels and their caricatures of the Inquisition, Hopkins's poems voice the harrowing celebration of violence and the suffering of religious bodies, from priests to nuns. He literalizes the cloister as a site of trauma by embodying overhearing and confession (Chapter 1), the thrall of confinement (Chapter 2), and fluctuating bodies (Chapter 3) through the trappings of Catholic life. Through Hopkins, we learn to take seriously representations of English Catholic life in literature, replacing the extremely limited fictive stereotypes perpetuated by Radcliffe, Monk, and others. Hopkins transforms the exaggerated Gothic figure of the foreign evil monk in British nineteenth-century literature by instead bringing home the real-life experience of an English Catholic priest. His spiritual, devotional verses recruit and embody Gothic forms to effect a convergence of his own English identity and Catholic faith. Reading Hopkins in such a way reveals the powerful anti-Catholic stereotypes that Victorian poetry inherited from Gothic fiction.

The conclusion takes a chronological step backwards, considering the poetry of Emily Brontë to reassess how Gothic forms function in her poems at the midpoint between the 1790s and 1890s, cast between Romantic "Old Gothic" or Victorian "New Gothic." For many critics, Emily Brontë's novels model a new mode of self-referential "anti-Gothic" (e.g. *Villette, Wuthering Heights*) that resist or satirize the traditional Gothic themes utilized in her comparatively neglected poems. This chapter revises that reception, bridging the gap between Emily Brontë's prose and poetry through a focus on her Gondal and non-Gondal poems. Tracing the strong influence of Gothic romance that permeated the Brontë household through periodicals and print culture, I show how Emily Brontë's verses embody the Radcliffean "Gothics of the everyday" through her superimposition of a violent, foreign Gothic landscape onto the Haworth moors of northern England. Reading Brontë's poetry of the 1840s alongside the prison lyrics and confessionals of Elizabeth Barrett Browning, Christina Rossetti, and G. M. Hopkins compels us to recognize a corpus of Victorian poetry, infused and imprinted with Gothic forms, that is intrinsically and characteristically Gothic in its construction.

As a way of marking and recalibrating historical shifts in verse developments, this book traces how poetic forms, to borrow Harold Bloom's terms, "bend and break" in new social worlds.[55] Theodor Adorno, reflecting on the paradox of lyric as a space of isolation, emphasized the importance behind "the social interpretation of lyric poetry," showing the universality of lyric as social in nature.[56] To consider the power of lyric in the context of a Gothic social world is to redefine a new gothicized sense of lyric poetry, defining, for instance, new terms of "Gothic overhearing" or "Gothic sonnets." To place formal universalities within a historical, social context invites us to blend readings that privilege formalist analysis with a historical poetics approach, considering various literary moments between 1790 and 1860. Thus, the chapters that follow, rather than reify assumptions of "lyric domination" surrounding a "timeless" poetic ideal from the Romantic era, in fact complicate them head on by showcasing the important element of parody and camp at moments thirty, forty, and fifty years after the advent of 1790s Gothic.[57] We see stagings of lyric song in Chapter 1—quite literally, verses sung against the strumming of a lute or lyre—in chivalric scenes of heroes professing their love in Radcliffe's and Lewis's novels. Chapter 2, which focuses on women's sonnets, tackles assumptions surrounding the troubadour's ideals of fifteenth-century poetic expression through nineteenth-century concerns of complicated childbirth and motherhood, where lyric song is the baby's or mother's cry. In all these ways, ideas of Gothic overhearing, Gothic confinement, and Gothic fluctuation complicate the historical poetical development of lyric, showcasing particular moments among the "fits and starts of the nineteenth century" chronicled and explored by other scholars of lyric.[58] The Gothic's contribution to the development of lyric is the ironization of those very ideals that would become fossilized as default assumptions of lyric poetry after the New Criticism: utter unconsciousness of a listener (Mill); poetry that "depends upon the phenomenalization of the poetic voice" (De Man); and an intensely subjective and personal expression (Hegel).[59]

Notes

1. William Wordsworth, "Preface to the Lyrical Ballads," 2nd edn (1800), in *Lyrical Ballads 1798 and 1800: William Wordsworth and Samuel Coleridge*, ed. Michael Gamer and Dahlia Porter (Toronto: Broadview, 2008), 177.
2. James Watt, *Contesting the Gothic: Fiction, Genre, and Cultural Conflict, 1764–1832* (Cambridge: Cambridge University Press, 2004), 8.
3. Wordsworth, "Preface," 171, 184. One defining formal element of the Gothic is its excess: the Gothic itself is a highly self-reflexive genre that deals in hyperbole and satires of its own conventions. It is purposefully derivative and recycles the same "mysterious" tropes of skeletons, buried secrets, and ancestral discovery, which often descend into camp.

This is central to the distinction between "old" and "new" Gothic, a binary theorized by Robert Heilman, where the old "primitive" Gothic seeks just "the relatively simple thrill or momentary intensity of feeling," but "new Gothic" challenges and satirizes these patterns by engaging in "anti-Gothic" realism. Robert Heilman, "Charlotte Bronte's 'New Gothic,'" in *From Jane Austen to Joseph Conrad: Essays Collected in Memory of James T. Hillhouse*, ed. Robert Rathburn and Martin Steinmann Jr. (Minneapolis: University of Minnesota Press, 1958), 118–32.

4. "Terrorist Novel Writing," *The Spirit of the Public Journals for 1797*, 2nd edn (London: James Ridgway, 1799), 225.
5. Ian Duncan and James Watt remind us that the term "Gothic" is a twentieth-century designation, whereas most of the texts in English prose fiction referred to themselves as "romances." Walpole famously established the hybridity of Gothic by presenting it as a "blend [of] the two kinds of Romance, the ancient and the modern." Horace Walpole, Preface to *The Castle of Otranto: A Gothic Story*, 5th edn (London: J. Dodsley, 1786), xiv. Gary Kelly asserts that Gothic romance "was not so much a coherent authentic genre as an ensemble of themes and formal elements which could be taken over and adapted in whole or in part by other novelists and writers." By "formal elements," he means a "vocabulary of character-types and plot motifs," which I essentially consider thematic characteristics. Gary Kelly, *English Fiction of the Romantic Period 1789–1830* (New York: Routledge, 1989), 49. Cited in Watt, *Contesting the Gothic*, 4.
6. Watt, *Contesting the Gothic*, iv.
7. George Haggerty tackles the question of locating Gothic form, but does so only attending to its affective function: "Gothic form, then, is affective form . . . these works are primarily structured so as to elicit particular responses in the reader . . . Gothic fiction therefore cannot have specific meaning: indeterminacy is inherent to its nature." One useful structural characteristic that Haggerty identifies, however, is the functional role that Gothic tales play within longer novels. George Haggerty, *Gothic Fiction / Gothic Form* (University Park: The Pennsylvania State University Press, 1989), 8, 11.
8. James Watt has argued that the heterogeneous genre of Gothic does not hold together as a continuous tradition. Scholars who read Walpole's preface to the second edition of *The Castle of Otranto* as a manifesto for a new literary genre give an "illusory stability" to the category of Gothic romance. Watt, *Contesting the Gothic*, 1.

For more on Radcliffe and Romantic women's travel writing, see Jane Stabler, "Taking Liberties: The Italian Picturesque in Women's Travel Writing," *European Romantic Review* 13, no. 1 (2002): 11–22; Benjamin A. Brabon, "Surveying Ann Radcliffe's Gothic Landscapes," *Literature Compass* 3, no. 4 (2006): 840–5; George Dekker, *The*

Fictions of Romantic Tourism: Radcliffe, Scott, and Mary Shelley (Stanford: Stanford University Press, 2005); and Marshall Brown, "In Defense of Cliché: Radcliffe's Landscapes," in *The Gothic Text* (Stanford: Stanford University Press, 2005).

For considerations of Radcliffe's Gothic heroines as Romantic poet figures, see Ingrid Horricks, "'Her Ideas Arranged Themselves': Re-Membering Poetry in Radcliffe," *Studies in Romanticism* 47, no. 4 (2008): 507–27 and Beatrice Battaglia, "The 'Pieces of Poetry' in Ann Radcliffe's *The Mysteries of Udolpho*," *DQR Studies in Literature* 39, no. 1 (2007): 137–51.

9. Marjorie Levinson, "What is New Formalism?" *PMLA* 122, no. 2 (March 2007): 558–69. Kramnick and Nersessian conclude that "the inconsistency with which the term ["form"] is used . . . over the long haul of the discipline [expresses] the discipline's good standing, not its crisis" (668). Jonathan Kramnick and Anahid Nersessian, "Form and Explanation," *Critical Inquiry* 43 (Spring 2017): 650–69.
10. Heather Dubrow, "Guess Who's Coming to Dinner? Reinterpreting Formalism and the Country House Poem," *Modern Language Quarterly* 61 (2000): 65.
11. Clune criticizes Levine's *Forms* for conflating forms with ideas, while Langdon Hammer finds problematic the way that in Levine's book, "forms, not people, do things . . . forms 'meet' or 'encounter' each other, like people in a coffee shop" (1204). Michael Clune, "Formalism as the Fear of Ideas," *PMLA* 132, no. 5 (October 2017): 1195–9; Langdon Hammer, "Fantastic Forms," *PMLA* 132, no. 5 (October 2017): 1200–5.
12. Stephanie Sandler, "Rhythms, Networks: Caroline Levine Meets Susan Howe and Marina Tsvetaeva," *PMLA* 132, no. 5 (October 2017): 1229.
13. "Form, in poetry, ceases to be trope only when it becomes topos, only when it is revealed as a place of invention. This revelation depends upon a breaking. Its best analogue is when any of us becomes aware of love just as the object of love is irreparably lost." Harold Bloom, "The Breaking of Form," in *The Lyric Theory Reader: A Critical Anthology*, ed. Virginia Jackson and Yopie Prins (Baltimore: Johns Hopkins University Press, 2014), 276.
14. Robert Hume has compared Gothicism to a poor, illegitimate relation of Romanticism that has been consigned to the margins. Robert D. Hume, "Gothic Versus Romantic: A Revaluation of the Gothic Novel," *PMLA* 84, no. 2 (March 1969), 282.
15. In fact, Lewis used the excuse of youth to apologize for the indiscreet language and themes in his earlier versions of *The Monk*. The fourth edition of the novel makes many changes to mitigate the charges of scandal against Lewis's writing. In this version, there are fewer references to sexual lust, with Ambrosio described as an "intruder" rather than a "ravisher." The moment of rape itself, expressed in the

words that Ambrosio "indulged in excesses" in the first three editions, becomes described as "committed an error" in the fourth edition. This supports the notion that Gothic content and machinery can be censored out or excised for more mature iterations of a text.

16. Recent criticism on Victorian Gothic tends to approach the subject, for instance, from a perspective of marginality or niche studies, such as Ardel Haefele-Thomas's *Queer Others in Victorian Gothic* (2012), Melissa Makala's *Women's Ghost Literature in Nineteenth-Century Britain* (2013), and Julian Wolfreys's *Victorian Hauntings: Spectrality, Gothic, the Uncanny and Literature* (2001).

17. The work of this book especially invites collaboration between scholars of Gothic and those interested in the development of specific Victorian poetic forms, such as the dramatic monologue (Britta Martens, Linda Hughes, Dorothy Mermin, Glennis Byron), women's sonnets (Angela Leighton, Marjorie Stone, Amy Billone, Constance Hassett), and Pre-Raphaelite artists (David Riede, Florence Boos).

18. Fred Botting (ed.), *Gothic: The New Critical Idiom* (London: Routledge, 1996); Emma Clery, *The Rise of Supernatural Fiction 1762–1800* (Cambridge: Cambridge University Press, 1995); Michael Gamer, *Romanticism and the Gothic: Genre, Reception, and Canon Formation* (Cambridge: Cambridge University Press, 2000); Diane Long Hoeveler, *Gothic Feminism: The Professionalization of Gender from Charlotte Smith to the Brontës* (Pennsylvania: Pennsylvania State University Press, 1998); Jerrold E. Hogle, ed., *The Cambridge Companion to Gothic Fiction* (Cambridge: Cambridge University Press, 2002); Robert Miles, *Ann Radcliffe: The Great Enchantress* (New York: Manchester University Press, 1995); David H. Richter, *The Progress of Romance: Literary Historiography and the Gothic Novel* (Columbus: The Ohio State University Press, 1996); Angela Wright, *Britain, France and the Gothic, 1764-1820: The Import of Terror* (Cambridge: Cambridge University Press, 2013); Angela Wright, *Gothic Fiction: A Reader's Guide to Essential Criticism* (Basingstoke: Palgrave, 2007).

19. Edited collections and anthologies on Victorian Gothic, which tend to focus on 1890s writing, include *The Victorian Supernatural* (ed. Nicola Brown, Carolyn Burdett, and Pamela Thurschwell, Cambridge: Cambridge University Press, 2004), *The Victorian Gothic: An Edinburgh Companion* (ed. Andrew Smith and William Hughes, Edinburgh: Edinburgh University Press, 2012), *Victorian Gothic: Literary and Cultural Manifestations in the Nineteenth Century* (ed. Ruth Robbins and Julian Wolfreys, Basingstoke: Palgrave, 2000), and *Gothic Evolutions: Poetry, Tales, Context, Theory* (ed. Corinna Wagner, Toronto: Broadview, 2014). Monographs on Victorian Gothic include Kelly Hurley's *The Gothic Body: Sexuality, Materialism, and Degeneration at the Fin de Siècle* (Cambridge: Cambridge University Press, 1996), Vanessa Dickerson's *Victorian Ghosts in the Noontide:*

Women Writers and the Supernatural (Columbia: University of Missouri, 1996), Gail Turley Houston's *From Dickens to Dracula: Gothic, Economics and Victorian Fiction* (Cambridge: Cambridge University Press, 2005), Hilary Grimes's *The Late Victorian Gothic: Mental Science, the Uncanny, and Scenes of Writing* (Aldershot: Ashgate, 2011), and Jamieson Ridenhour's *In Darkest London: The Gothic Cityscape in Victorian Literature* (Washington DC: Rowman & Littlefield, 2013).

Monographs that explore a Gothic influence on Romantic and Victorian writers focus almost exclusively on novels rather than poetry, including Judith Wilt's *Ghosts of the Gothic: Austen, Eliot, and Lawrence* (Princeton: Princeton University Press, 1980), Joseph Wisenfarth's *Gothic Manners and the Classic Manners* (Madison: Wisconsin University Press, 1988), Daniel Cottom's *The Civilized Imagination: A Study of Ann Radcliffe, Jane Austen, and Sir Walter Scott* (Cambridge: Cambridge University Press, 1985/2009), and Royce Mahawatte's *George Eliot and the Gothic Novel* (Cardiff: University of Wales Press, 2013).

20. "If 'Gothic' at first suggests a formal muddle, I hope to show in what sense that muddle is creative, not just formally but imaginatively as well." Haggerty, *Gothic Fiction*, 4.
21. Elizabeth R. Napier, *The Failure of Gothic: Problems of Disjunction in an Eighteenth-Century Literary Form* (Oxford: Oxford University Press, 1987); Robert Kiely, *The Romantic Novel in England* (Cambridge, MA: Harvard University Press, 1972), 9–72.

    R. S. Crane considered nineteenth-century works of Gothic more powerful because they were more compressed. R. S. Crane, *Critical and Historical Principles of Literary History* (Chicago: University of Chicago Press, 1971), 20, 41.
22. See Jackson and Prins, *The Lyric Theory Reader*, 5 and Marion Thain (ed.), *The Lyric Poem: Formations and Transformations* (Cambridge: Cambridge University Press, 2013); Barbara Herrnstein Smith, *On the Margins of Discourse: The Relation of Literature to Language* (Chicago, University of Chicago Press, 1978), 33; Marjorie Perloff, "Can(n)on to the Right of Us, Can(n)on to the Left of Us: A Plea for Difference," in *The Lyric Theory Reader*, 467.
23. Susan Wolfson, *Romantic Shades and Shadows* (Baltimore: Johns Hopkins University Press, 2018), 3.
24. Terry Castle, *The Female Thermometer: Eighteenth-Century Culture and the Invention of the Uncanny* (Oxford: Oxford University Press, 1995), 234
25. Patrick O'Malley, *Catholicism, Sexual Deviance, and Victorian Gothic Culture* (Oxford: Oxford University Press, 2006).
26. Wolfson, *Romantic Shades*, 3.
27. Ibid.

28. Eve Kosofsky Sedgwick, *The Coherence of Gothic Conventions* (New York: Arno Press, 1980), 4.
29. Ibid.
30. Ibid. 5.
31. Ibid. 7.
32. Ibid. 14.
33. Ibid. 12.
34. Sedgwick, *Coherence of Gothic Conventions*, 13.
35. Shaw showed the parallels between Coleridge's conversation poems and Browning's and Tennyson's monologues. Knoepflmacher has read Browning's monologues as an ironization and inversion of female projection seen in Keats. That overhearing lyric and dramatic monologue are variations of the same poetic model, rather than counterpoints, is a seminal contribution of Tucker to studies of the genre. David W. Shaw, "Lyric Displacement in the Victorian Monologue: Naturalizing the Vocative," *Nineteenth-Century Literature* 52, no. 3 (1997): 302–25; Ulrich C. Knoepflmacher, "Projection and the Female Other: Romanticism, Browning, and the Victorian Dramatic Monologue," *Victorian Poetry* 22, no. 2 (1984): 139–59; *Victorian Hybridities: Cultural Anxiety and Formal Innovation* ed. Ulrich C. Knoepflmacher and Logan D. Browning. (Baltimore: Johns Hopkins University Press, 2010); Herbert F. Tucker, "From Monomania to Monologue: 'St. Simeon Stylites' and the Rise of the Victorian Dramatic Monologue," *Victorian Poetry* 22, no. 2 (1984): 121–37.
36. Anne McCarthy, *Awful Parenthesis: Suspension and the Sublime in Romantic and Victorian Poetry* (Toronto: University of Toronto Press, 2018); Monique Morgan, *Narrative Means, Lyric Ends: Temporality in the Nineteenth-Century British Long Poem* (Columbus: The Ohio State University Press, 2009); Dino Franco Felluga, "Novel Poetry: Transgressing the Law of Genre," *Victorian Poetry* 41, no. 4 (Winter 2003): 490–9.
37. Radcliffe first found widespread success with her third novel, *The Romance of the Forest*. *Gaston de Blondeville* was published posthumously in 1826.
38. Miles, *Ann Radcliffe*, 8.
39. Compare this to William Godwin's payment of 10 pounds by William Lane for *Imogen: A Pastoral Romance. In Two Volumes. From the Ancient British* in 1784. Radcliffe's payments from T. Cadell and W. Davies in 1797 and from G. G. J. and J. Robinson in 1794 are the two highest known receipts for novels written between 1770 and 1799. See Table 7, "Surviving Receipts to Novelists for Surrender of Copyright, 1770–1799" in Raven and Forster (eds), *The English Novel 1770–1829: A Bibliographical Survey of Prose Fiction in the British Isles*, Volume 1: 1770–1799 (Oxford: Oxford University Press), 52–3.

40. John Keats, Letter to George and Georgiana Keats, 14 February to 3 May 1819, in *The Letters of John Keats: Volume 2, 1814–182*, ed. Hyder Edward Rollins (Cambridge, MA: Harvard University Press, 1958), 62.

41. See Franz J. Potter, *The History of Gothic Publishing, 1800–1835: Exhuming the Trade*, (New York: Palgrave, 2005), 15. Minerva authors, prominently female, included Eliza Parsons, Anna Maria Bennett, Isabella Kelly, Regina Maria Roche, Ann of Swansea, and Sarah Sheriffe, with myriad contributors publishing anonymously as well. Among the more obviously plagiaristic titles are works by male authors which received unfavorable reviews, including *The Romance of the Cavern* (1793) by George Walker and *Santa-Maria; or, the Mysterious Pregnancy* by Joseph Fox. (Dorothy Blakey, *The Minerva Press 1790–1820*, London: The Bibliographic Society of Oxford University Press, 1939; Graham Law, "Minerva Press," *The Oxford Companion to the Book*, ed. Michael F. Suarez and H. R. Woudhuysen, Oxford: Oxford University Press, 2010.)

Even Mary Robinson's *Hubert de Sevrac* was appraised by S. T. Coleridge as too obviously imitative of Radcliffe: "It is an imitation of Mrs. Radcliffe's romances but without any resemblance that may not be attained by a common pen." (Samuel Taylor Coleridge, Review of *Hubert de Sevrac*, *Critical Review* 23 (August 1798): 472.)

"This strange farrago is copied from various popular novels. The Romance of a Forest gave it the name; the Recess its heroes; and Ferdinand Count Fathom has supplied some of its most interesting events . . . The whole is absurd and improbable: we had begun to mark the inconsistencies of the story; but they would have filled a volume: its own weight is sufficient to sink it. The events astonish without interesting: the heroes are sunk in despair, or raised to happiness, without the reader's feeling a pang or transport." (Review of *The Romance of the Cavern; or, The History of Fitz-Henry and James*, *Critical Review* 10 (March 1794): 349, quoted in Raven and Forster, *The English Novel*, 599–600.)

Arthur Aikin reviewed Joseph Fox's *Santa-Maria; or, the Mysterious Pregnancy* for the *Monthly Review*, deeming it "a very poor and evident imitation of the style and character of Mrs Radcliffe's romances. Here are wonders that excite no surprise; horrors which are destitute of interest; and a pompous phraseology that only betrays the barrenness of the sentiments." (*Monthly Review* (1797): 210–11, quoted in *The English Novel 1770–1829*, vol. 1, 712–13.) Meanwhile, the *Critical Review* praised *The Romance of the Forest* (1791): "The novel . . . engages the attention strongly, and interests the feelings very powerfully: the general style of the whole, as well as the reflections, deserve also commendation . . . every thing is consistent, and within the verge of rational belief." (Review of *The Romance of the Forest*, *Critical Review* 4 (April 1792): 458–9, quoted in *The English Novel*, 543).

The prolific imitations of Radcliffe stumped book reviewers, who lacked the language to muster up new and interesting summaries. In a review for *Austenburn Castle*, published in two volumes for William Lane in 1795, written anonymously "by an unpatronized female," the *Critical Review* wrote: "Since Mrs. Radcliffe's justly admired and successful romances, the press has teemed with stories of haunted castles and visionary terrors; the incidents of which are so little diversified, that criticism is at a loss to vary its remarks. The present work will not be found devoid of entertainment by those who have taste for such compositions." (Review of *Austenburg Castle. In two volumes. By an unpatronized female. Critical Review* 16 (February 1796): 222, quoted in *The English Novel*, 629.)

42. T. J. Horsley Curties admitted that his novel *Ancient Records, or, The Abbey of Saint Oswythe* (Minerva, 1801) owed much to the "Udolpho's unrivalled Foundress," quoted in Peter Otto, "Radcliffe and her imitators." Gothic Fiction: Rare Printed Works from the Sadleir-Black Collection of Gothic Fiction at the Alderman Library, University of Virginia. Available at <http://www.ampltd.co.uk/digital_guides/gothic_fiction/Contents.aspx> (last accessed 15 December 2019).

43. See Miles, *Ann Radcliffe*, 1995; Rictor Norton's *Mistress of Udolpho: The Life of Ann Radcliffe* (London: Leicester University Press, 1999); Juliann E. Fleenor (ed.), *The Female Gothic* (Fountain Valley, CA: Eden Press, 1983); Hoeveler, *Gothic Feminism*; E. J. Clery, *Women's Gothic: From Clara Reeve to Mary Shelley* (Tavistock: Northcote House, 2000); Patricia Murphy, *The New Woman Gothic: Reconfigurations of Distress* (Columbia: University of Missouri Press, 2016); Andrew Smith and Mark Bennett (eds), *Locating Ann Radcliffe* (London: Routledge, 2019); Dale Townshend and Angela Wright (eds), *Ann Radcliffe, Romanticism and the Gothic* (Cambridge: Cambridge University Press, 2014); "Radcliffe at 250: Gothic and Romantic Imaginations – An International Conference at the University of Sheffield on June 27–29, 2014," sponsored by BARS (British Association for Romantic Studies) and the University of Stirling; Jakub Lipski and Jacek Mydla (eds), *The Enchantress of Words, Sounds and Images: Anniversary Essays on Ann Radcliffe, 1764–1823* (Washington DC: Academica Press, 2015).

"Mighty magician" comes from T. J. [Thomas James] Mathias, *The Pursuits of Literature: A Satirical Poem in Four Dialogues. With Notes*, 8th edition (Dublin: J. Milliken), 15, quoted in Townshend and Wright, *Ann Radcliffe*, 15.

44. 1809 saw the publication of *Manfroné; or, The One-Handed Monk. A Romance* by one Mary Ann Radcliffe. The title was later claimed by Louisa Theresa Bellenden Ker. *The Mysterious Baron, or the Castle in the Forest, A Gothic Story* (1808) was written by an Eliza Ratcliffe. Catherine Cuthbertson's 1809 French translation of *Romance of the*

Pyrenees (1803) was spuriously attributed to Ann Radcliffe. *The English Novel*, 168.

See Dale Townshend and Angela Wright, "Gothic and Romantic Engagements: The Critical Reception of Ann Radcliffe, 1789–1850," in *Ann Radcliffe, Romanticism, and the Gothic*, 14–15, for a more detailed account of the hack writers whose plagiarisms "augmented rather than tarnished" Radcliffe's reputation.

45. The greatest evidence of actual reading tastes over time—Bell's, Lackington's, and Lane's Libraries—give us a vision of Gothic readership today; in 1802, Minerva Library in London advertised 17,000 volumes. (Ann W. Engar, "The Minerva Press; William Lane," in *The British Literary Book Trade, 1700–1820*, ed. James K. Bracken and Joel Silver. Detroit: Gale Research, 1995.) See Potter, *History of Gothic Publishing*, 18. See also Elizabeth Neiman and Tina Morin (eds), "The Minerva Press and the Romantic-Era Literary Marketplace," *Romantic Textualities: Literature and Print Culture, 1780–1840*, no. 23 (Summer 2020). Available at <http://www.romtext.org.uk/issues/issue-23/> (last accessed 1 November 2021).

46. The term "Female Gothic" was first coined by Ellen Moers (1977), who emphasized the Gothic genre as a genre founded by women and written for women. See Ellen Moers, *Literary Women: Great Writers* (New York, Doubleday, 1976), 90. The "female Gothic" plot usually consists of an orphan in search of an absent mother, threatened by a feudal patriarchal figure, courted by a weak suitor figure. Male Gothic plots are purportedly more violent and Oedipal. See Robert Miles, "Ann Radcliffe and Matthew Lewis," in *A Companion to the Gothic*, ed. David Punter (Malden: Blackwell, 2000), 43.

47. "Without introducing into her narrative any thing really supernatural, Mrs. Radcliffe has contrived to produce as powerful an effect as if the invisible world had been obedient to her magic spell; and the reader experiences in perfection the strange luxury of artificial terror, without being obliged for a moment to hoodwink his reason, or to yield to the weakness of superstitious credulity." William Enfield, Review of *Mysteries of Udolpho*, *Monthly Review* 15 (November 1794): 280.

48. Deborah Rogers, *The Matrophobic Gothic and Its Legacy: Sacrificing Mothers in the Novel and in Popular Culture* (New York: Peter Lang, 2007), 165. Michael Gamer uses "Goody Blake & Harry Gill" as a model of how Wordsworth and his readers could indulge in supernatural stories while maintaining an "enlightened" distance. Gamer, *Romanticism and the Gothic*, 97.

49. "More than any other 'Gothic' writer, [Radcliffe] sought to dignify or elevate romance by subsuming elements of higher literary genres, and appealing to the prestigious discourse of aesthetics." Watt, *Contesting the Gothic*, 4.

See especially Jane Stabler, "Ann Radcliffe's Poetry: The Poetics of Refrain and Inventory," in *Ann Radcliffe, Romanticism and the Gothic*, ed. Townshend and Wright, 185–202.
50. "The gloom of these shades, their solitary silence, except when the breeze swept over their summits, the tremendous precipices of the mountains, that came partially to the eye, each assisted to raise the solemnity of Emily's feelings into awe; she saw only images of gloomy grandeur, or of dreadful sublimity, around her; other images, equally gloomy and equally terrible, gleamed on her imagination . . . Emily lost, for a moment, her sorrows, in the immensity of nature . . . From this sublime scene the travellers continued to ascend among the pines, till they entered a narrow pass of the mountains, which shut out every feature of the distant country, and, in its stead, exhibited only tremendous crags, impending over the road, where no vestige of humanity, or even of vegetation, appeared . . ." Radcliffe, *The Mysteries of Udolpho* (1794), Oxford World's Classics, ed. Bonamy Dobrée (New York: Oxford University Press, 2008), 224–5.
51. Mary Wollstonecraft, *A Vindication of the Rights of Men, in a Letter to the Honourable Edmund Burke, occasioned by his Reflections on the Revolution in France*, 2nd edn (London: J. Johnson, 1790), 9–10.
52. David Punter and Elisabeth Bronfen reconsider the Gothic genre in terms of trauma theory in "Gothic: Violence, Trauma and the Ethical," in *The Gothic*, ed. Fred Botting, 7–21.
53. Michelle A. Massé, *In the Name of Love: Women, Masochism and the Gothic* (Ithaca: Cornell University Press, 1992).
54. David Quint, *Epic and Empire: Politics and Generic Form from Virgil to Milton* (Princeton: Princeton University Press, 1993), 9.
55. Bloom, "Breaking of Form," 276.
56. Theodor W. Adorno, "On Lyric Poetry and Society," in *The Lyric Theory Reader*, ed. Jackson and Prins, 340.
57. Jackson and Prins, "Avant-garde Anti-lyricism," in *The Lyric Theory Reader*, 452.
58. Jackson and Prins, *The Lyric Theory Reader*, 2.
59. Paul de Man, "Lyrical Voice in Contemporary Theory: Riffaterre and Jauss," in *Lyric Poetry: Beyond the New Criticism*, ed. Chaviva Hošek and Patricia Parker (Ithaca: Cornell University Press, 1985), 55, quoted in Perloff, "Can(n)on to the Right of Us," 453.

Chapter 1

Gothic Overhearing: Inquisition, Confession, and Accusation in Browning's Dramatic Monologues

> That song has always seemed to us like the lament of a prisoner in a solitary cell, ourselves listening, unseen in the next.
>
> J. S. Mill, "What is Poetry?"

> And yet God has not said a word!
>
> Browning, "Porphyria's Lover"

"That's my last Duchess painted on the wall, / Looking as if she were alive."[1] So vaunts the wealthy Duke of Ferrara in Robert Browning's famous dramatic monologue, alluding to the young wife whose likeness he captured in a painting before commanding her murder. Cunning, collected, and ruthless, the Duke is a master of nuanced speech and emotions; he controls the pacing of his speech as he does the suspenseful plot that unfolds. As readers, we feel frightened of his machinations but also culpable as unwitting spectators to his understated crime—much like the poor unsuspecting page who brokers the Duke's next marriage. In many ways, the Duke from "My Last Duchess" looms as a gatekeeper to this book, standing as an imposing presence in Victorian poetry, but also as a symbol of Gothic villainy. He joins the ranks of cruel, unsavory speakers from many nineteenth-century poems, including Tennyson's "St. Simeon Stylites" and Browning's 1842 collection, *Dramatic Lyrics*.

But such memorable villains are not native to nineteenth-century lyrics. More than just a landmark figure in the development of the dramatic monologue, the Duke embodies the Gothic character of the iniquitous patriarch. Here we have an Italian aristocrat who celebrates, with elegance, the expediency of his wife's murder. He gestures towards the figure of a woman who has been silenced, murdered, and frozen within a frame. His confession takes the form of calculated boasts. He recalls the murderous villains from spectacularly popular Gothic novels of the 1790s, including those by Ann Radcliffe and Matthew Lewis, from *The Mysteries of Udolpho*'s evil Count Montoni to Father Schedoni of Matthew Lewis's *The Monk*. When it comes to the Victorian dramatic monologue, critics have, for the most part, been oblivious to the fact that Gothic villains have been staring us in the face the entire time.

Why has the history of criticism chosen not to notice something so obvious: that the lineage of this most famous poetic voice is as much a Gothic villain as it is the lyric speaker of the Romantic conversation poem? What has been the investment of lyric studies in overlooking this connection?[2] In addition to crossing the divide of genre, from the novel to the poem—as well as class, from lowly Gothic to high Victorian—formal assignations of style have also played a role in obfuscating this line of inheritance. The Gothic novel is typically associated with excess, while proper Victorian poetry is marked by the art of restraint. Yet in what follows, I subvert this narrative by emphasizing the shared poetics of containment, restriction, and confinement that pervade these texts. This restraint, sometimes so tensely bound in its formal strictures as to bubble up to the surface, reaching a pitch of intensity and excess, is what the Gothic and Victorian poetry share: a potent, often violent poetics of enclosure.

* * *

Many of Browning's poems are recognizably Gothic, notably those composed at the beginning of his career.[3] From *Pauline* (1833) to "Porphyria's Lover" (1836) and "Johannes Agricola in Meditation" (1836), these poems are populated with Gothic personae, particularly the two stock characters of the tyrannical, jealous husband and the egomaniacal cleric—both of whom are self-justifying, God-defying firebrands. While some critics identify the disturbing elements in Victorian poetry as grotesque, drawing on John Ruskin and Walter Bagehot's aesthetic theorizations, these features are also unmistakably Gothic in their inheritance. Not only can we consider Browning's dukes and counts as descendants of Gothic fiction for their dark, menacing characters as charismatic anti-heroes. Nor is it only because so many poems share the Catholic, Italian, sixteenth-century settings of so many Radcliffean novels. Aside from any thematic similarities, "My Last Duchess" is chilling and memorable due to the Duke's formal pyrotechnics. Manipulating the audience and divulging his crimes through a slow reveal, he borrows formal structures and rhetorical patterns, including strategies of display and concealment, or dramatic accusations, that are definitive of the Gothic novel and its setting of inquisition trials. These elements comprise the suspenseful machinery of 1790s Gothic fiction: overhearing, imprisonment, and forced confession. Browning's Duke casually orchestrates the incorporation of such tropes and devices into his speech—glibly, inconspicuously, and without acknowledging the Gothic tradition.

By republishing his first dramatic monologues as a pair entitled "Madhouse Cells" in 1842, Browning was calling attention to a genealogy of insanity, criminality, and confinement in his poems.[4] Herbert Tucker, without explicitly citing the Gothic, makes clear that the heritage of these speakers is anything but genteel, calling the dramatic monologues "the most daemonic poems written in English during the last two hundred years," remarkable for their "nearly naked aggression."[5] Browning's speakers create a blanket of oppressive discomfort for their audience through their presentation of the murderous act, by way of an offhand remark or some pointed braggadocio celebrating a nefarious accomplishment. This discomfort is often predicated upon the structure of overhearing, which forms the basis of the dramatic monologue through a triangulation of speaker, auditor, and audience.

These "daemonic" poems share a formal dynamics of inquisitional overhearing, confession, and accusation, starring a Gothic cast. We see this explicitly in various models of what I call "Gothic overhearing": self-conscious, overwrought scenes of eavesdropping and discovery that challenge and even satirize the typical ideal structures of lyric utterance. Often rooted in failure, and sometimes verging on bathos, Gothic overhearing draws on repetition and exaggeration as techniques to ironize the Gothic's aesthetics of excess and failure. Gothic overhearing doesn't take itself too seriously: it is imperfect; it is a series of trials; it plays upon stylistic failures of composition. In fact, the lengthy format of Gothic romance lent authors the freedom to experiment by creating staged scenes of thwarted miscommunication that pass as mistakes in plot: in *The Mysteries of Udolpho*, characters confuse Monsieur Dupont for Valancourt and St. Aubert's sister for Lady Laurentini. In *The Italian*, Ellena and Vivaldi cross signals in a romantic encounter, just as *The Monk*'s Antonia and Lorenzo do. As I will argue, such instances of failed overhearing posed a meaningful model of lyric experimentation that Victorian poets, too, performed forty years later in their own writing.

Gothic overhearing exists in a world of constant social threat, since the Gothic world is one in which there is no God or benevolent patriarch actively enforcing moral standards of behavior. The dramatic monologue, then, a relatively brief, contained speech-act that often terminates in interruption, often cuts off the potential for moral intervention or audience participation. In Gothic, one can only hope that one's words are overheard by the correct person in a benevolent context, lest they be misconstrued, misinterpreted, and used against them.

Why focus on structures of overhearing? The Victorian dramatic monologue has traditionally been understood as a form that was developed simultaneously, though independently, by Tennyson and Browning in the 1830s as an alternative to the universalizing voice of Romantic lyric.[6] Victorian poets re-envisioned the egotistical sublime of the Wordsworthian poet-speaker, instead staging poems in which the speaker is distinctly *not* the poet. The easiest way to achieve this was by assuming the voice of speakers "in extremis," in compromising situations, with the earliest speakers manifesting, as Tucker has shown, as "monomaniacs" in monologue.[7]

A chorus of critical voices has since posed different categorizations to dissect and taxonomize the dramatic monologue, in an attempt to define the form in its various iterations. In 1947, Ina Beth Sessions determined key characteristics that separated a "perfect dramatic monologue"—epitomized by "My Last Duchess"—from what she labeled as "imperfect," "formal," or "approximate" dramatic monologues. The seven elements compromising perfect dramatic monologues are: (1) speaker, (2) audience, (3) occasion, (4) interplay between speaker and audience, (5) revelation of character, (6) dramatic action, and (7) action taking place in the present.[8] Other terms, such as "dramatic lyrics" or "mask lyrics," have also proven useful in labeling variations of the imperfect dramatic monologue, each of which Glennis Byron surveys comprehensively in her 2003 study of the form.

For many scholars, the novelty of the dramatic monologue lies in a reader's response and interaction: Robert Langbaum conceived of dramatic monologue as a form in which the reader is affectively engaged in "sympathy or moral judgment" of the speaker.[9] Dorothy Mermin and Jennifer Wagner-Lawlor emphasized the presence of a silent auditor in the poems, exploring the complication of power dynamics between speaker, auditor and audience.[10] The role of the auditor, whether absent, present, implied, or replaced by God, provides another point of critical contention for scholars such as Angela Leighton and W. David Shaw.[11]

One major point of critical departure is the efficacy and intentionality of the character's speech act. For Tucker, dramatic monologists always betray themselves, because more often than not, "what Browning's speakers say gains ascendancy over what they set out to mean."[12] Dramatic monologists carry on so far as to lose control of their initial intentions, giving away more than they mean to. This ironic character revelation is key: "In the practice of reading, we recognize Browning's 'Madhouse Cells' as dramatic monologues because in both of them the self as authoritative voice fares so ill that the poems simply cannot be the lyrics we, or their initial public, might at first have taken."[13] Cornelia Pearsall, diverging from this view, gives credit to the authority and intentionality of the monologist, whose artful speech acts execute exactly what they set out to perform: "the speakers themselves knowingly, even willfully, set these transformations into motion by the force of an intensely ambitious discourse."[14]

This rich critical tradition, negotiating such an array of terms and conditions, exposes the difficulty of defining such a wide-ranging form. Joining the conversation, I propose a model for understanding the formal identifiers of the dramatic monologue not through a list of characteristics, but through a unified, literary-cultural lens of an important literary precursor: Gothic romance, with its repeated patterns of confessions, accusation, and inquisitional trial, is a powerful framework for understanding the many key poetic components of dramatic monologue that have previously been identified by scholars of the form.

In this chapter, I argue that scenes of eavesdropping and overhearing, as modeled in numerous scenes from 1790s Gothic novels, formalize a poetics of guilt, suspicion, and collusion that become important formal pillars of later Victorian dramatic monologues. These Gothic elements are structurally embedded in the poetic form and its triangulation of speaker, audience, and auditor. This coherence of Gothic conventions, which Eve Sedgwick describes as an aesthetic based on pleasurable fear, is a compelling literary and cultural source that we can use to understand that discomfiting, fear-based "unspeakability" of dramatic monologue speakers.[15] The implied threat of collusion on the part of the poetic audience emerges directly from the dramatic situation of a criminal on trial, where one's innocence is always being negotiated in a speech act of self-defense: in an inquisitional trial hall—often an unjust and bastardized version of the proper, lawful courtroom—we have the accused, the judge, and God. The model of Gothic overhearing merges the thematic and structural elements of guilt found in this singular poetic form.

In other words, Browning does not only borrow a cast of characters from 1790s Gothic novels in order to create his speakers "in extremis"; in utilizing these figures, he also inherits a structural framework of overhearing, accusation, and confession inherent to the fictional contexts of Gothic romance. Whether this overhearing is framed as an act of compromised romantic confession (which provides a sense of humiliation, shame, and failure), or of criminal confession (which provides a sense of grandstanding, self-vindication, and guilty collusion), these Gothic elements all contribute to the criminality, suspense, and suspicion so prevalent in early Victorian dramatic monologues, especially those by Robert Browning.

We can see poetic negotiations unfold in parallel within Gothic romance and Browning's poems: Where do we draw the line between poetic song and noise, or beauty and pain? When exactly do speeches of self-defense become acts of self-incrimination? How does one adjudicate between innocence and guilt when the judge and jury themselves are corrupt? Such deliberations about intent, morality, innocence, guilt, and free will reflect the pressing political concerns of Victorian authors writing in an era of Arnoldian doubt and religious re-examination. Linking these questions to historical developments in the judicial conceptions of liability and blame, particularly tort law, I trace the poetics of Gothic overhearing through a range of nineteenth-century dramatic monologues. Moving from poems that are ostensibly Gothic in theme to those that might even be called "anti-Gothic," I revisit Browning's poems chronologically through a lens of Gothic overhearing, from *Pippa Passes* to "The Confessional," "The Soliloquy of the Spanish Cloister," "Andrea del Sarto," and "Mister Sludge, 'The Medium.'"

Articulating this Gothic connection alters our readings of Browning's non-sensational poems in two ways. First, even in dramatic monologues that do not reveal some wrongdoing in plot, the poems still take on the mode of confession and criminality, evoking the suspicion and guilt inherent in the triangulation of Gothic overhearing. Like the many egotistical villains that populate Gothic fiction, dramatic monologists consistently risk betraying themselves, their confessional performances potentially unfolding as self-incriminations as they are on trial. In other words, we can understand both Sessions's and Tucker's formal characteristics of dramatic monologues through a specifically Gothic framework. The villainies and transgressions of Gothic are also a useful recasting of the "lyric pathology" recognized by Marion Thain in late-Victorian Decadent poems.[16]

Second, regardless of the innocence or guilt of a speaker's character, wrongdoing and suspicion pervade Browning's dramatic monologues because the reader too is incriminated as a guilty overhearer. That infamous line of Porphyria's lover, "And yet God has not said a word!" is a refrain shared by Browning's assassins, mad monks, and evil dukes. That refrain echoes throughout fictional prisons of the Inquisition, by victims and Grand Inquisitors alike, both the innocent and the guilty. It signals a Gothic universe where values of right and wrong become distorted, forcing individuals to navigate between godlessness and moral order. The Gothic is a mirror for the fluctuations of Victorian doubt, where good and evil, sympathy or judgment, shift back and forth in an unstable world. Ultimately, the Victorian dramatic monologue reconceptualized Romantic lyric by dismantling ideals of poetic expression: it undermined the ideal of lyric confession as truthful or authentic speech, simply by showing the power of rhetorical manipulation behind *all words*, and calling into question the purity of any single speech act. In the realm of the dramatic monologue—an intrinsically Gothic world—poetry can no longer pass as innocent verbal transmission, for words can always be recontextualized, reframed, or triangulated to incriminate both speaker and listener.

Romantic Confession

At a moment situated on the cusp of the 1790s Gothic novel craze and Victorian innovations of the dramatic monologue, John Stuart Mill articulated a now-classic definition of poetry as it was conceived in 1833: "Eloquence is *heard*; poetry is *overheard*." "Poetry is feeling confessing itself to itself in moments of solitude." "All poetry is of the nature of soliloquy." "The peculiarity of poetry appears to us to lie in the poet's utter unconsciousness of a listener."[17] The moment that a speaker acknowledges his audience cheapens this project, and the ideal of overheard poetry becomes compromised. Poetry gives way to "mere eloquence"; pure confession descends into staged performance.

To be sure, Mill's ideal functions best in some sort of poetic vacuum. But what happens when these poetic moments fail? Even in a fictional setting, the line between true poetry and mere eloquence is a thin one at best. In the novels of both Radcliffe and Lewis, scenes of overhearing abound that complicate, challenge, or mock the notion of "unconscious" speech. Such stagings of overhearing are ubiquitous throughout 1790s Gothic novels where heroines, prying about the castle, overhear suspicious plots in which they are embroiled. This narrative trope propels plot in particularly useful ways when characters hear confessions across some threshold, whether a castle turret, prison wall, or trapdoor. Key information, overheard, may reveal the location of a buried object or the identity of a missing ancestral link, or it may convince a doubtful heroine that her suitor does, in fact, love her.[18] But these scenes just as often result in misunderstanding, humor, and bathos. They are marked by irony and failure.

Such scenes can be understood as scenes of *failed* overhearing—where verbal transmission somehow goes askew, compromising Mill's poetic ideal. They result in a series of compact situational dramas, not unlike those that would be staged by Browning and Tennyson in their dramatic monologues. Once we recognize that this basis for compromised overhearing was established in Gothic novels forty years prior to Browning and Tennyson's "reinnovation" of the poetic form, we can begin to understand the presence of many critical components that are inherently associated with the Victorian dramatic monologue but not with Romantic lyric at play in nineteenth-century poems: collusion, cruelty, and silence.

Scenes of overhearing are so frequent in the Gothic novel as to become a rehearsed and tired trope. This element of excess, of repetition and ridiculousness is important to the characterization of what I term "Gothic overhearing." Gothic overhearing entails a self-reflexive treatment of the trope itself; it subverts and questions the typical structures of eavesdropping found in novels and plays. Gothic overhearing is marked by three factors: the ironic impossibility of unselfconsciousness; the sense of guilt transferred from speaker to unwitting auditor; and a potential sense of sympathy for the speaker, no matter how guilty he may be. Thus, the trope becomes compromised in a self-conscious treatment of its staging, pointing towards the various situational elements that might cause it to stray from the ideal.

In the following section, I examine four scenes of Gothic overhearing, drawn from prose passages of Gothic romance: each instance, featuring staged eavesdropping and ironic character revelation, imitates but complicates an ideal of successful overhearing. These passages proleptically show how lyric convention could become, in the hands of later dramatic monologists, ironized and criminalized. Radcliffe provides an anticipatory model for the Victorian experimentalists who follow in her wake, writing a parody of Romantic poetic conventions *avant la lettre,* staging Gothic versions of overhearing in its various imperfections and deformations.

Take 1: Utter Unconsciousness of a Listener

In our first example, drawn from Radcliffe's *The Italian,* a true poet effuses genuinely and spontaneously without regard for any audience or auditor, attempting to offer up true poetry in proto-Millian fashion. In the following passage, the dashing Vincentio de Vivaldi woos Ellena di Rosalba, the novel's heroine, through the chivalrous songs of a troubadour:

> From the bowery lattices of a small pavilion within the orangery, he perceived a light, and the sudden hope, which it occasioned, of seeing Ellena, almost *overcame* him. It was impossible to resist the opportunity of beholding her, yet he checked the impatient step he was taking, to ask himself, whether it was honorable thus to steal upon her retirement, and become an *unsuspected observer* of her secret thoughts. But the temptation was too powerful for this honorable hesitation; the pause was momentary; and, stepping lightly towards the pavilion, he placed himself near an open lattice, so as to be shrouded from observation by the branches of an orange-tree, while he obtained a full view of the apartment. Ellena was alone, sitting in a thoughtful attitude and holding her lute, which she did not play. She appeared *lost to a consciousness* of surrounding objects, and a tenderness was on her countenance, which seemed to tell him that her thoughts were engaged by some interesting subject. Recollecting that, when last he had seen her thus, she pronounced his name, his hope revived, and he was going to discover himself and appear at her feet, when she spoke, and he paused.
> . . .
> Vivaldi, when he listened to this, was immovable; he seemed as if entranced; the sound of her lute and voice recalled him, and he heard her sing the first stanza of the very air with which he had opened the serenade on a former night, and with such sweet pathos as the composer must have felt when he was inspired with the idea.
> She paused at the conclusion of the first stanza, when Vivaldi, *overcome* by the temptation of such an opportunity for expressing his passion, *suddenly* struck the chords of the lute, and replied to her in the second. The tremor of his voice, though it restrained his tones, *heightened its eloquence.* Ellena instantly recollected it; *her colour alternately*

> *faded and returned*; and, before the verse concluded, *she seemed to have lost all consciousness.*
>
> ...
>
> One evening that Vivaldi sat with Ellena and Signora Bianchi, in the very pavilion where he had *overheard* that short but interesting *soliloquy*, which assured him of regard, he pleaded with more than his usual *earnestness* for a speedy marriage.[19]

This scene seems to boast all the qualities Mill values in poetry, posing a standard model of conventional, romantic overhearing where a speaker professes his feelings in "utter unconsciousness of a listener." These lines, complete with "eloquence," "overhear[ing]," "soliloquy," "passion" and "earnestness," deploy the very same vocabulary later used by Mill in "Thoughts on Poetry and its Varieties." Radcliffe stages here a scene of romantic confession we might deem worthy as true poetry: Ellena is perfectly pure and unassuming in her utterances; Vivaldi is thoroughly shrouded from observation; the two figures perfectly play the role of earnest speaker and accidental overhearer. With the lute strumming, Radcliffe choreographs a scene of lyric expression that is spontaneous and unadulterated. Vivaldi, certainly no guilty voyeur, proves through actions that his intentions are pure: "He was going to discover himself and appear at her feet, when she spoke and he paused."

Yet even if this scene is cast as spontaneous, without any sense of theatrical manufacturing, it is hyperbolic in its delivery. Ellena is not only unaware before professing the name of her lover that he will hear her—she is unconscious to an even more comic extent: "before the verse concluded, she seemed to have lost all consciousness." Vivaldi, similarly, is "immovable" and "entranced." Within this perfect avowal of love is a touch of the ridiculous, with its heavy-handed description of "earnest" lovers who are "unsuspecting" to the point of stupor—and here we slip into the bathos of Gothic as the heroine falls into a fainting fit, one so comically recursive that "her colour alternately faded and returned." In full lyric overdrive (or overkill), this scene boasts not one, but two lutes (or lyres), one played by the female love object and the one by the male professor of love. The incorporation of double lutes is overly aggressive in its staging of lyric poetic clichés.

Beyond this, we learn that Vivaldi has actually choreographed his moment of overhearing: "He placed himself near an open lattice, so as to be shrouded from observation by the branches of an orange-tree, while he obtained a full view of the apartment." Positioning himself strategically on the set, Vivaldi shows just how deliberate and unspontaneous this occasion of poetry truly is. Ellena, seemingly catatonic by the end of the passage, showcases the ridiculousness of "utter unconsciousness." This scene of ironized overhearing, in every sense of Mill's delineation, smacks of eloquence.

Take 2: Mistaken Speaker in Udolpho

Next, we visit a humorous instance of failed overhearing from *The Mysteries of Udolpho*. In a scene that stretches our anticipation over the course of several chapters, the heroine Emily St. Aubert is finally united with an anonymous fellow prisoner whose voice she has continually overheard while trapped for days in Count Montoni's castle. She has listened to his strumming and singing from her bedroom, imagining their romantic reunion, and arranges through her servants, Annette and Ludovico, to finally meet him face to face. She is certain, of course, that this soliloquizer is her beloved fiancé, Monsieur Valancourt. Serendipitously, in a moment of sudden danger and distress, the lyric serenader escapes from his prison cell and rescues Emily. It turns out that the mystery singer is not Valancourt, but a newly introduced character named Monsieur DuPont, an admirer who has also loved Emily from afar. The shock against her romantic and poetic expectations is so great that Emily falls unconscious (yet again) to the floor. Upon reviving, she says nothing but bursts into tears and struggles away from DuPont, while Annette, in loud outbursts, expresses the exasperation and disappointment felt by all three:

> 'O, sir!' said she, in a voice, interrupted with sobs; 'O, sir! You are not the other Chevalier. We expected Monsieur Valancourt, but you are not he! O Ludovico! How could you deceive us so? My poor lady will never recover it—never!' The stranger, who now appeared much agitated, attempted to speak, but his words faltered; and then striking his hand against his forehead, as if in sudden despair, he walked abruptly to the other end of the corridor.[20]

In this scene, the ideal of romantic lyric as true feeling confessing itself in solitude becomes debased and devalued. Readers are meant to register DuPont as a foppish foil to Valancourt, Emily's true love. Contrary to any Romantic "spontaneous overflow of powerful feelings," here, the anonymity and authority of the lyric "I" is negated, as is any assumed familiarity or comfort in recognition of the poetic speaker.²¹ Suddenly, it matters exactly *who* is speaking, unlike in Keats's "Ode to a Nightingale," for example, where the poet-speaker poses an unspecified but all-subsuming voice. In fact, DuPont's presumption that he will play the role of Emily's rightful hero proves a parody of the idea behind a Wordsworthian "egotistical I." The pitiable Monsieur DuPont proves that a lyric poem, imperfectly overheard, can be one big mistake; and what is more, a lyric speaker can be an unwanted confessional voice. In this experience of failed lyric—awkward, inconvenient, and embarrassing—"true feeling," or what J. S. Mill defined to be poetry, is made ridiculous and discounted. Unlike a Romantic lyric poem, which deals with universals, context is of paramount importance in this scene. Mistaken context spoils the entire lyric set-up.

I argue that this scene in *Udolpho* anticipates the degradation of Romantic lyric—from having one speaker and one projected listener—into a triangulated monologue, overheard by an audience. Radcliffe reminds readers that love songs and love poetry, meant for a lover's ears only, are always in danger of becoming triangulated and overheard in compromising ways. In this moment of ironized sentimental overhearing, DuPont falls victim to the cruel reception of his auditors, while the communal disappointment of Annette, Emily, and Ludovico contribute to the comedy of this scene. Acknowledging his embarrassment through faltering speech and comical choreography—striking his forehead and walking abruptly away—DuPont's reaction also implicates the cruelty of his listeners. By the novel's end, DuPont's dignity and standing is never quite salvaged. *Udolpho* concludes in traditional Radcliffean fashion, with a happy marriage for Emily, all inheritance and property restored to the rightful female heir. Readers are meant to forget about the only loser of the story in terms of plot, the slighted lyricist, Monsieur DuPont.

Monsieur DuPont's particular variation of lyric failure teaches one lesson that deflates Mill's lofty poetics: dramatic overhearing *must* be carefully staged; the poet's "utter unconsciousness of a listener" is an impractical ideal. DuPont exhibits the kind of lyric isolation Herbert Tucker might describe as "a kind of sublime idiocy," while his failed romance puts pressure on yet more lines from Mill's essay: "Poetry which is printed on hot-pressed paper, and sold at a bookseller's shop, is a soliloquy in full dress and on the stage. It is so; *but there is nothing absurd, in the idea of such a mode of soliloquizing.*"²² Browning's dramatic monologues, discussed below, feature exactly this Radcliffean scenario: speakers made absurd by their mode of soliloquizing. The poetic speaker as egotistical braggart—a mainstay of Victorian dramatic monologues—exposes the risk of lyric failure built into the very model of overheard speech. The braggadocio of later monologists helped dramatize the suspicion and distance Victorian poets felt towards their Romantic counterparts.

Take 3: Absent Overhearer in The Italian

What might a profession-of-love lyric look like without a lover to overhear it? In *The Italian*, Radcliffe presents another a failed attempt at romantic confession when the dashing Vincentio di Vivaldi and a musical compatriot aim to profess his love through the time-honored technique of the troubadour, but without success. The two men shift awkwardly from window to window; they sing and play for more than one hour; but the staged romantic set-up fails and the suitors leave, disappointed and physically fatigued from their failed conquest:

> On this night, enthusiasm inspired [Vivaldi] with the highest eloquence, perhaps, which music is capable of attaining; what might be its effect on Ellena he had no means of judging, for she did not appear either at the balcony or the lattice, nor give any hint of applause . . . The musicians, unsuccessful in their first endeavour to attract attention, removed to the opposite side of the building, and placed themselves in front of the portico, but with as little success; and, after having exercised their powers of harmony and of patience for above an hour, they resigned all further effort to win upon the obdurate Ellena. Vivaldi, notwithstanding the feebleness of his first hope of seeing her, now suffered an agony of disappointment . . .[23]

Any reader would agree that Vivaldi fails as a poet in this scene; yet here the poor suitor even fails at mere eloquence, for he fails to realize his audience has left from earshot. The language of Radcliffe's description of Vivaldi's romantic confession again anticipates some of the lofty romantic ideals from Mill's essay: earlier in the passage, the suitor sings with a "fine tenor," "exquisite delicacy," and the "most simple and pathetic expression," "so tender, so imploring, yet so energetic." Yet the failure in spontaneous effusion, complemented by the embarrassing practical and physical details of their endeavors, again plunges the scene into bathos. This particular variation of lyric failure teaches one lesson that deflates the ideal of overheard transmission: dramatic overhearing *must* be carefully staged; "utter unconsciousness of an audience" is an impractical ideal.

With no overhearer to complete the familiar and formulaic trope, lyric overhearing falls flat and is made absurd. Once again, like DuPont, Vivaldi exhibits Tucker's "sublime idiocy," since "lyric isolation from context distempers character and robs it of contour . . ."[24] What is more, Vivaldi is a major male character and love interest in *The Italian*, unlike the character of Monsieur DuPont—proving the democratizing nature of ridiculousness via failed overhearing in Gothic novels. Here, the plot thickens: as we will later see, the Victorian dramatic monologue not only imports such scenes of romantic failure, but builds and improves upon them. Unlike Vivaldi, who fails at true poetry, the calculating Duke of Ferrara knows when to rhyme and when not to, offering up a scripted masterpiece that, to unsuspecting ears, sounds like natural conversation, not eloquence. The monologists in Browning's "Madhouse Cells," *Men and Women*, and *Dramatis Personae* cater to their audiences, tailoring each line of their speech in order to manipulate and persuade a specific overhearer. Only they succeed in passing off eloquence as poetry. This test case in *The Italian* begins with the basics, reminding us of the first prerequisite for successful lyric through triangulation: the verified presence of an overhearer who is present and within earshot.

Take 4: Unassuming Auditor in The Monk

For lyric confession to function effectively, an overhearer must also properly perceive the song he or she happens to hear with some degree of understanding. In the following passage from Matthew Lewis's *The Monk*, romantic overhearing is thwarted not due to any fault of the lyric singer, but because the unassuming auditor thinks the song must be for her neighbor instead. The young Antonia, supposing she hears the strains of her lover Lorenzo, rushes to the casement. Down below, Lorenzo offers up serenades to reassure her of his affections, even though he has not obtained her uncle's consent for an official attachment.

> His stratagem had not the desired effect. Antonia was far from supposing, that this nightly music was intended as a compliment to her: She was too modest to think herself worthy such attentions; and concluding them to be addressed to some neighbouring Lady; she grieved to find that they were offered by Lorenzo. [Followed by lyrics to the serenade.][25]

Amusingly enough, Antonia fails to receive the lyric communication because she is overly insecure of her own worthiness as the poet's addressee. Too humble and self-deprecating, she misses out on the lyric outpouring that is rightfully hers to overhear. In other words, Antonia has downshifted herself from the rightful role of "hearer" to mere "overhearer," listening in on what she thinks is someone else's love lyric. Here, Lewis mocks the traditionally silent female figure as the focal point of troubadour songs and other forms of lyric love poetry. This object of affection should be unassuming, coy, and out of reach, yet not so demure as to entirely miss the point. Unfortunately, Antonia is modest to the point of obliviousness, causing the poetic moment to fail within its own empty formalism. The structural formula for overhearing again fails. As we can see from the last several examples, the triangulated overhearing of lyric is not so easily "spontaneous," but must be staged and orchestrated in order to include all the essential pieces so carefully taxonomized by dramatic monologue scholars.

Reading passages of Radcliffe, Lewis, and Browning together shows how the many technical characteristics of dramatic monologues that have concerned critics—the presence of an unwitting auditor, the utter unconsciousness of a speaker, revelation of character, etc.—were elements that novelists too could grapple with, especially authors of the Gothic romance. By tracing this connection, we see that dramatic monologues and dramatic lyrics draw on a generic hybridity borrowed from novels as well as from plays.

The ubiquity of overhearing scenes in 1790s novels, aside from providing comic relief, stretches the limits of lyric communication, often ironizing the Romantic poetic ideals through irony, parody, and exaggeration. They are experiments that contribute, I argue, to the same formal project as Browning's and Tennyson's 1830s poems, testing the bounds of how far lyric can be pushed. Each variation results in an example of lyric failure that, collectively, paves the way for the dramatic monologue. Tucker has aptly described dramatic monologue as a form that alternates between "historical line" and "punctual lyrical spot," producing "a plot of lyricism resisted": "Lyric, in the dramatic monologue, is what you cannot have and what you cannot forget."[26] For Ulrich Knoepflmacher, the act of ironizing Romantic models of female expression by Keats was essential to Browning's development and eventual perfection of the dramatic monologue, especially those that adopted the voice of a female speaker.[27] For Marion Thain, "the mid-Victorian problematization of lyric" is predicated upon parody, which she recognizes in "Porphyria's Lover": "A parody of the lyric subject's immortalization of the beloved lyric addressee in literary form, the woman is preserved as a love object—idolized, silenced, and eternally beautiful."[28] While scholars have identified key poetic elements transformed in the transition from Romantic to Victorian lyric, Radcliffe and Lewis had already done similar work forty years earlier. In the same vein as Browning, authors of Gothic romance used the space of the novel—and the baggy, circuitous plots that the lengthy genre afforded—to poke fun at clichés of pure poetic confession as Mill would later imagine them.

Pippa Passes

Showcasing the importance of four minor, yet important variables—unconscious audience, mistaken speaker, absent overhearer, and unconfident auditor, each instance of thwarted overhearing in Radcliffe and Lewis tests the limits of lyric transmission. This kind of experimentation is mirrored in Browning's early work, *Pippa Passes*, which offers a methodical exploration of lyric song through a series of parallel scenes. Published as the first volume of *Bells and Pomegranates* in 1841, the dramatic verses present four instances of a lyric speaker who is accidentally overheard, each one resulting in serious consequences concerning love, life, or death in a small Italian village. Pippa is a young silk-winder who spends New Year's Day musing about the "Four Happiest Ones" in the town of Asolo: Ottima, the rich silk-mill owner; Jules, a French art student; Luigi, an Italian patriot; and the Monsignor. Inspired by Browning's 1838 trip to Italy, the poem captures the activity of Asolo's foreign art students, political conspirators, clerics, and Austrian policemen. In hopes that she will feel the blessings of God's love, Pippa looks forward to her one day off from work in the entire year: "I will pass each, and see their happiness, / And envy none" (203–4). With no intended audience for her songs other than herself, all who hear her are automatically overhearers.

As a sort of lyric bird, Pippa plays a useful role in a set of exercises that test the trope of overhearing. This flat character is a mouthpiece for generic song. Unaware of the meaning of her own opening lyric, she innocently asks, "What does New-year's hymn declare? / What other meaning do these verses bear?"[29] Pippa empties out lyric of its contents, allowing the poet to examine what he is left with—the form itself—such that Browning easily subjects her songs to overhearing in different circumstances. Quite simply, *Pippa Passes* is an exercise in dramatic irony. This verse drama turns away from the universalizing voice of the Romantics, creating scenes of context-specific, incident-driven poetry instead. I suggest that the lyric experimentation Browning performs within *Pippa Passes*, isolating the structure of overheard song, is analogous to the various trials that Radcliffe and Lewis perform within the space of their novels. They plop speakers in multiple fictional contexts to see how they fare, yielding scenarios that explore the repercussions of overhearing through the staged triangulation of characters, in a series of dramatic-poetic vignettes.[30] These assorted situations, seemingly repetitive but each a slight variation, serve as metaphorical Petri dishes in a scientific experiment to determine the outer limits of lyric overhearing. If Sessions's "perfect dramatic monologue" serves as a kind of control group, those examples of failed overhearing—with absent auditors or mistaken speakers—veer us into the territory of what critics have alternatively labeled "dramatic lyrics," "mask lyrics," "imperfect dramatic monologues," or "approximate dramatic monologues."[31] Such a range of labels and terminology reflects the wide spectrum of all the different ways in which lyric expression can be compromised and recalibrated, all possibilities which Radcliffe, Lewis—and, here, Browning—explore.

The readings below challenge traditional readings of Pippa as "a bona fide messenger from God," a spiritual force of benevolence who represents the innocence of the child.[32] The 1909 silent short film adaptation renamed Browning's subtitle as *Pippa Passes, or, the Song of Conscience*.[33] David Riede puts it best when he writes:

> Pippa is the ultimate puppet in the play in terms of Browning's experiment in genre. She thinks she is God's puppet, but her mere instrumentality in the extreme artifice of the play makes it clear that she is in fact the author's puppet. She is repeatedly trotted out as a sort of *regina ex machina* to bring scenes to a climax; she is the string that moves the other puppets. Her lack of more than superficial characterization further signifies her mere instrumentality. She can hardly be said to have her own voice.[34]

Pippa's character here is a tool, a mechanism perhaps clumsily utilized or "trotted" out. This parallels the "messy bag of tropes" model associated with Gothic writing, which granted authors the formal latitude to trot new characters in and out without the restrictive commitment to a realistic plot. Specifically, the often-circuitous plots and the Gothic romance's tolerance for repetition and excess made these novels a convenient and forgiving space to experiment, providing fecund soil for the nurturing of new, hybrid poetic forms.[35]

As we can see by juxtaposing the two, scenes of overhearing in the Gothic novel and *Pippa Passes* are both breeding grounds for what would become perfected as the dramatic monologue. What was incubated in the genre of the novel fully bloomed forty years later within the genre of poetry.

* * *

The Gothic bones of the plot of *Pippa Passes* are significant to its structural, formal experimentation. Quaint as the village may seem, Asolo is filled with criminals, and its universe is ultimately a Gothic world. The play's characters are each embroiled in criminal transgressions of some kind. Ottima and Sebald are hypocritical adulterers who have committed murder. The Monsignor is a scheming cleric who has embezzled property in the mode of Count Montoni. Pippa is a dispossessed maiden who, like the best of Radcliffe's heroines, will assumedly be restored her fortune and recognized as the cardinal's niece and true owner of church property. Luigi and his mother contemplate regicide, while Jules and Phene are victims of the sort of cruel prank and mistaken set-up seen in *Udolpho* with Monsieur DuPont. The Monsignor conspires with the insidious Intendant (the murderer of the Monsignor's brother Pasquale), who offers to "make away with [Pippa] for you."[36] Although critics have not considered Asolo's "Happiest Four" as Gothic villains, they have certainly recognized the "egoistic drives and individualistic goals" that make up their characters.[37] Moreover, like a Gothic heroine, Pippa is revealed by the end of the play to be the niece of a bishop and heiress to a great estate. But as we will soon see, the young Pippa inherits all these Gothic implications formally, and not just through plot.

The trial and error of her overheard songs, as she unknowingly rubs shoulders with criminals and murderers, shows Pippa navigating the ambiguities of a Gothic world, in which the moral authority of right and wrong, God and Satan, are confounded. In *Pippa*, Browning "was not merely subverting conventional dramatic form, but devising an experiment in decentered form" to develop a poetic structure "more appropriate to a world with no stable truths."[38] What Browning's verse drama demonstrates is that in multiple contexts, within an ever-shifting framework, there exists no constant value of innocent or guilty. The Gothic world is not one in which God is dead, but where God remains passive and silent: he is a mere spectator in the face of crime and evil, a passive overhearer of guilty criminals' boasts.

As Pippa *passes*, physically visiting different scenes and characters throughout her day, she sets off a butterfly effect that embroils her in the other characters' criminality: Her song of innocence causes discord between the lovers, Ottima and Sebald, who, shortly after hearing her, come to hate and curse one another.[39] Her song about Kate the Queen is overheard by Jules, who reflects upon the story and decides to come to a woman's aid, eventually marrying the model Phene.[40] Her song about the old king who "no need . . . should ever die" is overheard by Luigi, who reconsiders his plans of regicide. Luigi repeats Pippa's lines, "No need that sort of king should ever die! . . . That king should still judge sitting in the sun!"[41] He then leaves for Vienna, which saves him from being captured by the police. As Pippa passes these characters—in a play structure delineated by sections labeled Morning, Noon, Evening, and Night—her songs have unintended after-effects. These various overhearings—which we might read as Takes 1, 2, 3, and 4—show that even the simplest verses can never be free from complicity, if overheard by a guilty other.

But guilt or innocence is not solely hinged upon criminal action or inaction; the very structure of overhearing is indicting enough. In the case of the adulterers Ottima and Sebald, the coincidence of overhearing Pippa's song interrupts their romantic collusions, causing Sebald to re-evaluate the guilt and innocence of their actions. The two conspirators have likely arranged the murder of Ottima's husband Luca, and the lovers begin to turn against one another:

From without is heard the voice of Pippa, *singing—*

The year's at the spring
And day's at the morn;
Morning's at seven;
The hill-side's dew-pearled;
The lark's on the wing
The snail's on the thorn;
God's in his heaven—
All's right with the world!

[Pippa *passes.*]

Sebald. God's in his heaven! Do you hear that? Who spoke? You, you spoke!
Ottima. Oh—that little ragged girl!
She must have rested on the step . . . Sh!
She does not hear: call you out louder![42]

Here, Pippa sings freely, perched on a step, while the guilty couple is physically ensconced in a position of eavesdropping. This scenario's aura of guilt and complicity is built into the very positioning of the furtive listener. As Ann Gaylin explains:

> "to eavesdrop" originally meant to stand within the "eavesdrop," or the space under the eaves of a building likely to receive rainwater from the roof. The word contains within it the concept of being near a private space (a house) and its secrets, and suggests a punishment for being so positioned; a person in the "eavesdrop" is likely to get wet.[43]

This implied punishment likewise makes the experience of reading a dramatic monologue implicitly tinged with culpability and punishment: he or she will be rained upon, simply for engaging in the act of overhearing—whether intentionally or not.

An archetype for childhood and innocence, Pippa famously starts off her day with naïve optimism: "God's in his heaven; all's right with the world!"[44] Yet the ending of *Pippa Passes* abruptly turns to a passage shrouded in the trappings of Gothic. When Pippa finally returns home to sleep at the end of the day, readying herself for another continuous year of work, overtly Gothic imagery begins to appear.

> Oh what a drear dark close to my poor day!
> How could that red sun drop in that black cloud?
> Ah Pippa, morning's rule is moved away,
> Dispensed with, never more to be allowed!
> Day's turn is over, now arrives the night's.
> Oh lark, be day's apostle
> To mavis, merle and throstle,
> Bid them their betters jostle
> From day and its delights!
> But at night, brother howlet, over the woods,
> Toll the world to thy chantry;
> Sing to the bat's sleek sisterhoods
> Full complines with gallantry:
> Then, owls and bats,
> Cowls and twats,
> Monks and nuns, in a cloister's moods,
> Adjourn to the oak-stump pantry![45]

This passage poses the binary of a godly, ordered world against a universe where God seems absent. Though the garb and physical trappings of religion are present throughout this passage in the cloisters, cowls, and chantry, here, God is not present, nor is he securely "in his heaven," as he is in Pippa's famous refrain throughout the play. Instead, this Gothic passage in Pippa's evening song, often glossed over by critics, resonates more with the line of Porphyria's lover: "God has not said a word!" The transition from day to night marks a quick reversal from light to dark, good to evil. Pentameter converts to trimeter, lending a hypnotic, chant-like feel to the young Pippa's voice ("owls and bats, / Cowls and twats, / Monks and nuns)." The aggregation of spondees in lines 82–3 herald the darkness and storm clouds to come, like spondaic cracks of thunder: ("drear dark close" "poor day"; "red sun drop" "black cloud"). This bedtime speech signals Pippa's own place in a guilty and foreboding world. It highlights her politically and philosophically problematic existence: she exists within a framework where mere juxtaposition, cohabitation, and mild lyric interaction with criminal parties are enough to incriminate her.

It is significant that Pippa's otherwise benevolent lyrics take on a suspicious and Gothic tone before ending in cheerful naïvety. This buried Gothic passage represents the troubling extent of Pippa's effect on others. She is a key player in the lives of Asolo's citizens, an instigator who seemingly bears no responsibility for her indirect influence upon others. Yet her refrains indirectly inspire others to renounce their sins or escape punishment.[46] As an unintentional meddler who ultimately influences life or death, Pippa helps Browning confront larger metaphysical questions about the power of speech and the culpability of actions and inactions. Her character questions the consequences of cause and effect, of agency and interactions, between characters that in fact can indirectly "touch" and "move" one another:

> Now, one thing I should like to really know:
> How near I ever might approach all these
> I once fancied being, this long day:
> —Approach, I mean, so as to touch them, so
> As to . . . in some way . . . move them—if you please,
> Do good or evil to them some slight way.[47]

Formally, *Pippa Passes* raises interesting questions about the placement and contextualization of poetic structures: What is the difference between lyric carefully situated and lyric that just floats around? What dangers do decontextualized lyric pose? Does overheard, triangulated speech, if not firmly framed, expose poets to the danger of being grossly misinterpreted? What is the poet's responsibility, in the event that his poems and speakers get interpreted in morally ambiguous or destructive ways? One way to address these questions is through a legal frame, particularly by linking *Pippa Passes* to the idea of tort law, the legal rule of liability that prosecutes "negligence as fault." At the turn of the twentieth century, American tort law was derived from English common law, including, as an illustrating example, "the improbable but actual effects of a farmer's cow straying onto the road and causing a highway accident."[48] Torts fall under three types: negligence, liability, and intention. A consideration of torts frames the question of Pippa's guilt and complicity in terms of legal liability: "A harm does not cease to be a harm simply because one had not known the person whom one harmed or hadn't committed an action with the intention of harming them."[49]

According to tort laws, Pippa is liable for the good or harm she may inspire in those around her, even if it is not her "fault" that others misinterpret her for their own means. The presumed power of the disembodied lyric voice, muses Clyde de L. Ryals, is that it puts the poet "at a monologic remove from listeners, exercising power over them but abnegating his obligation to them."[50] As Riede writes, "The other characters do not take Pippa's songs as authoritative revelations: they act on misrepresentations of these songs rather than on what they actually say . . . each character accepts Pippa's song as somehow authoritative, but interprets it in such a way as to authorize his own limited and self-aggrandizing selfhood."[51] In other words, the power of words risks becoming more dangerously influential when overheard in various, uncontrolled contexts. Even if Pippa does not understand the meaning of her own verses, she may be liable for her influence on the actions of Jules, Phene, Ottima, Sebald, and the Monsignor.[52] Neither ignorance nor personal innocence exculpates one from the responsibility of harm inflicted.

In her discussion on unintentional crimes and unintended harm, Frances Ferguson draws on the evolution of tort law as a "law of the road" that reflects Jeremy Bentham's understandings of utilitarian value. By amassing judgments from all members in different facets of society, it created legal standards out of practice and social data, rather than relying on "any fixed principles of contractual, transcendental right or wrong."[53] Because tort law is determined from experiences in context, "it almost completely bypassed a transcendental argument that implicitly established some version of contract—or an appeal to the durability of intentions—as the basis of law . . . it emphasized a law of physical persistence over time and space."[54] This de facto, practical formation of moral standards prevails in *Pippa Passes*. Riede again: "The other characters do not take Pippa's songs as authoritative revelations: they act on misrepresentations of these songs rather than on what they actually say . . . each character accepts Pippa's song as somehow authoritative, but interprets it in such a way as to authorize his own limited and self-aggrandizing selfhood."[55] Much like Pippa's four encounters, each Act taking place in Morning, Noon, Evening, and Night, tort law amasses authority through its abundance of examples, rather than any philosophical standard of argument. Put in poetic terms, each new speech act by each new character in Browning's collections of dramatic monologues adds to the compendium of overhearing scenarios, contributing to an encyclopedic "book of torts" where there is never one consistent answer to the question of sympathy or judgment; each case must be tried on its own according to time and place and context.

In terms of social relations, tort law "projects a social world that links harmer and harmed—no matter how much they may be strangers to one another. In this sense, tort law establishes a new social group that includes both groups. It attempts to assign a value to sociality without sociability."[56] It is telling that Ferguson's text for discussion is the Marquis de Sade's *Justine*, a work of Gothic sadomasochism. As we encountered in the Introduction, Gothic plots often follow a sadistic model of cyclic violence between "the beater and the beaten," posed here as the harmer and the harmed.[57] A gothically inflected reading shows that Pippa is not Mill's solitary nightingale, singing lyric in a vacuum, nor simply the brainless lark and dramatic tool, left untouched, that critics have made her out to be. Rather, Pippa's seemingly harmless words carry the weight of guilt by association and the risk of liability for her lyrics. Speech risks becoming compromised and misinterpreted, its messages potentially abused depending on context. Poets, in turn, risk losing control of the effects of their own poems—verse is unleashed into a world of misinterpretations and egotistical manipulations. It is clear then that the Gothic elements found throughout *Pippa Passes* are not coincidental, but embedded in its formal blueprint. The very structure of her overheard speech renders Pippa a real hand in justice. This lyric songbird unintentionally assumes the role of Shelley's poet as an "unacknowledged legislator[] of the world," even when the poetic structure claims indifference or merely "passing" effects.[58]

Criminal Confession

J. S. Mill: Overhearing the Prisoner Next Door

While there are a few straightforward sound bites that have survived from Mill's essays on poetry, (his deeming all poetry "overheard," "spontaneous," and "of the nature of soliloquy"), there is one sentence that holds a particular significance in the context of Gothic overhearing: "That song has always seemed to us like the lament of a prisoner in a solitary cell, ourselves listening, unseen in the next."[59] Herbert Tucker has zeroed in on this sentence (which Mill excised in revision) as absurd and impractical: "How many of us in that next cell?" asks Tucker. "Does one eavesdrop in company?"[60] Mill's trope of eavesdropping on a "prisoner next-door" is one that Radcliffe staged quite literally in her fiction: a lone suitor lamenting in a solitary cell with multiple overhearers, a singing damsel trapped in a castle or convent listened in on by her captors, or a victim in the jails of the Inquisition, spied upon by Catholic jurors. In these cases, the original lyric set-up has become tainted, uncomfortable, and threatening. It has garnered, in effect, all the trappings of a dramatic monologue. One can conceive of the space of the dramatic monologue—choreographed and staged—as an inquisitional examination room, in which the demands on speakers force them to contort lyric, pushing it to extremes. This model of the poetic speaker as a victim—imprisoned, trapped, and outnumbered by his or her auditors—embodies the affective and formal elements of Browning's signature poems, including cruelty, disappointment, and imprisoned surveillance.

Criminality and overhearing are persistently conjoined in Gothic, particularly inflected by the context of the Spanish Inquisition in sixteenth-century Catholic Italy. In novels such as *The Italian* and *The Monk*, scenes abound where the machinations of guilty monks are overheard, proving them to be greedy conspirators rather than holy men. Even in Gothic romance novels with no inquisitional subtext, scenes of overhearing implicate those confined within a space of guilt and collusion, whether the Gothic castle or the mysterious monastery. In *The Romance of the Forest*, Adeline frequently listens through the door of the abandoned castle where she has sought refuge, gathering from snippets of conversation that her supposed protector will trade her to a libidinous marquis in exchange for exoneration from his ruinous debt. In *The Mysteries of Udolpho*, Emily St. Aubert eavesdrops from doorway to doorway within the castle trying to glean information about her situation, and hears sobs, murmurs, and groans. It is only upon leaving Udolpho and its environment of secrecy and overhearing that she feels relief from the guilt of mere proximity: "Emily, when the gondolier dashed th[e] oars in the water, and put off from the steps of the portico, felt like a criminal, who receives a short reprieve."[61] Because Gothic heroines are imprisoned and kept in ignorance of their futures, they naturally eavesdrop and overhear at every opportunity. As seen in the example from *Udolpho*, innocent parties (such as Emily, Annette, and Ludovico) are cast in the position of being awkward eavesdroppers, experiencing a mixture of Langbaum's sympathy and judgment.[62] They become cruel listeners of an unwitting speaker. Like these young maidens, Pippa too becomes embroiled in scenes of criminality and guilt. Despite being innocent in any criminal context, they are forced into a realm of transgression by assuming the role of eavesdropper. This confusion between the roles of victim and criminal, of innocence and guilt, will become a thematic centerpiece for each of Browning's dramatic monologists, who elicit sympathy from an audience despite their incorrigible character flaws.

Speakers of dramatic monologues are never fully innocent, and Victorian poems are peppered with charismatic scoundrels. From Porphyria's lover, to Johannes Agricola, the Bishop at St. Praxed's Church, and the Spanish Monk, Browning's murderers and hypocritical monks end up indirectly confessing to damning sins, if not outright crimes. Even those who are not criminals suffer the torture of their own narcissistic fantasies. But the dramatic monologue itself is never innocent, and this is because the very basis of overhearing confession is shrouded in guilt. There is no better way to understand this than through the important context of the Catholic Inquisition, a favorite setting of Gothic novels and an ideal occasion for playing out varied versions of performed and extracted speech.

In such scenes, the threat of forced confession poses the cruelest version of religious confessional, before an audience of judges. In both *The Italian* and *The Monk*, the jails of the Inquisition pose a dangerous peril; here, torture instruments brutally extract confessions of guilt from their victims, whether guilty or innocent. With no guarantee of justice under the powerful bureaucracy of a corrupt Catholic Church, innocent characters are often coerced into confession: to incriminate other guilty parties by name or indict themselves in order to avoid physical torture. The narrator of *The Monk* explains the general practices of the Inquisition to an unfamiliar reader:

> In these trials neither the accusation is mentioned, or [sic] the name of the Accuser. The Prisoners are only asked, whether they will confess: If they reply that having no crime they can make no confession, they are put to the torture without delay. This is repeated at intervals, either till the suspected avow themselves culpable, or the perseverance of the examinants is worn out and exhausted: But without a direct acknowledgment of their guilt, the Inquisition never pronounces the final doom of its Prisoners.[63]
>
> . . .
>
> That day [of Ambrosio's Trial] arrived. At nine in the morning his prison door was unlocked, and his Gaoler entering, commanded him to follow him. He obeyed with trembling. He was conducted into a spacious Hall, hung with black cloth. At the Table sat three grave stern-looking Men, also habited in black: One was the Grand Inquisitor, whom the importance of this cause had induced to examine into it himself . . . Ambrosio was beckoned to advance, and take his station at the lower end of the Table. As his eye glanced downwards, He perceived various iron instruments lying scattered upon the floor. Their forms were unknown to him, but apprehension immediately guessed them to be engines of torture. He turned pale, and with difficulty prevented himself from sinking upon the ground.[64]

The threat of physical violence impels the monk on trial to either "sing like a canary" or withhold speech and choose torture, releasing groans of pain instead. Historically, during the Spanish Inquisition beginning in 1542, one could be anonymously accused without knowing the identity of the accuser. Upon arrival in a town, the soldiers of the Inquisition would first call for people to offer up statements of self-incrimination, after which they would receive tips from informants, who were often merely acting upon personal grievances and rivalries. Subtitled "The Confessional of the Black Penitents," *The Italian* places great purchase on silence and the economy of coercing, withholding, or extracting speech.[65]

In such a world, the actuality of a prisoner's innocence or guilt has no bearing; word is more important than action or deed, as all judgment is predicated upon one's self-confession instead. Within these walls, a compelling performance of remorse, even if false, might lessen one's punishment of torture. Performance and eloquence, not truth, reign supreme.

> When the Executioners prepared to put him to the question, when He saw the engines of torture, and remembered his pangs, which they had already inflicted, his resolution failed him entirely. Forgetting the consequences and only anxious to escape the terrors of the present moment, He made an ample confession. He disclosed every circumstance of his guilt, and owned not merely the crimes with which He was charged, but those of which He had never been suspected.[66]

Here, the threat of violence induces the monk Ambrosio to invent fictions and become a poetic speaker who can innovate, extemporize, and proliferate stories upon demand. In the torture chamber, self-accusation or vindication is physically extracted: the more heartfelt the confession, the greater the likelihood that mercy might be afforded the victim.

When Vivaldi is first incarcerated in the prison of the Inquisitions, "he distinguishe[s] half-stifled groans, as of a person in agony" or detects "indistinct sounds, which yet appeared to [him] like lamentations and extorted groans."[67] Such noises highlight the moment of transition between a bodily, guttural sound of struggle and the emergence of sensical speech. In other words, the jails of the Inquisition elicit disfigured or impure lyric, spontaneous noises emitted from a speaker who is hardly in the physical position to produce carefully chosen words of poetry or eloquence. Browning recruits these sounds of disfigured lyric in his dramatic monologues. The trope of the inquisitional trial embodies a compelling nexus of violence and self-defense, of coercion and exculpation, lending the Victorian dramatic monologue its particular flavor of suspicion and guilt.

"The Confessional"

Browning's *Dramatic Lyrics* (1842) includes a rarely anthologized work, "The Confessional," which dramatizes the terror of the Inquisition in a narrative poem of iambic tetrameter.[68] Under the heading of *France and Spain*, this poem exhibits the same Catholic villainization seen in Radcliffe's and Lewis's novels. Though the poem begins with a romantic confession, it soon becomes the tale of an unwitting inquisitional informant.[69] Its disordered syntax also reveals how inarticulate poetic speakers become under the stress of inquisitional demands of confession. The speaker tells the story of how she has been betrayed by the church and her confessor. Much like *The Monk*'s Antonia, who turns to the church for compassion, she decides to confess her intimacies with her lover Beltran.⁷⁰ At first promised help and forgiveness, she is then tricked into divulging the crimes of her lover, only to find his corpse hanging in the city streets the next day. The speaker's grief and fury are vividly expressed in the opening stanza, with grammatically fraught lines of hysteria:

> I.
> It is a lie—their Priests, their Pope,
> Their Saints, their . . . all they fear or hope
> Are lies, and lies—there! through my door
> And ceiling, there! and walls and floor,
> There, lies, they lie—shall still be hurled
> Till spite of them I reach the world!⁷¹

In this frantic speech, the words "there" and "lies" perform grammatical double duty. The word "lies" denotes the actual "lie" told, but also the verb indicating their fixed location ("There . . . they lie"). Lies become physical weapons, like arrows or darts, hurled about by priests, popes, and saints; and strewn across the door and ceiling and lying around the room as tangible evidence. The confessor's condensed syntactical scrambling ("There, lies, they lie") reveals her shock from her religious betrayal: "All they fear or hope / *Are* lies [(noun)], *and* lies [(verb)]." "There" serves as a demonstrative, physical indicator ("There lies Beltram") but also as an ejaculation expressing indictment and exasperation ("There!"). Zeugma and syntactic ambiguity mirror the unstable world around her, where confessors double as informants and executors. Even nouns and verbs betray her with double meanings and double roles.

Grammatically disordered lines, forced accusation, and hysteric repetition of her speech are all at odds with flowing, lyric expression. This Gothic mode of poetic speech offers a stark counterpoint to the easy outpouring of a Romantic poetic ambling through the Lake District. Through grotesque versions of lyric, amidst the backdrop of inquisitional trial and torture, Gothic provides the template for what poetry might become in its most violent, coerced permutations. In forcing communication to its extremes, the scenes in these Gothic novels thus anticipated what Tennyson and Browning achieved by creating dramatic monologues that abandoned the familiar, safe standards of spontaneous effusion. They preview the Gothic, dark underside to the value of pure lyric and show how frightening or dangerous spontaneity of poetic speech can truly be.

The violence at the ending of "The Confessional" recalls the brutality of the Inquisition. The speaker's sudden stops and inarticulations reflect the dehumanization she has endured. She has deteriorated from a pretty young girl into an inhuman creature without flesh or blood:

> II.
> You think Priests just and holy men!
> Before they put me in this den
> I was a human creature too,
> With flesh and blood like one of you,
> A girl that laughed in beauty's pride
> Like lilies in your world outside.[72]

This Gothic body, seemingly discombobulated, resonates with Kelly Hurley's discussion of the "abhuman"—a body marked by ruination and abjection, abased and outcast.[73] By the final stanza, the speaker has become physically imprisoned by the church, with no recourse or escape: "No heaven with them, no hell!—and here, / No earth, not so much as space as pens / My body in their worst of dens."

> XI.
> Nor next night: on the after-morn,
> I went forth with a strength new-born.
> The church was empty; something drew
> My steps into the street; I knew
> It led me to the market-place:
> Where, lo, on high, the father's face!
>
> XII.
> That horrible black scaffold dressed,
> That stapled block . . . God sink the rest!
> That head strapped back, that blinding vest,
> Those knotted hands and naked breast,
> Till near one busy hangman pressed,
> And, on the neck these arms caressed . . .
>
> XIII.
> No part in aught they hope or fear!
> No heaven with them, no hell!—and here,
> No earth, not so much space as pens
> My body in their worst of dens
> But shall bear God and man my cry,
> Lies—lies, again—and still, they lie![74]

The anaphora of "That" (ll. 67–9) and "no" (ll. 73–5), overlaid upon tight, rhymed couplets, only increases this stifling sense of her confinement. Recounting the haunting, traumatic vision slows the reader's pace of discovery, akin to moments of revelation in a Radcliffe novel: "That horrible black scaffold . . . That stapled block . . . That head strapped back . . . Those knotted hands . . . these arms caressed."[75] Here we have the "slow reveal" inherent to both Gothic suspense plots and dramatic monologue form.

Yet it is not just the gruesome scene of the contorted corpse that poses the dramatic climax of the poem. The figure of the priest or "father" is a haunting vision, which Browning approaches with a rhythmical climax in Stanza 11, only to then refuse description. We hear suspenseful enjambment that increases the pace leading up to the moment of shock: "The church was empty; something drew / My steps into the street; I knew / It led me to the market-place: / Where, lo, on high, the father's face!"[76] Early on in "The Confessional," the father is described in terms that resemble Coleridge's Ancient Mariner and the "hermit good" who "shrieves" him: "That father's beard was long and white, / With love and truth his brow seemed bright."[77] He is one who might make an encouraging confessor and a good listener. By the poem's ending, however, "the old mild father" has undergone a complete transformation. His startling visage reveals him to have been the accuser and instigator, ultimately wreaking the Inquisition's trademark violence and torture. The figure of the father or priest, typically poised as a moral protector, in Gothic contexts becomes a threat who upends moral standards of chivalry and religion.

"Soliloquy of the Spanish Cloister"

The conflation of the innocent and guilty is best seen in the Gothic trope of the mad or evil monk. In *The Monk* and *The Italian*, the confessor, ostensibly meant to listen in on the peccadilloes of the devout, instead assumes the role of the deepest sinner. He performs soliloquies that either express remorse for crimes committed or help him muster up the courage to strike again. By casting the character of the monk as the tormented villain, Lewis and Radcliffe confound the roles of confessor and confessee, forgiver and transgressor. This subject-object confusion is aggravated by the ambiguity in the meaning of the word "confessor," which can denote either the monk authorized to take confession, or the parishioner professing sins. The figure of the unholy cleric is a model for memorable Browning characters, including the monk of the Spanish Cloister, the Bishop who orders his tomb at St. Praxed's Church, Giuseppe Caponsacchi in *The Ring and the Book*, and the Monsignor in *Pippa Passes*. More importantly, it establishes the formal model of sanctimonious confession and bastardized prayer. These compromised modes of lyric expression reflect a society where fathers and priests are villains and criminals; it is a Gothic world where the protections of a religious order are unavailable to the weak and vulnerable.

Criminality and Catholicism converge powerfully in Radcliffe's *The Italian* (1797), where the perpetrator of sins is the covetous monk Schedoni. This novel, drawing upon the anxieties of a xenophobic, English Protestant audience, begins with a frame narrative featuring a group of tourists who visit an Italian cathedral in 1758. They express disbelief upon learning that a suspicious-looking man appearing near the confessional booth is in fact a murderer who has taken refuge in the church. The opening of the novel appeals to a reader's disdain of Catholic indulgence:

> "An assassin!" exclaimed one of the Englishmen; "an assassin and at liberty!"
> An Italian gentleman, who was of the party, smiled at the astonishment of his friend.
> "He has sought sanctuary here," replied the friar; "within these walls he may not be hurt."
> "Do your altars, then, protect the murderer?" said the Englishman.
> "He could find shelter nowhere else," answered the friar meekly.
> "This is astonishing!" said the Englishman; "of what avail are your laws, if the most atrocious criminal may thus find shelter from them! ... Never!"[78]

Responding with judgment rather than sympathy, the Englishman is appalled by the moral leniency of a confessor content to forgive and protect a murderer. His shock betrays his affront at the moral violation committed by the church's promise that sanctuary is guaranteed "within these walls."

At the heart of the Englishman's surprise is the fact that an assassin could even recruit the sympathy of an audience. In his mind, a criminal's speech should fall on deaf ears, with only God to judge his confessional outpouring. It should not be a strategic statement engineered to secure safety from an abbot who receives the request. The expectation of audience reception degrades civilized prayer into barbaric custom. Cast in Mill's language, the Englishman is offended by the eloquence of the confessing speaker, who should instead be soliloquizing: "Eloquence is feeling pouring itself out to other minds, courting their sympathy, or endeavoring to influence their belief, or move them to passion or to action."[79] Read in national terms, English poetry is posed against Italian eloquence.

It is this space of safety that emboldens the more brazen of Browning's monologists, such as Porphyria's lover, to gloat that "God has not said a word!"[80] This protected space of the confessional booth or church sanctuary, formally construed, is in fact the dramatic monologue—it is a site of lyric confession where the most ribald statements can find sympathy rather than judgment. The bastardized prayer of characters in Gothic novels of the 1790s set a crucial formal example for Browning's dramatic monologists, who sanctimoniously convert the lyric site for soliloquy and confession into a staged trial, waged against the petty accusation of others.

* * *

In "Soliloquy of the Spanish Cloister," the monk's guttural "Grrr's" straddle the fine line between noise and speech. Much like the sound one might hear from the lips of a prisoner in the jails of the Inquisition, these angry consonants reveal the limitations of finished speech, presenting the very minimum of what might be considered lyric expression. Such bestial groans are usually signals of Gothic transformation, as in William Godwin's 1794 novel *Caleb Williams*: "As I opened the door, I heard at the same instant a deep groan expressive of intolerable anguish . . . a voice that seemed supernaturally tremendous . . ."[81] Certainly no beautiful lyric, nor wholehearted confession, this monologue is a series of choppy self-interruptions that presents the monk as a self-betraying speaker:

> *Gr-r-r*—there *go*, my heart's abhorrence!
>   Water your damned flower-pots, *do*!
> If hate killed men, Brother Lawrence,
>   God's blood, would not mine kill you!
> *What*? Your myrtle-bush wants trimming?
>   *Oh*, that rose has prior claims—
> Needs its leaden vase filled brimming?
>   Hell dry you up with its flames![82]

Despite the regularity of *abab cdcd* rhyme, we do not hear poetic sonority but rather blotched bursts of anger that chokes the speaker up: "Gr-r-r- . . . go . . . do! . . . What? . . . Oh."[83] Any constant momentum of trochaic tetrameter is thwarted by halting ejaculations. This stuttering speech enacts the spastic tensions that seem to come from deep within the monk's body, like the groans of a torture victim. As if possessed by a supernatural anger, the monk demonstrates a visceral hatred for Brother Lawrence (who sips his juice impiously) that seems on the one hand humanly immature and quibbling but deeply demonic on the other.

The monk's fragmented thoughts result in tangled language that renders him possessed by other beings. The last stanza, which invokes the devilish hex of "Hy Zy Hine," shows a disordering of text in its scrambling of the angelus prayer, which should read "Ave Maria, plena gratia." Here, Browning remixes the prayer with the ending of the Salve Regina prayer.[84]

> . . . Hy, Zy, Hine . . .
> 'St, there's Vespers! *Plena gratia*
> *Ave, Virgo!* Gr-r-r—you swine![85]

The unholy mixing of Latin prayer with invective and cacophonous syllables reflects his fragmented sense of self. He fails in his holy office and appears instead as a cursemonger, grunting out mystical babble in the vein of William Beckford's Vathek. The Gothic world is a fiendish one in which even monks try to outsmart, bully, or taunt God into action.

Metrical regularity, in fact, signifies the monk's inauthentic performance. If we are to distinguish between Mill's "poetry" and mere "eloquence," the verses of the poem that are full of cacophonous sounds denote true lyric, while the metered lines betray his false religiosity, where he only pretends to follow rules. In his "holier than thou" tirade, the Spanish monk allows his daily actions to be dictated by exacting routine (three sips)—not in the glory of God or the Holy Trinity, but to keep his antagonism in check. He suffers more than Brother Lawrence, who imbibes his juice freely, aloof from any rivalry or hypocrisy. Thus the monk's self-regulated behavior is but a performance. Steady trochaic tetrameter in the middle stanzas of the poem belies his saccharine obedience, enacting a sense of order: "Oh, those melons? If he's able / We're to have a feast! So nice! / One goes to the Abbot's table, All of us get each a slice."[86] Easy tetrameter echoes immature children's chant:

> When he finishes refection,
>   Knife and fork he never lays

> Cross-wise, to my recollection,
>   As do I, in Jesu's praise.
> I the Trinity illustrate,
>   Drinking watered orange-pulp—
> In three sips the Arian frustrate;
>   While he drains his at one gulp.[87]

But the monk lets loose his demonic inner self in the opening and ending stanzas. The *abab cdcd* verse pattern is obscured by his grunts and interrupting dashes ("Gr-r-r—"; "'St")[88] and guttural, extracted sounds. These opening and closing growls thus comprise the most lyrically "pure" sections of the poem, enacting true spontaneity in the first and final stanzas, while the middle stanzas exhibit forced constraint and self-coercion.

Browning's Spanish monk embodies the Gothic's inversion of innocence-criminality because he doles out accusation and invective rather than forgiveness: "Hell dry you up with its flames!"[89] In his failure of religious office, the monk confounds the roles of holy confessor and bitter accuser, with peccadilloes of his own to reveal. This betrayal of a religious figure's moral integrity feeds the danger of a Gothic, inquisitional world, where evil priests or nuns become inquisitional accusers and subject their victims to punishment and torture. We can thus reconsider Langbaum's paradigmatic contest between judgment and sympathy in a new way: as an iteration of the verdicts delivered in Gothic trials, where Grand Inquisitors dispense rulings of mercy or condemnation. "The Soliloquy of the Spanish Cloister," by raising central questions about the power of vile accusation, of malevolence masquerading as benevolence, provides a useful lens with which to read other dramatic monologues—including poems that feature female monologists, such as Augusta Weber's "Jeanne d'Arc."[90] Accusing others of mistreating him, the Spanish monk practices self-victimization and plays the starring role of false martyr. The poem models a sacrilegious speech act that features triangulation through the exchange of poetic roles: speaker, auditor, and audience map onto the accuser, jury, and defendant of an inquisitional trial. In both cases, the dramatic monologue is centered around false accusation and driven by emotion and spectacle, appealing to the rhetorical desires of an avid audience.

Poets thus have a morally ambiguous power: through their various framings of lyric, their monologues determine the relative innocence or guilt of their speakers in an unstable world of shifting perspectives. The multiplicity of overhearing scenes in novels, drama, and poems is not just absurd or comedic; it presents a dark reality about the manipulation of speech. Even monks and father figures deform and disfigure truth to play the roles of villain or martyr, rather than protector. This in turn raises questions about the figure of the poet and its social responsibilities. If Browning understands purely authentic, spontaneous speech to be impossible, then his role as a poet is drastically compromised. The poet is no longer a vatic poet or a priest figure professing lyric truth, simply voicing the sounds of a Coleridgian or Keatsian nightingale. Instead, Victorian authors grappled seriously with the risk of authorial liability imbedded in the dismantling of this Romantic ideal. Despite even their most careful constructions of contextualized lyric, their words could be overheard and misinterpreted. They too could potentially be incriminated in a dangerous dissemination of various shades of truths, indirectly sinning each time they put pen to paper.

"Andrea del Sarto"

By the end of Browning's major phase with the collection *Men and Women* (1855), his dramatic monologists bear little thematic resemblance to the stock Gothic characters seen in *Dramatic Lyrics* (1842). Instead of Italian counts, maddened monks, and murderous lovers, we are introduced instead to a cast of musicians, artists, and grammarians—speakers much less fanatical, less driven to extreme actions, who often exhibit a certain world-weariness. "Andrea del Sarto" features a technically skillful but underachieving painter who challenges the philosophy of imperfection. Deemed "the faultless painter," he is a Renaissance artist of the humanist tradition. Yet in this poem, we see Browning recruit the formal structures of Gothic overhearing without saturating his poem with Gothic themes. Andrea del Sarto may lack the trappings of Browning's monks and dukes, but he nonetheless masters the art of the inquisitional trial. Throughout the monologue, he performs an inquisitional hearing that triangulates accusations as deftly as the Duke of Ferrara and the Spanish monk. As many scholars have discussed, Andrea's conscious exploitation of hearing and overhearing reveals his precocity and awareness of a third party, his audience of readers. Yet his complex layering of triangulated speech, manipulating both audience and auditor, read differently when understood as part of a larger trajectory that includes the Gothic. Recognizing the Gothic prehistory to Andrea's manner of inquisitional accusation reshapes what we already know about Andrea and his monologue.

Andrea del Sato always tries less than he is capable of; but despite his easy-going nature, he recruits the structures of an inquisitional trial. His speech is driven by an obsession with reward roles, featuring accusation, confession, judgment, and punishment. He employs the art of deflection to manipulate multiple levels of audience. Thus, Andrea not only triangulates speech, hearing, and overhearing, he triangulates blame as well. He plays all three functions of defendant, informer, and judge. To recognize Andrea as an inquisitional figure requires a more subtle reading of his secrets and crimes than traditional criticism provides. He confesses to the past embezzlement of royal funds. He also casts himself in a location of confinement, consistently emphasizing the four walls that surround him in attempts at self-victimization.[91]

Though Andrea is a technically flawless painter, the task of his monologue is to distract, seduce, and persuade the audience of his moral faultlessness. He consciously plays the role of the defendant on the judgment block.

> Their works drop groundward, but themselves, I know,
> Reach many a time a heaven that's shut to me[92]
> . . .
> My father and my mother died of want . . .
> They were born poor, lived poor, and poor they died:
> And I have laboured somewhat in my time
> And not been paid profusely.[93]
> . . .
> Well, less is more, Lucrezia: I am judged.[94]

In his insincere confession, Andrea seems to live under the constant scrutiny and judgment of Lucrezia, God, and his fellow painters. However, his self-positioning as the object of judgment is merely a ploy. He strokes the ego of his listeners, elevating us to the role of judge and thereby ensuring a compassionate audience: "I do not boast, perhaps: yourself are judge."[95] This is all in preparation for his plan of last-minute deflection, when Andrea secures the good will of his audience to redirect judgment onto his wife Lucrezia. Here he takes on the role of prosecutor as well, like an inquisitional victim who exculpates himself and avoids confession by accusing another instead.

In a basic reading of the poem that is "heard" by Lucrezia, the silent auditor, Andrea is the victim, put on trial and judged by God, Lucrezia, his fellow painters, and French royalty. A seeming failure and underachiever, Andrea defends himself by creating a speech-act that serves as self-exculpation and excuse. The faultless painter understands this role and revels in it. Yet Andrea manipulatively creates a second layer of narrative, reshuffling the roles of Lucrezia, the reader, and himself. In this second narrative, it is Lucrezia who is on trial, with the audience positioned in the role of overhearer. Though Andrea is modest and non-violent, unwilling to point fingers in a blind rage, he has carefully utilized a rhetoric of blame in which he exculpates himself, deflecting blame onto Lucrezia in a series of accusations instead. These accusations, though sprinkled out throughout the monologue, sound almost inquisitional when posed sequentially:

You don't understand / Nor care about my art . . .[96]
. . .
You don't know how the others strive
To paint a little thing like that you smeared
Carelessly passing with your robes afloat, —[97]
. . .
Had you enjoined them on me, given me soul,
We might have risen to Rafael, I and you!
Nay, Love, you did give all I asked, I think—
More than merit, yes, by many times.
But had you—oh, with the same perfect brow,
And perfect eyes, and more than perfect mouth,
And the low voice my soul hears, as a bird
The fowler's pipe, and follows to the snare—
Had you, with these the same, but brought a mind!
Some women do so. *Had the* mouth there urged . . .
I might have done it for you. So it seems:
Perhaps not.[98]
. . .
And *had you not grown restless* . . . but I know—
'T is done and past; 't was right, my instinct said.[99]
. . .
If you would sit thus by me every night
I should work better, do you comprehend?
I mean that I should earn more, give you more.[100]

Throughout these lines, Andrea plants the seeds for his overhearing reader to judge Lucrezia, shifting the roles of defender and accuser. Minor as they seem, these accusations are often formulated in the subjunctive: "If you had . . . then I might have . . ." In the third, longer instance, Andrea alternates between accusation, forgiveness, and accusation again. Here we can see Andrea manipulating his audience on various levels. On the first level, akin to Mill's conception of poetry, Andrea speaks directly to his wife and seems to have little regard for who may or may not be overhearing his words. On the second level, however—eloquence—we can almost be sure that he understands the power of his words in the greater context of an overhearing, judging audience. Though Andrea relies here on our role as overhearers, he does not betray his acknowledgment of our presence. He skillfully speaks and works simultaneously in both worlds, within and outside of the walls of the dramatic monologue. That expectation of judgment, that knowing that one's fate will be decided by listening jurors who also might misunderstand or misinterpret, forces one into a state of performance—creating an unavoidable staging for guilty inauthenticity.

Indeed, much of Andrea's depth of character rests in his nuanced fluctuations of tone. Like a Gothic figure, he can seem pathetic and cowering at first but suddenly transform into a spiteful and threatening double of his weaker self. Accordingly, his speech wavers, line by line, from the rhetoric of self-deprecation to ireful invective. Within his speech, one can hear the cowering subservience of monks in the early chapters of Radcliffe's and Lewis's Gothic novels, as well as the virulent accusation of figures like the Duke of Ferrara or the monk of the Spanish cloister. In this sense, modesty is but a shield, a tactic that reveals Andrea's expertise as a speaker of dramatic monologue form: it functions adequately in the realm of direct speech and hearing, but truly dazzles in the realm of indirect speech and overhearing. In Alan Sinfield's term, the "feint" moves closer or further from the poet's "I."[101] As in *Udolpho*, we are led to overlook pivotal facts—we momentarily forget Andrea's own failures, and perhaps, his crime of embezzlement, as he thrusts attention and blame onto his wife instead. Thus, in this monologue, Andrea outwardly offers confession, but masterminds a potential confession from Lucrezia as well.

Despite posing as a victim and confessee of his personal flaws in a secular context of humanism, Andrea actually plays the role of a Grand Inquisitor, calling on God and the reader to witness a confession, while refusing to perform the accusation outright, pressuring his wife towards self-incrimination instead. In his underlying aggression, Andrea plays all three functions of defendant, informer, and judge, the very roles of the inquisitional trial as portrayed in *The Monk* and *The Italian*. In many ways, the poet, too, is responsible for the texts he produces regardless of their dissemination, reception, and possible misinterpretation, liable for what harm may come by way of his poetry.

Aside from Andrea, there is one more figure lurking in the shadows, that of Lucrezia's "cousin" or lover. "That Cousin here again? he waits outside? . . . Ah, but what does he, / The Cousin! what does he to please you more? . . . Again the Cousin's whistle! Go, my Love" (ll. 220, 242–3, 267). In a humorous caricature of romantic confession, the cousin's serenade is a mere whistle, a comically abbreviated form of lyric. Though not particularly sophisticated, it serves as a successful lyric act to secure his courted lover. This poses an easy mockery of romantic confession and lyric speech, akin to the laborious serenading that Vivaldi performs under Ellena's window or that DuPont performs in hopes of winning Emily, cited earlier in this chapter. This minimalist form of lyric poetry—a mere whistle, emptied out of romance, verbal articulation, and musical complexity—is almost crude. But in comparison to Andrea's complex speech act, the cousin's simple whistle is inarguably more effective. In the fashion of the Gothic novel, Browning's dramatic monologues satirize lyric expression and successful overhearing through this simple caricature.

Once Andrea del Sarto is cast as a figure rapt in the manipulative roles of victimization, accusation, punishment, and reward, many figures from Browning's *Men and Women* (1855) and *Dramatis Personae* (1864) can follow suit. This poetics of blame and self-preservation can be closely linked to Fra Lippo Lippi, Browning's Grammarian, Caliban, and Bishop Blougram, as well as the lovers and romantic confessors from "The Statue and the Bust," "The Last Ride Together," "James Lee's Wife," "Two in the Campagna," and "Dis aliter Visum." Indeed, the inquisitional framework appears even in an overtly anti-Gothic poem, one that seeks to debunk the mystical or supernatural trappings often associated with Gothic fiction.[102] As a final test case, this chapter ends with a reading of just such a poem.

Mr. Sludge, "The Medium"

Mr. Sludge, "The Medium" (1864) is a poem that harnesses the power of Gothic form, despite debunking the supernatural in its message. As we will see, this poem raises the stakes of Andrea del Sarto's masterful inquisitions by conducting a complicated and messy conflict of three-fold accusation and overhearing. This results in a chaotic poem in which speaker, auditor, and audience are all at odds with one another—even breaking into physical discord—and incriminating everyone at the scene through the familiar discourse of Gothic guilt and blame. With the characters of Mr. Sludge, Hiram Horsefall, and "little David," Browning further complicates the Gothic inquisitional paradigm, with yet more innovations in the role of auditor and overhearer. The poem's complicated layers of triangulation result in an inquisitional exercise that ultimately wages a critique of readers of Gothic, even while recruiting the key inquisitional aspects of Gothic form.

Deemed "the most famous Victorian attack on mediumship as quackery," *Mr. Sludge, "The Medium,"* a poem set in Boston, skewers the infamous Daniel Dunglas Home, an American, self-professed medium whom Browning met and considered a charlatan.[103] Home could professedly levitate at will and captivated the attention of prominent Victorians by conducting private seances, which often featured rapping sounds and knocks around the house. According to Arthur Conan Doyle, Home was exceptional for his ability to perform mediumship on four distinct levels: *direct voice* (the ability to let spirits audibly speak); *trance speaker* (the ability to let spirits speak through oneself); *clairvoyance* (the ability to see things that are out of view); and *physical medium* (moving objects at a distance).[104] Browning disapproved of his wife's interest in spiritualism, a passion she described in her letters as a "hot spring [of interest that] grows hotter [still]."[105] Even so, Barrett Browning's enthusiasm for the fad only began to subside in the 1850s, when she reported "a chasm between believing that there are spirits . . . and believing that these spirits are infallible . . . or even authentic."[106] By June 1857, she still regarded Home as "the electric wire" between the material and spiritual worlds, but judged him "a weak, commonplace, foolish young man!"[107] *Mr. Sludge, "The Medium"* is thus a pragmatic disavowal of supposedly spiritual happenings, in the same vein of the explained supernatural in Ann Radcliffe's novels. It also serves as a critique of readers who crave Gothic sensation, ultimately arguing that performers and audiences are jointly culpable in the proliferation of these sensational acts. Such brazen eloquence—selling out truth for spectacle—is achieved through the role of the medium, who pretends to deliver whatever it is the audience craves.

Along with "A Death in the Desert," *Mr. Sludge, "The Medium"* is one of the two longest dramatic monologues in the relatively brief collection *Dramatis Personae*. Each offers opposing commentaries on the resurrection of the dead.[108] Mr. Sludge, the medium character based on Home, admits to using deceitful tactics to execute his performances. The poem opens with the speaker caught red-handed, like Fra Lippo Lippi, but he pleads guilty right away.[109]

> Now, don't, sir! Don't expose me!
> Just this once! This was the first and only time, I'll swear,—
> Look at me,—see, I kneel,—the only time,
> I swear, I ever cheated,—yes, by the soul
> Of Her who hears—(your sainted mother, sir!)
> All, except this last accident, was truth—
> This little kind of slip!—and even this,
> It was your own wine, sir, the good champagne,
> (I took it for Catawba, you 're so kind)
> Which put the folly in my head![110]

Sludge cowers like Caliban under the rock, begging his patron for money, forgiveness, and protection from disrepute. He admits outright the phoniness behind spiritual happenings around the house: signs from the patron's dead mother, for example, are actually rappings of his foot.

Yet Sludge's defense naturally turns into aggressive attack, and hence the Gothic poetics of blame ensue. Much like Andrea, Mr. Sludge sets up his monologue by playing the role of victim while Hiram. H. Horsefall plays the violent Grand Inquisitor. Accusation soon shifts in a familiar pattern, as Sludge resorts to self-exculpation by laying blame on those around him. He represents himself as a wronged pet or boy, "only a fractious child," "cockered, cosseted / And coddled," bullied and kept "from the kennel."[111] Soon after, Sludge attacks the "audience" as an entire group. He vehemently directs blame towards those who crave hearing stories of the supernatural. It is the audience, not the spiritualist, who perpetuates the lies and wrongdoing.

As Isobel Armstrong has outlined, the monologue falls into three sections: Sludge's confessions of how he has deceived his patron and his supplications for forgiveness; Sludge's justification of his position, where he compares himself with God; and finally, Sludge's claim for the fictional "truth" behind his deceptions, where he compares himself to a poet.[112] In each of these framings, we can identify the voices of earlier Browning figures who fit the Gothic model. Part One presents the demented prayer of an unabashed criminal pandering for mercy from a confessor rather than from God. Sludge kneels in line 3, then swears not to God, but to his swindled client Hiram H. Horsefall and the ghost of his mother, "by the soul / Of Her who hears."[113] Part Two mirrors the heedless self-exculpation of Johannes Agricola or Porphyria's lover, figures that elevate themselves to God's level. Part Three reveals a maniacal speaker's conscious, even aggressive recognition of his overhearing audience, as seen in "Caliban upon Setebos."

Mr. Sludge, "The Medium" provides an atypical model for the roles of auditor and overhearer in Browning's dramatic monologues. In "The Pragmatics of Silence, and the Figuration of the Reader in Browning's Dramatic Monologues," Wagner-Lawlor describes how an auditor's silence helps to define the reader's own reaction to the speaker in a poem, and how in this relationship, the "silence of intimidation" can topple over into a silence of resistance. The sooner a reader recognizes his separation from the poem's "you," "the sooner the ambiguity of silence may clarify into the active silence of dissent," undermining the power of a coercive speaker.[114] In *Mr. Sludge, "The Medium"* however, the auditor is not silent or demure, like the envoy in "My Last Duchess," but rather abusive and punishing. He is more present than most auditors; and we can infer the tone of his voice and his exact words by the way that Sludge repeats him. He yells, "Get up!," scowls, and throttles the speaker, who painfully responds, "You still inflict on me that terrible face? / You show no mercy? . . . Aie—aie—aie! / Please sir! Your thumbs are through my windpipe, sir! / Ch-ch!"[115] Here, the terrible looks and iron arm reveal an auditor who is actively violent and punishing, imposing physical threat of violence upon the speaker. The numerous players in the poem wrangle in noisy chorus and physical conflict, eking out the forced speech and physical grunts of gothicized lyric we have encountered earlier.[116] The layers of triangulated overhearing only complicate matters, with no mediator to deescalate their accusation and attacks.

A medium, who can supposedly glean information from another world and hear voices of the dead, presents an important figure in a new structure of triangulation that this poem offers. Mediums serve as a bridge between the world of the living and the world of the dead. But upon pretending to overhear the words of dead spirits, they offer up an eloquent performance before the living—pandering to the demands of a Gothic audience that is equally guilty in demanding the exporting of lies. They are participant in the process of promoting false fictions. Here, the figure of the medium, conjured by audience demand, is also represented by the character of little David. This hypothetical young lad, "say a help's son in your house," randomly chosen but representative all the same, is the figure who listens at keyholes. He claims to hear fragments of the medium's performance, then reports them back to the audience surrounding him, all too eager to hear about the spiritualist spectacle going on inside the next room. The men and women of Beacon Street crave overhearing the activity of "signs and wonders, the invisible world" and "the unexplained *phenomena!*"[117] "How good men have desired to see a ghost."[118]

> But let the same lad hear you talk as grand
> At the same keyhole, you and company,
> Of signs and wonders, the invisible world . . .
> . . . If he break in with, "Sir, *I* saw a ghost!"
> Ah, the ways change![119]

David here is a stand-in for the character of the poetic overhearer. First and foremost an eavesdropper, he is then forced to become a medium at one remove, repeating what he hears to an audience that craves illicit content. Rather than translate from one world to another, he relays information from one room to the next. He is thrust, momentarily, into the position of Gothic storyteller.

Browning's poem thus presents three layers of triangulation, outlined in Table 1.1, with three mediums who each takes on a particularly interesting double role. Mr. Sludge, a professed spiritualist, can overhear spirits from the world of the dead, then transmits their words to a credulous audience of Victorian luminaries. Little David, the young boy perched at the keyhole, listens in on what the gossipers crave hearing, then reports back exactly what these "birds of prey" desire—details of Sludge's antics. Browning, in orchestrating this poem, ventriloquizes words of the actual spiritualist David Home, creating a poem that caters to the kind of sensational details we crave.

Table 1.1 Triangulation of speaker, overhearer, and audience in "Mr. Sludge, 'The Medium'"

Layer	Speaker	Medium ← *overhearing*	Medium *eloquent performance* →	Audience
1°	World of the Dead	Mr. Sludge		Horsefall and others in the drawing room
2°	Mr. Sludge, the "medium"	David		Beacon St. birds of prey
3°	David Home	Browning		Readers (us)

The poem's diverse bird imagery paints colorful scenes to convey Browning's disdain for the showmanship of spiritual mediums and, worse yet, a hungry audience that craves spectacle. David's listening audience, judgmental and hungry for more Gothic excitement, is described as a group of "birds of prey," "perched and prim," waiting in suspense for a good story.[120] David, upon assuming the role of a second-hand sensational speaker, stands not upon a soapbox, but rather "what I call your peacock-perch, pet post / To strut, and spread the tail, and squawk upon!"[121] Sludge compares David's faltering speech to momentary rufflings of feathers. This peacock speaker is no bird of prey, nor a lyric bird like Pippa or the Romantics' nightingales, but an empty vessel, a mere medium, a visually dashing figure all stuffed and fluffed and egged on by his audience. The speaker and poet figure are created and manipulated by a controlling audience that devours him whole in avaricious gluttony: "Then, you just have shut your eyes, / Opened your mouth, and gulped down David whole, / You!"[122]

David merely conjures up stories to keep his listening audience off his heels, in much the same way that Mr. Sludge must develop more innovative ploys to amuse his audience. This game of cat and mouse defines the constructive relationship between the Gothic author and reader. We find this model too in Coleridge's portrayal of Radcliffe in his 1794 review of *The Mysteries of Udolpho*, where he commends her ingenuity by comparing her to a locksmith who is forced to escape her thieving readers. The Gothic author is hurried along from room to room in an unending race to create more fanciful twists and turns with which to satiate her readers:

> Curiosity is kept upon the stretch from page to page, and from volume to volume, and the secret, which the reader thinks himself every instant on the point of penetrating, flies like a phantom before him, and eludes his eagerness till the very last moment of protracted expectation. This art of escaping the guesses of the reader has been improved and brought to perfection along with the reader's sagacity; just as the various inventions of locks, bolts, and private drawers, in order to secure, fasten, and hide, have always kept pace with the ingenuity of the pickpocket and housebreaker, whose profession is to unlock, unfasten, and lay open what you have taken so much pains to conceal. In this contest of curiosity on one side, and invention on the other, Ms Radcliffe has certainly the advantage. She delights in concealing her plan with the most artificial contrivance, and seems to amuse herself with saying, at every turn and doubling of the story, "Now you think you have me, but I shall take care to disappoint you."

In his explanation of the curious reader chasing after the innovative author, it is the audience that provides the source of momentum and inspiration. Coleridge presents himself as a Gothic reader agonized by the guilt ensnaring him in a moral and fugitive limbo. The reader is posed as a guilty housebreaker, whom the author must outwit and flee. As a fugitive and intellectual mastermind, assuming the mentality of a thief, the Gothic reader is necessarily villainized and posed as a predatory, though productive force.

The inherent linking of criminality and curiosity is a token of the Gothic genre. Curiosity, personified, (super)naturally flies like a phantom. But Coleridge's extended metaphor for authorial innovation takes the form of theft and escape artistry. There is no actual stealing or housebreaking involved, only encouragement of imagination. Positive inspiration is cast as transgression. Curiosity is always incriminated, such that guilt and collusion become an inextricable part of the reading and writing experience. The very models of Gothic innovation and consumption—whether modeled by Ann Radcliffe or Douglas Home and their fans—are configured as a chase between fugitive and pursuer, prey and predator. There is no innocent party in this framework: both reader and author are implicated.

Mr. Sludge, "The Medium" is a critique of Gothic readers who crave the supernatural. The poem serves as an explanation of why a Gothic taste for literature and incident is so persistent in everyday culture. Sludge's deflection of culpability recruits a familiar rhetoric of allegation; it argues that the Gothic mode should not be blamed on spiritual figures who are "chosen" or "possessed," but rather, it is fueled by the general public, the flock of predatory birds and their common taste for a colorful, fantastical show of peacock feathers. "Fol-lol-the-rido-lddle-iddle-ol! /You see, sir, it's your own fault more than mine; / It's all your fault, you curious gentlefolk!"[123] But Horsefall blaming fans of spiritualism—or Browning blaming his readers—is simply another example of the Gothic's deflection of guilt and accusation.

Ultimately, Gothic confabulation lies not in the hands of a select few, but is perpetuated by a community of writers, mediums, and a demanding audience who share in a guilty participation. Thus, like Radcliffe's endings, Mr. Sludge's monologue affirms the Gothic of the everyday. Here, the "explained supernatural" demystifies the possibility of magical arts; Gothic machinery becomes the joint artistic production of Hiram Horsefall and his Beacon Street neighbors, as channeled through mediums like Sludge, David, and even Browning himself. As in Coleridge's description, we too are potentially criminalized as Gothic readers who crave sensation and excitement, forcing a creative speaker to report on his latest overhearings. Sludge and David are not members of a spiritual elect, but mere victims of a quotidian and mainstream desire for Gothic speech and overhearing.

The Gothic thus provides a thematic, structural, and cultural framework to better understand Victorian dramatic monologues, in ways that complement existing conceptualizations of the form, including Robert Langbaum's sympathy and judgment, or Cornelia Pearsall's rapture, in its many senses of loaded violence, religiosity, and rhetorical "rapt" attention. From the seemingly innocent lyric bird in *Pippa Passes*, Browning's proto-dramatic monologue experiment—to the guttural, forced confession of the monk in "The Soliloquy of the Spanish Cloister"—to the humanist staging of inquisitional trial in "Andrea del Sarto"—to anti-Gothic poems like *Mr. Sludge, "The Medium,"* we can see Browning innovating upon a poetics of guilt and accusation to full fruition. Through each of these variations, he adds cases and precedents, (as in a book of torts), to bank more information that can be used to parse out a world without stable guidelines for right and wrong, without clear, universal rulings for sympathy and judgment. While many of Browning's monologists may take on the thematics of Gothic characters, it is especially his characters who seem to resist and evade Gothic characterizations that prove how all overheard speech is not merely beautiful and lyrical, but tinged with guilt and liability. We learn this lesson best not necessarily from the monks and dukes, but from the young silk-winders, humanist painters, and debunkers of supernaturalism: overheard speech is powerful because transgression and collusion are inherent in its very structure, through a gothically charged dynamic among speaker-auditor-audience that incriminates even us, the reader. The world is more Gothic than we think, and dramatic monologues equip us to recognize these Gothics of the everyday.

Notes

1. Robert Browning, "My Last Duchess," in *The Poetical Works of Robert Browning. Volume 3: Bells and Pomegranates I–VI*, ed. Ian Jack and Rowena Fowler (Oxford: Clarendon Press, 1988), 186–8.
2. In regards to the use of the term "lyric," Yopie Prins and Virginia Jackson have called attention to contemporary tendencies to privilege lyric poetry over other forms, resulting in a "super-sizing" of lyric that

conflates lyric with all of poetry. (Virginia Jackson and Yopie Prins (eds), *The Lyric Theory Reader*, Baltimore: Johns Hopkins University Press, 2014, 5.) In my discussions of John Stuart Mill, in Chapter 1 especially, I use lyric (overheard) in contradistinction to "dramatic monologue" (heard), while fully acknowledging the impossibility of Mill's own ideal, as well as the hybridity of the dramatic monologue's development out of lyric precursors. The chapter's references to a "lyric I" are couched in the sense of Mill's conceptions of the term, along with that of his contemporaries. My use of "lyric" thus does not encourage a flattening of the term nor assume it "to have transhistorical, typological validity" across periods and into the present day. Throughout this book, I invoke "lyric" in the more capacious sense that John Addington Symonds came to use the term by 1889: "But what a complex thing is this Victorian lyric! It includes Wordsworth's sonnets and Rossetti's ballads, Coleridge's 'Ancient Mariner' and Keats's odes, Clough's 'Easter Day' and Tennyson's 'Maud,' Swinburne's 'Songs before Sunrise' and Browning's 'Dramatis Personae,' Thomson's 'City of Dreadful Night' and Mary Robinson's 'Handful of Honeysuckles,' . . . The Kaleidoscope presented by this lyric is so inexhaustible . . ." (John Addington Symonds, "A Comparison of Elizabethan with Victorian Poetry," *Fortnightly Review* 45, no. 265 (January 1889): 55–79, 63–4).

As Marion Thain points out, lyric "was by the end of the nineteenth century not a particular song form of poetry, but was gradually encompassing a variety of forms and modes" (Marion Thain, "Victorian Lyric Pathology and Phenomenology," in *The Lyric Poem: Formations and Transformations*, Cambridge: Cambridge University Press, 2013, 158.) This kaleidoscopic range of lyric content, perhaps disorienting and frustrating for Symonds, points to some of the prolific developments of poetic forms covered in the chapters of this book.

3. Adam Roberts reads Browning's dramatic monologues as verbal resuscitations of the dead, "a quasi-Spiritualist voicing of dead men and women" where he recognizes Browning's "necromancer poetics" in the way that he returns "again and again to figures that straddle life and death." Adam Roberts, "Browning, the Dramatic Monologue and the Resuscitation of the Dead," in *The Victorian Supernatural*, ed. Nicola Brown, Carolyn Burdett, and Pamela Thurschwell (Cambridge: Cambridge University Press, 2004), 109, 112.

4. In "Porphyria's Lover" "the speaker himself attempts to enter into the consciousness of another, of Porphyria, but his appropriation of her consciousness reduces her to a mere puppet, figuratively at first, and then literally as he props up her murdered body . . . Such utter appropriation of another's consciousness, such desire to speak for another, is clearly insane, but of course Browning could not be unaware that he himself, claiming to speak from within the consciousness of a lunatic, was performing a similar act." David G. Riede, *Allegories of One's*

Own Mind: Melancholy in Victorian Poetry (Columbus: The Ohio State University Press, 2005), 157–9.
5. Herbert F. Tucker, "From Monomania to Monologue: 'St. Simone Stylites' and the Rise of the Dramatic Monologue," *Victorian Poetry* 22, no. 2 (Summer 1984): 137.
6. Critics have since revised the notion that Tennyson and Browning "invented" the dramatic monologue in the Victorian period. A. Dwight Culler, Alan Sinfield and Robert Pattison remind readers that the dramatic monologue existed long before the 1830s, beginning with Theocritus, and used to great effect by Ovid and Shakespeare. A. Dwight Culler, "Monodrama and the Dramatic Monologue," *PMLA* 90 (1975): 368–74. Alan Sinfield, *Dramatic Monologue* (London: Methuen, 1977). Robert Pattison, *Tennyson and Tradition* (Cambridge, MA: Harvard University Press, 1979).

    Isobel Armstrong (1993) and Kate Flint (1996) have attributed the Victorian revival of the dramatic monologue to female poets of the 1820s. Isobel Armstrong, *Victorian Poetry: Poetry, Poetics and Politics* (New York: Routledge, 1993). Kate Flint, "'. . . As a Rule, I does Not Mean I': Personal Identity and the Victorian Woman Poet," in *Rewriting the Self: Histories from the Renaissance to the Present,* ed. Roy Porter (London: Routledge, 1997), 156–66.

    Dorothy Mermin, *The Audience in the Poem: Five Victorian Poets* (New Brunswick: Rutgers University Press, 1983), Cynthia Scheinberg (1997), and Glennis Byron (2003) argue for an opening up of the canon to contextualize Tennyson and Browning's contributions within an earlier moment dominated by these women poets. Cynthia Scheinberg, "Recasting 'Sympathy and Judgment': Amy Levy, Women Poets, and the Victorian Dramatic Monologue," *Victorian Poetry* 35, no. 2 (1997): 173–91. Glennis Byron, *Dramatic Monologue* (London: Routledge, 2003).
7. Tucker, "From Monomania to Monologue," 123.
8. Ina Beth Sessions, "The Dramatic Monologue," *PMLA* 62 (1947): 503–16.
9. Robert Langbaum, *The Poetry of Experience: The Dramatic Monologue in Modern Literary Tradition* (New York: Random House, 1957).
10. Mermin, *The Audience in the Poem*. Jennifer A. Wagner-Lawlor, "The Pragmatics of Silence, and the Figuration of the Reader in Browning's Dramatic Monologues," *Victorian Poetry* 35 (1997): 287–302.
11. Angela Leighton, *Victorian Women Poets: Writing Against the Heart* (Charlottesville: University of Virginia Press, 1992). W. David Shaw, *Origins of the Monologue: The Hidden God* (Toronto: University of Toronto Press, 1999). W. David Shaw, "Lyric Displacement in the Victorian Monologue: Naturalizing the Vocative," *Nineteenth-Century Literature* 52, no. 3 (December 1997): 302–25.
12. Tucker, "From Monomania to Monologue," 125.

13. Ibid. 126.
14. Cornelia Pearsall, *Tennyson's Rapture: Transformation in the Victorian Dramatic Monologue* (Oxford University Press, 2008), 22.
15. Eve Kosofsky Sedgwick, *The Coherence of Gothic Conventions* (New York: Arno Press, 1980).
16. "While lyric may have been unwittingly, and perhaps regretfully, pathologized by Mill, and deliberately so by Browning, Decadence was able to reclaim the genre through its own deep affinity with the very terms of that pathology." Marion Thain, "Victorian Lyric Pathology and Phenomenology," 164.
17. All passages by Mill refer to John Stuart Mill, "Thoughts on Poetry and Its Varieties (1833)," in *The Collected Works of John Stuart Mill*, vol. 1: *Autobiography and Literary Essays*, ed. John M. Robson and Jack Stillinger (Toronto: University of Toronto Press, 1981), 348–9.
18. We may also reframe Mill's distinction between poetry and eloquence through the distinction between overhearing and eavesdropping. For Ann Gaylin, there exists a clear difference between intentional and inadvertent overhearing, where listening is often morally valenced: "evil characters deliberately eavesdrop, whereas good characters happen to overhear information that frustrates villains' plots." Gaylin's discussion of eavesdropping is situated in the context of the Victorian novel, where the social rules of eavesdropping reflect coded forms of behavior "that insure the stability of the social order; middle-class overhearing thus regulates criminal eavesdropping." In either case, however, the audience of a dramatic monologue has no way to intervene in the actions of a poem; we cannot rush in to warn the envoy or the Duke's next wife of her impending doom. Ann Gaylin, *Eavesdropping in the Novel from Austen to Proust* (Cambridge: Cambridge University Press, 2002), 7.
19. Ann Radcliffe, *The Italian, or the Confessional of the Black Penitents: A Romance*, ed. Frederick Garber (New York: Oxford University Press, 1998), 26, 37.
20. Ann Radcliffe, *The Mysteries of Udolpho*, (New York: Oxford University Press, 2008), 447.
21. William Wordsworth, "Preface to the Lyrical Ballads, 2nd edn (1800)," in *William Wordsworth and Samuel Coleridge, Lyrical Ballads 1798 and 1800*, ed. Michael Gamer and Dahlia Porter (Toronto: Broadview, 2008), 183.
22. Herbert F. Tucker, "Dramatic Monologue and the Overhearing of Lyric," in *Lyric Poetry beyond the New Criticism*, ed. Chaviva Hosek and Patricia Parker (Ithaca: Cornell University Press, 1985), 230.

    J. S. Mill, "Thoughts on Poetry and its Varieties," 350.
23. Ann Radcliffe, *The Italian*, 17.
24. Tucker, "Dramatic Monologue and the Overhearing of Lyric," 230.
25. Matthew Lewis, *The Monk: A Romance*, ed. Howard Anderson (New York: Oxford University Press, 2008), 296–7.

26. Ibid. 230, 235.
27. "Browning's perfection of the dramatic monologue allowed him both to ironize the Romantic process of projection and yet to restore prominence to a Female Other on which both he and the Romantics had projected their desire." Ulrich C. Knoepflmacher, "Projection and the Female Other: Romanticism, Browning, and the Victorian Dramatic Monologue," *Victorian Poetry* 22, no. 2 (1984): 139–59, 143. See also Linda Shires, "Browning's Grafts," *Studies in English Literature, 1500–1900* 48, no. 4 (Autumn 2008): 769–78, which explores Browning's letters to Euphrasia Fanny Haworth to trace the role of impersonation and gender relations of lyric and context.
28. Marion Thain, "Victorian Lyric Pathology and Phenomenology," 163.
29. Browning, *Pippa Passes*, ll. 1881–9, in *The Poetical Works of Robert Browning*, vol. 3, 21–91.
30. Critics have recognized the experimental nature of *Pippa Passes*. David Riede reads the play as "an extraordinary experiment in the politics of genre, an experiment that calls into question the moral authority of both lyric and drama" (50). Tucker describes *Pippa Passes* as an experiment in genre. David G. Riede, "Genre and Poetic Authority in 'Pippa Passes'," *Victorian Poetry* 27, no. 3/4 (1989): 50. Herbert F. Tucker, *Browning's Beginnings: The Art of Disclosure* (Minneapolis: University of Minnesota Press, 1980), 122.
31. Sessions, "The Dramatic Monologue," 508.
32. Riede, "Genre and Poetic Authority," 54.
33. Daniel Karlin also resists the reading of Pippa as wholly innocent. Contrasting Pippa with Wordsworth's Highland lass from "The Solitary Reaper," Karlin reads Pippa as a songbird with pointed motivations. "In her conscious, self-pleasing artistry, [she has] a psychological motive for that artistry. The framing scenes of the drama tell of her struggle to accept her poverty, alienation, and lack of love, and imply that she finds in her singing a mode of compensation if not transcendence." Daniel Karlin, *The Figure of the Singer* (Oxford: Oxford University Press, 2013), 91.
34. For Riede, the adjudication of Pippa as either a queen or a puppet girl reveals the political ramifications of Browning's take on republicanism and the authority of speech. Ultimately deeming Pippa as a hybrid "puppet-queen girl," Riede reads *Pippa Passes* as a critique of lyric authority. David G. Riede, "Genre and Poetic Authority."
35. Arthur Hallam had called Tennyson's poems "a new species of poetry, a graft of the lyric on the dramatic," while Tucker recognized early on the hybridity of the dramatic monologue through this metaphor of grafting plants, or implants. As Tucker has recognized early on, "the dramatic monologue is an eminently Romantic form once we recognize the hybrid genre of it . . ." Tucker, "Dramatic Monologue and the Overhearing of Lyric," 237–8.

"The hybrid dramatic monologue, as a result of its aim to make the world and subjectivity safe for each other in the interests of character, has proved a sturdy grafting stock for flowers of lyricism; and the governing pressures of the genre, just because they governed so firmly, had bred hothouse lyric varieties of unsurpassed intensity. These lyrical implants it was left to a new generation of rhymers, scholars, and anthologists to imitate, defend, and excerpt in a newly chastened lyric poetry, a severely purist poetics, and a surprisingly revisionist history of poetry." Arthur Henry Hallam, in *The Writings of Arthur Hallam*, ed. T. H. Vail Motter (London: Oxford University Press, 1943), 197.

36. "Sir, I will make away with her for you—the girl—here close at hand; not the stupid obvious kind of killing; do not speak—know nothing of her nor of me!" (*Pippa Passes*, "Night," ll. 146–8).
37. Dale Kramer, "Character and Theme in *Pippa Passes*," *Victorian Poetry* 2 (1964), 244, 249, quoted in Marvin P. Garrett, "Language and Design in 'Pippa Passes'," *Victorian Poetry* 13, no. 1 (1975), 48, 49.
38. Riede, "Genre and Poetic Authority," 53–4.
39. "My brain is drowned now—quite drowned." *Pippa Passes*, "Morning," l. 276.

    All quotations from *Pippa Passes* refer to *The Complete Works of Robert Browning*, vol. 3, ed. Ian Jack, Margaret Smith, and Rowena Fowler), 13–88.
40. "What name was that the little girl sang forth? / Kate? The Cornaro, doubtless, who renounced / The crown of Cyprus to be lady here / At Asolo . . . Yes, a bitter thing / To see our lady above all need of us; . . . Here is a woman with utter need of me, – / I find myself queen here, it seems!" (*Pippa Passes*, "Noon," ll. 271–82).
41. *Pippa Passes*, "Evening," ll. 178, 204.
42. *Pippa Passes*, "Morning," ll. 221–36.
43. Gaylin calls attention to the physical aspect of eavesdropping as a theatrical device borrowed from drama and imported into the novel. The German, Russian, Polish, French, Italian, and Spanish synonymous expressions all indicate a sense of physical space (under, next to, beside); a proximity to walls, doors, or other structures of separation; and/or the element of hiding (*lauschenig; pod slushivanye; podsluchiwanie and przysluchiwanie; écouter aux portes; origliare alla porta; ascoltare di nascosto/udire per caso, di nascosto; escuchar a escondidas*). Scenes of eavesdropping "dramatize the ways in which identity is shaped by forces of rumor, innuendo, suggestion, and discussion. It literalizes the concept of distance between self and other—between others' position and place of cognition and our own—and reminds us that our conception of ourselves is dependent on our specific place in a physical and psychological world." Gaylin, *Eavesdropping in the Novel*, 3.
44. Browning, *Pippa Passes*, Part 1, "Morning," ll. 227–8.

45. Ibid. "Night," ll. 82–98. According to the *Oxford English Dictionary*, Browning used the word "twat" erroneously in line 96, writing "under the impression that it denoted some part of a nun's attire." *Oxford English Dictionary, s.v.* "twat," <https://www.oxfordenglishdictionary.com/definition/english/twat> (last accessed 3 January 2020).
46. Soon after overhearing Pippa's song, Sebald, repeating the lines in a refrain, extracts himself from his conspiracies and returns to a sense of moral righteousness. He renounces his sin, ready to pay for the price of justice, and curses Ottima: "*That little peasant's voice / Has righted all again.* Though I be lost, / I know which is the better, never fear, / Of vice or virtue, purity or lust, / Nature or trick! *I see what I have done, / Entirely now! . . . / I, having done my deed, pay too its price!* / I hate, hate—curse you! *God's in his heaven!*" "Morning," ll. 261–9, italics mine.
47. *Pippa Passes*, "Night," ll. 280–6.
48. Robert J. Kaczorowski, "The Common-Law Background of Nineteenth-Century Tort Law," *Ohio State Law Journal* 51, no. 5 (1990): 1127–99.
49. Frances Ferguson, *Pornography, the Theory: What Utilitarianism Did to Action* (Chicago: University of Chicago Press, 2004), 26.
50. Clyde de L. Ryals, *Becoming Browning: The Poems and Plays of Robert Browning, 1833–1846* (Columbus: Ohio State University Press, 1983), 137.
51. Riede, "Genre and Poetic Authority," 57.
52. "Not only was ignorance of the law, in the materialist account of tort law, no excuse; one could never really be anything but ignorant of the law so long as the future remained invisible. And therefore the notion of rewards and punishments for actions—indeed, the very notion of actions—was considerably refashioned." Ferguson, *Pornography, the Theory*, 67.
53. Ferguson, *Pornography, the Theory*, 68.
54. Ferguson emphasizes the importance of tort law following the development of mercantilism, rendering individuals responsible for the consequences of their property: "tort law came to hold persons responsible for their effects and for the effects of their objects. The paradigmatic early cases established a law of the road by claiming that a person's carriage did not cease to be his/her carriage even when it was out of his/her control." Ibid., 67.
55. Riede, "Genre and Poetic Authority," 57.
56. Ferguson, *Pornography, the Theory*, 26–7.
57. Michelle A. Massé, *In the Name of Love: Women, Masochism and the Gothic* (Ithaca: Cornell University Press, 1992).
58. Percy Bysshe Shelley, "A Defence of Poetry," in *Shelley's Poetry and Prose*, 2nd edn, ed. Donald H. Reiman and Neil Fraistat (New York: W. W. Norton, 2002).
59. John Stuart Mill, "Thoughts on Poetry and Its Varieties," 349.

60. Tucker, "Dramatic Monologue and the Overhearing of Lyric," 228. Richard Stein writes of Michel Foucault's model: "if we feel as if we are within the cell, we also seem to be peering into it with the intensity of a keeper." This conceit becomes important for my argument in Chapter 2 on confinement in Victorian women's sonnets, where the captive plays the role of imprisoner. Richard L. Stein, *Victoria's Year: English Literature and Culture, 1837–1838* (New York: Oxford University Press, 1987), 33.
61. Lewis, *The Monk*, 223.
62. Langbaum, *The Poetry of Experience*, 85.
63. Lewis, *The Monk*, 423.
64. Lewis, *The Monk*, 422.
65. See also the Inquisition scene from Chapter 11 of *Melmoth the Wanderer*: "One of the judges, trembling on his seat, (while his shadow, magnified by the imperfect light, pictured the figure of a paralytic giant on the wall opposite to me), attempted to address some question to me. As he spoke, there came a hollow sound from his throat, his eyes were rolled upwards in their sockets,—he was in an apoplectic paroxysm, and died before he could be removed to another apartment." Charles Maturin, *Melmoth the Wanderer*, ed. Douglas Grant (New York: Oxford Univeristy Press, 2008).
66. Lewis, *The Monk*, 430.
67. Radcliffe, *The Italian*, 197.
68. Robert Browning, "The Confessional," in *The Poetical Works of Robert Browning. Volume 4: Bells and Pomegranates VII–VIII*, ed. Ian Jack, Rowena Fowler, and Margaret Smith (Oxford: Clarendon Press, 1991), 89–93.
69. Female heroism in Gothic romance lies not in action, but in silence and stoicism, refusing self-incrimination. Even at her moment of arrest by the Inquisition, Ellena of *The Italian* does not speak in her own defense, but gasps inarticulately and falls senseless; it is Vivaldi who utters her disavowal on her behalf: "She acknowledges no crime," replied Vivaldi; "she only perceives the extent of the malice that persecutes her." A female character must not admit to any crimes "to save [her]self from undeserved sufferings," [lest she] "should then incur deserved ones." As Ellena asserts, "The very dissimulation which I should employ in self-defence, might be a means of involving me in destruction." Radcliffe, *The Italian*, 96.
70. Generally, female characters are pressured to self-incrimination through verbal threat and extortion, while male characters risk having confession physically extracted from their bodies through methods of torture. Margaret Davison discusses torture chambers and the "paraphernalia of confinement" in her article "Haunted House/Haunted Heroine," where she recognizes the use of Spanish Inquisition imagery to symbolize the marriage institution as a definitive aspect of the

Female Gothic tradition. Carol Margaret Davison, "Haunted House/ Haunted Heroine: Female Gothic Closets in 'The Yellow Wallpaper'," *Women's Studies* 33, no. 1 (2004): 59.
71. Browning, "The Confessional," ll. 1–6.
72. Ibid. ll. 7–12.
73. Kelly Hurley, *The Gothic Body: Sexuality, Materialism, and Degeneration at the Fin de siècle* (Cambridge: Cambridge University Press, 1996).
74. Browning, "The Confessional," ll. 61–78.
75. Ibid. ll. 68, 69, 70, 72.
76. This mirrors the device employed in so many Gothic tales, where the moment of unveiling is thwarted with a dash, exclamation point, or chapter break. This mechanism for narrating a heinous discovery is famously utilized in Coleridge's *Christabel* ("A sight to dream of, not to tell!") and in Volume II, Chapter 6 of *Udolpho*, where Emily faints at the initial sight of a rotting face and the narrator withholds a visual description.
77. Browning, "The Confessional," lines 43–4. "By thy long grey beard and glittering eye / Now wherefore stopp'st thou me?" Samuel Taylor Coleridge, "The Rime of the Ancient Mariner," in *The Complete Poetical Works of Samuel Taylor Coleridge. Volume 1: Poems*, ed. Ernest Hartley Coleridge (Oxford: Oxford University Press, 1912), line 3.
78. Radcliffe, *The Italian*, 2.
79. Mill, "Thoughts on Poetry and Its Varieties," 349.
80. Browning, "Porphyria's Lover," in *The Poetical Works of Robert Browning*, vol. 3, 244–8, lines 99–101.
81. As Herbert Tucker notes, "The monk literally growls his way into utterance and out again, ending his poem in the unspeakable hatred with which he has started. 'Gr-r-r—there go, my heart's abhorrence!' These sounds are an inversion of those in the prayer, '*Ave, Virgo!* Gr-r-r—you swine!' (72)." Tucker, *Browning's Beginnings*, 155.
82. William Godwin, *Caleb Williams*, ed. David McCracken (New York: W. W. Norton, 1977), 7.

Readers can readily witness similar examples of poetic expression under physical duress in Victorian dramatic monologues where speakers offer triangulated speech while imprisoned or tortured, from Browning's "Caliban upon Setebos" to Charles Kingsley's "Saint Maura," in which a woman speaks the entirety of the poem to her husband Saint Timothy as they both endure crucifixion until dawn. The groans of her husband reveal his bodily pain, but also his inexpressibility of speech, which is the true sign of his martyrdom. In Kingsley's poem, while the auditor is understood to grunt from physical torture, the speaker is articulately expressive, and this jarring difference in linguistic capacity represents the ideological riff between the couple in their last living moments. Here, as in The *Monk* and *The Italian*, Saint Timothy represents a martyr denied the ability of articulation. See also Elaine Scarry, *The Body In Pain* for the differing role of pain for victims and torturers. Elaine Scarry, *The Body in Pain: The Making and Unmaking of the World* (New York: Oxford University Press, 1985).

83. All quotations from "Soliloquy of the Spanish Cloister" refer to *The Poetical Works of Robert Browning. Volume 3: Bells and Pomegranates 1–VI*, 199–203. Here, lines 1–8, italics mine.
84. Archibald C. Knowles, "Memorial of the Incarnation, or 'The Angelus'," in *The Practice of Religion: A Short Manual of Instructions and Devotions* (New York: Edwin S. Gorham, 1918), 175.
85. Browning, "Soliloquy of the Spanish Cloister," lines 70–2.
86. Ibid. ll. 41–4.
87. Ibid. ll. 33–40.
88. Ibid. ll. 1 and 71.
89. Ibid. line 8.
90. Augusta Webster's "Jeanne d'Arc" raises the Spanish monk's laughable show of martyrdom to a serious pitch, testifying to the very real and physical consequences of true martyrdom. About to be burned at the stake, Jeanne must try to vindicate herself against accusations of heresy through a speech act of self-defense. The question of her hypocrisy—she is either a saint or a fiend—positions her as a female counterpart to the Gothic's guilty monks. Augusta Webster, "Jeanne d'Arc," in *Augusta Webster: Portraits and Other Poems*, ed. Christine Sutphin (Peterborough, ON: Broadview, 1999), 47–52. See also Note 102.
91. See Eleanor Cook, *Browning's Lyrics: An Exploration* (Toronto: University of Toronto Press, 1974), 126–7 and Lee Erickson, "The Self and Others in Browning's 'Men and Women'," *Victorian Poetry* 21, no. 1 (1983): 53. Cited in Erik Gray, "Andrea del Sarto's Modesty," in *Robert Browning's Poetry: A Norton Critical Edition*, 2nd edn, ed. James F. Loucks and Andrew M. Stauffer (New York: W. W. Norton, 2007), 643–50.
92. Browning, "Andrea del Sarto," lines 83–4. All quotations from "Andrea del Sarto (Called 'The Faultless Painter')" refer to *The Poetical Works of Robert Browning*, vol. 5, *Men and Women*, ed. Ian Jack and Robert Inglesfield (Oxford: Clarendon Press, 1995), 259–74.
93. Ibid. ll. 250–5.
94. Ibid. ll. 78.
95. Ibid. l. 64.
96. Ibid. ll. 54–5.
97. Ibid. ll. 73–5.
98. Ibid. ll. 118–33.
99. Ibid. ll. 165–6.

100. Ibid. ll. 205–7.
101. "Dramatic monologue feigns because it pretends to be something other than what it is: an invented speaker masquerades in the first person which customarily signifies the poet's voice." Sinfield, *Dramatic Monologue*, 25. Pattison, *Tennyson and Tradition*.
102. The application of the Gothic inquisitional framework to a reading of dramatic monologue extends to poets beyond Browning, from Tennyson to Augusta Weber. In particular, Webster's "Jeanne d'Arc" shows a woman on trial. The question of her hypocrisy—she is either a saint or a fiend—positions her as a female counterpart to the Gothic trope of guilty monks. About to be burned at the stake, Jeanne must try to vindicate herself against accusations of heresy through a speech act of self-defense: "They say / I commune with the Fiend and he has led / My way so high. Yes, if he could do this, / And I, deserted as I am of God, / Might cease to war with him and buy my life."

    As Helen Luu writes, "And yet, in response to Jeanne's prayer, God does not say a word. The poem ends with the prayer, leaving Jeanne's subject status in question by leaving in doubt the status of her speech" (31). At the end of the poem, Joan of Arc is visited by nightmares or Gothic dreams. Helen Luu, "A Matter of Life and Death: The Auditor-Function of the Dramatic Monologue" *Victorian Poetry* 54, no. 1 (Spring 2016): 19–38.
103. Adam Roberts, "Browning, the Dramatic Monologue and the Resuscitation of the Dead," in *The Victorian Supernatural*, ed. Brown et al., 109–27. For more on this topic, see Emma Clery, *The Rise of Supernatural Fiction 1762–1800* (Cambridge: Cambridge University Press, 1995).
104. Arthur Conan Doyle, *The History of Spiritualism*, vol. 1 (New York: George H. Doran Company, 1926), 204–5.
105. Robert Browning and Elizabeth Barrett Browning, *The Brownings' Correspondence*, ed. Philip Kelley, Edward Hagan, and Linda M. Lewis (Winfield, KS: Wedgestone Press, 2016), 155, quoted in Beverly Taylor, "Guide to the Year's Work: Elizabeth Barrett Browning," *Victorian Poetry* 55, no. 3 (Fall 2017): 339.
106. *The Brownings' Correspondence*, 155.
107. *The Brownings' Correspondence*, 84.
108. Roberts, "Browning, the Dramatic Monologue and the Resuscitation of the Dead," 109. Roberts's essay focuses on Browning's "necromancing, resurrectionist poetics" that fuel his "great many death-bed poems" and poems where speakers describe the process of dying, die in the process of voicing their monologue, or give voice to the dead (125, 144).
109. In lines 107 to 125, the young lad David is wrongfully accused of stealing money. Like Andrea, Sludge's defense is one of self-victimization: "I cheat in self-defense / And there's my answer to a world of cheats!"

All quotations from *Mr. Sludge, "The Medium"* refer to *The Complete Works of Robert Browning*, vol. 6, ed. John C. Berkey, Allan C. Dooley and Susan E. Dooley (Athens: Ohio University Press, 1996), 285–351.
110. Browning, *Mr. Sludge, "The Medium,"* ll. 1–10.
111. Ibid. ll. 391, 387–8, 393.
112. Isobel Armstrong, "Browning's *Mr. Sludge, 'The Medium,'*" *Victorian Poetry* 2, no. 1 (Winter 1964), 3.
113. Browning, *Mr. Sludge, "The Medium,"* ll. 4–5.
114. Wagner-Lawlor, "The Pragmatics of Silence," 292.
115. Browning, *Mr. Sludge, "The Medium,"* ll. 15–17. These ejaculations of pain are closest to "true poetry" or genuine speech in Sludge's monologue.
116. After Horsefall refuses to shake hands and storms off at the end of the poem, Sludge allows for a true enunciation of his feelings: "R-r-r, you brute-beast and blackguard! Cowardly scamp! . . . Confound the cuss!" lines 1280, 1392. This growling, passionate voice, like that of the Spanish monk and Caliban, is not the sign of a primitive speaker, but rather one that utilizes alliteration and enjoys the guttural sound of strong consonants. These noisy moments, as angry as they may be, offer far better occasions of poetic meaning-making than the lyrical and gleeful sounds of the earlier Sludge, acting on his best behavior before Horsefall: "Fol-lol-the-rido-lddle-iddle-ol!" "illy-oh-yo," and "rub-a-dub," lines 83, 284, 302.
117. Ibid. ll. 98, 132, 152.
118. Ibid. ll. 135, 144.
119. Ibid. ll. 130–2, 138–9.
120. Ibid. l. 139.
121. Ibid. ll. 156–7.
122. Ibid. ll. 212–14.
123. Ibid. ll. 83–5.

Chapter 2

The Gothic Poetess: Self-Confinement in the Sonnet Cell

"'The sanctuary is prophaned,' said Ellena, mildly, but with dignity: 'it is become a prison.'"

Ann Radcliffe, The Italian

"Thus am I mine own prison."

Christina Rossetti, "The Thread of Life"

Ann Radcliffe's *The Mysteries of Udolpho* (1794), in addition to over six hundred pages of prose, is also, as its subtitle reminds us, "A Romance; interspersed with some pieces of poetry." It contains sporadic verses passed off as poetic musings of the heroine Emily St. Aubert, who throughout the novel pens poems in moments of solitude, reflection, and often imprisonment. Emily composes mundane, occasional poems titled "Shipwreck," "The Bat," and "Go, pencil!" These poems, according to Samuel T. Coleridge in a 1794 review, were "some beautiful, all pleasing, but rather monotonous."[1] It is easy to disregard these poems as middling verses of escapist poetry. Subsumed by the prolific prose that surrounds them, they serve as signals of overwrought melancholia in scenes sometimes melodramatic to the point of satire.[2] But the fact that Radcliffe's Gothic heroines are also elegiac sonneteers allowed her novels to exert a poetic influence in ways that critics have not previously considered. By posing Gothic heroines as sometime-poetesses, Radcliffe's astonishingly popular works established sentimental clichés that came to shape a succeeding generation of sonneteers, particularly women writers who inherited these Gothic conventions.

Romantic and Victorian poets recruited gendered tropes of imprisonment as a means for expressing the perversity of female domestic confinement: the state of being trapped within the "Bastille" of marriage or doomed to the risks of childbirth. Contorting their bodies and modifying their voices to negotiate the constraints of separate spheres, female poet-speakers evoked the language of captivity and thralldom, departing from the typically soft, harmonious lamentations of elegy. We hear, in their metasonnets, a new range of images and sounds emerge from women writers that mirror the constraints of their situation, establishing the Gothic voice of the professional Victorian poetess. This is a voice that sings and enacts, in myriad ways, a poetics of Gothic enclosure.

In this chapter, I argue that 1790s Gothic novels helped define the cultural image of the nineteenth-century poetess, contributing to the myth of the female sonneteer by modeling specifically Gothic modes of form and restraint, through embodied images of violence, fetishized confinement, and thwarted motherhood. I propose using the 1790s Gothic novel as a lens to trace a poetics of captivity that haunts the figure of the female sonneteer in fiction, poetry, and literary history. The trope of the damsel in distress recurs in many nineteenth-century metasonnets, "sonnets on sonnets" that offer commentary on the form itself. Utilized by major poets of the 1800s, the trapped woman—in a castle turret, dungeon, or abbey cell—becomes a familiar physical figuration, where the sonnet's form serves as a metaphor for prison and the image of a trapped woman is used to justify, or even celebrate, such prosodic strictures. Creativity in confinement becomes a generative trope for Romantic and Victorian poets alike, embodied in a tradition of what I call "Gothic sonnets": sonnets that thematically and formally utilize the imagery of female bondage, both thematically and structurally, as an analogy for the structural limitations of the form's fourteen lines, rigid rhyme scheme, and strict meter.

The sonnet, construed as a gothically bound woman, becomes a complex node connecting Romantic Gothic novels to works of the major Victorian poets. We can trace an evolution in three stages, beginning with the Romantic sonnet revival and the popularity of professional poets such as Charlotte Smith and Anna Seward. Upon their success, sonneteers of the 1770s and 1780s joined the ranks of the mythicized poetess, immortalized through succeeding representations in biography, criticism, fiction, and poetry. But it was ubiquitous appearances in Gothic novels and poems at the turn of the century that firmly established the elegiac sonneteer as a victimized damsel or a trapped nun. Then, by the early 1800s, we can see poets such as Wordsworth and Keats leveraging the Gothic imagery of a male jailor and female victim to defend sonnet form. This figure begins as a victim, but she comes to embody and even perpetrate her own confinement, eventually calling for more bonds and chains. Finally, half a century later, Victorian women writing in the 1840s and 1850s bore the burden of confronting this legacy of the poetess under duress. But rather than reject this figuration, they actively exploited Gothic modes of confinement in their verses, representing suffering and pain, liberation and escape, through a new vocabulary of sounds. Construing the sonnet as both a prison and a womb, these poet-speakers emulate the captivity showcased in Gothic fiction, echoing trapped nuns in convents, pregnant mothers in monasteries, and maidens threatened by live burial.

This woman, then, has a Gothic double: not only does she represent the poem itself, embodying the physical prison; she is also the female poet who creates and enforces these punishing spaces. In what follows, I demonstrate how Gothic formulations of form and restraint dominate the tradition of nineteenth-century metasonnets, redefining the cultural phenomenon of the Victorian professional poetess. This takes the form of two arguments: first, that the sonnet cell is a Gothic prison; and second, that the Victorian poetess is a Gothic heroine. Borrowing from 1790s novels by Ann Radcliffe, Matthew Lewis, and Mary Wollstonecraft, male and female poets alike consistently deployed clichés of elegy and women's writing, particularly in their representation of women as imprisoned bodies, as melancholy sonneteers, and as beneficiaries rather than victims of their confinement.

The poetess is a nexus of signs and symbols that converge across fiction and history, spanning from the ancient to modernist versions of herself. Critics have recognized the convergence of the many identities subsumed in this figure, including Sappho, Anna Seward, Charlotte Smith, Mary Robinson, Lydia Huntley Sigourney, Felicia Hemans, Letitia Elizabeth Landon, Eliza Cook, Frances Harper, Adelaide Anne Proctor, Emily Dickinson, H.D., Sylvia Plath, and Madame de Staël's Corinne.[3] She is a product of every female poet's literary reception, sentimental biography, and fictional caricature over time.[4] As Tricia Lootens has recently suggested, the mythic poetess

> emerges, most famously, within the poems, introductions, and interstices of volumes ... That she takes the form within criticism is a given; that she lives on through fiction seems at least as clear. As students of nineteenth-century literature now learn, after all, hers is a dangerous, part-fictional heritage—and, in this, a heritage of great power.[5]

In their various studies of the poetess, Angela Leighton, Susan Brown, Dorothy Mermin, Virginia Jackson, Tricia Lootens, and Yopie Prins have shown how the poetess figure is haunted by her past and condemned to a fate of self-negation and erasure. The more she proliferates through myth and hagiography, the more she dissipates from any real or fixed identity.

What all mythic poetesses share, not only throughout the Victorian era but across centuries, are stereotypical associations of sentimentality and the elegiac, the masterful "performance" of a self-consciously professional figure, and a prowess in negotiating public and private spheres. But to recognize the Victorian poetess as inherently a Gothic heroine—one who revels in her own captivity, and in fact stages it, all while recognizing her own participation in this cultural cliché—affords us with the capacity to recognize a new array of perverse sounds and images available to the author. We can hear how she supplants conventions of the sweet, harmonious songs that earn her laurels with discordant tones of painful utterance instead. The Victorian writer, through her "poetess performance," reveals another facet of herself as a formal contortionist, yielding new Gothic shapes and structures.

In this chapter, the mythos of the poetess-damsel is triply refracted: in poets of the post-1770s sonnet revival after whom these Gothic heroines are modeled; in the caricatures of young, pensive women penning sonnets in 1790s Radcliffean fiction; as well as in the highly self-conscious Victorian variations of this mythical poetess. This dark variation on the poetess figure, first as a Gothic damsel, and later, as we will see, as a nun, haunts the image of the elegiac sonneteer as a professional poet who is not simply trapped but actively seeks out her own restraints.

Poetess-damsel figures of the long nineteenth century

1770s–1780s: female sonneteers of the Romantic Sonnet Revival
  (e.g. Hannah More, Charlotte Smith, Mary Robinson, Anna Seward)
1790s: fictional Gothic heroines who write sentimental poems, especially from prisons or castle cells
  (e.g. Emily St. Aubert, Ellena di Rosalba, Agnes de Medina)
1840s: Victorian sonnet writers who formalize imprisonment
  (e.g. Elizabeth Barrett, Christina Rossetti)

Analyzing, first, the sonnet's space as a Gothic prison and, next, the sonneteer as a Gothic maiden, I use as my case examples major metasonnets by poets whose literary careers were shaped by their publication of sonnets: William Wordsworth, John Keats, Elizabeth Barrett Browning and Christina Georgiana Rossetti. By juxtaposing canonical works of high Romantic and Victorian poetry with popular fiction, I show how nineteenth-century poets relied on popular Gothic fiction to help express the exigencies of domesticity, religion, and femininity in their time. This chapter has three parts, beginning with Romantic rationales for the return of sonnet form. Part One establishes the Gothic message of "creativity in confinement" found in Radcliffe's novels and utilized in Wordsworth's "Nuns Fret Not" (1806) and Keats's "If By Dull Rhymes" (1819), recognizing the feminization and fetishization of the sonnet by male authors. William Beckford's mockeries of women's elegiac writing reveal how the female poetess, in the sentimental Romantic tradition of Smith and Seward, was already fodder for parody within a Gothic tradition that pitted "Male Gothic" against "Female Gothic" writing. Part Two explores how women writers confronted the Gothic trope of female imprisonment by figuring female poetic production in terms of childbirth. Elizabeth Barrett's metasonnets from her 1844 *Poems* and *Aurora Leigh* recruit the language of the prison, embodying themes of Gothic motherhood borrowed from Wollstonecraft's novel *Maria*: pregnancy, miscarriage, childbirth, infanticide, and suicide. In these poems, the sonnet is not just a room, it is recast as a site of failed reproduction: a cell, cloister, womb, or grave. Part Three traces a poetics of predetermined endings in Christina Rossetti's "The Thread of Life" and her novella *Maude* (1850), focusing on her composition of sonnet triptychs and *bouts-rimés*, a party parlor game. From these examples, we can see that by the middle of the nineteenth century, the figure of the Victorian professional poetess—an often-parodied descendant of the Romantic figure of the elegiac sonneteer—is in fact a Gothic heroine whose fate of self-negation is predetermined by the myth that defines her. The Victorian poetess is a haunted figure who cannot escape an inevitably Gothic end.

Female poets portrayed female confinement in stark, physical language, their formal choices mirroring the domestic demands that nineteenth-century women faced. Fraught debates surrounding marriage and reproductive rights of the time led to the 1857 Matrimonial Causes Act and the 1870 Women's Marriage Property Act, as well as medical and legal developments redefining femininity, childbearing, and maternity. These acts partially expanded women's rights to dissolve marriages, seek protection from violent husbands, and own property. Yet the poetic constriction and restraint so prominent in women's poetry serve as constant reminders that any seeming victories along the lines of women's freedom were minimal at best. Their poems formally stage spaces of oppression, echoing within chambers of the "domestic carceral," while at the same time, they redefine self-imprisonment as a space of their own construction. This poetics of self-enclosure becomes a source of Gothic power and agency.[6]

I. Creativity in Confinement: The Prison as Refuge

"Nuns fret not at their convent's narrow room," Wordsworth reassures readers of his 1807 *Poems*.[7] Defending the sonnet form, he insists upon the pleasure and productivity of "convents," "cells," and "citadels" in which nuns, hermits, and students are each confined: "In truth, the prison, unto which we doom / Ourselves, no prison is." In 1819, Keats extolled the rewards of choosing one's own means of restraint: "If by dull rhymes our English must be chained," and "if we may not let the Muse be free, / She will be bound with garlands of her own."[8] This recurring image of a sonnet, "chain'd," "fetter'd," prison-like, and "doom[ed]," is the poetic embodiment of a Gothic trope ubiquitous throughout major metasonnets of the nineteenth century: damsels in distress and sequestered nuns, representing modes of domestic and religious bondage all too familiar from the works of Ann Radcliffe and Matthew Lewis.

From Radcliffe's *The Mysteries of Udolpho* and *The Romance of the Forest*, to Lewis's *The Monk*, William Godwin's *Caleb Williams*, and Mary Wollstonecraft's *Maria, or, The Wrongs of Woman*, Gothic novels deploy two stock sites of thematic crisis and punitive oppression: the prison and the convent cell. These spaces challenge their protagonists' ability to preserve selfhood and liberty within excruciating confines. The layered images of sonnet, prison, and sanctuary represent not only a thematic transfer from 1790s Gothic conventions into Victorian poetry, but also a shared logic of defending trapped spaces, celebrating confining forms, and even advocating self-imprisonment—all tactics that were marvelously useful for poets choosing to write in a form that had fallen out of favor over the course of the eighteenth century.[9]

Radcliffe's novels are populated by female victims forcibly trapped in castles, dungeons, and convents, including Emily St. Aubert, Madame Montoni, and Signora Laurentini from *The Mysteries* of *Udolpho*; Ellena de Rosalba and Sister Olivia from *The Italian* (1797); and Adeline from *The Romance of the Forest* (1791). These captive heroines, though solitary in their cells, are in good company across the genre, including Agnes from *The Monk* (1796) and Wollstonecraft's eponymous *Maria* (1798). While the jailed female victim is a familiar one, the novelty of this Gothic trope lies in the contention that although her room might serve as a prison, this prison is actually a safe haven. Radcliffean damsels are taught to seek retreat within their prisons, constantly reassured that the confines of a cell are far preferable to the violence and lust of Italian banditti outdoors.

This moral of safety despite imprisonment resounds forcefully when preached to heroines, who, offered the solace of a private space, no matter how small, gain the opportunity for reflection and elegiac expression, often in the form of music or poetry. The abbey or castle cell serves as a space for literary creativity, meditative peace, and safety, promoting the reactionary notion that incarceration can be more liberating than it first seems. Such rooms offer protection from a world without borders, order, or beneficent patriarchal rule. The Apennines, Alps, and Italian forests, rife with banditti and murderers, prove far more disastrous for lone women characters than the castle bedrooms or Catholic convents to which they are banished. In their cells, the young women can at least enjoy a space of privacy and reflection; they can even compose poetry or elegize upon their lutes.

The sonnet's structure provides a meaningful convergence of Gothicized form and content within the genre of elegy in particular. The elegiac sonnet, famously championed by Charlotte Smith, becomes a key mode of writing that links women's writing with the plight of female domesticity, often assuming the authority of autobiographical authenticity. The sonnet, featuring an insular prosodic space, provides both a physical model and outlet for that plight. Once this space becomes colored by the violent imagery of confinement, the *stanza* becomes not only a room, but a veritable cell. The idea of sonnet form as formally confining, yet safe and thus liberating, thus echoes the often-overwrought moral that prevails at the end of countless Gothic novels: that what often seems like a prison actually serves as a refuge for young women in a dangerous world. The sonnet is analogous to the space of isolated captivity inhabited by young fictional heroines, paving the way for a new strain of "Gothic sonnets" that emerged in the early nineteenth century.

In *The Romance of the Forest*, Monsieur La Motte, an exile of Paris, rehearses a persistent Gothic argument, insisting that the cells of the basement in which they are trapped are actually "not so small." In the following scene, the La Motte family must downgrade from the upstairs rooms of a deserted abbey and go into yet further hiding within a secret lower level. Adeline and La Motte participate in a mutual defense of confinement, gratefully portraying it in desirable terms:

> When they reached the cells, Madame La Motte wept at the necessity which condemned her to a spot so dismal. "Alas," said she, "are we, indeed, thus reduced! The apartments above, formerly appeared to me a deplorable habitation; but they are a palace compared to these."
> "Let the remembrance of what you once thought them, soothe your discontent now; these cells are also a palace, compared to the Bicètre, or the Bastille, and to the terrors of farther punishment, which would accompany them: let the apprehension of the greater evil teach you to endure the less: I am contented if we find here the refuge I seek."
> . . . Adeline, forgetting her late unkindness . . . felt so thankful that La Motte was now secreted within this recess, that she almost lost her perception of its glooms and inconveniences.[10]

Here, our heroine Adeline reaffirms the moral of patience and forbearance despite confinement. Although she soon stumbles upon an abandoned manuscript and even the skeleton of a former prisoner murdered in this very spot, the dungeons prove a more palatable option than "her late unkindness," the lust and violence of her aggressor, Monsieur Montalt, awaiting her upstairs.

This message is reinforced by the endings of Gothic novels in particular, when mysterious occurrences are explained by mundane realities: evil tyrants, if not absolved, are at least exposed or even excused. Radcliffe's formulaic plots are rife with such eleventh-hour realizations that promote patriarchal order and dismiss female fears as hysteria or overthinking. In *The Mysteries of Udolpho*, we learn that Montoni is not a murderer but merely a bandit; Monsieur St. Aubert is not an adulterer, but a loyal brother who mourned over the portrait of his lost sister. The greatest oppressors of Radcliffe's heroines (Monsieur LaMotte, Montoni, Schedoni) actually prove to be these young maidens' greatest protectors from physical harm, practically speaking. The dungeon is a shelter, in the same way that the jail is a refuge.

This conservative message, when applied to poetic structure itself, becomes a particularly useful tool for poets of the Romantic sonnet revival who found themselves defending the use of such a structured or limiting form. In what would become landmark Romantic sonnets that promote and defend the sonnet form, two metasonnets by Wordsworth and Keats perpetuate the moral of female forbearance in favor of confinement. Drawing on the Gothic machinery of locks, chains, and distressed damsels, these poems formally fetishize captivity, evoking a masochistic aesthetic that celebrates pleasure in restriction.[11]

"Nuns Fret Not"

Wordsworth's "Nuns Fret Not" (1806), presented as the "Prefatory Sonnet" to his 1807 *Poems*, begins by making the case for spiritual liberty despite physical confinement.[12] The poem reifies the familiar, conservative lessons perpetuated in the eleventh-hour undoing of Radcliffe's romance plots, where Gothic dangers and insidious suspicious are explained, discounted, or swept under the rug.[13]

> Nuns fret not at their convents' narrow room;
> And hermits are contented with their cells;
> And students with their pensive citadels;
> Maids at the wheel, the weaver at his loom,
> Sit blithe and happy; bees that soar for bloom,
> High as the highest Peak of Furness Fells,
> Will murmur by the hour in foxglove bells:
> In truth, the prison, unto which we doom
> Ourselves, no prison is: and hence for me,
> In sundry moods, 'twas pastime to be bound
> Within the Sonnet's scanty plot of ground;
> Pleas'd if some Souls (for such there needs must be)
> Who have felt the weight of too much liberty,
> Should find brief solace there, as I have found.[14]

Of course, Wordsworth's "narrow room" (l.1) or "prison" represents the sonnet form itself, with its circumscribed fourteen lines of five iambic feet each. However, through the loose parataxis of increasingly expansive imagery, Wordsworth "beguiles" the reader away from the sorrow of confinement, just as Smith's *Elegiac Sonnets* did.[15] From the calm nuns, to the obedient students, productive weavers, and finally free-soaring bees, each successive example of confinement becomes diluted in intensity. Each poses an ever-shrinking unit, relegated to less space on the page: the nuns, hermits, and students are allotted one line each, but the maids and weaver are allotted only half this space, as heard in the double-time and parallelism of shortened clauses in line 4. Subtle alliterations (in "wheel," and "weaver"; "blithe" and "bloom"; "cells" and "citadels") artfully transcend these individuated units of space, suggesting spaciousness. The enjambment across "doom / Ourselves" undermines the tyranny of end-stopped lines. Wordsworth's examples of confinement also transition from indoor rooms and an artisan's working chamber to open fields and meadows outdoors in nature. This clever manipulation on the part of the poet-speaker makes it almost impossible, by the end of the line 7, to notice how far we have strayed from his initial example, when we finally detect the rhyme of "cells" with "Furness Fells" and "foxglove bells."

But while Wordsworth's poem easily glides from narrow rooms to wide open spaces, its mode of imaginative expansion garnered suspicion from some readers. Leigh Hunt famously responded to "Nuns Fret Not" with a reminder that "thousands of nuns, there is no doubt, have fretted horribly, and do fret; and hermitages have proved so little satisfactory, that we no longer hear of their existence in civilized countries."[16] In Hunt's literal reading, the suffering within harsh, claustrophobic conditions eclipses Wordsworth's intended message of productivity despite confinement. Hunt keys into a frantic, Gothic suspicion that proclaimed safe havens are often but a step away from prisons or dungeons; with strong anti-Catholic sentiment, he insinuates that the inhumane conditions of solitary confinement make them more akin to inquisitional cells of torture than peaceful rooms for respite and meditation.

The Gothic is further invoked in the masochistic tendencies of Wordsworth's speaker, where to be bound within the sonnet's strictures is both painful and pleasurable. "For me, / In sundry moods, 'twas pastime to be bound / Within the Sonnet's scanty plot of ground" (ll. 9–11), he claims, as if the feeling of interment or entombment is physically pleasing. This sonnet's plot of ground echoes the "beauteous heap . . . just half a foot in height," "so like an infant's grave in size" in "The Thorn," a particularly Gothic contribution by Wordsworth to the *Lyrical Ballads*.[17] The thorn is a site of burial that marks the infanticide of Martha Ray, who like many mothers of Gothic novels, points to sites of reproductive failure, negating the assurance of safe, productive spaces that Wordsworth's sonnet seems to promise.

The sonnet's inherent expectations for clear change and progress also belie a formal contraction of space. Whereas a ballad featuring stanzaic repetition looks stifling but actually allows for narrative progress and gradual change, the octave, volta and sestet of the sonnet structure all promise the potential for a sudden turn. Thus, Wordsworth's sonnet poetically performs the confinement that many Gothic novels celebrate: artfully juxtaposing form and content, pitting prosody against imagery, his sonnet convinces a reader that downsizing from the octave to the sestet does not indicate physical enclosure (a diminution from eight lines to six) but poetic expansion (from "cells" and "scanty plots" to open fields and "liberty").

Wordsworth's overinsistence on enjoying "solace" and freedom in spite of enclosure parallels the dismissive claims of Radcliffe's Gothic tyrants who belittle the cry of pleading damsels. In *The Italian*, Ellena di Rosalba is kidnapped by the Marchesa and Monk Schedoni, then held captive in the San Stefano convent by a cruel abbess. The heroic climax of her incarceration comes with her defamation of the very nun who is meant to protect her: "'The sanctuary is prophaned,' said Ellena, mildly, but with dignity: 'it is become a prison.'"[18] She indicts this mother figure for her failure to preserve a space of safety and comfort. Similarly, in *Udolpho*, the captor's response is simultaneously a threat and promise of protection:

> "I find," said [Montoni], "that you were not in your chamber, last night; where were you?" Emily related to him some circumstances of her alarm, and entreated his protection from a repetition of them. "You know the terms of my protection," said he; "if you really value this, you will secure it." His open declaration, that he would only conditionally protect her, while she remained a prisoner in the castle, shewed Emily the necessity of an immediate compliance with his terms . . .[19]

This apologetic rationalization for captivity, rehearsed over and again in Gothic plots, reifies patterns of female oppression, discounting any protestations as overreactions or misunderstandings. The overwhelming dismissal of the victim's experience, replaced by suggestions for female forbearance, is in effect the "lesson learned" at the end of Radcliffe's novels and Lewis's *The Monk*.

"If By Dull Rhymes"

If Wordsworth's "Nuns Fret Not" advocates accepting one's lot within the convent cell, Keats's "If By Dull Rhymes" goes even further, celebrating the masochistic endurance of a bound figure. Keats not only argues that a narrow cell "no prison is"; he goes so far as to seek out more chains, more fetters, and more constraint. Comparing the Muse to the mythical Andromeda, whose bondage represents the fate of the English sonnet, he makes claims of ecstasy despite physical restraint, of creativity despite limitations of form. This intensifies the relationship between psychic enthrallment and physical thralldom.

The poem fetishizes a mode of self-imposed confinement that mixes pleasure with constraint:

> If by dull rhymes our English must be chain'd
> And, like Andromeda, the Sonnet sweet,
> Fetter'd in spite of pained loveliness;
> Let us find out, if we must be constrain'd,
> Sandals more interwoven and complete
> To fit the naked foot of Poesy;
> Let us inspect the Lyre, and weigh the stress
> Of every chord, and see what may be gain'd
> By ear industrious, and attention meet;
> Misers of sound & syllable, no less
> Than Midas of his coinage, let us be
> Jealous of dead leaves in the bay wreath crown;
> So, if we may not let the Muse be free,
> She will be bound with garlands of her own.[20]

Keats's imagery invokes Gothic tropes through Andromeda, the damsel in distress of classical mythology. The sonnet sensually details the "naked" foot of the chained Muse and mixes erotic and violent vocabulary: "sweet" (l. 2), "pained" (l.3), "fetter'd" (l. 3), "constrain'd" (l. 4), "jealous" (l. 12) and "naked" (l. 6). Rather than calling for freedom or delivery, the poem sexualizes the bound Muse, which is all the more alluring under the duress of captivity.

The lovely female figure, chained helplessly to a rock, is mirrored in the character Ellena of *The Italian*, who is kidnapped and held by the sea, then nearly murdered by her father Schedoni. We find yet another Radcliffean iteration of Andromeda in Adeline, the heroine of *The Romance of the Forest*:

> [A man] entered, leading, or rather forcibly dragging along, a beautiful girl, who appeared to be about eighteen. Her features were bathed in tears, and she seemed to suffer the utmost distress . . . He now seized the trembling hand of the girl, who shrunk aghast with terror, and hurried her towards La Motte . . . She sunk at his feet, and with supplicating eyes, that streamed with tears, implored him to have pity on her. Notwithstanding his present agitation, he found it impossible to contemplate the beauty and distress of the object before him with indifference . . . Pale and exhausted, [she] leaned for support against the wall. Her features, which were delicately beautiful, had gained from distress an expression of captivating sweetness: she had
> "An eye
> As when the blue sky trembles thro' a cloud

Of purest white" . . .

Part of her hair had fallen in disorder, while the light veil hastily thrown on, had, in her confusion, been suffered to fall back. Every moment of farther observation heightened the surprise of La Motte, and interested him more warmly in her favour.[21]

A prisoner throughout the entirety of the novel, Adeline is an object of desire to countless characters, including Theodore, Louis, Monsieur de Montalt, and even Madame La Motte, particularly due to her vulnerability. Similarly attractive in thrall is Keats's "Sonnet sweet, / Fetter'd in spite of pained loveliness" (ll. 2–3).

By the end of the sonnet, much as in "Nuns Fret Not," Keats's speaker offers the promise of free choice as a consolation for physical imprisonment: "She will be bound with garlands of her own" (l. 14). Yet choosing one's own prosodic fetters is hardly a just consolation. For all the measured, metapoetic words in "If By Dull Rhymes," ("inspect the Lyre" [l. 7], "weigh the stress" [l. 7], "ear industrious, and attention meet" [l. 9]), the poem ends describing the Muse's physical binding, enwreathed by a crown of dead leaves. This rapture and enrapture, thralldom and enthrallment, mirrors the process described in Wordsworth's 1800 Preface to *Lyrical Ballads*, where measurement and numbers allow for the transformation from a memory of pain into an experience of pleasure.[22] Such arguments for measurement use rhetorical rationalization to deflect attention away from the violence of coercion that pervades Keats's poem. The poet figure in "If By Dull Rhymes" perpetrates oppression but cleverly re-envisions this violence as a heroic act of self-restraint.

Keats's final image of self-binding garlands is particularly potent because it not only ensnares female figures, but gothicizes the sign of female poets, the garland. Alluding to "dead leaves in the bay wreath crown" (l. 12), he points to the male tradition of great sonneteers.[23] But to extend the image of the laurel crown to that of bound garlands invokes a distinctly female image of entwining and asphyxiation.[24] Garlands and tendrils, recurring images woven throughout the *Elegiac Sonnets*, both connect the elegiac sonnets of Smith to one another and serve as a shared trope among women poets more broadly. Smith's opening sonnet of the collection describes garlands amid a welcome path for female-inspired poetry:

> The partial muse has, from my earliest hours,
> Smiled on the rugged path I'm doomed to tread,

And still with sportive hand has snatched wildflowers
To weave fantastic garlands for my head;[25]

Anna Seward similarly invokes the language of garlands in conversation with a female interlocutor in "Sonnet XLIII: To May, in the Year 1783":

Nymph, no more
Is thine to mourn beneath the scanty shade
Of half-blown foliage, shivering to deplore
Thy garlands immature, thy rites unpaid;
Meads dropt with gold again to thee belong,
Soft gales, luxuriant bowers, and wood-land song.[26]

The fecund language of laurels, garlands, and bands are also used by Mary Robinson, Letitia Elizabeth Landon, and later, by Elizabeth Barrett and Christina Rossetti as well. Keats renders their legacy in the form of an inanimate symbol, utilizing it as a weapon or tool for the imprisonment of the female figure. The language of being "bound" (l. 14) connects Keats's poem to Wordsworth's sonnet ("'twas pastime to be bound / Within the Sonnet's scanty plot of ground" (ll. 10–11)), as well as to Rossetti's "The Thread of Life" (1881) ("Thou too aloof bound with the flawless band / Of inner solitude; we bind not thee; / But who from thy self-chain shall set thee free?" (ll. 5–7)).[27]

This violence invokes a peculiarly gendered revision of imprisonment. While Wordsworth's and Keats's sonnets feature a male poet's enthrallment of a female figure, both poems also argue for a female's confinement of herself: "So, if we may not let the Muse be free, / She will be bound with garlands of her own" (ll. 13–14). As Jennifer Ann Wagner has observed, the struggle with formal closure in this poem is a trope to express the sonnet's formal awareness of its own historicity; the "primary innovation [of "If by Dull Rhymes"] is the *suspension* of closure by introducing at the end a new quatrain, a new beginning."[28] Keats's call for a female figure to imprison herself can thus be interpreted as a strategic deflection: here, a male poet recasts his own subjugation by a female entity (a poet bound by his muse) as a narrative of a female self-entrapment instead. This insistence on female self-confinement serves as a sounding point for the female sonneteers explored in the remainder of this chapter.

It is no coincidence that Wordsworth and Keats rely on the feminization and fetishization of sonnet form to establish themselves as prominent sonneteers on the heels of the Romantic sonnet revival, which was spearheaded by women poets such as Robinson, Smith, and Seward. To shackle the muse and construe the sonnet as a suffering female figure was a strategic way for male poets to assert themselves on the literary scene, forging what would becoming enduring nineteenth-century portrayals of "the Sonnet sweet, / Fetter'd, in spite of pained loveliness." Of course, Wordsworth, likely fraught with anxieties about the minorness of the tradition, did not always admit to his appropriation of Gothic motifs. Though he contributed several poems in *Lyrical Ballads* that gesture to the supernatural, including "Goody Blake and Harry Gill" and "The Thorn," he publicly disdained Gothic writing of the "school of terror," which he blamed for churning out writing of lowly scandal and gross stimulation.[29] His 1802 Preface to the *Lyrical Ballads* famously laments the influence of "frantic novels, sickly and stupid German Tragedies, and deluges of idle and extravagant stories in verse" for "blunt[ing] the discriminating powers of the mind" and reducing them "to a state of almost savage torpor."[30] Considering that *The Mysteries of Udolpho* (1794) sold over twenty thousand copies by 1816 and reached an even wider audience of readers through imitative chapbooks of the Minerva Press, Wordsworth's mission to cultivate a new readership, one that could learn to be excited without "gross and violent stimulants," was an improbable task. We see in his "Lucy" poems a turn instead, in compensation, to a quieter and more subtle Gothic of "the uncanny."

Even Coleridge, who took credit for the supernatural poems included in the *Lyrical Ballads,* actually sought, (with much hypocritical self-consciousness,) to marginalize Gothic forms. In an 1804 letter rejecting the inclusion of his Gothic poem titled "The Mad Monk" in a new anthology, he dissociated himself from the maligned tradition, writing, in a panicked epistle:

> My dear Miss Robinson! I have a wife, I have sons, I have an infant Daughter—what excuse could I offer to my own conscience if by suffering my name to be connected with those of Mr. Lewis ... I was the *occasion* of their reading the Monk? ... Should I not be an infamous Pander to the Devil in the seduction of my own offspring?—My head turns giddy, my heart sickens, at the very thought of seeing such books in the hands of a child of mine.[31]

The twee "*Who, me?*" theatricality of this response somehow reeks of both sarcasm and genuine contrition.

Keats, upon completing "The Eve of St. Agnes" and *Isabella, or the Pot of Basil* in 1819, jovially referred to his spurt of Gothic poems in a letter to his brothers that credits the names of his stories, both affectionately and disparagingly, to "Mother Radcliff."[32] A year earlier, he had written to Benjamin Reynolds, telling him to

> cosset your superstition . . . Buy a girdle—put a pebble in your Mouth—loosen your Braces—for I am going among Scenery whence I intend to tip you the Damosel Radcliffe—I'll cavern you, and grotto you, and waterfall you, and wood you, and water you, and immense-rock you, and tremendous sound you, and solitude you.[33]

Despite paying a kind of mocking respect due to Radcliffe, Wordsworth, Coleridge, and Keats actively distanced themselves from the lowbrow tradition of Grub Street authors who produced works of Gothic sentimental "trash," disavowing any shared literary audience with that genre.[34]

Interestingly enough, scholars too have embraced a similar, gendered "safety" narrative as that rehearsed in Gothic novels. Our expanded critical view of the Romantic sonnet revival now credits the rebirth of the sonnet to poets like Smith, Seward, Robinson, and Anna Laetitia Barbauld, rather than to male poets like Samuel Bowles or Wordsworth. According to Paula Feldman and Daniel Robinson, whose anthology, *A Century of Sonnets* (1999), features the works of such women poets, the choice to participate in an outmoded form like the sonnet was a conscientious attempt at "self-canonization," a way for women to situate themselves apart from contemporary male poets but thrive within a stable, established subgenre of English literature.[35] Amy Billone's *Little Songs* (2007) argues that women poets of the long nineteenth century turned to the sonnet form particularly because they were "drawn to the form's structural affinity for reticence."[36] Such formulations aptly suit not just female poets, but female sonneteers especially. The formally defined features of the sonnet helped to carve out a niche defined by the textual space in which women poets could rule over their own ground, without competing or threatening the space of male poets.

Perhaps expectedly, critics and reviewers frequently subscribed to the idea of productivity under duress, applying this narrative to the lives of women writers. We can detect echoes of Radcliffe and her trapped maidens in biographies of Charlotte Smith, emphasizing her laborious, astoundingly productive literary output alongside the feat of birthing twelve children.[37] Rumors circulated the suspicion that Smith, who in fact composed much of *Elegiac Sonnets* (1784) within the confines of a debtor's prison, was eventually driven to death by her dissolute husband and merciless editor, who pressured her to publish at an unrelenting rate until the end of her life. On the other hand, Smith's success can be cast in a positive light, demonstrating, as Wordsworth writes, that "the prison, unto which we doom / Ourselves, no prison is" (ll. 8–9). In this version, the sonnet's "scanty plot of ground" (l. 11) provided Smith with pastime and short solace, a path towards fame and an independent living that provided her with the ability to support her family. Thus, the trope of safety within the sonnet's modest space reveals a critical tendency to impose Gothic trappings upon the life and afterlives of the elegiac sonneteer, which emerge across fiction, biographies, and criticism.

Gothic Clichés: Satirizing the Poetess

Perhaps the most common misunderstanding about Gothic novels, which resulted in the decades-long critical disregard of authors like Radcliffe, is the failure to recognize the deliberate uses of repetition, cliché, and sentimentality in passages otherwise attributed to the "bad style" of some eighteenth-century women's writing.[38] Radcliffe has long suffered this slight in comparison to novelists of commendably "good" style, such as Austen. Just as Radcliffe's long, loco-descriptive scenes of landscape and banditti both invoke and caricature the picturesque tradition, the passages of elegiac poetry sprinkled throughout her novels both recruit and parody female sentimentality. The critical tendency to gloss over or resist analyzing such passages eschews exactly what Tricia Lootens reminds us not to recoil from: "the task of working through and beyond the sentimental squirm." To recognize "the "click of the cliché" and to "seek[], not skim[]" these sentimental moments allows us to recognize the Gothic energies fueling them.[39]

Recognizing Radcliffe's self-conscious play within these gendered literary traditions is key to understanding her novels. It is precisely in 1790s Gothic novels that we see early, outright satirizations of the elegiac poetess figure. A budding and struggling poet-heroine, *Udolpho*'s Emily St. Aubert pens wistful sonnets like "The Bat" and "Go, pencil!" that are pensive and melancholy, yet almost laughable and trivial in content. Sentimental to a fault, these scenes border on the ridiculous. The clicking cliché sounds for us whenever heartfelt elegiac expression by a poetess tips over into overwrought, manufactured melodrama.

Radcliffe's novels expertly exploit the comical disharmony between a seasoned, world-weary author-poet and her inexperienced, melodramatic poet-heroine. Her sonnets are at once poems by an immature, sentimental character like Emily and the work of a veteran writer like Radcliffe herself—with a fascinating counterpoint emerging from this overlap. The sonnets embedded throughout *The Mysteries of Udolpho*, praised as fine touches of poetry, were also occasions for acerbic ridicule. To be sure, Emily, as a fictional stand-in for all the Charlotte Smiths and "poetesses" of England, can be read as over-sensitive and self-wallowing; she is admonished by her equally sensitive father to check her emotions all through the beginning of the romance. St. Aubert's final words are a reminder for his daughter not to "indulge in the pride of fine feeling, the romantic error of amiable minds. Those, who really possess sensibility, ought early to be taught, that it is a dangerous quality, which is continually extracting the excess of misery, or delight, from every surrounding circumstance."[40] But St. Aubert's equally melodramatic death scene at the end of Chapter 7 parodies his earlier message against oversensibility and elegy. In this vein, the mundane premise of poetic effusion in "Go, pencil!" is hardly less ridiculous than William Beckford's satirical "Elegiac Sonnet on a Mopstick," a cheeky nudge at the domestic travails of women poets.[41]

   Sonnet. [from Udolpho]
      Go, pencil! faithful to thy master's sights!
      Go—tell the Goddess of this fairy scene,
      When next her light steps wind these wood-walks green,
      When all his tears, his tender sorrows, rise:
      Ah! paint her form, her soul-illumin'd eyes,
      The sweet expression of her pensive face,
      The light'ning smile, the animated grace—
      The portrait well the lover's voice supplies;
      Speaks all his heart must feel, his tongue would say:
      Yet ah! not all his heart must sadly feel!
      How oft the flow'ret's silken leaves conceal
      The drug that steals the vital spark away!
      And who that gazes on that angel smile,
      Would fear its charm, or think it could beguile![42]

   "Elegiac Sonnet to a Mopstick"
      Straight remnant of the spiry birchen bough,
      That over the streamlet wont perchance to quake
      Thy many twinkling leaves and, bending low,
      Beheld thy white rind dancing on the lake—
      How doth thy present state, poor stick! awake
      My pathos—for, alas! even stripped as thou

> May be my beating breast, if ever forsake
> Philisto this poor heart; and break his vow.
> So musing on, I fare with many a sigh
> And meditating then on times long past,
> To thee, lorn pole! I look with tearful eye,
> As all beside the floor-soiled pail thou art cast;
> And my sad thoughts, while I behold thee twirled,
> Turn on the twistings of this troublous world.[43]

Beckford, the author of the orientalist tale *Vathek* (1786) and, along with Matthew Lewis, a key figure of the Male Gothic tradition, mocks the sensibility of elegiac women sonneteers found in heroines of Female Gothic. His "mopstick" poem was included in *Azemia*, a burlesque of women's writing that he published under the pseudonym "Jacquetta Agneta Mariana Jenks." The "[s]ad thoughts" and "pathos"—awaken[ed]" by the "poor stick" and "beating breast"—show Beckford disrespectfully assuming a woman's voice to juxtapose male and female sexual organs, making a male mockery of female sentimentality. The simultaneously metapoetic and sexual puns on the "twirl[s], "turn[s]" and "twistings" of the "pole" lend the faux-elegy crude humor. The "floor-soiled pail," a prop for a Cinderella figure, is a rude allusion to female domestic labor, while ridiculous neologisms like "troublous" insinuate the writing of bad, immature poets who twist words around poorly, without direction. Here, elegy and sonnet form, much like the Gothic prison or convent cell, becomes a site of laughable female effusion and overcharged melodrama. The misogyny of Beckford's parodies is predicated upon the enduring double standards of the male and female sonneteer. Whereas the success of the male poem hinged upon the authentic identity of the poet, female poetesses forever negotiate their professional writing along public and private spheres, reconciling their professional careers with their domestic roles as mothers, wives, and daughters. And in his Freudian dig, Beckford's implication that an Emily St. Aubert or an Ann Radcliffe is better off substituting her "pencil" for a "mopstick" is not a subtle one.

II. Elizabeth Barrett: Gothic Motherhood and the Womb as Prison

But how does the creative female figure appear within the space of the nineteenth-century sonnet itself? By the 1840s, Elizabeth Moulton Barrett (hereafter EBB) could be considered an established leader of a new female tradition that made emboldened uses of the sonnet form, particularly in more elaborate collections like *Sonnets from the Portuguese* (1850).⁴⁴ Through a study of the Gothic strains in EBB's earlier sonnets, we can see that her innovation lies not in resisting the plight of the imprisoned damsel, but rather in intensifying this premise of oppressive confinement, assuming the role of the jailor herself. In a counter-intuitive turn, Victorian women sonneteers invert the power dynamics of female thralldom by recruiting the Gothic language of justified imprisonment.⁴⁵

EBB's metasonnets reimagine the discourse of form and restraint, entrapment and liberation, through the trope of Gothic motherhood, with the prison emerging as the essential site of the womb. By drawing out the curse and benediction of motherhood, she portrays the sonnet as a productive, yet confined space of punishment, pain, violence, and incarceration. Here, Gothic motherhood symbolizes a model of female lyric creation where the poet-mother both generates and contains her infant (the song and poem itself), while also serving as the very space or prison from which it is delivered. Rather than focus on the oft-discussed *Sonnets from the Portuguese*, I turn here to two metasonnets from the two-volume *Poems* of 1844 that established EBB's reputation as a professional poetess, "The Prisoner" and "The Soul's Expression."⁴⁶ I then revisit an embedded metasonnet in her highly autobiographical epic, *Aurora Leigh* (1857).

"The Prisoner"

The anxieties of self-imprisonment are present in EBB's 1844 "The Prisoner," which describes the experience of a speaker trapped indoors and deprived of a fresh world of nature outside. Listening from inside, she fixates on a range of sounds, from "all things summer-mute" to "nature's lute," the shutting of a door, and "a strange wild music to the prisoner's ears." This sensory overdrive is similar to that expressed in the manuscript that Adeline discovers in Radcliffe's *The Romance of the Forest*; it is the journal of a former prisoner in the ruined abbey whose entries boil over in fear each time he detects a sound from the outside.⁴⁷ While "The Prisoner" draws on EBB's personal experiences as a patient confined to bed rest, it consistently links the sonnet form to the space and duration of a prison sentence.

> I count the dismal time by months and years
> Since last I felt the green sward under foot,
> And the great breath of all things summer-mute

> Met mine upon my lips. Now earth appears
> So strange to me as dreams of distant spheres
> Or thoughts of heaven we weep at. Nature's lute
> Sounds on, behind his door so closely shut,
> A strange wild music to the prisoner's ears,
> Dilated by the distance, till the brain
> Grows dim with fancies which it feels too fine:
> While ever, with a visionary pain,
> Past the precluded senses, sweep and shine
> Streams, forests, glades, and many a golden train
> Of sunlit hills transfigured to divine.[48]

The sonnet is sprinkled with metapoetic touches. The prisoner waits out the days of her extended sentence, "count[ing] the dismal time of months and years." A reader can hear in this the enumeration of a formally conscientious poet who measures metrical pacing in iambic feet. For this prisoner-poet, liberty and poetic creation are memories of the past, much time having passed "since last I felt the green sward under foot." These feet, yearning to take steps of freedom, crave lyric inspiration from "the *great breath* of all things summer-mute" (*inspirare*: to breathe in). Yet the poetic freedom, inspiration, and roving feet are now but a distant memory; the speaker endures a punitive sentence, measuring time in units of "months," "years," and iambic feet.

The sonneteer is a prisoner, and this poem assumes the compact space of a Gothic cell. Reminiscent of a lonely dungeon, the sonnet's setting is closed off from the vivid world of the sun, streams, forests, and glades. From a historical perspective, the punitive isolation represented in EBB's "The Prisoner" most likely draws upon fictive examples of incarceration, as solitary imprisonment was not yet actively practiced in a widespread manner across England.[49] Cultural-historical studies such as *The Self in the Cell* by Sean Grass have worked to revise the misconception of solitary confinement as a common experience of nineteenth-century prison life. Until the 1860s, when jails featuring solitary confinement began to be built more regularly throughout England, the prison was actually an area of bustling activity and community.[50] EBB, writing in 1844, would not have conceived of this sort of lone imprisonment within the context of her time.[51] The poetic setting of EBB's prisoner was thus likely drawn from earlier, fictional representations of confinement, including Gothic ones.

The speaker's confinement within a prison gives way to hallucination or madness, with visions that are even "too fine" for the speaker to comprehend. Imprisonment has not only blunted her lucidity ("the brain / grows dim") but also worn away her refinement, causing the poetic music of nature to sound wild and strange to her ears. This representation of the feral prisoner recalls the dark, unpublished endings of William Godwin's *Caleb Williams* and Wollstonecraft's *Maria*, where the final scenes of isolated confinement cause the psychological decline and unraveling hysteria of their protagonists. EBB's poem, with its "strange wild music" supplanting the conventions of Keats's "Sonnet sweet," conveys a more muted expression of bondage, evoking instead the language of restraint and frailty.

Though "The Prisoner" is not an overt defense of the sonnet, the metapoetic allusions throughout the poem signal EBB's participation in the larger tradition of Gothic metasonnets I have outlined. Her reference to a "visionary pain" echoes Wordsworth's "visionary gleam" at the end of the Intimations Ode,[52] while the list of "streams, forests, glades, and many a golden train / of sunlit hills transfigured to divine" echoes the famous spondees of Wordsworth's "Ships, towers, domes, theatres, and temples [that] lie."[53] Through these echoes, Barrett Browning responds to the rhythmic patterns of Wordsworth in the mode of "undersong" as John Hollander, Angela Leighton, and Elizabeth Helsinger conceive of it: undersongs are poems "haunted not only by a poem's own sound patterns . . . but also by the sounds of other poems—and . . . of songs: specific kinds of musical song and sometimes the rhythm of a particular tune."[54] However, in an important inversion, EBB's speaker negatively invokes lines that show such vistas and poetic range; in her version, this strong spondaic line enumerates just what is deprived from her senses due to her captivity indoors. The sonnet-prison bars the speaker from nature's majesty, from its "streams, forests, glades" and "sunlit hills." It instead relegates her within the indoor space of darkness, dimmed senses, and visionary pain.

Physical limitation is likewise gendered in other sonnets of EBB's 1844 *Poems*. In "George Sand: A Desire," which appears two poems before "The Prisoner," Sand must perform before an "applauded circus." The following poem, "George Sand: A Recognition," acknowledges the captivity of women whose genius is constrained by mere ornamentation and decorative bands: "True genius, but true woman! dost deny / Thy woman's nature with a manly scorn, / And break away the gauds and armlets worn / By weaker women in captivity?"[55] In contrast, Wordsworth appears in the third sonnet of EBB's collection: "On a Portrait of Wordsworth by B. R. Haydon" positions him high up on Helvellyn mountain with a limitless vista.[56] In the 1844 *Poems*, sonnets seem to physically free men but confine women.

"The Soul's Expression"

"The Soul's Expression" serves as the opening sonnet of EBB's breakthrough 1844 collection, and it forcefully embodies the plight of a female poet-speaker who is both an imprisoner and deliverer. Within the first two lines of this poem, we hear the strenuous effort of a mother giving birth in a cluster of alliterated "s," "st," and "sh" sounds:

> With *st*ammering lips and in*s*ufficient *s*ound
> I *st*rive and *st*ruggle to deliver right
> That music of my nature, day and night
> With dream and thought and feeling interwound,
> And inly answering all the *s*enses round
> With octaves of a my*s*tic depth and height
> Which *st*ep out grandly to the infinite
> From the dark edges of the *s*en*s*ual ground.
> This *s*ong of *s*oul I *st*ruggle to outbear
> Through portals of the *s*ense, sublime and whole,
> And utter all myself into the air:
> But if I did it,—as the thunder-roll
> Breaks its own cloud, my fle*sh* would peri*sh* there,
> Before that dread apocalypse of soul.[57]

In this sonnet, the act of poetic creation as childbirth ("to deliver right" [l. 2]) is ridden with insecurity and anxiety. The birth of a poem, a child, music, or one's "song of soul" becomes a struggle not just to "bear out," as one would express in conventional English, but rather to "outbear," a variation of the verb chosen to fit the sonnet's rhyme scheme (l. 9). This term, which means both to carry out and to endure suffering, demonstrates the "stammering," "striv[ing]," and "struggl[ing]" of this poem's difficult birth, as well as the pain it inflicts upon the mother-poet.[58] The inverted positioning of the syllables "bear" and "out," reminiscent of a baby that emerges from the womb feet first, creates the experience of struggle for a reader encountering this word for the first time.

Through this metaphor of grueling labor, the sonnet represents both the offspring (the poem birthed) and the space of the mother's womb. Barrett Browning draws attention to the spatial volume of the sonnet through mention of an "octave," which alludes to the poet's musical range and the first eight-line section of the sonnet. Meanwhile, "depth" and "height" suggest the metric (horizontal) and fourteen-line (vertical) requirements of stanza form (l. 6). This dimensional configuration of the sonnet draws attention to the space of a womb, from which the poet and her poem "step out grandly" into the world (l. 7). But this space from which the child emerges, the womb-like mouth from whence the poem is released, becomes vague and foreboding, described as "the dark edges of the sensual ground" (l. 8). With one final cry of labor pains, the poetess "utter[s] all [her] self into the air" (l. 11), exhaling her being. The last two lines impart a foreboding sense of the mother's self-negation, as if she will expire from the trauma of labor: the thunder-roll breaks its own cloud, and her "flesh" might "perish," yoked together through assonance. The verb "breaks" draws attention to the physical violence and tearing of the mother's flesh (l. 13).

The dangers of miscarriage or mortality from childbirth were not merely poetic figurations. Inaccessibility to contraception and abortion at the turn of the nineteenth century indeed rendered marriage a prison for many women, while pregnancy could pose a death sentence.[59] Duncan Wu describes Charlotte Smith's profoundly prolific career in light of her marriage at sixteen, which "began a child-bearing career that would span the next twenty-two years, producing twelve children." Smith described her own marriage as akin to being "sold, a legal prostitute."[60] Incremental reforms through the Matrimonial Causes Act of 1857 improved the lot of women suffering domestic abuse at the hands of their husbands but slightly, and the 1869 repeal of the 1864 Contagious Diseases Acts, spearheaded by the Ladies National Association (Elizabeth Wolstenholme and Josephine Butler) defended prostitutes as victims of social injustice rather than punishing them as criminals. Still, the high risks of venereal disease and maternal mortality rendered motherhood a Gothic prospect that threatened one's own negation, particularly for women of lower classes without access to comprehensive medical care.

If "The Soul's Expression" likens the creation of a poem to the delivery of a child, it also conceives of delivery in terms of liberty and freedom. For the speaker to bring this baby into the world would free the child from its confines. To "deliver *right*" further emphasizes the pride of justice achieved through liberation, though it may not be an easy or natural birth. The etymological proximity between "deliverance" and "liberation" vindicates the anguish of pain, all for a higher cause, heralded through the language of the "sublime" (l.10), "infinite" (l. 7), and the "grand" (l.7). Yet, the baby's delivery is the deliverance from a tyrant who could only possibly be the mother herself. Still further, if this baby is born a girl, once delivered into this world, she merely exchanges the womb for another "room"— the sonnet stanza or a confining cell, representative of the woman's limited world.

One of her generation's most vocal abolitionist poetesses, EBB recounts the maternal experience of slaves in political poems such as "The Runaway Slave at Pilgrim's Point" and "A Curse for a Nation." Her activist commitments are corroborated in her letters, most recently in Volume 23 of the Wedgestone edition of *The Brownings' Correspondence*, which reveals the poet's preoccupations with social injustices between July 1856 and January 1857.[61] EBB's political concerns during this year revolved around such issues as "workhouses, physical abuse of women, and the married woman's property petition . . . [She] expresses her high aspirations that *Aurora Leigh*, with its narration of Marian's rape and illegitimate child, will 'raise the spiritual above the natural' for readers."[62] While the 1857 Matrimonial Causes Act still greatly favored husbands over wives in cases of divorce, it did allow separation for wives on grounds of cruelty, adultery, or desertion. These concerns with women's rights in 1856 coincided with EBB's revisions of the fourth edition of her *Poems*.[63] Of course, Victorian women's groups were among the most active players in the anti-slavery movement, relying on an intersectional consciousness of overlapping oppressions across slavery, race, and women's domestic rights.[64]

Gothic Motherhood

The inevitable doom of female creation, through the convergence of motherhood, childbirth, and confinement, comprises what I define as Gothic motherhood. In the Gothic tradition, female literary production is often inextricable from grotesque, abortive imagery and the language of miscarriage, pitched within the context of imprisonment, suicide, and infanticide. Whereas Deborah Rogers explores Gothic *matrophobia* as the fear of mothers, fear of becoming a mother, and fear of separation from the maternal body, I focus more specifically on childbirth and original poetic production as symbolic negations of the female self.[65]

As prisoner (of her soul's expression), deliverer (the mother in labor), and the prison itself (the pregnant body and womb), the speaker of "The Soul's Expression" embodies the plight of Gothic motherhood within the space of fourteen lines. The competition for voice, air, and life becomes a dramatic struggle. Her need to birth herself and "utter all myself into the air" (l. 11) creates an unnatural paradox, resonating with EBB's famous statement that she "look[ed] everywhere for grandmothers and s[aw] none."[66] This powerful utterance creates an expected union of sounds: the birthing pains of the mother overlap with the expected cry of the baby's first breaths. Childbirth is compared to a foreboding storm in nature; like the thunder-roll breaking its own cloud, it creates the sounds of a noisy growl and impending danger, not easeful music. In this sonnet, we hear a new range of Gothic utterance, articulating discomfort and pain more akin to the snarls and growls of Robert Browning's monk of the Spanish cloister heard in the previous chapter. The mother-poetess, imprisoned and pregnant, generates sounds of pain akin to those uttered by Gothic fiction's Inquisitional victims of torture.

Andrea Gazzaniga has noted that for Barrett Browning, "the sonnet's tight dimensions would seem to prohibit dual occupancy and, indeed, its tradition suggests that fourteen lines are barely enough to hold a single ego, let alone two."[67] This mother-child struggle appears in countless Gothic tales of the suicidal and infanticidal mother, from the "The Mad Mother" and the legend of Martha Ray in "The Thorn" from *Lyrical Ballads* (1798), to the young Agnes who gives birth in the catacombs of *The Monk*. As Agnes is led down to her prison vault, the Domina shows no pity for the yet unborn child:

Expect no mercy from me either for yourself, or Brat. Rather pray, that Death may seize you before you produce it; Or if it must see the light, that its eyes may immediately be closed again for ever! No aid shall be given you in your labour; Bring your Offspring into the world yourself, Feed it yourself, Nurse it yourself, Bury it yourself.[68]

Agnes's infant, who starves soon after birth, moves directly from the mother's womb, to a prison, to a grave. The most graphic rape scene in *The Monk* by Matthew Lewis takes place within the catacombs, where Antonia is imprisoned: "He longed for the possession of her person; and even the gloom of the vault, the surrounding silence, and the resistance which He expected from her, seemed to give a fresh edge to his fierce and unbridled desires."[69] In these stories, mothers are represented as hysterical or suffering victims, intent upon murder or suicide as the only options of rest and liberation for their offspring. In many Gothic plots, the location of birth and then infanticide is often one and the same—the graveyard.[70]

Gothic motherhood emerges most politically in Wollstonecraft's *Maria, or the Wrongs of Woman* (1798), which begins with its protagonist distracted by phantasmal visions of her infant child while she is immured in a prison cell. Maria's womb is a safe, internal prison housing the baby girl before the child's deliverance into a life of figurative bondage. Wollstonecraft's language in *Maria* is famously charged with a socio-historical indictment: "Marriage has bastilled me for life"; "the world is a vast prison, and women born slaves."[71] Though *Maria* remained a fragment, Wollstonecraft had planned out the tragic ending in note form: "Pregnancy—Miscarriage—Suicide."[72] According to these drafts, Maria's suicide is motivated by dead visions of her infant: "She swallowed the laudanum . . . Her murdered child again appeared to her, mourning for the babe of which she was the tomb."[73] Eventually, in the published version, Maria is reunited with her infant child and decides to live; yet her maternal instincts are still tinged with the threat of infanticide: "She caught her to her bosom, and burst into a passion of tears—then, resting the child gently on the bed, as if afraid of killing it,—she put her hands to her eyes, to conceal as it were the agonizing struggle of her soul."[74] As in EBB's poem, the soul and womb become sites for "agonizing struggle"; they are sources of reproductive power but more so a prison of suffering.

For women writers assuming the role of professional poetess, poetic output was constantly underscored by models of motherhood borrowed from Gothic fiction, featuring suicide, abortion, or death through childbirth. Recruiting the language of motherhood to describe authorial production, William Godwin, in the role of editor, describes the composition of *Maria* in terms of anguished fertility: "In reality, these hints, simple as they are, are pregnant with passion and distress. It is the refuge of barren authors only, to crowd their fictions with so great a number of events, as to suffer no one of them to sink into the reader's mind."[75] Casting uninspired authors as fertile mothers, Godwin champions great writing that follows a difficult and painful childbirth: a good author is not pregnant with joy and life or blessed by easeful production, but wrought with passion and distress. In the same vein, the link between reproduction and literary production lends women's poetry a repertoire of perverse and ominous sounds: the echoed cries from within a prison cell and the guttural groans of birthing pains.

In her preface, Wollstonecraft defends her composition of *Maria* while resisting the image of a mad mother driven by hysteria and suffering: "Surely there are a few, who will dare to advance before the improvement of the age, and grant that my sketches are not the abortion of a distempered fancy, or the strong delineations of a wounded heart."[76] Following her death from complications in childbirth, the author's capacity for motherhood was notoriously attacked by detractors who construed her death as punishment by divine will. For Wollstonecraft, whose personal history included two suicide attempts, Maria's progression of "pregnancy—miscarriage—suicide" encapsulates a predetermined narrative of the mother-author figure that spells out the demise of female domestic bliss.

This applies of course not only to Wollstonecraft, but extends more broadly across generations of women writers cast as gothicized mother figures. The language of abortion pervades Mary Shelley's *Frankenstein*, in both the novel and the author's preface. We can recognize the condemnation of female creation even in the legacy of Sappho, the original ancient poetess, who (in a later tradition beginning with Menander) leaps to her death. For Yopie Prins, writing within the paradox of the poetess myth, meant

> ironically giving birth to a female subject that is produced by bearing the pain of the past and reproduced by bearing this pain into the future. Sappho is not cured, then, but doomed to leap again and again without ever dying; because the leap has not killed her, she must repeat it, endlessly.[77]

Christina Rossetti recognizes this too in her dramatic monologue, "What Sappho Would Have Said Had Her Leap Cured Instead of Killing Her": "It is vain; is all in vain; / I must go forth and bear my pain."[78] The echo of "it is vain" repeats the poetess's expectations of a life marked by the female forbearance of pain.

Thus, the ease of female poetic expression, a cliché established through the staggeringly prolific verse of Smith, More, Robinson, and Hemans, is negated when we recognize the poetess as a Gothic victim. Here, wistful, elegiac song is recast as the painful utterances of a difficult childbirth, where delivery is always colored by the threat of barrenness, abortion, or suicide. As if answering Keats's call that the Muse "be bound with Garlands of her own" (l. 14), EBB builds upon Wollstonecraft's example of prisons that are not simply created by men but built and guarded by women jailers. But for women writers, the confinement of adhering to the sonnet form is no longer romanticized or fetishized. *Maria* casts the womb as a metaphorical cell to represent the oppressive world into which all women are born, while Barrett Browning recreates the prison within the space of the sonnet, circumscribing the poem as a site from which the music of her soul must deliver itself. The overlap between womb, prison, and sonnet yields a locus of competition between productivity and oppression.

EBB bookends the sonnets of her 1844 *Poems* with strong examples of painful, laboring "delivery" by a female poet marked by physical and womb-like confinement. While "The Soul's Expression" begins the collection with a model of a stammering, self-struggle to "outbear" her song, the last two sonnets of the section are "The Prisoner" and "Insufficiency," in which the poet-speaker's utterance overtakes her body with all-consuming undulations: "When I attain to utter forth in verse / Some inward thought, my soul throbs audibly/ Along my pulses."[79] Here, again, the speaker's voice is stifled, with a double meaning in the word "conceive": "And what we best conceive, we fail to speak."[80] Recruiting the language of embodied struggle from within the sonnet cell, EBB ends this final poem with a couplet yearning for delivery and liberation: "And then resume thy broken strains, and seek / Fit peroration, without let or thrall."[81]

* * *

EBB's Gothic metasonnets appear even in the midst of epic, where sonnet form manifests but momentarily, though still invoking the language of imprisonment. Naomi Levine identifies a hidden sonnet within *Aurora Leigh* in lines 223 to 236 of Book V, where the poet-protagonist questions the rationale behind the numbers of poetic forms: Why do five acts make up a play?[82] Why not fifteen, ten, or seven? Why are there fourteen lines in a sonnet? In a deliberate answer to her own challenge that evades formal fixity, EBB composes the loose "sonnet" below, comprised of fifteen lines. In these verses, too, the problem of formal restraint becomes a question of "imprison[ment]" and "embodiment" (ll. 226 and 227):

> What form is best for poems? Let me think
> Of forms less, and the external. Trust the spirit,
> As sovran nature does, to make the form;
> For otherwise we only imprison spirit
> And not embody. Inward evermore
> To outward,—so in life, and so in art
> Which still is life.
> Five acts to make a play.
> And why not fifteen? why not ten? or seven?
> What matter for the number of the leaves,
> Supposing the tree lives and grows? exact
> The literal unities of time and place,
> When 't is the essence of passion to ignore
> Both time and place? Absurd. Keep up the fire,
> And leave the generous flames to shape themselves.[83]

With this metasonnet, Aurora Leigh warns against overdetermined forms, advocating that poets trust the spirit to give shape to words instead: "Keep up the fire, / And leave the generous flames to shape themselves . . . For otherwise we only imprison spirit / And not embody."[84] This resonates with the Gothic impetus we see in "The Prisoner" and "The Soul's Expression," the call to take ownership of formal or spatial confinement and embody it, lest the female figure simply become victim to the bondage of Keats's shackled muse. By playing the roles of poet and imprisoner, dictating the structures and strictures themselves, women poets assume the agency to control—contrary to expectations—either the openness of the sonnet form or the closed form of blank verse. This injunction to construct forms that "embody" the spirit, rather than "imprison" it, remains a central concern for women's sonnet writing of the nineteenth century. The Gothic heroine's task, after all, is to find refuge and spaciousness while in captivity.

III. Christina Rossetti: Gothic Endings and Enclosures

In the works of Christina Rossetti, the figure of the female poet is creatively thwarted by an inevitability of self-enclosure that entraps her, both formally and biographically. Like EBB in her sonnets, Rossetti also invokes prison imagery, even when experimenting with forms that expand her prosodic landscapes.[85] This poetics of Gothic enclosure assumes the heavy weight of doom and apocalypticism, where the fate of predetermined endings is simultaneously performed on various scales: in her individual sonnets, in triptychs like "The Thread of Life," and in sonnet sequences of fourteen or twenty-eight poems. In particular, she is interested in composing not simply single sonnets, but elaborate narrative sequences that bind her. This dead-end aesthetics fuels the Gothic undercurrent of her novella *Maude*, which features the parlor game of *bouts-rimés*. In this story, the sonnet compositions that the girls partake in produce *bouts-rimés* in rounds of three. Throughout Rossetti's oeuvre, in both her small and large-scale sonnet works, the figure of the female sonneteer cannot escape the inevitable fate of Gothic self-negation.

While Rossetti's early collections incorporated relatively few sonnets, her later works, especially *A Pageant and Other Poems* (1881), included so many that she composed a prefatory sonnet to justify the presence of the "many" in the collection: "Sonnets are full of love, and this my tome / Has many sonnets: so here now shall be / One sonnet more . . ."[86] As if in response to Keats's call for sandals "more interwoven and complete," she composes sonnet sequences to expand the limits of her verse, but then stages yet more confinement across these poems through her signature repetition of sounds. This is especially evident in the three sonnets that make up "The Thread of Life," published in 1881, which recruits the familiar imagery of blooming flowers, laurels, and garlands definitive of women's poetry.[87] By grouping together three sonnets, Rossetti widens her poetic field (14 x 3 = 42), providing more lines for cross-stitching and interweaving, but also for further self-constriction.

"The Thread of Life"

In "The Thread of Life," the patterned end rhymes of typical sonnet form become overshadowed by unexpected instances of internal repetition, which emerge from the speaker's fixation on tightly binding the sonnets together with an aural chain. In the first sonnet, echoes across lines 1, 2, 8, and 9, as well as anaphora in lines 9, 10, 12, 13, and 14 enact the declaration in Sonnet Two of a conscious formal choice: "Thus am I mine own prison."[88] Rather than "*my* own prison," the choice of "mine" securely locks together the last three words through terminal consonance: "mi*n*e," "ow*n*," and "priso*n*." Here, writing within sonnet conventions (fourteen lines of rhymed iambic pentameter) seems so natural and uninhibited for Rossetti that the real formal restriction, particularly the limitation of vocabularic expansion and aural sounds, emerge from a single line within the poem. Bondage is not an external circumstance but a personal one: "We bind not thee; / But who from thy self—chain shall set thee free?" (1.6).

> 1
> *The irresponsive silence* of the land,
> *The irresponsive sounding* of the sea,
> Speak both one message of one sense to me:—
> *Aloof, aloof*, we stand *aloof*, so stand
> Thou too *aloof* bound with the flawless band
> Of inner solitude; we bind not thee;
> But who from thy self-chain shall set thee free?
> *What heart shall touch thy heart? what hand thy hand?*—
> *And I* am *sometimes proud* and *sometimes meek*,
> *And* sometimes I remember days of old

When fellowship seemed not so far to seek
And all the world and I seemed much less cold,
And at the rainbow's foot lay surely gold,
And hope felt strong and life itself not weak.

2
Thus am I mine own prison. Everything
Around me free and sunny and at ease:
Or if in shadow, in a shade of trees
Which the sun kisses, where the gay birds sing
And where all winds make various murmuring;
Where bees are found, with honey for the bees;
Where sounds are music, and where silences
Are music of an unlike fashioning.
Then gaze *I* at the merrymaking crew,
And smile a moment and a moment <u>*sigh*</u>
Thinking: Why can *I* not rejoice with you?
But soon *I* put the foolish fancy <u>*by*</u>:
I am not what *I* have nor what *I* do;
But what *I* was *I* am, *I* am even *I*.

3
Therefore *myself* is that one only thing
I hold to use or waste, to keep or give;
My sole possession every day I live,
And still *mine own* despite Time's winnowing.
Ever mine own, while moons and seasons bring
From crudeness ripeness mellow and sanative;
Ever mine own, till Death shall ply his sieve;
And still *mine own*, when saints break grave *and sing*.
And this *myself* as king unto my King
I give, to Him Who gave Himself for me;
Who gives Himself to *me*, and *bids me sing*
A sweet new song of His redeemed set free;
He *bids me sing*: O death, where is thy sting?
And sing: O grave, where is thy victory?

    The three sonnets in "The Thread of Life" are marked by frequent anaphora and repetition, which Eric Griffiths recognizes as moments when Rossetti's "verbal needle seems stuck in a groove."[89] The "threads" in the title serve as binding garlands and "flawless bands" (1.5) where Rossetti's formal choices perform a determinism that time and again ends in a thematic and structural self-enclosure of the speaker-poet's "my," "mine" and "I."⁹⁰ Joseph Phelan recognizes the aggregation of the word "I" in Sonnet Two as self-confinement: "It is just this 'I' she has created for herself through her poetry," he suggests, "that has become her 'prison.'"⁹¹ In Sonnet Three especially, incessant repetitions of words internal to the lines create a new form and aural pattern, drawing our attention away from the end-rhymes of sonnet form.

We see in "The Thread of Life" the same paradox of spaciousness and claustrophobia at work as in Rossetti's more complex sonnet structures: the intertextual binding of threads and layered meanings are exponentially on display in sequences like *Monna Innominata*, where she expands the metasonnet construction into 14 x 14 to create a sonnet of sonnets, and *Later Life: A Double Sonnet of Sonnets*, with twenty-eight consecutive poems.⁹² The choice of expansion and multiplication ironically allows for greater occasions of intertwining and binding.⁹³

Maude: *The Predetermined Endings of* Bouts-Rimés

Even in works of prose, Rossetti employs poetic strictures as a driving plot device. Her novella *Maude: A Story for Girls*, written in 1850 but published posthumously in 1897, recounts a year in the life of Maude Foster, who leaves London to attend a birthday party and reunite with her cousin and friends. It features a budding poetess's experimentation with *bouts-rimés*, a game that Dante, William and Christina Rossetti played as children. In this game, cards with word rhymes are selected at random and each player constructs a sonnet using the mandated end-words. The characters Mary, Agnes, Magdalen, and Maude undertake this spontaneous exercise of sonnet writing, each producing a poem different from the last. Together, they enjoy "sundry tarts" with "unlimited strawberries and cream" and chatter while at their toilets, fixing flowers and sprigs of bay in their hair.⁹⁴ Maude has a talent for writing and often pens sonnets in her "writing-book," which is "neither commonplace-book, album, scrap-book, nor diary, [but] a compound of all these, [which] contained original compositions not intended for the public eye, pet extracts, extraordinary little sketches, and occasional tracts of journal."⁹⁵

Maude is a poetess novella, a *Bildungsroman* in miniature of a character aspiring to become a sonneteer. But I also read *Maude* as a Gothic novel in miniature, a work of Radcliffean satire that deliberately employs scenes of female elegiac writing and exaggerated sentimentality. This Gothic novella narrates the slow annihilation of a young Victorian poet as she confronts the burdens of her profession, inhabiting both sides of separate spheres. Scenes of "poetess performance" showcase moments where Maude is forced to face her audience, reciting poems and exposing herself as the person behind her compositions, followed by her melodramatic death. What Rossetti reveals in this novella—as EBB demonstrates in her metasonnets—is that the Mythic Poetess is a Gothic Heroine, a legacy that inherits Radcliffe's novelistic representations of elegizing damsels in captivity. *Maude* both enacts and satirizes the Romantic clichés of women's writing and the professional poetess figure.

While much of the novella takes place in high society, featuring birthday parties and ladies' luncheons in the setting of a Victorian middle-class home, critics still recognize Maude's "uncanny," "self-mortifying impulse" and her Lacanian death drive.[96] Maude's spiritual crisis around Christmas Eve is particularly Gothic, as she surrenders in her struggle to "come right," her final days of poetic production cast in terms of sickness and sterility. Retiring from the company of family and friends, she retreats to her bedroom to compose more poems, an act represented in terms of vampiric enervation. She refuses to take Holy Communion for fear of profaning Holy Things. Uneasy about her nightly prayers, "Maude lay down harassed, wretched, remorseful, everything but penitent . . . Gradually the thick, low sobs became more rare." Her cousin Agnes finally discovers her "weeping bitterly," headached, overtired, and writing in the cold.[97] A year later, on the way to Mary's wedding, Maude suffers from an undescribed wound after a carriage accident, which is shortly followed by her mysterious death.[98]

But the Gothic is prevalent even in the playful sections of the novella that feature Victorian parlor games. *Bouts-rimés* contributes to a poetics of inevitability and determined endings from the story's beginning to end. In the round they play, each contestant cannot help but imprint a damning biographical impulse upon the poem she writes. Of the four girls, Mary refuses to partake in the challenge, and at the end of the story is the only girl who ends up happily married. Magdalen composes a poem that imagines the dutiful work of "good fairies dressed in white" completing menial tasks to keep all right with nature and the world; she ends up taking orders and joining a convent by the story's end. Agnes's poem, which dips into dimeter and tetrameter, is criticized by Maude for lacking metric stability: "Might I however venture to hint that my sympathy with your sorrows would have been greater, had they been expressed in metre?"[99]

As one who does not adhere easily to formal regulations, she is the only character who, a year later, is neither married nor committed to a convent. By abstaining, she escapes the poetics of predetermination that the other girls could not. Maude's poem, cast in perfect iambic pentameter with insistent anaphora in the first quatrain, reveals a dogged insistence for cataloging the world. A commentary on the types of people and their dress, or rather, form and content, her sonnet is tinged with Maude's signature cruelty and a touch of violence. Her comic-apocalyptic poem conjures images of deluge or last judgment, as punishment for something as simple as one's clothing choice.

[Agnes:]

>   Would that I were a turnip white,
> Or raven black,
> Or miserable hack
>   Dragging a cab from left to right;
>   Or would I were the showman of a sight,
> Or weary donkey with a laden back,
> Or racer in a sack,
>   Or freezing traveller on an Alpine height;
> Or would I were straw catching as I drown,
>   (A wretched landsman I who cannot swim,)
>   Or watching a lone vessel sink,
>   Rather than writing: I would change my pink
> Gauze for a hideous yellow satin gown
>   With a deep-cup scolloped edges and a rim.

[Magdalen:]

>   I fancy the good fairies dressed in white,
> Glancing like moon-beams through the shadows black;
> Without much work to do for king or hack.
>   Training perhaps some twisted branch aright;
>   Or sweeping faded Autumn leaves from sight
> To foster embryo life; or binding back
> Stray tendrils; or in ample bean-pod sack
>   Bringing wild honey from the rocky height;
> Or fishing for a fly lest it should drown;
>   Or teaching water-lily heads to swim,
>   Fearful that sudden rain might make them sink;
>   Or dyeing the pale rose a warmer pink;
> Or wrapping lilies in their leafy gown,
>   Yet letting the white peep beyond the rim.—

[Maude:]

> Some ladies dress in muslin full and white
> Some gentlemen in cloth succinct and black;
> Some patronize a dog-cart, some a hack,
> > Some think a painted Clarence only right.
> > Youth is not always such a pleasing sight,
> Witness a man with tassels on his back;
> Or woman in a great-coat like a sack
> > Towering above her sex with horrid height.
> If all the world were water fit to drown
> > There are some whom you would not teach to swim,
> > Rather enjoying if you saw them sink;
> > Certain old ladies dressed in girlish pink,
> With roses and geraniums on their gown:—
> > Go to the Bason, poke them o'er the rim.—[100]

It becomes evident that the real challenge of *bouts-rimés* here is for Rossetti, the single author behind these compositions. Using the same building blocks and poetic form, she must create three distinct poems that match the characters of Agnes, Magdalen, and Maude. Each round of the game is an occasion for Rossetti to display her technical skill and, most importantly, her skill of matching three similar-looking poems on the page to the character of each girl, all while using the same words of "white," "black," "hack," "right," "sight," "back," "sack," "height," "drown," "swim," "sink," "pink," "gown," and "rim." The poems "written" by Agnes, Magdalen, and Maude, like "The Thread of Life," represent three sonnets interwoven with repeated words that are indicative of an underlying single author bound to herself.

The dictated end rhymes of *bouts-rimés* no doubt intensify the typical strictures of sonnet composition. But overriding this is the unavoidable personality revealed in the poems of each young poetess. In the novella, they do not, in fact, choose the poems they compose; the word endings dictate a sort of fictional, literary fate that chooses them instead. Their plot endings align, respectively, with Magdalen's dutiful nature, Agnes's inexperience, and Maude's dark broodings. Ultimately, the autobiographical "I" of the poetess performer overpowers each exercise in sonnet writing. The characters in *Maude* enact this self-realization not in the positive sense of traditional *bildung*, but, instead, through a poetics of predetermination and gloomy inevitability played out through their marriage or spinsterhood, as we will later see.

The dramatic irony of the single poet behind multiple speakers becomes Rossetti's central challenge behind each round of parlor games: Are these *bouts-rimés* a creative array of poems forged by a single hand and the work of a true improvisatrice? Or are they merely interchangeable duplications of one another, unconvincing variations in a poetic exercise? As we will see, establishing the individual personality of a female poet is a thankless, impossible task, since the myriad of poetess figures throughout literary tradition blend into one another to form a single symbol.[101]

Collapsing Separate Spheres

As a self-reflexive Gothic text, *Maude* critiques the obstacle of reception that the poetess must face, countering stereotypes of elegiac authenticity, autobiography, and hagiography. To borrow a phrase from Lootens, "Poetess parallax" makes it impossible to see each poetess for who she is as an individual, rather than as a placeholder for a vast constellation of similar women.[102] Readers of *Maude* are presented with this contradiction between the experience of the author-poetess, Christina Rossetti, and the relative inexperience of the fictional character-poetess, Maude. This tension is itself a commentary on the practice of limiting women's writing in the elegiac tradition to reductive, biographical readings.

The ambiguity of Maude's personal suffering is precisely what renders the reception of her poems so bewildering to her fictional audience. Until the mysterious carriage ride towards the end of the novella, there is no ostensible loss or trauma that justifies her elegiac mode. Unlike Charlotte Smith, who bore the burdens of an adulterous husband, widowhood, and financial struggles, Maude suffers from no worldly problems but harbors an unarticulated and self-devouring sense of religious guilt. She feels unworthy of taking communion and stops receiving the Eucharist, which reflects biographically on Christina Rossetti's own Tractarian principles and spiritual crisis. As William Michael Rossetti mentions in his preface, his sister was, at the time of writing *Maude*, "overburdened with conscientious scruples. The worst harm she appears to have done is that when she had written a good poem she felt it to be good."[103]

But Maude's heavy morbidity, amidst the cheer of her sunny cousins, a stable family life, and joyful fêtes, presents a self-ironizing portrayal of the overly sensitive female protagonist. From the very beginning, the jarring mismatch between Maude's young, innocent character and her jaded life outlook baffles her friends and the narrator, who question whether her melancholy poems are fueled by real experiences actually worth lamenting:

> It was the amazement of every one what could make her poetry so broken-hearted as was mostly the case. Some pronounced that she wrote very foolishly about things she could not possibly understand; some wondered if she really had any secret source of uneasiness; while some simply set her down as affected. Perhaps there was a degree of truth in all these opinions.[104]

In other words, Maude is either a ridiculous Gothic heroine or a serious female poetess, or both—along with all the stereotypical poetesses who fit both molds—and the difficulty of reconciling these personas is the interpretive conflict for any reader of the novella. The product of quick drawing-room games, sonnet writing becomes an occasional, offhand task, something to be pieced together in a few minutes' leisure time. Written for pure entertainment, any seriously elegiac or devotional sonnet produced in a round of *bouts-rimés* suggests fabrication. The scene of young girls celebrating a fifteenth birthday without any true woes thus descends into a scene of caricature. Rossetti knows that we, as readers of elegy, cannot help but seek out biographical justifications for the misery in a poetess's verse.[105] Written in company rather than in solitude, Maude's sonnets ironize the autobiographical sonnets of Charlotte Smith or Letitia Elizabeth Landon. They foreshadow Amy Levy's "To a Dead Poet" as well as "A Minor Poet" (1884), her dramatic monologue about a suicidal writer.[106] At stake in this satirical devaluation of the elegiac tradition is the possibility of domestic life as an occasion for true misery. Conceived as a safe space, the middle-class home can evoke true danger to some, but melodrama and solipsism to others.[107] Maude's bedroom becomes a laughable prototype for Madame Bovary's French boudoir.

Rossetti sounds the "click of the cliché" each time the young girls in *Maude* and their poetic attempts echo the distraught heroines of Gothic novels. The heavy-handed representation of the poetess figure, in scenes of cloying femininity and stereotypical melodrama, are enough to elicit in us Lootens's "sentimental squirm."[108] When Maude is nearly forced to recite her poems aloud at the bequest of the aptly named Miss Savage, the narration spirals into a scene of panic. At the moment of recitation, public and private spheres collide:

> Poor Maude's misfortunes now came thick and fast. Seated between Miss Savage and Sophia Mowbray, she was attacked on either hand with questions concerning her verses. In the first place, did she continue to write? Yes. A flood of ecstatic compliments followed this admission: she was so young, so much admired, and, poor thing, looked so delicate. It was quite affecting to think of her lying awake at night meditating those sweet verses—("I sleep like a top," Maude put in drily,)—which so delighted her friends, and would charm the public, if only Miss Foster could be induced to publish. At last the bystanders were called upon to intercede for a recitation. A hasty answer was rising to her lips, the absurdity of her position flashed across her mind so forcibly that, almost unable to check a laugh in the midst of her annoyance, she put her handkerchief to her mouth . . .[109]

Here Rossetti stages the conflict of a young writer negotiating her own identity as a "professional poetess," forced to act her expected role in public.[110] Though the stakes seem relatively limited for Maude, (a drawing-room performance versus her bedroom private sulkings), the emotional negotiations are cataclysmic. This scene marks Maude's refusal to perform along separate spheres—demanding a rupture, break, or suspension on her own terms.[111] Thus, in this moment when separate spheres collide in *Maude*, the potential for satire is threefold. First, readers may harbor suspicions that a young female figure like Maude should ever be justified in composing genuine elegy from the comforts of house and home. Second, even if Charlotte Smith does serve as a paragon for true domestic elegy expressed in sonnet form, succeeding fictional versions of her fall short of impossible, mythic expectations. Third, the domestic sphere is such a boring, unproductive space, contrary to the Wordsworth's suggestion in "Nuns Fret Not," that it produces Maude's genuine irritability and her self-destructive ennui.

Maude's only sin is the unexplained melancholy she experiences from her spiritual crisis, which even she treats flippantly. We learn that, immediately upon completing a poem about suffering and heart-sickness, she simply "yawned, leaned back, and wondered how she should fill up the time till dinner."[112] Such juxtapositions between scenes of creative and domestic life—staged here as Maude's scaled-down version of private and public spheres in caricature—allow Rossetti to counter the assumption that women poets' literary work must necessarily overlap with their personal biography. As a young girl limited to her bedroom, birthday parties, and tea parlors, how can Maude transcend these limitations to embody the professional poet, evoking pathos without bathos? Rossetti's work still solicits divergent readings by critics today who understand her as both a young, riddling poet engaging in word games and a woman confronting vast theological issues on a catastrophic, apocalyptic scale.[113]

Ultimately, the young Maude understands that performing to meet the expectations of the poetess myth necessitates a Gothic negation of herself. Instead, she turns away, interrupting the satirical possibility that she is being led to perform. She refuses to embody the Gothic trope of the performing poetess. At the end of the scene with Miss Savage and Miss Mowbray, Maude covers her own mouth with a handkerchief and cuts the evening short, returning home "dissatisfied with her circumstances, her friends and herself." Here, the potential union of poet and speaker culminates in a moment of physical self-silencing, reminiscent of EBB's stammering speaker in "The Soul's Expression." The poetess's experience is indeed one necessarily marked by failure, erasure, and "infinitely repeatable loss."[114] As Lootens explains:

> I speak of "the Poetess"; but, in fact, I have come to believe there is no such thing. Less a heroine than a heritage, the Poetess is, as Yopie Prins memorably puts it, "the personification of an empty figure," "a trope, 'available for occupancy' yet also advertising its vacancy." To sign "Poetess" is, then, to practice signature as a form of erasure: it is to sign "Nobody."[115]

Gothic self-negation, through childbirth, self-imprisonment, self-silencing, or mysterious death, reverberates across iterations of the poetess figure across history. In the same vein, Prins's argument that Victorian poetesses—from Sappho leaping to her death, to her reincarnations in Letitia Elizabeth Landon, to *fin de siècle* poets like Amy Levy, to modernists like Sylvia Plath—can be understood as a long line of Gothic heroines continuing a tradition marked by suicide, matricide, abortion, or infanticide.

In a mode familiar to us from 1790s novels, Maude's illness, isolation, and eventual death mark the typical, melodramatic ending of the languishing Gothic damsel who never gets freed from her self-prison. The only difference is one of setting and tone: In Rossetti's novella, the Italian castles overlooking the Apennine mountains of Gothic romance are replaced by the middle-class Victorian bedroom. The difficulty of separating private from public, poet from speaker, continues to pose a problem for even the most conscientious critics and readers of women's poetry; and the entwining knots compromising this mythic web resemble Gothic bonds and chains more than laurels and threads. Yet by reading *Maude* as a Gothic text, we can recognize the ways Rossetti both replicates and resists assumptions surrounding female autobiography and hagiography, providing us with a means to break the patterns of tokenizing a conventional figure in rhetorically convenient ways.[116] An author can confront the impossible imperative of performing perfectly within separate spheres, of skillfully playing the angel in the house and the professional poetess, contorting her body and voice when called to assume the spaces demanded of her. She can orchestrate her own exit and refusals by self-consciously orchestrating her own Gothic endings.

Conclusion: "The Three Nuns"

If the mythic poetess is a Gothic heroine, she takes the form not only of imprisoned damsels, but nuns—women who, in taking orders, submit to spatial confinement as a commitment to their calling and career. In a counterpoint to the opening scene of *bouts-rimés*, Maude composes a final triptych of poems at the end of the novella. The poems are about herself and her two cousins, all cast as Catholic sisters. "The Three Nuns," individually titled 1°, 2° and 3°, is the final image of the three women, immortalizing them in a state of mythic saintliness: a stanza in the second poem reads, "Bury me in the Convent ground / Among the flowers that are sweet; / And lay a green turf at my feet, / Where thick trees cast a gloom around." The third poem begins, "My heart is a freeborn bird / Caged in my cruel breast, / That flutters, flutters evermore, / Nor sings, nor is at rest. / But beats against the prison bars . . ."[117] Despite their different fates and vocations, all three women appear here, elliptically and anonymously, as caged or buried bodies. Moreover, the figure of the nun, like the mythic poetess, is anonymous and indiscernible, such that in poetry, Mary, Magdalen, and Maude become subsumed as unrecognizable doubles of one author. Because they are all indistinguishable versions of the same, Maude must explain her composition: "The first Nun no one can suspect of being myself, partly because my hair is far from yellow and I do not wear curls; partly because I never did anything half so good as profess. The second might be Mary, had she mistaken her vocation. The third is Magdalen, of course."[118]

The message here is one of impending inevitability: each young girl becomes yet another version of a Gothic heroine—if not a damsel in distress, then a cloistered nun. The professional poetess, young or old, fictional or real, understands this predetermination of literary history. The story ends with Maude's death. In the final scene, Agnes intertwines tendrils of the girls' hair, echoing with this action the entwined laurels and garlands of so many mythic poetesses or the interweaving lines "The Thread of Life." She carries out Maude's final wishes, burning her verses so that no public will ever read them:

> The locked book she never opened, but had it placed on Maude's coffin . . . She next collected the scraps of paper found in her cousin's desk and portfolio, or lying loose upon the table, and proceeded to examine them . . . Piece after piece she committed to the flames . . . but it cost her a pang to do so . . . Agnes cut one long tress from Maude's head; and on her return home laid it in the same paper with the lock of Magdalen's hair . . . Amen for us all.[119]

By the end of the novella, only Agnes remains a witness to the fates of her cousin and friends. As if evaluating the poems from their round of *bouts-rimés*, we evaluate their lives, one year later in the novel: Mary has married and lives "a tale of happiness," Magdalen has taken orders into the Sisterhood of Mercy, and Maude expires.[120] One woman chooses the bonds of marriage and the protection of a husband; another chooses enclosure through allegiance to the church; while the aspiring poetess, hoping to pen verses in solitude, expires from her mysterious accident. The only survivors are those who have chosen the protection of female domestic or religious confines.

It is important in such a reading to emphasize the biographical and serious register of nuns as characters in *Maude* and not to read these figurations as Gothic tropes invoked offhand by the author as a plot device. The influence of the Oxford Movement on Rossetti's Anglican background intensified her Catholic connection. As Emma Mason reminds us, Rossetti believed that "what is Catholic underlies what is Christian," and "on the Catholic basis alone can the Christian structure be raised, even while to raise that superstructure on that foundation is the bounden duty of every soul within reach of the full Divine Revelation."[121] Rossetti was attracted to Tractarianism for its "promotion of a universal Catholicism founded on a unity of all living things," which we witness staged in the interconnections of "The Thread of Life" and "Three Nuns" poems.[122] *Maude* is not a Gothic text because it invokes nuns and omens but because it treats seriously the literary themes of female confinement, self-confinement, and heroism through the use of Gothic forms.

Looking back to the young reluctant wards in Radcliffe's Gothic convents, to the cruel Abbess and Domina who detain them, to Wordsworth's nuns who "fret not," and the young girls penning *bouts-rimés*, we see in this imagery of nuns an important Gothic variation on the poetess figure. If we attempt to suspend subscribing to separate spheres as a way to counter "Poetess parallax," to truly see beyond reductive constructions and perpetuate the myth, the nun poses a Gothic iteration of the mythic poetess that actively chooses confinement as a sign of her vocational commitment. (One thinks, for instance, of the prolific oeuvre of Sor Juana Inés de la Cruz.) Unlike the Gothic damsel, the nun's life of form and restraint is a professional choice. In Chapter 4, I will revisit nuns, cloistered confinement, and the sonnet form in readings of G. M. Hopkins's poetry; first though, I turn to Dante Gabriel Rossetti, and to the fluctuating bodies and framed women in artwork that define his Gothic poetics.

Notes

1. Samuel Taylor Coleridge, "The Mysteries of Udolpho, Review," *The Critical Review* (August 1794): 361–72.
2. Emily's poems may have been verses that Radcliffe composed but did not consider highly enough to publish separately in their own right at the time. Her verses were not published as a collection until 1816, as *The Poems of Mrs. Ann Radcliffe* (London: J. Smith, 1816). Charlotte Smith also included her own poems in the novels *Emmeline* and *Celestina*, portraying her heroines as sometime poetesses as well. Charlotte Smith, *Emmeline: the Orphan of the Castle* (London: T. Cadell, 1789); *Celestina: A Novel in Four Volumes* (London: T. Cadell, 1791).
3. Tricia Lootens, *The Political Poetess: Victorian Femininity, Race, and the Legacy of Separate Spheres* (Princeton: Princeton University Press, 2017), 2–3. See also Virginia Jackson, "The Poet as Poetess," in *The Cambridge Companion to Nineteenth-Century American Poetry*, ed. Kerry Larson (Cambridge: Cambridge University Press, 2011), 54–75.
4. Ann Radcliffe, for her second published novel, *A Sicilian Romance* (1790), appeared on the title page as "the authoress of *The Castles of Athlin and Dunbayne*," a choice likely made to dispel presumptions of male authorship while maintaining her anonymity. "Such attributions are fairly common throughout the reviewing practices of this literary period, but of all the novels produced in the years 1790 and 1791 (the two years in which Radcliffe and her publishers used this attributive construction), hers are the only ones that specify 'by the authoress' rather than 'by the author.'" Dale Townshend and Angela Wright, eds.

Ann Radcliffe, Romanticism and the Gothic (Cambridge: Cambridge University Press, 2016), 6–7.
5. Lootens, *The Political Poetess*, 3.
6. Paul Morrison, "Enclosed in Openness: *Northanger Abbey* and the Domestic Carceral," *Texas Studies in Literature and Language* 33, no. 1 (Spring 1991): 1–23.
7. William Wordsworth, "Nuns Fret Not," in *The Poetical Works of William Wordsworth*, vol. 3: *Miscellaneous Sonnets* (London: E. Moxon, 1841), 3.
8. John Keats, "If By Dull Rhymes," in *The Poetical Works of John Keats* (London: Moxon, Son and Co., 1871), 346.
9. See Mark Raymond's "The Romantic Sonnet Revival: Opening the Sonnet's Crypt," whose title itself has strong Gothic resonances. *Literature Compass* 4, no. 3 (2007): 721–36.
10. Ann Radcliffe, *The Romance of the Forest*, ed. Chloe Chard (New York: Oxford University Press, 2009), 57.
11. This glorified constriction is critiqued in Tennyson's "St. Simeon Stylites." The following readings of Wordsworth's and Keats's meta-sonnets may be considered a gendered transformation of the confined sonneteer in the Petrarchan tradition. See Heather Dubrow, *Echoes of Desire: English Petrarchism and its Counterdiscourses* (Ithaca: Cornell University Press, 1995).
12. For responses to Wordsworth's "Nuns fret not" by poets who composed sonnets on the sonnet, such as Capel Lofft (1807) and Thomas Doubleday (1827), see Jennifer Wagner, *A Moment's Monument: Revisionary Poetics and the Nineteenth-Century English Sonnet* (London: Associated University Presses, 1996), 115. Wagner provides contextualization for reading messages of nationalist morality behind Romantic vindications of English sonnet form on pages 117–23.
13. A poem that celebrates confinement over liberty, this particular sonnet has been associated with Wordsworth's increasingly conservative politics. Sir Henry Taylor, in 1841, recognized it as a "doctrinal poem," interpreting the message as one about duty, discipline, and moral restraint. Such a reading identifies Wordsworth's turn away from "too much liberty" towards the sonnet's more restrictive form as a signal of his political retirement and resignation. As Joseph Phelan has argued, "the sonnets are the crucible in which the 'Victorian' Wordsworth is formed, and they were recognized as such by his Victorian admirers and imitators." Joseph Phelan, *The Nineteenth-Century Sonnet* (New York: Palgrave Macmillan, 2005), 17.
14. Wordsworth, "Nuns Fret Not," 3.
15. "The little poems which are here called sonnets have, I believe, no very just claim to that title, but they consist of fourteen lines and appear to me no improper vehicle for a single sentiment . . . Some very melancholy moments have been beguiled by expressing in verse the sensations

those moments brought." Charlotte Smith, "Preface to the First editions," *Elegiac Sonnets* (Chichester: Dodsley, Gardner, Baldwin, and Bew, 1784), iii–iv.
16. Leigh Hunt, *The Book of the Sonnet*, ed. S. Adams Lee (Stanford: Stanford University Press, 1989), 431, quoted in Phelan, *The Nineteenth-Century Sonnet*, 18.
17. "The Thorn," in *The Complete Poetical Works of William Wordsworth* (London: E. Moxon, 1869), 153.
18. Ann Radcliffe, *The Italian, or the Confessional of the Black Penitents: A Romance* (1797), ed. Frederick Garber (New York: Oxford University Press, 1998), 179.
19. Ann Radcliffe, *The Mysteries of Udolpho*, ed. Bonamy Dobrée (New York: Oxford University Press, 2008), 436.
20. Keats, "If By Dull Rhymes," 346.
21. Radcliffe, *The Romance of the Forest*, 5–7.
22. Wordsworth, "Preface to the Lyrical Ballads", 2nd edn (1800), *Lyrical Ballads 1798 and 1800: William Wordsworth and Samuel Coleridge*, ed. Michael Gamer and Dahlia Porter (Toronto: Broadview, 2008), 172.
23. This line of male sonneteers is paid homage in Wordsworth's metasonnet, "Scorn not the Sonnet."
24. John Hollander offers definitions of "jealous" to mean "apprehensive, vigilant, mistrustful," while Jennifer Wagner adds the possibility of the meaning "zealous or solicitous for the preservation or well-being of something possessed or esteemed, vigilant or careful in guarding." For Wagner, this jealousy of dead leaves shares echoes with Wordsworth's jealousy of dead leaves, which prompted "Scorn not the Sonnet." John Hollander, *The Work of Poetry* (New York: Columbia University Press, 1997) 173; Wagner, *A Moment's Monument*, 95.
25. Charlotte Smith, "Sonnet I," in *Elegiac Sonnets*, 3rd edn (London: Dodsley, Gardner and Bew, 1786), 1, ll. 1–4.
26. Anna Seward, "Sonnet XLIII: To May, in the Year 1783," in *Original Sonnets on Various Subjects; and Odes Paraphrased from Horace* (London: G. Sael, 1799), 45, ll. 9–14.
27. Christina Rossetti, "The Thread of Life," in *The Complete Poems of Christina Rossetti*, vol. 2, ed. R. W. Crump (Baton Rouge: Louisiana State University Press, 1986), 122–3, ll. 5–7.
28. Wagner, *A Moment's Monument*, 96.
29. Wordsworth and Coleridge each attempted to write Gothic dramas in the German tradition for theatrical success on Drury Lane, but failed to achieve any sustained success. For more on the "school of terror," see Angela Wright, *Gothic Fiction: A Reader's Guide to Essential Criticism* (Basingstoke: Palgrave Macmillan, 2007).
30. William Wordsworth, "Preface to the Lyrical Ballads," 177.
31. Samuel T. Coleridge, quoted in Michael Gamer, "Gothic Fictions and Romantic Writing in Britain," in *The Cambridge Companion to Gothic*

32. "I shall send you the Pot of Basil, St. Agnes eve, and if I should have finished it a little thing call'd the 'eve of St. Mark' you see what fine Mother Radcliff names I have—it is not my fault—I do not search for them . . ." Though crediting his inspiration for names to Radcliffe, the use of "Mother" here is slightly disparaging in address, as in "Goody Blake." John Keats, Letter to George and Georgiana Keats, 14 February to 3 May 1819, in *The Letters of John Keats: Volume 2, 1814–1821*, ed. Hyder Edward Rollins, (Cambridge, MA: Harvard University Press, 1958).
33. Keats, Letter to J. H. Reynolds, 14 March 1818, in *The Letters of John Keats, Volume 1: 1814–1821*, 245.
34. William Lane's Minerva Press, which was most active from 1790 to 1820, became synonymous with what Jane Austen called "the trash with which the press now groans" in Chapter 5 of *Northanger Abbey*.
35. Paula R. Feldman and Daniel Robinson (eds), *A Century of Sonnets: The Romantic-Era Revival 1750–1850* (Oxford: Oxford University Press, 1999), 10.
36. Amy Billone, *Little Songs: Women, Silence, and the Nineteenth-Century Sonnet* (Columbus: Ohio State University Press, 2007).
37. Duncan Wu (ed.), biographical note for Charlotte Smith in *Romanticism: An Anthology*, 4th edn (Oxford: Blackwell, 2006), 78–9.
38. Marshall Brown is both appreciative and disparaging of Radcliffe's style, especially in his chapter "In Defense of Cliché": "Radcliffe's descriptive prose was widely admired in her own time, yet seems remarkably bloodless today." "If gothic writing doesn't positively define such second-rateness, it certainly exemplifies it: it is apprentice writing; you grow out of being a gothic novelist, rarely if ever into it . . . [Gothic prose] manifests a kind of self-consciousness. Often, it seems self-conscious in the negative sense—awkward, slightly embarrassed, even unintentionally funny." Marshall Brown, *The Gothic Text* (Stanford: Stanford University Press, 2005), 107, 162.
39. Lootens, *The Political Poetess*, 17.
40. Ibid. 80.
41. Skeptical readers of Charlotte Smith warned that such melancholia and solipsism could lead to dark, Gothic fantasies; Anna Seward, her rival poet, even accused Smith's elegiac poems of promoting "dark dreams of suicide." Duncan Wu, Introduction to "Elegiac Sonnets: the third edition. With twenty additional sonnets (1786)," in *Romanticism*, 85.
42. Radcliffe, *The Mysteries of Udolpho*, 7.
43. William Beckford, "Elegiac Sonnet to a Mopstick," in Feldman and Robinson, *A Century of Sonnets*, 91.
44. Elizabeth Barrett became Elizabeth Barrett Browning after her marriage in 1846. She was Elizabeth Barrett Moulton Barrett at the time

of publication for the poems discussed in this chapter—and is hereafter referred to as "EBB."

45. My Gothic model offers a darker alternative to that of Dorothy Mermin, who conceived of the woman's poet struggle as the desiring/desired and subject/object as assuming the role of both "the damsel and the knight." Dorothy Mermin, "The Damsel, the Knight, and the Victorian Woman Poet," *Critical Inquiry* 13, no. 1 (Autumn 1986): 64–80.

46. According to Marjorie Stone, 1844 was a time when Barrett Browning rebirthed herself after two years of sickness, without the support or influence of her mother. Marjorie Stone, *Elizabeth Barrett Browning* (New York: St. Martin's Press, 1995), 19.

47. "O sound of despair! O moment of unutterable anguish! The pang of death itself is, surely, not superior to that I then suffered. Shut out from day, from friends, from life—*for such I must foretell* it—in the prime of my years, in the height of my transgressions, and left to imagine horrors more terrible than any, perhaps, which certainty could give . . . Three days have now passed in solitude and silence . . . When I awake in the morning I think I shall not live to see another night; and, when night returns, that I must never more unclose my eyes on morning. Why am I brought hither—why confined thus rigorously—but for death! Yet what action of my life has deserved this at the hand of a fellow creature?" Radcliffe, *The Romance of the Forest*, 131–2.

48. Barrett Browning, "The Prisoner." Poems by Barrett Browning in *Poems* (1844) refer to *The Complete Works of Elizabeth Barrett Browning*, vol. 2, ed. Charlotte Porter and Helen A. Clarke (New York: Thomas Y. Crowell, 1900). Here, p. 240.

49. The use of solitary confinement was far more common in the U.S., which Dickens excoriates in *American Notes*, pointing specifically to Philadelphia's Eastern State Penitentiary. "The Twentieth Report of the Inspectors of Prisons" presented by the Earl of Shaftesbury provides a sympathetic portrayal of harsh prison conditions and calls for reform: "Lordships were bound to take all possible care that our prisons and houses of correction were made as effective as possible for the reform of the persons detained in them. If however, many of the prisons throughout the country were to continue in the state in which they now were, not only with respect to sanitary conditions, but likewise as to moral considerations, prisoners would issue forth from them in worse bodily health and in more degraded condition morally than they were when they entered within their walls." The report cites up to 85 male prisoners and 45 female prisoners relegated to cells that were meant to house only 30 and 25 respectively, proving the inadequacy of accommodation to meet continual demands. *Hansard's Parliamentary Debates*, 123–4.

50. In prisons like Newgate, families of debtors often lodged within the prisons, while merchants and prostitutes were free to enter and leave

the space as needed. The better-funded prisons "resembled marketplaces" complete with butchers, chandlers, surgeons, and tap-houses. Sean Grass, *The Self in the Cell: Narrating the Victorian Prisoner* (New York: Routledge, 2003), 6.

51. While D. A. Miller and Andrew Jaffe have called attention to panoptical modes of surveillance and judgment ubiquitous throughout the Victorian novel, Grass's book, which covers English attempts at prison reform from 1780 to 1840, reminds readers that Jeremy Bentham's panopticon, though intellectually groundbreaking, was never successfully implemented and thus not readily available in England. Grass, *The Self in the Cell*, 6.
52. "Whither is fled the visionary gleam? Where is it now, the glory and the dream?" William Wordsworth, "Ode: Intimations of Immortality from Recollections of Early Childhood," in *The Poetical Works of William Wordsworth*, 2nd edn, ed. Ernest de Selincourt (Oxford: Clarendon, 1959), lines 56–7.
53. William Wordsworth, "Composed upon Westminster Bridge, September 3, 1802," in *The Poetical Works of William Wordsworth*, line 6.
54. Elizabeth Helsinger, *Poetry and the Thought of Song in Nineteenth-Century Britain*, (Charlottesville: University of Virginia Press, 2015), 5. Angela Leighton, *Hearing Things: The Work of Sound in Literature* (Cambridge, MA: Harvard University Press, 2018), 505–6. Hollander, *The Work of Poetry*, 173.
55. Elizabeth Barrett Browning, "To George Sand: A Recognition," 239, ll. 1–4.
56. "Wordsworth upon Helvellyn! Let the cloud / Ebb audibly along the mountain-wind," lines 1–2. Elizabeth Barrett Browning, "On a Portrait of Wordsworth by B.R. Haydon," 228.
57. Elizabeth Barrett Browning, "The Soul's Expression," 227.
58. "outbear, v.3," *Oxford English Dictionary* Online, March 2019, Oxford University Press.
59. Contraception and abortion were not readily available to Victorian women. The first statutory prohibition of abortion was enacted through Lord Ellenborough's Act of 1803, which made abortion after quickening a capital crime. In 1823, John Stuart Mill was arrested for distributing pamphlets about birth control. In 1877, Annie Besant and Charles Bradlaugh were arrested for publishing Charles Knowlton's *The Fruits of Philosophy*, which advocated birth control. The 1861 Offences Against the Person Act outlawed abortion. See John Keown, *Abortion, Doctors and the Law: Some Aspects of the Legal Regulation of Abortion in England from 1803 to 1982*, Cambridge Studies in the History of Medicine (Cambridge: Cambridge University Press, 1988).
60. Wu, biographical note for Charlotte Smith, in *Romanticism: An Anthology*, 78.

61. *The Brownings' Correspondence*, vol. 23, ed. Philip Kelley, Scott Lewis, Edward Hagan, Joseph Phelan, and Rhian Williams (Winfield, KS: Wedgestone Press, 2016).
62. Beverly Taylor, "Elizabeth Barrett Browning," *Victorian Poetry 55*, no. 3 (Fall 2017): 337, quoting *The Brownings' Correspondence*, 34 and 74–5. See Jill Matus, *Unstable Bodies: Victorian Representations of Sexuality and Maternity* (Manchester: Manchester University Press, 1995); Carol Smart, "Disruptive Bodies and Unruly Sex: The Regulation of Reproduction and Sexuality in the Nineteenth Century," in *Regulating Womanhood*, ed. Carol Smart (London: Routledge, 1992); and Natalie J. McKnight, *Suffering Mothers in Mid-Victorian Novels* (New York: St. Martin's Press, 1997).
63. In 1856, Lord Brougham received a petition from 20,000 women, which he reported in a statement to the House of Lords: "But remember, I pray you, the lot of a woman toiling through days—not seldom nights too—of hard labour to support her own and her children's existence, whom an idle or a profligate husband has deserted, and doomed to see the little store which her exertions have gathered together swept away by that idler or good-for-nothing." Minutes to the House of Lords: "Property and Earnings of Women—Petition," 14 March 1856, in *Hansard's Parliamentary Debates*: Third series (London: Cornelius Buck, 1856), 120–1.
64. See Lootens, *The Political* Poetess, for considerations of the Victorian poetess as a black woman writer.
65. Deborah D. Rogers. *The Matrophobic Gothic and Its Legacy: Sacrificing Mothers in the Novel and in Popular Culture* (New York: Peter Lang, 2007).
66. "England has had many learned women, not merely readers but writers of the learned languages, in Elizabeth's time and afterwards—women of deeper acquirements than are common now in the greater diffusion of letters; and yet where were the poetesses? The divine breath which seemed to come and go, and, ere it went, filled the land with that crowd of true poets whom we call the old dramatists—why did it never pass, even in the lyrical form, over the lips of a woman? How strange! And can we deny that it was so? I look everywhere for grandmothers and see none. It is not in the filial spirit I am deficient, I do assure you—witness my reverent love of the grandfathers!" *The Letters of Elizabeth Barrett Browning*, ed. Frederic G. Kenyon (New York: Macmillan, 1898), 231–2.
67. Gazzaniga proposes a concept of "proximal poetics" that reimagines the conventionally isolated space of the sonnet as a place that might only accommodate one speaker. While she recognizes this second body sharing a confining poetic space as a husband rather than a child figure, her essay shows how "the proximate is both a space to occupy and a space to create . . . the space she has created for herself and a place

where others may stand next to her. In this way, she has successfully negotiated the intrusion of a beloved [other] . . . into the inviolate space of the sonnet without compromising her own power to author it." This construal of the sonnet as an intensely private physical and metaphysical "room" shows a lyric space that does not necessarily demand total isolation. Andrea Gazzaniga, "'This Close Room': Elizabeth Barrett Browning's Proximal Poetics in Sonnets from the Portuguese" *Victorian Poetry* 54, no. 1 (2016): 67–92. See also Emily Harrington, *Second Person Singular: Late Victorian Women Poets and the Bonds of Verse* (Charlottesville: University of Virginia Press, 2014).
68. Matthew Lewis, *The Monk: A Romance* (New York: Oxford University Press, 2008), 410.
69. Lewis, *The Monk*, 380.
70. See Irvine Loudon, *Death in Childbirth* (Oxford: Clarendon Press, 1992) and Robert Millward and Frances Bell, "Infant Mortality in Victorian Britain: The Mother as Medium," *The Economic History Review* 54, no. 4 (November 2001): 699–733.
71. Mary Wollstonecraft, *A Vindication of the Rights of Woman; and, The Wrongs of Woman, or, Maria* (New York: Pearson Longman, 2007) 316, 317.
72. Ibid. 202.
73. Ibid.
74. Ibid. 203.
75. Ibid. 204.
76. Wollstonecraft, "Author's preface" to *Maria*, 73.
77. Yopie Prins, *Victorian Sappho* (Princeton: Princeton University Press, 1999), 207.
78. Rossetti, "What Sappho Would Have Said Had Her Leap Cured Instead of Killing Her," ll. 59-60, in *Complete Poems*. See also Prins, *Victorian Sappho*, 204–5.
79. Barrett Browning, "Insufficiency," 240, lines 1–3.
80. Ibid. line 11.
81. Ibid. lines 13–14.
82. Naomi Levine, "Elizabeth Barrett Browning's Historiographical Poetics," *Modern Language Quarterly* 77, no. 1 (March 2016): 81–104. In this article, Levine shows that what critics found faulty as "paucity of rhyme" and "inadmissible" half rhymes were in fact a result of EBB's study of historiographical prosody and her engagement with the works of Henry Hallam. We can see in this example an "organic melding of sonnet and blank-verse form."
83. Elizabeth Barrett Browning, *Aurora Leigh*, ed. Margaret Reynolds (New York: Norton, 1996): 5.223–36.
84. Ibid. lines 335–6, 226–7.
85. Rossetti's lyrics seem to gesture towards an oppositional tension that pervades her oeuvre: the conflict between the playfulness of open-ended

riddles or a poetics of doom with predetermined endings. These two inclinations can be seen in recent readings of Rossetti's work: Adam Mazel reads the riddles of Rossetti's later lyrics in light of her experience with word games in *Marshall's Ladies Daily Remembrancer: For 1850*. These enigmas alternately invoke endings of "satisfying solutions" or the impossibility of solutions, which reflect her Tractarian aesthetics. On the other end of the spectrum, Nathan Hensley offers apocalyptic readings in which the poet's later-career concern with end times imagines catastrophic ends on both a small and large scale. Adam Mazel, "'You, Guess': The Enigmas of Christina Rossetti," *Victorian Literature and Culture* 44 (2016): 511–33. Nathan Hensley, "After Death: Christina Rossetti's Timescales of Catastrophe," *Nineteenth-Century Contexts* 38, no. 5 (2016): 399–415.

86. Christina Rossetti, "Dedicatory Sonnet," in *A Pageant and Other Poems* (London: Macmillan, 1881), 144.
87. Christina Rossetti, "The Thread of Life," *Complete Works*, 122–3.
88. Rossetti, "The Thread of Life," Sonnet 2, line 1.
89. Eric Griffiths, "The Disappointment of Christina G. Rossetti," *Essays in Criticism* 47, no. 2 (April 1997): 108. Angela Leighton proposes a purely aural response to these sounds of repetition, pointing towards the tautological or self-echoing effects. Angela Leighton, "On the 'hearing ear': Some Sonnets of the Rossettis," *Victorian Poetry* 47, no. 3 (Fall 2009): 505–16. "Instead of looking at the technical formalities of the sonnet, its lines, rhyme scheme, and meter, I want to try listening, to the way the sonnet becomes a shape in the ear, a sound-work or rhythm," 505.
90. By the 1890s, the scene of women's writing had evolved. Emily Harrington identifies Christina Rossetti as an influence for female *fin de siècle* poets, for whom Wordsworth's "scanty plot of land" is a fertile garden plot, and for whom Coventry Patmore's "bonds of verse" (meter) served as a means for both restraint and connection, especially in poems by Alice Meynell. For Harrington, Rossetti's poetry epitomizes the impersonal. "In writing a poetics of impersonal intimacy," *fin de siècle* women poets "took many cues from Christina Rossetti" who "unravel[s] the notion of a self, especially in poems whose utterances come from beyond the grave." She views late nineteenth-century women poets claiming back what are "presumably feminine and negative qualities such as silence, passivity, and submission." Harrington, *Second Person Singular*.
91. Phelan, *The Nineteenth-Century Sonnet*, 97. Elizabeth Helsinger likewise hears the internal rhythm and sense of time that satisfied neither Coventry Patmore's "poetics of (musical) time marked in equal measure" nor Ruskin's preferred regular beat of metrical verse. Instead, Rossetti "listened for an alternative music behind or beyond the

metrical surface of her verses." Helsinger, *Poetry and the Thought of Song*, 140.
92. William Going provides a list of sonnet sequences composed in the eighteenth and nineteenth centuries, reporting "some 260" sonnet sequences "containing almost 4800 sonnets." Going, *Scanty Plot of Ground: Studies in the Victorian Sonnet* (The Hague: Mouton, 1976), 157.
93. In a similar vein, Harrington identifies the "reverse apostrophe" at the poem's opening where objects talk to the speaker, rather than the other way around; she reads this mutuality as a demonstration of Rossettian intimacy, predicated on a balance of dominance and submissiveness to God. Harrington, *Second Person Singular*, 13.
94. *Maude*, in *Christina Rossetti: Poems and Prose*, ed. Simon Humphries (New York: Oxford University Press, 2008), 267–8.
95. Ibid. 265.
96. Suzanne Waldman identifies physical signs that Maude is possessed by other spirits, judging from the way her complexion pales and her eyes light up; a baby at the party even howls when Maude holds her. Suzanne Waldman, *The Demon and the Damozel: Dynamics of Desire in the Works of Christina Rossetti and Dante Gabriel Rossetti* (Athens: Ohio University Press, 2008) 47.
97. Rossetti, *Maude*, 283.
98. "My side is dreadfully hurt; I looked at it this morning for the first time, but hope never again to see so shocking a sight. The pain now and then is extreme, though not always so; sometimes, in fact, I am unconscious of any injury." Rossetti, *Maude*, 286–7.
99. Ibid. 270.
100. Ibid. 270–1.
101. This is also seen in Rossetti's reusing of the same name in various other poems in her collections, including "Sister Maude" and "Maude Claire."
102. Lootens, *The Political Poetess*, 8. For more on Rossetti's treatment of the Eucharist in *Goblin Market*, see also Marylu Hill, "'Eat Me, Drink Me, Love Me': Eucharist and the Erotic Body in Christina Rossetti's Goblin Market," *Victorian Poetry* 43 (2005): 455–72.
103. William Michael Rossetti, Prefatory Note to *Maude: A Story for Girls* (London: James Bowden, 1897), ix.
104. Rossetti, *Maude*, 266.
105. Reviewers of Smith's *Elegiac Sonnets*, for instance, either identified with the melancholy of the author ("We are sorry to see the eye which can shine with so much poetic fire sullied with a tear, and we hope the soothings of the favoured muse may wipe it from her cheek") or suspiciously questioned how genuine they were ("We cannot . . . forbear expressing a hope that the misfortunes she so often hints at,

are all imaginary. We must have perused her very tender and exquisite effusions with diminished pleasure, could we have supposed her sorrows to be real. It would be hard indeed if a lady, who has so much contributed to the delight of others, should feel any want of happiness herself.") *Critical Review* 61 (1786): 467–8; *Gentleman's Magazine* 56, no. 1 (1786): 333–4.

106. See Holly Laird, "The Death of the Author by Suicide: Fin-de-Siecle Poets and the Construction of Identity," in *The Fin de Siecle Poem: English Literary Culture and 1890s*, ed. Joseph Bristow (Athens: Ohio University Press, 2005), 116–51.
107. By the end of the nineteenth century, this drawing room scene in *Maude* would not have seemed as ridiculous. Women participated in "vigorous salon culture" analogous to the Rhymer's Club of male poets, as the poetess figure became a reality, such that Oscar Wilde wrote, "No country has ever had so many poetesses at once . . . The work done by women in the sphere of poetry is really of a very high standard of excellence," quoted in Harrington, *Second Person Singular*, 7. See also Talia Schaffer and Kathy A. Psomiades (eds), *Women and British Aestheticism* (Charlottesville: University Press of Virginia, 1999).
108. Lootens, *The Political Poetess*, 17.
109. Rossetti, *Maude*, 279.
110. Susan Brown, "The Victorian Poetess," in *The Cambridge Companion to Victorian Poetry*, ed. Joseph Bristow (Cambridge: Cambridge University Press, 2000), 180–202.
111. Lootens recognizes the suspension of separate spheres as necessarily Gothic in its sentimentality: "The continuous act of suspending spheres [is] not only sentimental but Gothic: indeed, as sentimental by right of being Gothic. The dying soldier's transition from abstract subject of the law of the State to cherished, irreducibly individual family member; the release of the dying 'Mother' from the exiled custodial labors of 'home,' into that 'Heaven' whose transcendent, yet historically contained, captive claims she has so strenuously protected: these present themselves, in some sense, as grounds for rejoicing. Still, even in the most ideal terms, each release requires a corpse. Sentimentality meets—and, indeed, requires—Gothicism, then," *The Political Poetess*, 87.
112. Rossetti, *Maude*, 266.
113. See note 85.
114. Prins, *Victorian Sappho*, 175.
115. Lootens, *The Political Poetess*, 4.
116. "'Step right up!' I now imagine us calling, across divides of nation and period. 'Have a look at this Genuinely Interesting Nineteenth-Century Woman poet: that is the one *I* study. See her subtle, ambitious work; note her splendid cultural figure. Here, my friends, is

the apotheosis of poetic negotiation with the demands of femininity! . . . Pay no attention to that shadowy form behind the curtain. That's only the Mere Poetess. Pure conventionality, that's what *she* has to offer: mere (fill in the blank: eighteenth-century / Romantic period / mid-Victorian / British / American) ideology. Don't worry! We'll have her offstage in no time.' And thus, foil to all and focus to none—obliquely seen, though never actually quite offstage—the privatized Poetess has attained a nearly magical staying power, quietly performing on behalf of separate spheres (and with them of racialized national sentimentality), even as controversies over feminism, literary theory, historiography, and philosophy have exploded around her." Lootens, *The Political Poetess*, 8. See also Tricia Lootens, *Lost Saints: Silence, Gender, and Victorian Literary Canonization* (Charlottesville: University of Virginia Press, 1996).
117. Rossetti, *Maude*, 291.
118. Ibid. 287.
119. Ibid. 115–22.
120. Ibid. 294, 285.
121. Emma Mason's study connects Rossetti's Tractarian commitments with her belief in "an ecological love command," providing ecocritical readings of her religious verse. Emma Mason, *Christina Rossetti: Poetry, Ecology, Faith* (Oxford: Oxford University Press, 2018), 36.
122. Ibid.

Chapter 3

Gothic Shock and Swap: Suspended Bodies and Fluctuating Frames in D. G. Rossetti's Double Works

> Emily . . . went towards the picture, which appeared to be enclosed in a frame of uncommon size, that hung in a dark part of the room. She paused again, and then, with a timid hand, lifted the veil; but instantly let it fall—perceiving that what it had concealed was no picture, and before she could leave the chamber, she dropped senseless to the floor.
>
> Ann Radcliffe, *The Mysteries of Udolpho*

Elements of D. G. Rossetti's early career smack of Gothic intrigue, from brushes with exhumed graves to Bluebeardian jealousy. After his wife Elizabeth Siddal died in 1862, possibly of suicide from a laudanum overdose, Rossetti buried his letters and poems twined with Elizabeth's hair in her grave at Highgate Cemetery. Seven years later, he infamously had the manuscript volume of his poems exhumed, "add[ing] a touch of the macabre to the life story."[1] With a nod to Gothic confinement, his well-known paintings such as *Water Willow* (1871) and *Proserpine* (1874) perpetuate the romantic fantasy that William Morris jealously kept his wife Jane away from Rossetti, a rival lover, under lock and key at Kelmscott Manor.

Certainly, a fixation on medieval and Gothic themes was a major draw for fans of the Pre-Raphaelite Brotherhood. The movement had revived the pleasures of medieval and Gothic romance among young Englishmen like Walter Crane, who reminisced on his early reactions to its enchanting aesthetic:

> The curtain had been lifted, and we had a glimpse into a magic world of romance and pictured poetry, peopled with ghosts of "ladies dead and lovely knights,"—a twilight world of dark mysterious woodlands,

haunted streams, meads of deep green starred with burning flowers, veiled in a dim and mystic light, and stained with low-toned crimsons and gold, as if indeed one has gazed through the glass of

Magic casements opening on the foam
Of perilous seas in faerylands forlorn.²

Yet Rossetti's later works shifted away from themes of Arthurian and Gothic romance, engaging with Gothic forms in more subtle ways. Distancing himself from the original group of Pre-Raphaelite Brothers from his early career, his later works progressed from works of Mariolatry to large, often full-bodied female portraits.

Rossetti's paintings of the 1860s often feature portraits of women who are oversized and seemingly ill-proportioned to the frame.³ These paintings are intensely stylized and aestheticized, set within a

Figure 3.1. Paintings from Rossetti's "double works," clockwise from top left: *Lilith, Sibylla Palmifera, Proserpine,* and *Astarte Syriaca*

Courtesy of Tate Gallery, London; Manchester City Art Gallery; Delaware Art Museum, Newark; and Lady Lever Art Gallery, National Museums Liverpool, Port Sunlight, United Kingdom

wide range of historical contexts. Yet the faces and bodies depicted unabashedly reveal the identities of the highly recognizable models who sat for those pieces: Fanny Cornforth, Jane Morris, and Alexa Wilding. From the viewer's perspective, the paintings are confrontational, jarring, and demanding. Are we looking at a biblical figure, a Greek goddess, or a studio model? These paintings command our attention, but almost resist interpretation—causing us to renegotiate our understanding of the image, particularly when read in conjunction with their accompanying poems. Building up to final close readings, I turn, in this chapter, to four examples (and two pairs) of Rossetti's Victorian "picture poems" from the 1870s: *Proserpine*, *Astarte Syriaca*, *Lady Lilith*, and *Sibylla Palmifera*. Each is an example of Rossetti's doubled works, paired poems and paintings composed under a unifying title. The works are meant to be appreciated in conjunction, the reader attending to both their textual and visual components. To interpret these works, I pose a connection between the "realist symbolism" of Pre-Raphaelite art and the "realist supernatural" of Radcliffean Gothic as a way of understanding texts that meld both painting and poetry.

The Radcliffean "realist supernatural," explored earlier in this book and revisited shortly hereafter, is best exemplified by the lifting of the veil in *The Mysteries of Udolpho* and the reader's complicated "confrontation" with a visual image—the infamous scene that serves as the epigraph to this chapter. For sometime-readers of Radcliffe, this passage is well recognized, but also, for many, it is a familiar scene that somehow also goes *unseen*: those who have not read all six hundred pages of *Udolpho* have only encountered it in passing reference, while even those who have read the chapters carefully understand that the reader's view of the image is denied when Emily drops senseless to the floor. As Radcliffe's novel progresses, the veiled imaged becomes a representative symbol, a sign of Female Gothic and the machinery of the explained supernatural.

The realist symbol, in contrast, a marker of Rossetti's nineteenth-century works, is located in pictorial and poetic elements that seem alternately spiritual or loaded with meaning, alternately fleshly and superficial. The problem of "symbolic realism" is that the viewer or reader must negotiate between considering these artistic details as either intrinsically meaningful or simply markers of realist detail, akin to Barthes's "reality effect." In both aesthetic models—the realist supernatural and realist symbolism—the indeterminacy between real and representational bodies, meaningful and meaningless detail, becomes a source of affective power, challenging the reader who must confront a simultaneously textual and visual object and its confounding fungibility.

Realist Symbolism and the Realist Supernatural

The best way to understand realist symbolism is through Dante Gabriel Rossetti's double work, "The Blessed Damozel." It is a classic example of a "picture poem," where the paintings are often mounted on a frame inscribed with key verses from the accompanying poem. As a painter and a poet, Rossetti composed poems with lines that alternate between figurative poetic imagery and concrete pictorial details, which at times harmonize and at times conflict.

Figure 3.2. D. G. Rossetti, *The Blessed Damozel*, Fogg Museum, 1943.202 Harvard Art Museums collections online, <https://hvrd.art/o/299805> (last accessed 20 December 2021)

> The blessed damozel leaned out
>   From the gold bar of Heaven;
> Her eyes were deeper than the depth
>   Of waters stilled at even;
> She had three lilies in her hand,
>   And the stars in her hair were seven.[4]

The damozel's eyes, "deeper than the depth" of stilled waters, indicate vague indescribability, resorting to linguistic tautology. But the next two lines are materially specific: she holds three lilies and has seven stars in her hair, which is "yellow like ripe corn" (l. 12). These descriptions alternately sway us in the directions of painting and poetry, the two "sister arts" central to works of the Pre-Raphaelite Brotherhood.

More than just combining the literary and the visual, "The Blessed Damozel" forces successive encounters with the fleshly and the symbolic. The damozel's robe is "ungirt from clasp to hem" (l. 8) as she looks down at her lover; by line 45, we learn of the passage of time and accumulation of her bodily warmth:

> And still she bow'd herself and stoop'd
>   Out of the circling charm;
> Until her bosom must have made
>   The bar she lean'd on warm,
> And the lilies lay as if asleep
>   Along her bended arm.

The damozel's bodily warmth famously raises epistemological questions of representation: Is she real or representational? Fleshly or ethereal? Human or angel? Is she a heavenly figure impervious to heat or cold, or an earthly body emitting heat?[5] Members of the Pre-Raphaelite Brotherhood sought to achieve an accurate and genuine representation of nature in their paintings and poetry, as made clear in their early "manifestos" in *The Germ*. Following the precepts of John Ruskin, they sought to "Go into nature in all singleness of heart, and walk with her laboriously and trustingly, having no other thought but how best to penetrate her meaning; rejecting nothing, selecting nothing, and scorning nothing."[6] Painters who depicted nature exactly as they viewed it, down to each detail, could penetrate nature's meaning, such that all natural things could be "symbols also in some deeper way."[7]

However, these details became ambiguous sites of simultaneous meaning and meaninglessness, serving as both representative symbols and realist detail. In an early article explaining "Rossetti's Significant Details," Jerome McGann sought to remedy the indifference of post-WWI critics to Rossetti's work by identifying how the poet leads his readers to experience Christian detail in a wholly sensational way, "purifying" them of prior symbolic associations.[8] While scholars have long established the necessity of reading Rossetti's double works simultaneously, interpreting both painting and poem in conjunction, I emphasize the oscillation between both modes, focusing on the experience of fluctuation between the poetic and the pictorial, the fleshly and the symbolic, the living and the dead—modeling a Gothic mode of uncertain readership that a reader or viewer must endure.

Pre-Raphaelite art specialist Elizabeth Prettejohn identifies realist symbolism as the "non-symbolizing symbol" or "the proliferating symbol," pictorial details that either resist or overwhelm with meaning.[9] The quandary of how to interpret such symbols intensifies when these sites of meaning or meaninglessness are *women's* bodies. From his early Art-Catholic[10] beginnings to the first and second waves of Pre-Raphaelitism, Rossetti's depictions of women's bodies evolved from iconic, reverent representations to more secularized and sensual ones. This can be traced from his early 1849 painting "The Girlhood of Mary Virgin" and its accompanying sonnets, which show "a chaste reverence for women and mystery" that for David Riede is typical of Pre-Raphaelite art.[11] By the 1850s and 1860s, however, Rossetti replaced Mariolatry with paintings of medieval romance, stylized oil paintings featuring exotic female beauty. The transitioning from Christian and Dantean religious themes to erotic, chivalric romance clearly shifted the moral tone of the Pre-Raphaelite movement, from one of holy purity in God and nature's works, to one closer to Aestheticism, openly resistant to Victorian standards of morality. The figure of Beatrice, for example, was not to be allegorized through Christian mysticism, but revered as a flesh-and-blood woman.[12] From the blessed damozel, with hair "yellow like ripe corn" and a warm body leaning over the gold bar (first painted in 1847), to Jenny, the sleeping prostitute (in the eponymous poem published in 1870), Rossetti's pictured women—his fleshly women painted in realist detail—challenge and confound viewers as to whether we should read them as breathing, living figures or mythic characters of symbolic significance.

* * *

How might reading scenes of the realist supernatural be akin to interpreting realist symbols? And why consider the two in conjunction?

In *The Mysteries of Udolpho*, the waxen figure of Signora Laurentini di Udolpho appears to be flesh when Emily draws the curtain back, and this unexpected presence of an actual woman in place of an artistic representation of one threatens us with the potential of a suddenly enlivened gaze. What we thought was fake is real; something we thought always inanimate was once alive.

The trope of uncanny body switches, what I am calling the device of Gothic "shock and swap," demands—even cultivates—a particular mode of Gothic reading that is integral to understanding Rossetti's double works: one of navigating the disorienting fluctuations between viewing art or viewing flesh. Hermeneutic confusion surrounding women's bodies leaves the reader-viewer in a state of suspended interpretation, in a phase of pregnant uncertainty, ready to be relieved through explanation and enlightenment. Such instances of "shock and swap" require a mode of readership that must withstand the discomfort of fluctuation, producing a feeling of unease and confusion integral to the Gothic reading experience. In Gothic novels, women are confined within a frame or coffin, presented as art objects or dead bodies—or both. Rossetti's paintings and poems elicit this same uncertainty of reading and viewing. The viewer's obligation to negotiate between myth and woman, figure and body, yields a state of uncertainty that re-enacts the Gothic challenge of navigating the realist supernatural.[13]

This chapter focuses on scenes of swap and suspense surrounding women's bodies to develop an affective theory of Gothic reading that can be applied to the double works of Dante Gabriel Rossetti. Reading across the long nineteenth century, from 1790 to 1860, I focus on the recurrence of framed women's faces and suspended bodies as dramatic occasions that mark a distinctly Gothic reading experience. These scenes are moments of mistaken visual interpretation that compel readers to surrender to their senses, resulting in a suspension of the viewer's judgment and interpretation. While the previous chapter focused on the Gothic trope of women pent up in cells, this chapter concentrates on the powerful effect that a framed, objectified woman can have upon a startled, frozen viewer who is, then, also cast in the position of stasis.[14]

Put differently, I explore commonalities in the hermeneutic reactions to Radcliffe's realist supernatural and to Rossetti's symbolic realism. In key scenes of culminating suspense in Gothic novels, readers are cast into a state of limbo when the climax is suddenly undercut, leaving them questioning what is real and what is not. More than just moral uncertainty, they experience a momentary crisis of representation and perception. That crisis is not quickly resolved and settled once and for all, but occurs again and again, as the tables continue to turn with new twists of plot and additional formal surprises. This unstable realism reflects the phenomenological instability of a Gothic world.

Exploring the Castle: Gothic Shock and Swap

Most often, in 1790s Gothic novels, the framed object in question is a woman's face or body, at first a marker of real fear and terror, but soon undercut as a mistaken assumption. The crisis of interpretation surfaces with confusions surrounding what may be a female corpse, a living body, or an art object. Time and again, the fearsome corpse of a woman turns out not to be one at all—it is, instead, the body of a castle guard, or a painting, or a sculpture. The framing of women's bodies, the sudden fears they incite, and the ensuing marginalization of these fears, are all defining features of the Radcliffean "realist supernatural," in which paranormal workings are explained away through logical coincidences by the novel's end. Amidst these confusions are key reversals of meaning and symbol that exchange real terrors for fake ones, real flesh for facsimiles, bodies for art, and vice versa.

Claudia Johnson, in *Equivocal Beings*, assembles readings based on the last-minute switches of wounded bodies or corpses. What Emily in *Udolpho* fears is the injured body of her aunt turns out to be the body of a dispensable male castle guard. This easy switch from assumed female to male body betrays the "equivocal" nature of gendered bodies in Radcliffe's text; Johnson astutely problematizes this hasty dismissal of otherwise very real female fears of bodily harm.[15] The following discussion focuses not on the conflation of male and female bodies in such scenes of Gothic suspense, but rather on the fungibility between original and facsimile, flesh and wax, picture and person. In these scenes, the reader-viewer must negotiate switches between reality and art, or the picturesque and the sublime. I begin with two scenes from 1790s Gothic novels, explicating what I regard as the two most important scenes of suspense in *Udolpho* and *The Monk*.

Gothic Swap #1: From Flesh to Wax in Udolpho

The most obvious example of Gothic shock and swap surrounding an ambiguous body is that of Lady Laurentini in *The Mysteries of Udolpho*, the scene to which I have gestured earlier in this chapter and in its epigraph. Hidden in Udolpho Castle, her image is the site of the novel's climax when Emily, upon lifting the curtain, sees a rotted face and drops senselessly to the floor. Approaching this object of terror, Emily had expected a definitively Burkean experience of the Romantic sublime:

> This brought to her recollection the veiled picture, which had attracted her curiosity, on the preceding night . . . A terror of this nature, as it occupies and expands the mind, and elevates it to high expectation, is purely sublime, and leads us, by a kind of fascination, to seek even the object, from which we appear to shrink.[16]

What she experiences, however, is a moment of failed spectatorship; perhaps Emily sees, but her moment of interpretation is cut short, her sublime experience short-circuited by terror. Readers, as a result, do not get to "see" the spectacle at hand.

> Emily passed on with faltering steps, and having paused a moment at the door, before she attempted to open it, she then hastily entered the chamber, and went towards the picture, which appeared to be enclosed in a frame of uncommon size, that hung in a dark part of the room. She paused again, and then, with a timid hand, lifted the veil; but instantly let it fall—perceiving that what it had concealed was no picture, and before she could leave the chamber, she dropped senseless to the floor.[17]

After a series of successive, teasing clauses, Emily immediately faints, rendered "senseless" from her feminine oversensibility. Her interpretive agency is undermined when all she can tell is that this image is "no picture." Ostensibly, it is Emily's runaway imagination that imposes her own image upon the body of the female victim: she identifies with what she believes to be the remnants of Laurentini, imagining herself as the next victim to fall under Montoni's cruelty. In this moment epitomizing Gothic fear, Emily risks the transformation from living flesh to a hanging object—a transformation that Browning immortalizes decades later with the framed duchess hanging on the Duke of Ferrara's wall.

Leading up to this moment of shock are the Gothic sensation novel's trappings of female hysteria, victimization, and helplessness. As readers, we must suspend our curiosity for another four hundred pages, when the explanation is finally offered:

> on lifting it, there appeared, instead of the picture she had expected, within a recess of the wall, a human figure of ghastly paleness, stretched

at its length, and dressed in the habiliments of the grave. What added to the horror of the spectacle, was, that the face appeared partly decayed and disfigured by worms, which were visible on the features and hands. On such an object, it will be readily believed, that *no person could endure to look twice*. Emily, it may be recollected, had, after the first glance, let the veil drop, and her terror had prevented her from ever after provoking a renewal of such suffering, as she had then experienced. Had she dared to look again, her delusion and her fears would have vanished together, and she would have perceived, that the figure before her was not human, but formed of wax . . . This image was so horribly natural, that it is not surprising Emily should have mistaken it for the object it resembled . . .[18]

By reading her own face in the place of Laurentini's, imagining the possibility that she too may be killed and hung to rot as a trophy of Montoni's cruelty, Emily exerts interpretive powers of self-identification. In this sense, she views the framed picture as if it were a mirror: She is horrified by the sheer grotesqueness of the aesthetic object, but also reads her own vulnerability in the image. This fear of becoming yet another victimized woman generates the overwhelming emotional impetus for the plot of the second half of the novel. The scene thus opens up to a feminist reading centered around the Gothic protagonist's self-awareness of her role within a distinct literary tradition. We see here the self-reflexive use of Gothic clichés: the heroine momentarily adopts the perspective of a seasoned Gothic reader. Emily seems to exhibit the self-awareness of a character who knows all too well how Gothic heroines end up.

At the same time, the framed female body alters the dynamics of viewer and object. In its own subversive way, the body resists rather than attracts a gaze. Gothic encounters with framed women consistently seem to undermine the agency of female characters. Heroines who sigh and faint upon uncovering mysterious images play into a tradition of female hysteria and Gothic sensationalism. But by staging reversals of the real and the representational, the Gothic novel complicates this topos of the female as either a framed, viewed object or a fumbling, mistaken spectator. The switch of perspective suddenly objectifies the viewer instead, demoting him or her to a position devoid of control or mastery. This creates a dramatic shift in the power of the female's role as gazer and gazed-upon.

Radcliffe enlivens the terrible power of the un-beautiful female body as an object upon which "no person could endure to look twice." And though it is clearly a "spectacle," it relies on the realness of her representation ("it was so horribly natural") to be so horrible as to reject female objectification ("disfigured by worms"). It is because of its terrifying verisimilitude that the object wields power. Laurentini's image shuts down its own objectification by forcing others to turn away or faint from shock. Therein lies the power of the framed woman's body that is lifelike but dead, exerting control and repelling a gaze. The momentary shift from representation to reality grants power to the framed object over its viewers, modeling a familiar Gothic trope of unsightly fascination, from *Christabel* to *The Picture of Dorian Gray*.

But soon, yet another fluctuation arrives at the novel's end, when the full trajectory of Emily's alternating impressions culminates in still more confusion. While the framed image is, upon first expectation, a picture or painting, Emily is then shocked to discover that it is "no picture," but rotting flesh; only to learn, after, that the figure is indeed just an image.[19] Playing the role of panicked, flustered viewers, and lacking the certainty of an authoritative, male gaze, Emily and her servant Annette alternately debate whether the object in question is a picture or no picture: "'Are you sure it is a picture?' said Emily, 'Have you seen it?—Is it veiled?' 'Holy Maria! Ma'amselle, yes, no, yes. I am sure it is a picture—I have seen it, and it is not veiled!'"[20] The oscillation of Annette's "yes, no, yes" represents the shared experience of characters who *think* they have seen the framed figure but haven't, much like the novel's readers. When the real story behind the image is uncovered in Radcliffe's usual fashion of the explained supernatural, the Gothic reader experiences a final, suspending swap. We learn that the waxen image is merely an old instrument for penance commissioned by the family and the Catholic Church, serving as a precaution against "some other sins" that have nothing to do with Emily or her plot line.

> A member of the house of Udolpho, having committed some offense against the prerogative of the church, had been condemned to the penance of contemplating, during certain hours of the day, a waxen image, made to resemble a human body in the state, to which it is reduced after death. This penance, serving as a moment of the condition at which he must himself arrive, had been designed to reprove the pride of the Marquis of Udolpho, which had formerly so much exasperated that of the Romish church . . .[21]

Emily's hysterical suspicions are dispelled. The extended narrative suspension, stretching two hundred pages, finally ends. The reader's suspension of disbelief is rewarded with explanations of the realist supernatural. But by now, much more than receiving a simple correction, the reader has been jostled back and forth and back again in a series of visual, epistemological fluctuations that challenge the ability to verify the truth as the veil is proverbially lifted each time: We go from picture, to "no picture," and back again to picture. The protracted process engenders a doubly disconcerting sense of instability, unacceptable in most narratives but typical of Gothic romance. This substantiates Terry Castle's monumental reading of *Udolpho* in *The Female Thermometer*, in which she recognizes confusion of the living and the dead as a part of what she calls "the spectralization of the other": "In the moment of Radcliffean reverie . . . the dead seem to 'live' again, while conversely, the living 'haunt' the mind's eye . . . Life and death—at least in the realm of the psyche—have become peculiarly indistinguishable."[22]

Certainly, the experience of the Gothic reader is one of consistent shock and re-evaluation. The plight of the Gothic reader, and also, I argue, of the Gothic heroine, is a crisis of her interpretative powers, or her potential failure to distinguish real corpses from mere pictures, the real from the representational. The successful Gothic reader, who is necessarily also a spectator of art objects, is thus one who can navigate sudden, repeated switches and swaps. He or she negotiates responses of terror and horror, pain and pleasure, suspense and relief. Put simply, the Gothic novel features objects cast in suspended animation—bodies, faces, or paintings—that then induce a similar reaction in the characters that confront them. They become, in turn, frozen and suspended too.

Gothic Swap #2: From Madonna to Matilda, Saint to Sorceress, in The Monk

The second example of Gothic "swap and shock" surrounding a framed female figure comes from Matthew Lewis's *The Monk*. At the beginning of the novel, the ostentatious though much-admired Father Ambrosio toes the line between religious zeal and lustful indecency in the way that he worships a detailed painting of the Madonna:

> "Yet hold! . . . Am I not a Man, whose nature is frail, and prone to error? . . . The fairest and noblest Dames of Madrid continually present themselves at the Abbey, and will use no other Confessor. I must accustom my eyes to Objects of temptation, and expose myself to the seduction of luxury and desire. Should I meet in that world which I am constrained to enter some lovely Female, lovely . . . as you Madona . . .!"

As he said this, He fixed his eyes upon a picture of the Virgin, which was suspended opposite to him: This for two years had been the Object of his increasing wonder and adoration. He paused, and gazed upon it with delight.

"What Beauty in that countenance!" He continued after a silence of some minutes; "How graceful is the turn of that head! What sweetness, yet what majesty in her divine eyes! How softly her cheek reclines upon her hand! Can the Rose view with the blush of that cheek? Can the Lily rival the whiteness of that hand? Oh! if such a Creature existed, and existed but for me! Were I permitted to twine round my fingers those golden ringlets, and press with my lips the treasures of that snowy bosom! . . . Never was Mortal formed so perfect as this picture."[23]

A staggering mix-up is revealed when Ambrosio learns that the framed image is not simply a picture of the Virgin Mary, but actually a portrait modeled after the seductress Matilda.[24] While the monk is lying sick on his deathbed, he overhears Matilda confessing her love for him and her libidinous hopes that Ambrosio might gaze with admiration upon her own fleshly body in the same way he worships the Madonna: "With what pleasure He views this picture! With what fervor He addresses his prayers to the insensible image! Ah!"[25] The Madonna transforms from a picture or object into a living, breathing figure of power and agency. At this moment, Ambrosio awakens from his sickly stupor and demands a full explanation from Matilda. She confesses:

> Accident has made you Master of a secret, which I never would have revealed but on the Bed of death. Yes, Ambrosio; In Matilda de Villanegas you see the original of your beloved Madona. Soon after I conceived my unfortunate passion, I formed the project of conveying to you my Picture: Crowds of Admirers had persuaded me that I possessed some beauty, and I was anxious to know, what effect it would produce upon you. I caused my Portrait to be drawn by Martin Galuppi, a celebrated Venetian at that time resident in Madrid. The resemblance was striking: I sent it to the Capuchin-Abbey as if for sale, and the Jew from whom you bought it, was one of my Emissaries. You purchased it. Judge of my rapture, when informed, that you had gazed upon it with delight, or rather with adoration; that you had suspended it in your Cell, and that you addressed your supplications to no other Saint. . . . I heard you daily extol the praises of my Portrait: I was an eyewitness of the transports, which its beauty excited in you.[26]

Upon learning of Matilda's "perfidy," Ambrosio soon spirals into a relationship of sexual enslavement with her, leading to his patterned behavior of rape, incest, and murder. As Patrick O'Malley describes it, Ambrosio "moves seemingly inexorably from a masturbatory adulation of a portrait of the Virgin Mary to the incestuous rape and murder of his sister on the church grounds themselves."[27]

In *The Monk*, the framed picture of a woman's face serves as a momentous site of confusion, corruption, and last-minute disavowal. The sudden exchange of the Madonna for Matilda inverts symbolic meaning at a moment's notice: What was the artistic depiction of a saint, no longer living but erotically regarded, becomes a locus of sexual desire for a female who is not only alive, but present, breathing, and ready to reciprocate. Moreover, Matilda has been watching Ambrosio's every move from close quarters under disguise as a monk-in-training. Here, unlike in *Udolpho*, the swap occurs from representation to reality, and the power of pornography and the control of the gaze is quickly handed over to Matilda, who makes Ambrosio succumb to her surveillance and her seductive powers.

The portrayal of Matilda as the villain at the beginning of the novel no doubt feeds into a politics of placing blame on female characters, familiar from the misogynistic archetypes of the witch or whore. This idea of the temptress preying upon a weak man, in the tradition of an Eve or Lilith figure, can be used to exculpate Ambrosio. Matilda's machinations are what unleash Ambrosio's otherwise repressed sexuality and sets him off on a tailspin of deceit, irreligiosity, and sexual addiction. The theme of woman as original sinner will reappear in discussions of Rossetti's paintings and poems in the next section, particularly of "Lady Lilith."

Paradoxically, the moment of discovery exposing Matilda as a villain in *The Monk* is also a thematically empowering one. Matilda exploits Ambrosio's religious zeal to fuel female authority. And by turning religious worship on its head, she exposes Ambrosio's sanctimoniousness more than her own. She manipulates male admiration and in so doing, frames the female body and its charms, exerting authorial control; she draws on the power of her image, harnessing the power of both the sublime and what I call "the Gothic picturesque"—an aesthetic explored in depth in the following section.

The fluctuations continue still, and Ambrosio's shock in *The Monk* does not end here. It is thereafter discovered that Matilda has been in the proximity of the monk all along, disguised as his apprentice, Rosario. Matilda not only exerts her mastery over Ambrosio in the form of artwork, she has donned male garb and furtively seduced him in person. By the end of the novel, Rosario/Matilda is revealed as neither male nor female, but as a sexless demon sent by Lucifer to seduce Ambrosio.[28] The sudden changes from Madonna to Matilda to Rosario in *The Monk* prove terrifying because each of the three iterations of her image subjugates this man in different ways: he first falls in love with a picture of the Madonna, then learns that this image is actually Matilda, and finally learns that Matilda is actually Rosario, his apprentice and ward. Each time, it is in fact Ambrosio who has been the watched figure, an object of Matilda's surveillance and manipulative gaze. These reversals in framing grant sublime powers to Matilda's image. Ambrosio's descent into villainy eventually launches him into an exultant state, a mode of the sublime where he experiences rapturous torrents of lust and malevolence. Yet, as this section has shown, his sublime evil on the scale of lurid Male Gothic stems from a single picture—a powerful image of the Gothic picturesque, painted by a male artist (Martin Galuppi), but orchestrated by a female mastermind (Matilda).

A Detour through the Lake District: Sublime, Picturesque, and the Gothic Picturesque

In his 1794 review of *Udolpho* for *The Critical Review*, Samuel T. Coleridge commends Radcliffe for her incorporation of "picturesque scenes of terror." He quotes at great length scenes in which terror is framed and anticipated, but all expectation is then thwarted after a final twist of the plot.[29] To connect the picturesque with terror is especially provocative, for the affective reactions of viewers to each are typically opposite. The sublime is ineffable; it takes control of a person, lifting one up to ennobling heights through the mysterious majesty of nature. Sublime landscapes can induce an expansion of the soul, followed by a sense of self-diminution in the face of nature's grandeur. The picturesque, in contrast, can be framed and contained. Spectators and painters acquire a sense of mastery over the pictured landscape or object, achieving a neat satisfaction.

Radcliffe's literary theorizations were closer in concept to ideas of sublimity and terror, and her novels are well known for their explicit use of Burkean language in describing natural scenes. Her essay, "On the Supernatural in Poetry," written for the *New Monthly Magazine*, stages a conversation between Mr. W. and Mr. S., who debate about the role of sublimity and terror in the banquet scene of *Macbeth*. For Mr. W., "the gloomy and sublime kind of terror" found in the ghost of Banquo relies upon "the union of grandeur and obscurity, which Mr. Burke describes as a sort of tranquillity tinged with terror, and which causes the sublime."[30] The lofty terror of the sublime is reflected in the majestic mountains of the Alps, the Dolomites, and Apennines, unlike the picturesque of English countryside and Lake District.

The "picturesque," first theorized by William Gilpin and elaborated upon by Richard Payne Knight, Uvedale Price, and John Ruskin, was derived from the Italian "pittoresco," (of or like a painter). It was a term recruited from the visual arts that was applied widely at the turn of the eighteenth century to gardening, landscape architecture, travel and tourism, distinct "types" of female beauty, and literature. The picturesque became an aesthetic ideal that blossomed into an obsession, especially for travelers undertaking a continental version of the Grand Tour. It redefined the connection between tourism, nature, and art, converting the amateur tourist into a composer of scenes or images. The work of a picturesque traveler was not simply to reproduce nature, but to enhance it through advantageous composition. In fact, the picturesque is defined as a middling state, considered a safe, milder category mediating the binaries of Burke's beautiful and sublime.[31] As Knight wrote, drawing on the ideas of Price, the picturesque "ought to signify that middle style, which is not sufficiently smooth to be beautiful, nor sufficiently rough and elevated to be sublime."[32] It is thus curious for Coleridge to identify in Radcliffe's novel "picturesque scenes of terror," mixing the picturesque with the terrible or sublime. To coin the phrase "picturesque scenes of terror" is to join two terms that are seemingly at odds with one another, pairing a philosophy of the unviewable (like Milton's "Death" in *Paradise Lost*) with that which is meant to be seen as a picture would. And picturesque travel literature and painting, another pairing of the sister arts, shared strong associations with Gothic romance.

Picturesque travelers sought out the ruins of abbeys, castles, and other such scenes romanticized in Gothic novels or poems; as James Buzard reports, the most popularly carried texts other than guidebooks were the works of Madame de Stael and Lord Byron.[33] As this fad developed, however, the hordes of "picturesque hunters" who descended upon the English countryside to capture idyllic views, pencils in hand, became a source of ridicule. Gilpin's tour book was particularly popular among travelers to the Lake District who scoured the vales with their easels and viewfinders to paint the perfect picturesque picture.[34] By the Victorian era, "picturesque" was broadly conceived of as a disparaging term, meaning excessively showy. Thomas Maitland, shielded under the pen name Robert Buchanan, in fact levied the term in his attack on the Fleshly School. Citing Rossetti's failure to gracefully import his ideas from the medium of painting into poetry, he writes: "Poetry is something more than painting, and the idea will not become a poem, because it is too smudgy for a picture . . . There and here are glimpses of actual thought and insight, over and above the picturesque touches which belong to the writer's true profession." Of course, in Buchanan's estimation, Rossetti's true profession should have been painting, not poetry.[35] In general, the "picturesque" has been considered a pleasing aesthetic, but one applied to lesser artists, and not to masters of the grand style.[36]

The picturesque is an important aesthetic constitutive of 1790s Gothic on various levels. First, the picturesque and the Gothic novel shared thematic clichés of poverty, ancient ruins, banditti, and gypsies. (The thematic element of architectural ruins and background banditti were mainstays of picturesque paintings, particularly those by Salvatore Rosa and Claude Lorrain.)[37] Within the Gothic novel, picturesque descriptions of landscape include incredibly lengthy loco-descriptive passages of sheepfolds, cottages, and pastures against the backdrop of beautiful vistas or terrifying cliffs.[38]

Female characters in confinement often look out a casement window to behold landscapes of beauty that alternately include elements of the sublime and picturesque. Echoing Chapter 2, such moments become ridiculous through repetition, and the figure of the Gothic heroine waxing Romantic at a castle casement becomes a familiar, framed scene—itself picturesque. The castle or monastery window becomes an aperture or tool for framing these pretty scenes, akin to the viewfinder that touristic travelers and "picturesque hunters" carried in their easels as they sought out the perfect landscape.

Second, throughout the Gothic novel, women's bodies and faces become framed objects of sublime and picturesque terror, especially at pivotal moments of anticipation or suspense. Such examples of what I call the "Gothic picturesque"—often moments of great importance to the novel's plot—feature the machinery of terrible, sublime, or supernatural expectation, undercut by a moment of realization and deflation that reduces the framed image to something merely picturesque, evacuated of death or power. It is this latter instance that is the main interest of this chapter.

What exactly, then, are "picturesque scenes of terror" or the "Gothic picturesque"? I define the "Gothic picturesque" as an aesthetic in which framed figures, women especially, become loci of intrigue and symbolic confusion, causing the fearful and sudden alternation in a viewer's reactions, forcing one to bounce back and forth between sublime fear and picturesque pleasure. Characterized by a loss of control, experiencing the Gothic picturesque forces a viewer to constantly shift one's prior framework of interpretation and ultimately surrender to hermeneutic uncertainty. I utilize this concept of the "terrible picturesque," inspired by Coleridge, to label pivotal scenes in which the visual framing of bodies and faces, particularly those of women, result in misunderstandings and revelations of shock and swap. In fact, the plots of *Udolpho* and *The Monk* are propelled by key moments of mystery and expectation surrounding sites of ambiguous framing by a picture frame, curtain, mirror, sheet, or veil. These climactic scenes all employ the Gothic picturesque.

What is the function of Gothic picturesque, or of "picturesque scenes of terror"? The picturesque is meant to capture detail to bring pleasure to viewers, whereas terror is produced through obscurity and darkness. This merging of terrible obscurity with picturesque detail thus poses a contradiction, uniting that which we turn away from with that which brings pleasure through specificity. The pleasure in approaching a "picturesque" scene of terror is the anticipation and excitement in approaching a framed object that is also, paradoxically, unviewable. The practice of *framing* the terrible or the sublime makes Burkean horror more palatable, rendering it picturesque and even delightful to our curiosity. "Picturesque scenes of terror" in fiction and poetry are thus images that serve as an anticipated locus for terrible or sublime expectation, made manageable through framing by a casement, curtain, or veil. When these objects of framed terror are women's bodies, this invites serious questions surrounding the threatening relationship of Gothic female figures to beauty and terror in the nineteenth century.

Matilda's sudden transformation from objectified image to living mistress in *The Monk*—or picturesque scenes of terror more generally—offers a way to reinterpret the many framed women in Pre-Raphaelite picture poems, particularly those of D. G. Rossetti. The ambiguity of female figures as guilty women or luckless victims is a central theme in many of Rossetti's framed paintings, from "Jenny" to "Found" (1869).[39] Poems such as "Lady Lilith," "Sibylla Palmifera," "Astarte Syriaca," and "Proserpina" are paired with paintings that accentuate these women in all their fleshliness, accentuating their sensuality as powerful seductresses or mythological figures. Like Lewis's Matilda/Madonna, the female face in Pre-Raphaelite paintings becomes framed and worshipped as both an aesthetic ideal and as a realist representation of a fleshly woman. Relying on the dualities of saint or seductress, madonna or whore, innocent or guilty, holy or satanic, Radcliffe's "explained supernatural" models the machinery of shock and surprise later recruited in Rossetti's "realist symbolism" of the so-called "fleshly school." Understanding a reader's hermeneutic confusions around the Matilda/Madonna image and surrounding "picturesque scenes of terror" equips us to more aptly consider the readers' responses of sublimity and ennoblement, of suspension and paralysis in Rossetti's late-career double works.

Suspension, Suspense, Pleasure, and Pain: Gothic Reader Response

The two previously discussed examples of swap and shock from Radcliffe and Lewis each model the affective discombobulation imposed upon Gothic readers: they are first made fearful, then regain solace after the evacuation of their fears, only to be disabused of both perceptions. The ultimate result of Laurentini's picture-to-flesh-to-wax evolution is the utter distrust of one's own interpretive powers. Beyond simple misinterpretation lies the dangerous impossibility of truthful interpretation at all. Here I draw on the work of Anne C. McCarthy, whose *Awful Parenthesis* explores the key role of suspension in the development of the sublime, from Romantic to later Victorian works. As a constitutive component of the sublime, suspension is both "paralysing and enabling, absorbing and jarring." Coleridgean suspension in particular marks a crucial discontinuity in a world "that cannot be fully recovered or resolved."[40] From this perspective, suspension becomes "the paradigmatic posture for meeting a world of 'constitutive discontinuity,'" a discontinuity which, I posit, is exemplified within a Gothic setting.[41]

McCarthy's connection between suspension and the sublime is beautifully typified in Radcliffe's *Udolpho*, where the unveiling of the terrible picture becomes a locus for suspension. Suspension manifests in three distinct but interrelated ways: First, the figure of Lady Laurentini is a female body in suspended animation—either a preserved corpse or a waxen figure. Upon viewing the object, Emily St. Aubert, too, immediately enters a state of imperception, becoming the second female body in a suspended condition: while gazing at a piece of artwork, in her attempt at interpreting it, her body too becomes marked by stasis and a stoppage of time. McCarthy offers two useful theorizations of artistic perception as suspended states, from Victor Shklovsky and Jonathan Crary, respectively: "A work is created 'artistically' so that its perception is impeded and the greatest possible effort is produced through the slowness of perception. As a result of this lingering, the object is perceived not in its extension in space, but, so to speak, in its continuity."[42] "The state of being suspended [is] a looking or listening so rapt that it is an exemption from ordinary conditions, that it becomes a suspended temporality, a hovering out of time . . ."[43] Finally, Emily is denied this moment of artistic interpretation, for upon seeing the image, she drops senseless to the floor, yielding our third instance of a body in suspension.

The literary trope of the fainting maiden, physically overwhelmed by sensation, is prevalent in Gothic and Victorian texts alike, from *Christabel* to Lucy in *Villette*.[44] Throughout *Udolpho*, Emily St. Aubert faints several times upon uncovering various corpses: "When her sense returned . . . the extreme languor of her spirits did not permit her to speak, or move, or even to feel any distinct fear."[45] Gothic romance is littered with the suspended bodies of fainting, dead, or framed women. For McCarthy,

> The suspended animation of a beloved female body—and the ending of that suspension in a return to life ([is] here implicitly distinguished from the continuation of that suspension into death) . . . The image of the fainting woman and its sense of domestic spectacle—[signals] a dislocation so profound that definitive reading becomes impossible . . .[46]

Matilda's face, frozen in posterity as a Madonna painted by Galuppi, also serves as an image in suspension, an unreadable and mistakenly interpreted female body.

It is important to note that Emily is only afforded two modes of response to the image of Laurentini: either interpretation or unconsciousness. Both are characterized by immobility or fixation. In fact, it is the very moment of interrupting this suspended state of sublime terror that would allow for true perception, resulting in a clarification of the real-representational dilemma: "Had she dared to look again, her delusion and her fears would have vanished together, and she would have perceived, that the figure before her was not human, but formed of wax."[47] To break the trance of paralyzing fear would be the only way for Emily to truly see. As McCarthy reminds us, suspension is "both paralyzing and enabling, absorbing and jarring."[48]

But what happens when the female body awakens from shock or comes to life is of utmost importance? Thomas De Quincey's essay "On the Knocking at the Gate in *Macbeth*" famously theorizes the potency of interruption after a period of suspended consciousness, drawing on one of Shakespeare's most Gothic plays:

> We must be made sensible that the world of ordinary life is suddenly arrested—laid asleep—tranced—racked into a dread armistice; time must be annihilated; relation to things without abolished; and all must pass self-withdrawn into a deep syncope and suspension of earthly passion . . . When the deed is done, when the work of darkness is perfect, then the world of darkness passes away like a pageantry in the clouds: the knocking at the gate is heard; and it makes known audibly that the reaction has commenced: the human has made its reflux upon the fiendish; the pulses of life are beginning to beat again; and the re-establishment of the goings-on of the world in which we live, first makes us profoundly sensible of the awful parenthesis that had suspended them.

De Quincey also narrates the return to ordinary life in feminine terms: "If the reader has ever witnessed a wife, daughter, or sister, in a fainting fit, he may chance to have observed that the most affecting moment in such a spectacle, is *that* in which a sigh and a stirring announce the recommencement of suspended life."[49] A woman's revival from unconsciousness, this moment of resuming life after a suspension of consciousness, is the bread and butter of every Gothic damsel who encounters picturesque scenes of terror at each castle turn.

Yet in the passages of Gothic picturesque that I explore, this witching hour, the key moment of being awoken from a state of suspension or sleep, is only the first step in a series of constant fluctuations. It is one thing to wake up from a Gothic dream and return to normalcy after a sudden fright; it is another to be relegated to a space of constant oscillation between one reality and the next with no finality nor stability. As we have seen earlier, the alternation between real and representational—with no markers to distinguish nightmare from reality—defines the Gothic reading experience. If the grating of carriage wheels or the reassuring embrace of a recently fainted maiden are moments that jog our consciousness into a realization of our previous suspended state, then what a Gothic world threatens is the absence of such grounding effects. The return to life, which De Quincey and McCarthy so aptly emphasize, is no return to the ordinary. Gothic characters—and Gothic readers—forever seek the navigational tools to distinguish illusions of terror from real life. There is no guarantee of a return to the ordinary, only a perpetual state of oscillation from which one can never find rest of interpretation until the novel finally ends.

What physiological and psychological toll does such suspense and suspension take on Gothic readers? To answer this question, I turn to an early theorization of narrative suspense as it functions within the Gothic. A 1773 essay by siblings John and Anna Laetitia Aikin (better known to us today as Anna Laetitia Barbauld) accounts for the pleasure that Gothic stories afford their readers. In their essay on terror, the Aikins distinguish between the gradual, prolonged "pain of suspense" one endures while reading a Gothic novel, and the acute pain of being terrified at a certain moment in the plot. Aikin and Aikin map out a difference of whether readers derive pleasure or pain from "terrible objects."

> How are we then to account for the pleasure derived from such objects? I have often been led to imagine that there is a deception in these cases; and that the avidity with which we attend is not a proof of our receiving real pleasure. *The pain of suspense, and the irresistible desire of satisfying curiosity, when once raised, [fuels] our eagerness to go quite through an adventure, though we suffer actual pain during the whole course of it*. We rather chuse to suffer the smart pang of a violent emotion than the uneasy craving of an unsatisfied desire. That this principle, in many instances, may involuntarily carry us through what we dislike, I am convinced from experience. This is the impulse which renders the poorest and most insipid narrative interesting when once we get fairly into it; and I have frequently felt it with regard to our modern novels, which, if lying on my table, and taken up in an idle hour, have led me through the most tedious and disgusting pages, while, like Pistol eating his leek, I have swallowed and execrated to the end. And it will not only force us through dullness, but through actual torture . . . When children, therefore, listen with pale and mute attention to the frightful stories of apparitions, we are not, perhaps, to imagine that they are in a state of enjoyment, any more than the poor bird which is dropping into the mouth of the rattlesnake—they are chained by the ears, and fascinated by curiosity.[50]

Here, reading Gothic texts is likened to physically excruciating experiences: Pistol swallowing and execrating his leek, and the bird descending into the mouth of the rattlesnake. But in the examples cited in this chapter, the Gothic reader is not rewarded for his or her pain with just a single pang of pleasure. Instead, this "torture" is experienced successively. The fluctuation of pain, pleasure, and their retraction are experienced many times. Relief does not arrive just once. That movement from pain to pleasure, from suspension to realization to realized mistakenness, creates a chain effect of oscillations that I recognize as central to the Gothic readership.

The function of the Gothic picturesque is to frame sites of terror, in order to delimit the sublime and lessen the disgust or pain which can be, in the Aikins' words, akin to eating leeks. But entangling the sublime and the picturesque in such scenes creates precisely that dynamic instability experienced in Gothic shock and swap. Looking back to *Udolpho*, Emily's apprehension in approaching the veiled object rebounds between expectations of the picturesque (what picture lies behind the veil?), to suspension and the sublime (paralysis from fear of a corpse), to the sublime (it is no picture!), and back to relief (it is but a picture). Similarly, in *The Monk*, the Madonna-Matilda-Rosario transformations elicit successively shocking reactions from Ambrosio, from aesthetic superficial admiration, to disgust, to deep and utter worship. Through these picturesque-sublime-picturesque switches, Gothic authors manufacture the reader's suspension of disbelief in a way that does not elicit "stuplimity," what Sianne Ngai identifies as a sense of numbness, awe, and boredom—or "the whatever factor."[51] Instead, Gothic readers are forced to accept the fungibility between real-life female bodies and artistic replications of them.

Over the course of the novel, a reader, like a Gothic heroine, is expected to be flexible when meaningful details are replaced with new information; or when initial assumptions are dispelled as his or her own misinterpretations or oversensitivity. The reader must surrender himself or herself to constantly exchanging symbolic image for arbitrary detail, and vice versa. A Gothic world is one in which beauty constantly shifts between the picturesque and the terrible sublime, the pleasurable and the painful. Readers' bodies run the gamut of affective responses to these ever-changing figures: between states of suspended interpretation and stillness (dilated eyes; bated breath; blood frozen in veins) and frenzied stimulation (chills running down the back; hair standing on end). Rossetti's female bodies, which seem alternately artistic and fleshly, also fluctuate between the picturesque and the sublime.

* * *

This chapter began with an investigation into the Gothic trope of "shock and swap" in two pivotal scenes: climactic moments of the "realist supernatural" from *The Mysteries of Udolpho* and from *The Monk*. Analyzing readers' reactions to this Gothic trope, I now apply this as a framework with which to read the appearance of Victorian women's bodies, framed and frozen with an arresting gaze, in the later works of Dante Gabriel Rossetti. His picture poems exemplify a union of the bodily and symbolic, which read against "realist symbolism" and the "realist supernatural," demonstrates the important afterlife of Gothic reading practices even in appreciating later Pre-Raphaelite works of the 1860s and 1870s.

Building upon aesthetic concepts from Gothic theory and Romantic landscape painting, I read Rossetti's double works of art to develop an affective theory of reading nineteenth-century poem paintings that simultaneously pose as literature and art objects. Using theorizations of the sublime and picturesque, terror and horror, Female and Male Gothic, pain and pleasure, suspense and suspension, I draw on discussions of the Aikins, Burke, and De Quincey, and contemporary critics Anne McCarthy, Claudia Johnson, Frances Ferguson, and Terry Castle. The stakes of these readings are to re-envision what might be understood as a kind of formal violence performed upon the reader—with its sudden shocks and pulls—and to appreciate the flexibility and fungibility demanded of an assenting audience, thus redefining what it means to be a Gothic reader. Willing readers of "shock and swap," much like readers who willingly "suspend their disbelief," must surrender to a Gothic framework: they must admit the impossibility of recognizing the difference between realist and symbolic depiction, of illusion or the supernatural. A truly Gothic world exacerbates the difficulty of maintaining spectatorial control amid such representations. As Victorian Pre-Raphaelite artists famously wrestled with anxieties surrounding the impossibility of truthful representation that are "true to nature," we see this play out not only in their depictions of flora and fauna, but most starkly in their depictions of women's bodies.

The Art Gallery: Rossetti's Framed Women

Rossetti's framed women stand out for their seemingly physical warmth and palpability conveyed through realist depiction, but also for a jarring presence on the page that transcends the simple objectification of a woman's body. Like Gothic passages of female bodies in flux, these "fleshly" poems and paintings rely on a surfeit of details that embody both the corporeal and the spiritual. Such "double works" vacillate continually between portraying the female form in all its bodily detail or as a revered ideal. Approaching these works as a Gothic reader helps to make sense of the discomfort and uncanniness induced by Rossetti's painting-poems. The explained supernatural offers a model for ways in which audiences might also waver or fluctuate between different states, rather than simply cast this doubleness as ambivalence or aesthetic failure.

The main criticism of Rossetti, from both his contemporaries and critics of the past forty years, was predicated upon his strained commitments to symbol and flesh. Viewers underscored the discomfort stemming from the ambivalent straddling between aesthetic realism and artistic symbolism. Can we see the Venus figure in his paintings, wholly appreciating her mythological dimension, without discerning the familiar face of Alexa Wilding staring back at us? Is she goddess or woman, virgin or experienced model? Rossetti's figures suggest both, and the frustration with his "inconsistency" has fueled disparate criticism, from Robin Sheets's reading of "Jenny" as potential pornography, to Harold Weatherby and John McGowan's critiques that Rossetti fails to unite form and content, superstition and religiosity.[52] For Weatherby, a main weakness of "The Blessed Damozel" is "the problem of meaning in relationship to the reality or unreality of the supernatural . . . It is impossible to tell exactly what Rossetti expects you to believe or disbelieve, for the poem is neither fully committed to the supernatural . . . nor ironically detached."[53] Indeed, the negotiation between real-life fleshliness and other-worldly, symbolic meaning has often been cast in terms of aesthetic failure, or as an unholy objectification and worship of women.[54] For the Yale University Art Gallery's 1976 exhibit of "Rossetti's Double Works of Art," art historian Susan P. Casteras defined Rossetti's double works as pieces where "real-life features were infused with hallucinatory, abstract qualities in portraiture." In Rossetti's productions of the late 1860s especially, Casteras identifies "a barrier of self-conscious artifices" where "art seems to be mirroring art or a dream of life more than it reflects actual life."[55]

The double works' teeter-tottering between woman and dream vision, flesh and art, has furthermore been connected to Rossetti's megalomania and its misogynistic undertones. To Casteras, Rossetti's paintings are marked by his obsessive desire to seize the image—"to remember it, to love it, and to own it."[56] Rossetti's interest in certain female models betrays a strain of possessive narcissism, seen particularly in his strange self-identification with Elizabeth Siddal, whom he nicknamed "Guggums." With Siddal, Rossetti "fostered a curious symbiosis of passion and shared identity," to the extent that when he drew countless drawings of her in one sitting, his friend Ford Madox Brown was taken aback, noting in a diary entry that "Rossetti showed me a drawer full of 'Guggums': God knows how many . . . it is like a monomania with him."[57]

The sexual liaisons between artists and their "mistress-models" at Tudor House in the artists' district of Fitzroy Square in Chelsea are well documented, including trysts between Rossetti and Fanny Cornforth, on the one hand, and James McNeil Whistler and Joanna Hiffernan, on the other.[58] Rossetti biographers have used each model to symbolize a different phase in the artist's life, with Siddal representing his youth and idealism in the early 1850s, embodying Dante's Beatrice; Cornforth representing the opposite, vice over virtue, mistress over wife, in the later 1850s; and Jane Morris as a reconciliation of the two extremes in the later 1860s, "unit[ing] the spiritual with the sensuous, to heal the rupture in Rossetti's nature."[59]

Embodying Rossetti's uniform femme fatale type, Fanny Cornforth "brazenly stares out at the viewer," just as Jane Morris "gazes mesmerized at the beholder" in paintings like *Bocca Baciata, Fair Rosamund, The Blue Bower, Monna Vanna,* and *Astarte Syriaca*.[60] Carl Peterson locates a marked change in Rossetti's works after 1858 and 1859, noting that "all of the women based on various models share a trancelike, heavy-lidded expression and seem to beckon with overt sexual allure from within their crowded niches or from behind their parapet windows."[61] The proliferation of these "trancelike, heavy-lidded" women invites a Gothic reading approach to Rossetti's oeuvre. As Terry Castle writes of Gothic doubles and overlapping characters, such similitude compromises a natural world, contributing to the supernaturalization of the everyday: "When everyone else looks like everyone else, the limit between mind and world is again profoundly undermined, for such obsessive replication can only occur, we assume, in a universe dominated by phantasmic imperatives. Mirroring occurs in a world already stylized, so to speak, by the unconscious."[62]

David Riede recognizes elements of Gothic supernaturalism in Rossetti's poems such as "The Portrait," in which the portrait of his beloved is "miraculously lifelike," especially in line 440: "Gaze hard, and she shall seem to stir . . . I gaze, till I am sure / That I behold thee move."[63] Citing the picture *How They Met Themselves*, in which "a pair of lovers meet their doubles, outlined in light, in a wood at twilight—a sure presage of death," Riede writes that "Rossetti is having the supernatural both ways, using the Christian imagery of angels, and the gothic of doubles."[64] The presence of doppelgängers are frequent in Rossetti's later works where Christian imagery is increasingly secularized, most obviously in works based on Poe, such as *Ulalume* (1847–8) and his illustration to "The Raven," titled *Angel Footfalls* (1846).[65] The indistinguishability between copy and original shocked Henry James, who upon first meeting Jane Morris in March 1869, wrote, "When such an image puts on flesh and blood, it is an apparition of fearful and wonderful intensity. It's hard to say [whether] she's a grand synthesis of all the pre-Raphaelite pictures ever made—or they a 'keen analysis' of her—whether she's an original or a copy."[66]

We find elements of Gothic shock and swap even in Rossetti's compositional process and in his relationship with the models who sat for him. The artist's obsessive attachments with his models and his peculiarly flippant attitude towards swapping out their body parts on canvas display a problematic pattern for feminist scholars especially. Rossetti was known to use various models for a single painting, alternating between Alexa Wilding and Jane Morris in *La Pia d' Tolomei* (1868), between Wilding and Ellen Smith in *A Loving Cup* (1867), and painting Wilding's face over the features of a different "giantess," whom Rossetti had noticed on the street and asked to pose for *Venus Verticordia* (1867).[67] In 1872, he repainted his original 1864 painting *Lady Lilith* but with a different model. Even in this second version, he replaced the face of one model with another.[68] McGann's note on the production of the 1868 painting explains:

> Model: Fanny Cornforth
> Note: Begun in 1864 with Fanny Cornforth as the model; completed in 1868. Stephens' description was made of the picture in its original state, with Fanny Cornforth as the model.
> Model: Alexa Wilding
> Note: In 1872–3 when Rossetti repainted it at Kelmscott, the head of Alexa Wilding was substituted
> Repainting: 1872–3
> DGR replaced the original face, of Fanny Cornforth, with the face of Alexa Wilding.[69]

In his own version of Gothic body swaps, Rossetti creates a final product that coheres despite a series of surprises and corrections. Though he selected Fanny Cornforth as the original model, he then swapped her out for Alexa Wilding, whose head he used as a model in the second version eight years later—only to later replace Wilding's face with Cornforth's.

This cryptic practice echoes the disembodiment and dismemberment of women's body parts from the world of Gothic fiction. In his article "Rossetti's 'Jenny': Aestheticizing the Whore," Lawrence Starzyk recognizes Jenny as kindred to the Duke of Ferrara's Duchess, whom he deems "the most famous aestheticized object of Victorian culture."[70] Moreover, Rossetti's practice merges the legend of Zeuxis selecting models with the foundational text of Gothic creation: the converging of disparate body parts from separate select specimens recalls the graveyard constructions of Victor Frankenstein's creature. Still, the interchangeability in Rossetti's painting process does not so much promote a sense of equivalence between the women's bodies, faces, and heads; rather it insists on their difference and specificity.[71] More than the simple objectification of women's bodies, these constant replacements and reframings also exemplify the mode of fluctuation and vacillation that Rossetti underwent in his artistic conception of these works. Replacing Cornforth's head with Wilding's and Wilding's face with Cornforth's was of incomparable importance to Rossetti, in the same way that Emily's and our understanding of *Udolpho* is irrevocably altered when we learn that a body is wax, not rotting flesh. The symbolic details matter, as these Gothic-like body swaps attest to his commitment to symbolic realism.

* * *

Three features might be observed in Rossetti's 1860s double works: the engaging gaze of the female figures; their position near a window or mirror; and the meta-artistic themes in the accompanying poems. The following section explores four sets of paired poems and paintings that began as "Sonnets for Pictures" but were later included in *The House of Life*. These brief analyses pay special attention to the female gaze, windows, and mirrors—all defining aspects of Rossetti's double works of the 1860s—while borrowing ideas of suspension and sublimity, oscillation and fluctuation, and picturesque scenes of Gothic to navigate the reader-viewer's experience.

In the four paintings, *Proserpine*, *Astarte Syriaca*, *Lady Lilith*, and *Sibylla Palmifera*, as well as their accompanying poems, the featured women seem to come alive, taking on artistic agency and exhibiting a self-consciousness of their own place within a work of art. Each is each empowered by her outward gaze, which repositions the viewer of the painting as an object instead. In Rossetti's works, three elements of composition can work to short-circuit the male gaze of a female subject and its traditional power dynamics: A scene may be composed in which (1) the female figure looks out a window, gesturing to the outside; (2) she gazes outside of the painting's frame, recognizing a viewing audience outside of her plane; and (3) she gazes into a mirror, as if acknowledging her own status as a viewed object.[72] The practice of positioning framed women near window frames emphasizes their power as viewers themselves, not simply objectified figures, but figures of depth with viewing and interpretative powers. As Brian Donnelly argues, "What [Rossetti's] women know . . . is the implicit content of the answering gaze with which they confront anyone compelled to view or to read them."[73] This possibility of suddenly recasting the viewer as viewed object is a key feature of Rossetti's framed women paintings, which build upon the same heuristic of reading Gothic "shock and swap" where uncertainty and fear are most starkly produced through sudden changes in framing. Rossetti's painting-poems elicit gothically inflected responses from the reader/viewer, who is negotiating between affective experiences of suspension, shock, and sublimity. The framing, positioning, and gaze of each woman overturns expectations of viewer and viewed, artist and object. This effect is often produced by the painting's particular juxtaposition against the poem. As we will see, a reader might navigate elements of shock and swap in Rossetti's aesthetic by mediating between picture and poem, or between octave or sestet, in order to balance various readings without settling on just one.

Proserpina and "Proserpine"

It took Rossetti more than eight versions to depict the Roman goddess of fertility and crops to his satisfaction in the painting *Proserpine* (Figures 3.3 and 3.4). Forced to stay in the underworld with Pluto each winter, the figure of Proserpina (or Persephone) is associated with both confinement and abduction. At the same time, she is a figure of liminality, alternating between the underground and the earthly world each winter and spring, and serving as a guide between the living and the dead. Having tasted the pomegranate and eaten from the fruit of life, Proserpina is no longer a pure or virginal figure, but one edified by experience. She straddles two worlds and alternately serves as devoted wife and daughter, mother and maiden. The painting includes a window, but the leaves at the left of the window, posed against the objects on the table, confound any clear sense of what is indoors or outdoors. A backdrop of Earth or the underworld is difficult to discern in relation to the framed scene. Rather than

Gothic Shock and Swap 173

Figure 3.3 D. G. Rossetti, *Proserpine*, 7th Version, 1874, Tate Gallery, London

Figure 3.4 D. G. Rossetti, *Proserpine*, 7th Version, with frame, 1874, Tate Gallery, London

looking out through the window, Proserpina's gaze is subtly directed towards the direction of where the viewer or painter might be standing. If we are to consider the possibility of her looking out any window at all, it would be the frame of the painting itself. The name Proserpina, a Latinized form of the Greek "Persephone," comes from the verb "proserpere," meaning "to creep forward." While this may allude to the growth of crops blessed by the goddess of fertility, seen in the creeping ivy of Rossetti's composition, the impulse for crossing thresholds and encroaching forward is also captured in the body language of Proserpina, who seems to simultaneously draw back with her hands but lunge forward with an expression of longing or disdain.

The sublime and the picturesque converge in this painting. The goddess figure, Proserpine, is mythical, elevating, and sublime; but at the same time, Rossetti clearly sought to "improve upon nature" in the depiction of details layered on after painting the model's body. Similar to the women discussed in the passages of Radcliffe and Lewis, Proserpina is a body suspended in animation, trapped not solely in a confined location, but in a distinct space of liminality. The window on the left, the poem parchment painted on the top right corner, and Rossetti's signature scroll at the bottom underneath the incense bowl provide three rectangular fixtures to mark the limits of the painting. (The surrounding picture frame in Figure 3.4 offers yet another border that boxes her in.) In addition to this, the unnatural position of her arms makes her appear folded onto herself, as if crammed within the dimensions of the canvas. The hands are clasped in an unconventional position of restraint: one hand holds the pomegranate, while the other hand holds the opposite wrist. Her right hand even looks as if it could belong to someone else. The texture of her dress suggests its heaviness; it seems to impede easy movement. *Proserpine*, a painting in three-quarter length ratio, is not placed in a position of natural rest or movement, but instead wrapped and enfolded to fit, almost coffin-like, within the frame.

With its rich detail of tendrils, leaves, pomegranate, and incense bowl, Rossetti's work sends viewers into a back-and-forth negotiation between the realist symbols and symbolic meaning of the painting. Catherine Golden performs just this type of negotiation, ultimately deciding in her reading that "the pomegranate becomes less a symbol and more a literal object blending with the surrounding objects."[74] The model in this painting is very recognizably Jane Morris, who is fixated on a view of her own, holding a mesmerized and alluring gaze, "locked in a moment of reverie."[75] Her impression of uneasy suspension emanates from a body that is not at rest. The hands and chin point, like arrows, towards the pomegranate as the focal center of the painting, rather than her own face or body. The gaze is stern and intensely questioning. But it is also marked by evasion, as she deflects attention off to the left and forefront from the plane where she stands. Her eyes are not focused on an object within the painting, nor does she stare back directly at us. Instead, she is fixated uncomfortably on some middle plane, expanding the perspective of the painting from solely what we see to the very plane where we stand, undermining our authority as viewers and pointing to the liminality of her own position between two spatial planes.

The actual framing of the picture contributes to this self-consciousness of the female figure as a model or painting subject. That Proserpina seems to be looking out beyond the frame, outside, or to the side of it, as Jane Morris might have done while Rossetti was painting her, draws attention to the physical frame attached to this painting. The poem was inscribed on the canvas, as can be seen in the upper right-hand corner. Rossetti was aware that dealers often separated paintings from their frames and, to prevent this, he made it a practice to customize his frames by including verses from the corresponding poem. This particular painting was first accompanied by a sonnet in Italian, which Rossetti then translated to English, entitled "Proserpina (For a Picture)." The 1874 and 1877 versions of the painting include the full Italian sonnet inscribed on a frame, while the 1882 version includes the full sonnet in English inscribed on the canvas itself. The physically bound nature of the double work—a sonnet bound to a painting in its very frame—finds a symbolic parallel in the myth of Proserpina, who is confined within Pluto's underworld after she tastes the fruit.[76]

PROSERPINA
(FOR A PICTURE)

Afar away the light that brings cold cheer
    Unto this wall,—one instant and no more
    Admitted at my distant palace-door.
Afar the flowers of Enna from this drear
Dire fruit, which, tasted once, must thrall me here.
    Afar those skies from this Tartarean grey
    That chills me: and afar, how far away,
The nights that shall be from the days that were.

Afar from mine own self I seem, and wing
   Strange ways in thought, and listen for a sign:
   And still some heart unto some soul doth pine,
(Whose sounds mine inner sense is fain to bring,
Continually together murmuring,)—
   "Woe's me for thee, unhappy Proserpine!" [77]

In the opening lines of this poem, Proserpina's voice betrays the artistic knowledge of a painter or a seasoned model, whose understanding of "light," angles, "distan[ce]," background, and walls offers her an agency far beyond that of an aesthetic object. Her subtle delineation of a "Tartarean grey" reveals the artistic precision of one who perhaps understands the technical choices behind each expression. Moreover, line 5 rings with the self-consciousness of a woman who understands her own entrapment as punishment for having tasted of knowledge and irretrievably crossed a threshold: "this drear / Dire fruit, which, tasted once, must thrall me here."

While the octave offers a strong sense of visual self-consciousness, the sestet offers an astute aural sense of self-positioning and distancing, "listen[ing] for a sign," with "murmuring" and sounds heard by her "inner sense." This heightened self-awareness as an artistic object has not been lost on other readers. As Jerome McGann has noted, "The sestet of the sonnet then develops an uncanny sense that Proserpine is listening for the sounds and signs of the very poem she herself appears to be authoring/speaking, and hence that the final line is giving us Rossetti's words, here reported back from the underworld."[78] But Proserpina exhibits a doubled sense of self-consciousness too: she is trapped within a poem *and* a painting, locked into the symbolic imagery of her legend *and* the physicality of the picture frame. Meanwhile, throughout one's experience of the double work, the bodily reality of Jane Morris always threatens to subvert the mythic effect of the legend. Viewers are left in a state of suspension and indecision, negotiating the artistic depiction from fleshly body, recalibrating their gaze upon a flickering scene of representation and reality. We can already begin to see the sublime and the picturesque at work in Rossetti's double works.

The doubleness of the *Proserpina* picture-poem is further augmented by the fact that this poem is both a sonnet and a dramatic monologue. It is part of a lyric tradition that objectifies the woman as an idealized image and love object, as well as one that lends the speaker a distinct voice, character, and potential for dramatic action. Even the poem's title, "Proserpina: *For a Picture*" suggests the layered interiority and self-consciousness of a monologist playing a dramatic role (italics mine). The figure seems aware of herself as a sitting model, posing "for a picture" and framed by this tradition. Proserpina sees herself as an art object, as she says in the poem upon viewing her own image: "Afar from mine own self I seem."[79] Her awareness and self-distancing (markers of dramatic monologue speakers) is reinforced by the necessarily differentiated words so similar in meaning, "mine," "own," "self," and "I"—all which complement the protective stance and posturing in Rossetti's painting, along with her stern, guarded gaze.

Astarte Syriaca and "Astarte Syriaca"

The gaze of *Proserpine* is even more intensified in *Astarte Syriaca* (Figures 3.5 and 3.6), another painting for which Jane Morris

Figure 3.5 D. G. Rossetti, *Astarte Syriaca*, 1877, Manchester City Art Gallery, Manchester

Figure 3.6 D. G. Rossetti, *Astarte Syriaca*, with frame, 1877, Manchester City Art Gallery, Manchester

modeled. *Astarte Syriaca*, also titled *Venus Astarte*, is considered one of the most illustrious portraits of Morris executed by Rossetti, who here chose to represent her as the Mesopotamian goddess of fertility, sexuality, and war. While the sonnet is rife with biblical allusions from the Book of Revelation (17:5 "Babylon the Great, Mother of harlots and abomination of the earth" and 12:1 "woman clothed with the sun"), the painting is best known as a work that combines symbolic meaning and corporeal realism. The Venus figure before us poses an ideal representative of beauty, love, and godliness, but is also very recognizably the woman and model Rossetti's circle would have known as William Morris's wife. For William Michael Rossetti, *Astarte Syriaca* united the meanings of *Lady Lilith* and *Sibylla Palmifera*.[80] Dante Gabriel Rossetti had made two attempts at the painting, claiming he wasn't sure whether the British public could appreciate his "experiments in flesh-painting." He anticipated the reactions of critics like Theodore Watts-Dunton, who in his essay "The Truth About Rossetti" observed how "the corporeal part of man seemed more and more to be the symbol of the spiritual."[81] The bright skin and sinewy muscles, particularly in the arms of the three women, accentuate the corporeal and human basis of these bodies. Painted on a 182.8 x 106.5 inch canvas, the three-quarter length figure towers six feet high. W. M. Rossetti described his brother's decision to work at larger dimensions in this way: "He had aimed to make it equally strong in abstract sentiment and in physical grandeur."[82] At the same time, however, the Venus figure in the center is clearly more human and present than the transcendent figures that appear in lighter, diluted colors in the background. These two attendants operate on a higher plane and assume a more mythical position in the painting, flanking the protagonist to frame her image.[83] Astarte Syriaca, front and center, gazes directly out of the painting, as if staring at us, the viewer, while the other two gaze upwards, distantly above, towards the heavens.

This direct confrontation between Astarte Syriaca and the viewer creates a scenario similar to that we have seen in *Udolpho* and *The Monk*, where what we expect to be the framed, unknowing female figure looks back at us in return, as if recognizing her presence within the frame and threatening to invert the roles of gazer and gazed-upon. We might thus consider *Astarte Syriaca* an example of the "picturesque scenes of terror" or the "Gothic picturesque" discussed earlier, which short-circuit the audience's gaze. As in earlier scenes with Lady Laurentini and with Matilda, we recognize here a female body that simultaneously represents a real woman in all her fleshliness and a goddess as a mythological ideal. Jane Morris is a locus for sensuality, sexual confidence, and eroticism, at the same time that Astarte Syriaca or Venus serves as a metonymy for these female traits. Like a Gothic reader, a viewer of Rossetti's many Venus paintings necessarily experiences the bodily-artistic swaps staged by Radcliffe and Monk, where representations of legendary female characters cannot be removed from that familiar, knowing gaze of the models. In this particular painting, the Venus figure seems ready to step out of the picture and into our plane, her legs poised in an almost warlike stance, ready to take a stride forward and leave the realm of the two attendants behind her. At first, we can consider the framed woman—both model and painted subject—as a body suspended in animation. But her potential movement in turn freezes the viewer in a state of suspension, as we evaluate the woman staring out at us from the painting. This challenge of interpretation poses the question of De Quincey's *Macbeth*: What happens at the moment when life resumes? What happens when Astarte Syriaca strides out of the painting and her two attendants are unfrozen?

Many critics have already undergone some version of Gothic shock and swap, negotiating reality and artifice in their analyses and readings of Rossetti's double works. Meaning and context changes based on reading sequence, for instance, depending on whether one approaches the painting first and the accompanying painting second, or vice versa. Focusing on certain portions of the sonnet—the octave versus sestet—also changes the balance and emphasis of the poem's relative "fleshliness," in cases where Rossetti selectively inscribed certain verses onto his frames. *Astarte Syriaca* provides an interesting case study because of the importance of the physical frame to this painting, which Rossetti designed himself and to which he also appended lines from his sonnet.

ASTARTE SYRIACA
(FOR A PICTURE)

Mystery: lo! betwixt the sun and moon
    Astarte of the Syrians: Venus Queen
    Ere Aphrodite was. In silver sheen
Her twofold girdle clasps the infinite boon
Of bliss whereof the heaven and earth commune:
    And from her neck's inclining flower-stem lean
    Love-freighted lips and absolute eyes that wean
The pulse of hearts to the spheres' dominant tune.

Torch-bearing her sweet ministers compel
    All thrones of light beyond the sky and sea
    The witnesses of Beauty's face to be:
That face, of Love's all-penetrative spell
Amulet, talisman, and oracle,—
    Betwixt the sun and moon a mystery.[84]

In an important 1988 reading of Rossetti's double works as analogous to his famous "two-sided coin," Catherine Golden demonstrates the ways in which the meaning — in particular, the fleshliness — of *Astarte Syriaca* alters: when contextualized with just the painting itself, when paired with the sestet of the accompanying sonnet, or when read against the octave of the sonnet.[85] While a full sonnet was attached to the canvas of *Proserpine*, only a portion of the sonnet "Astarte Syriaca: For a Picture" is attached to the base of the frame that Rossetti designed for the painting. This is significant because the excluded octave emphasizes the eroticism of the Syrian goddess's figure, while the sestet offers the flip side of the coin, emphasizing her face and gaze. As Golden observes, the accompanying sonnet "saves the picture from erotica by immediately informing us that the female subject is the goddess of fertility, sexual love, and the moon." Thus, while the sestet contextualizes Jane Morris's body within legend and tradition, rehabilitating the painting from pure fleshliness, Golden considers the painting alone to be "an overly erotic portrait."[86] Because the appended octave of the sonnet accentuates this eroticism, the figure of Astarte Syriaca can appear overwhelmingly fleshly when judged without the full sonnet. Moreover, Golden's reading reveals that one cannot read a painting and a poem at the same time. One must come before the other, and this sequencing makes inevitable the oscillation of our reading response. Golden's reading of the two-sided coin (like the coins depicted on Rossetti's gold-colored frames) parallels the Matilda/Madonna divide. A reader and viewer's experience thus fluctuates, much like Ambrosio and Emily's do in the Gothic novel when confronted with "picturesque scenes of terror." All the meanwhile, the female figure's gaze upon us is locked in a fixed, commanding stare, a stark counterpoint to her viewer's state of interpretive instability. To reconcile the sublimity and picturesque elements of Astarte Syriaca/Jane Morris's image is a disorienting affective experience.

Recruiting Gothic language to describe "Astarte Syriaca," the French critic Théodore Duret, in his review for the *Gazette des Beaux-Arts*, surrenders to her power of fascination and identifies this woman as an image of terror:

> a colossal being, having on a large neck a head strongly accentuated, with salient lips and an enormous head of luxuriant hair. This creature, a kind of sibyl, siren, or melusine, has none of the delicate graces of woman; she is nonetheless very living and, when one has gazed at her for some time, she becomes unforgettable; she exercises a kind of fascination, but mixed with inquietude; one is afraid to come too close to her, one fears that if she took you by the arms, she would make your bones crack.

Duret conceives of Astarte Syriaca as a Frankensteinian creature, beginning with the "enormous head of luxuriant hair," and ending in fear of his own physical destruction. In between, though, is a fearful recognition of her female powers of fascination. What physical reactions do we experience in response to the poem's depictions of her "inclining neck," "love-freighted lips," "absolute eyes," and "two-fold girdle [that] clasps the infinite boon / Of bliss"? The terror then, inherent in the challenge of Rossetti's model's pose, is the dubious question of how, at the key De Quinceyan moment, life will resume. In both the painting and the poem versions of *Proserpine* and *Astarte Syriaca*, a particular attention to the frame and framing yields sudden shifts in perspective, authority, and agency—sending the reader/viewer in a series of suspended fluctuations.

In Rossetti's double works, as in the two examples of Gothic shock and swap from Radcliffe and Lewis, the pictured object exerts control over the viewer. The "picturesque" object surprisingly dominates the spectator in sublime fashion, while the surrender of the Gothic reader—one's loss of power over a visual object or textual character—exemplifies one of the many upsetting reversals of Gothic shocks and swaps.

* * *

The final pair of double works I will investigate is Rossetti's poem based on the painting *Lilith* (Figures 3.7 and 3.8), followed by his poem based on the 1866 painting *Sibylla Palmifera* (or *Venus Palmifera*) (Figures 3.9 and 3.10). Each poem accompanying the paintings had alternate titles: "Body's Beauty" was also called "Lady Lilith"; "Sibylla Palmifera: For a Picture" (1870) was published as "Soul's Beauty" in 1881. The two sonnets appended to the paintings came to be incorporated in *The House of Life* as Sonnets 77 and 78, respectively. "Body's Beauty" seems to represent the aesthetic and fleshly side of Rossetti's works, while the figure in "Soul's Beauty" embodies deeper meaning and purity. Yet it is clear that these double works were not meant for simplistic moralizing, so simply contrasting two allegorical women. Instead, the layered representations of each woman through both poem and painting reveal her ability to be far more than just body or soul. Rossetti again imbues both figures with the potentiality for artistic agency and an uncanny consciousness of her own place within a framed work.

The two paintings appear to embody the familiar Victorian dichotomy between Madonna and Magdalena, wife and whore; yet as Prettejohn suggests, "the symbols of virtue and vice are oddly assorted between the two images [such that] Rossetti's pictures also

Figure 3.7 D. G. Rossetti, *Lady Lilith*, 1866–8 (altered 1872–3). Oil on canvas 39x34 in., Delaware Art Museum, Samuel and Mary R. Bancroft Memorial, 1935

refuse to offer a clear choice."[87] The "rose and poppy," virginal white dress, white daisies, white roses, red roses, red robe, and veil complicate any reductive message of spiritual purity or sensual love.

Lady Lilith *and "Body's Beauty"*

In almost every aspect of this painting, Lilith presents as a highly aestheticized subject surrounded by objects that accentuate or reference her beauty. Positioned idly in a dressing room brushing her hair, she is surrounded by decorative items that clutter the space around her.

Figure 3.8 D. G. Rossetti, *Lady Lilith*, 1866–8 (altered 1872–3). Oil on canvas 39x34 in., frame: 53 ¼ x 48 in., Delaware Art Museum, Samuel and Mary R. Bancroft Memorial, 1935

The braided tassel around her wrist, the necklace or garland on her lap, as well as the flowers below, above, and in front of her contribute to a feeling of overcrowding. The flowers and trees, again blurring the distinction between indoors and outdoors, serve as decoration and adornment. The sumptuous bare shoulders and exposed skin under her white gown, blending into the white blanket underneath her, all contribute to a central image of uniform color. Any distinction among body, clothing, and blanket is only delineated through differences in texture, demanding an intimate proximity between picture and viewer. Lilith, representing "Body's Beauty," personifies vanity as she contemplates her own reflection and admires her painted lips and long, luscious locks.

The folklore surrounding Lilith is alternately a source of misogynistic or feminist inspiration. Lilith is villainized as the original temptress, a woman who abandoned her role as Adam's partner and came to be portrayed as the ultimate seductress, accused of sexual incontinence and even infanticide. This murderess, described in letters to Rossetti as a "queen of the demons," depicted a "Modern Lilith" exhibiting a supernatural kind self-fascination: "a *Modern Lilith* comb[s] out her abundant golden hair and gaz[es] on herself in the glass with that complete self-absorption by whose fascination such natures draw others within their circle."[88] At the same time, she is a subversive figure, even more so than Milton's Eve. Created from the Earth as man was, she claimed equal footing as one of God's direct creations. As with Matilda in *The Monk* and Jane Morris in various Rossetti paintings, female beauty is both an incriminating feature and a source of power and agency for women. Griselda Pollock's pivotal feminist rereadings of Rossetti's art in *Vision and Difference* (2005) reaffirm the symbolic references of the feminine as powerful reinforcements of the male gaze, which complement readings of Lilith as the first female rebel and, as "the first strong-minded woman . . . the original advocate of women's rights."[89]

In terms of Rossetti's compositional technique, this painting again includes a window in the background, from which Lilith chooses not to look outside. Nor does she seem to gaze out of the painting's frame in a way that challenges the viewer objectifying her body. Instead, Lilith looks into a smaller frame of a different sort: the mirror she holds, with which she can control the composition and perspective in her view. With a twitch of her hand, Lilith might alter the angle of the image she sees and of the painting she inhabits, cropping and framing her own face or figure as an artist might do to his model. Brush in hand, she might even alter the details of the framed female subject: she can comb her hair and can adjust the content of the image. The damsel-like maiden contemplating her own beauty is an oft-used trope in paintings by Rossetti's circle, including Simeon Solomon's *The Toilette of a Roman Lady* (1869), Aubrey Beardsley's *The Toilette of Salome* (1893), (an illustration of Oscar Wilde's drama), James McNeill Whistler's *The Little White Girl* (1864), and Rossetti's *Fazio's Mistress* (1863).[90]

The mirror's possibilities of compositional framing multiply yet further. As D. M. R. Bentley points out, besides opening to an outside forest scene, the window in the background also serves as a partial mirror, creating three sets of reflections: the two lit candles mounted on the windowpane, a rose and a rosebud in the arrangement that surrounds Lady Lilith, and a forest scene that lets in the natural light illuminating her. This window and its partial reflection present important questions to a careful viewer: "Shouldn't there be a reflection of the artist in the mirror? If not a reflection of the artist, shouldn't there be a reflection of the spectator? Is the spectator meant to be understood as being in the room with Lady Lilith but slightly to the right of the window and mirror where the painting asks the viewer to stand?"[91] The illogic behind the image, and the vampiric lack of reflection, suggest Gothic echoes behind the composition. In asking these questions, Bentley also demonstrates the way in which Lady Lilith, even without gazing outwards at the viewer, challenges the place of the female figure within the frame as an object affixed with meaning, in a similar way that the framed women's faces in Radcliffe and Lewis are not passive, inanimate art objects. "By mobilizing these sorts of questions, *Lady Lilith* invites the (male) viewer to recognize the situation of the voyeur who is unacknowledged, either because it is undetected or undesired."[92] Lilith emerges here as a legitimate spectator herself, without acquiescing to the demands of our expectations and our eyes resting upon her.

A simple or moralistic reading would simply view the mirror in the painting as a symbol of Lilith's narcissism, conceit, and superficiality. But Lilith utilizes the mirror as a tool to subvert the delimiting power of the painting's very canvas and frame. This mirror, as a foil to the picture frame, grants Lilith the agency of the traditionally male viewer, wresting control back to herself, thus forcing that viewer to question his or her own position vis-à-vis the art-object. Playing her role as the subject of a painting entitled "Body's Beauty," she is a self-conscious model whose deliberate self-objectification is reinforced by the text of the poem. The verses reinforce the reading that Lilith understands the potentiality of her own beauty as power.

"Lady Lilith" or "Body's Beauty"

Of Adam's first wife, Lilith, it is told
   (The witch he loved before the gift of Eve,)
     That, ere the snake's, her sweet tongue could deceive
And her enchanted hair was the first gold.
And still she sits, young while the earth is old,

> And, subtly of herself contemplative,
>   Draws men to watch the bright web she can weave,
> Till heart and body and life are in its hold.
>
> The rose and poppy are her flowers; for where
>   Is he not found, O Lilith, whom shed scent
> And soft-shed kisses and soft sleep shall snare?
>   Lo! as that youth's eyes burned at thine, so went
>   Thy spell through him, and left his straight neck bent
> And round his heart one strangling golden hair.[93]

"Body's Beauty" flatly accuses Lilith of being a witch and a spider, likening her to a murdering Porphyria, or even a weaving Lady of Shalott. Yet the poem also helps to confirm that Rossetti's painting of Lilith is not simply a warning against female vanity.[94] The sonnet presents a thoughtful, self-reflective character, as Lilith brushes her hair, "subtly of herself contemplative." Featuring a legendary figure whose bodily objectification is the very source of her power and control over men, the painting and sonnet require the reader/viewer to negotiate the realistic, quotidian aspects of the texts and the grand mythological archetype they evoke. We readily recognize the faces of Fanny Cornforth and Alexa Wilding, while the interior setting looks like a Victorian parlor room rather than some setting from biblical lore. Just as the image of the Countess de Villeroi alternately presents as a rotting corpse and waxen image over the course of the novel, Rossetti's work invokes a wavering between two worlds upon his readers/viewers. Conjuring the supernatural, he invokes snakes, enchantments, and poppy to present Lilith as a "witch."

For Harold L. Weatherby, "the peculiar and perhaps unfortunate thing about Rossetti . . . is that he had a strong predilection for the supernatural, as strong indeed as his predilection for the flesh (and the two go hand in hand)."[95] In the sonnet, this "witch" self-consciously exerts a pull on men's gazes, but not in a confrontational way; rather, she emits a passive and yet more powerful enchantment: "still she sits . . . and, subtly of her self contemplative, / Draws men to watch the bright web she can weave, / Till heart and body and life are in its hold." Here, punning on the word "draws," Rossetti illuminates the way in which, with this beauty, Lilith entraps men through the eyes. This entrapment is bolstered by the language of feminine weaving and spider's webs. She eventually takes control over a man's heart, body, and life, drawing another's gaze into her web "till heart and body and life are in its hold." The pun on the artist's capacity to "draw" demonstrates the female figure's ability to usurp the role of gazer and artist.

Lady Lilith, as the downfall of the male viewer and the male artist, thus embodies the stereotype of the Gothic enchantress casting "spells"—drawing up stratagems and weaving webs—with her supernatural beauty. She renders them in a state of stupefaction through her witchery. On the one hand, this serves as a warning to other male viewers who, like Adam, will fall to her enchantments. Rossetti's speaker continually attempts to "write" the female within the male-dominated traditions of the sonnet, biblical tales ("it is told"), and blazon (describing her tongue, hair, and scent). In each of these forms, the author offers Lilith up for other male gazers to view as well. On the other hand, the poem's final line, boldly reminiscent of Browning's "Porphyria's Lover," portrays Lilith as a master of feminine physical strength and linguistic seduction. The alliterative accumulation of soothing "s" sounds ("O Lilith, whom shed scent / And soft-shed kisses and soft sleep shall snare?") culminates in a violent act which, with a final stroke, does not even require Lilith to meet the youth's gaze.[96] Her attack is cold, quick and effective: "As that youth's eyes burned at thine, so went / Thy spell through him . . ."[97] In these stark, monosyllabic lines, Lilith enchants her victim precisely at the moment when he is the most vulnerable prey—a viewer with his eyes locked and burning for the female subject he sees.

A reader of this double work can hardly resist identifying with Adam in these final lines. The viewer of the painting can little help playing the role of "that youth" whose "eyes burned at thine" in line 12. This moment of the spell interrupts Adam's suspended moment of interpretation: his eyes burn ablaze when her spell goes through him. Like Matilda in *The Monk*, Lilith wields the power of her image that both fixates and interrupts a male gaze, breaking his suspended state and limiting his powers as viewer and artist—the double role that Rossetti himself played. The poem "Body's Beauty" suggests the extent to which Rossetti was in fact at the mercy of his models, complicating long-standing readings of his megalomaniacal artistic practice.

Sibylla Palmifera *and "Soul's Beauty"*

If *Lady Lilith* represents the body's beauty, *Sibylla Palmifera* (Figures 3.9 and 3.10) is Rossetti's counterpoint to that physical emphasis, celebrating the soul's beauty instead. This 1866 painting, also entitled *Venus Palmifera*, depicts a holy woman rather than a femme fatale. With a

Figure 3.9 D. G. Rossetti, *Sibylla Palmifera*, 1870. Courtesy of Lady Lever Art Gallery, National Museums Liverpool, Port Sunlight, United Kingdom

palm frond in her hand, representing the triumph of Christ's resurrection, the sibyl purportedly possesses prophetic powers; she hovers between a divine and human state, and between Christian and classical Greek values of salvation and beauty. The sonnet to *Sibylla Palmifera*, which references both Dante and Sandro Botticelli in lines 10 and 11, gestures towards the double nature of Rossetti's works, uniting historical figures of poetry and painting.

However, *Soul's Beauty* is not necessarily a composition that hinges any less upon physical beauty than *Lady Lilith* does. Again, we have

Figure 3.10 D. G. Rossetti, *Sibylla Palmifera*, with frame, 1870. Courtesy of Lady Lever Art Gallery, National Museums Liverpool, Port Sunlight, United Kingdom

a woman depicted as the classic Rossetti "type" with long, flowing hair; fair skin against dark, rich-colored clothing; long, white hands; and a haunting gaze. As in *Astarte Syriaca* and *Proserpine*, the Venus figure looks directly outside of the frame, as if fixated on something or someone in the viewer's plane. Though the clothes hang more loosely on the body here than in *Lady Lilith*, the detailed folds upon the garment alert viewers to the palpability of the material and the body beneath it. Here, the simultaneously realistic and other-worldly features of the sibyl create an uncanny effect.

Critics have previously noted the excess and sense of uneasiness in *Sibylla Palmifera*. McGann describes this painting as lacking dignity, considering it "more grotesque than it perhaps ought to be, given its elaborate classical accessories."[98] (The language of the grotesque reappears in discussions of *Pia de' Tolomei*, where the elongated neck seems almost dislocated.) Considering *Sibylla Palmifera*, Mary Bennett points to the presence of the skull, winged sphinx, and "many-headed serpent" in the sibyl's background, which contribute to an "almost crepuscular atmosphere [resulting] from the strange juxtaposition of artificial and natural forms." The "strange color arrangements" also include gold and flesh-colored tones that offer an uneasy combination of the "splendid and simple."[99] The sibyl figure inhabits a liminal position between realism and symbolism, the natural and artificial, classical and Christian, sensual and holy. This state of uncertainty, of course, is reinforced by the unstable boundary between picture and reality.

As with the other three paintings we have seen, the presence of background objects, including butterflies, lamps, olive branches, poppies and roses, creates doubt as to whether the setting is earthly or celestial. These elements ultimately also contribute to a sense that the sibyl is trapped and crowded within the frame. Though there is no window painted in the background of the scene, the sibyl seems to be gazing out of the picture frame itself. Her positioning is pregnant with the potential of looking beyond and even stepping out of the picture, much like in *Astarte Syriaca*. Leaning forward and to our left, with eyes directed to our left, the sibyl looks through or past the opening of the frame, possibly at us. Like *Proserpine*, *Sibylla Palmifera* was attached to a signature frame with three concentric circles that make up the "roundels" on the frame with tiered molding. This gilded frame was used by Rossetti from 1868 on and is an essential component of the painting as a whole; the gold of the frame complements the gold hues seen at the top left and right of the painting, as well as at the bottom left, completing the composition and reflecting a similar light.

Furthermore, the palm frond in the sibyl's hands—the only other part of her body besides her face that is exposed and featured in brighter light—is held in the position of a pen. Rossetti referred to the frond as a "palm-sceptre," which he had "bestowed on the lady to mark the leading place which I intend her to hold among my beauties."[100] Viewers are not meant to appreciate *Sibylla Palmifera* for the beauty of her soul *rather* than her body in this case; instead, the palm frond effectively serves as a beauty trophy in a pageant of Rossetti's pictured women. Moreover, the palm frond represents the woman's capacity as a painter or poet herself. As Deborah Cherry has shown, Elizabeth Siddal was a painter in her own right, having produced several watercolors during an intensely productive year that saw the creation of a strong portfolio of watercolors, pen and ink and pencil, as well as oils. These included works from 1857, such as *Lady Clare*, *Lady Affixing a Pennant*, and *Clerk Saunders*, which was exhibited at Russell Place in an exhibition of Pre-Raphaelite art.[101]

Here, in *Sibylla Palmifera*, we are presented with a figure who seems to resist the captivity of the framed female body in three ways: her body is positioned towards the picture frame as if towards a window from which she might escape her objectification; her gaze challenges the viewer, as she assumes the role of viewer herself; and the palm frond or "scepter" she holds signals the triumph and power of her own beauty. My reading of the accompanying poem expands on this power of the palm frond as a symbol and tool.

SOUL'S BEAUTY[102]

Under the arch of Life, where love and death,
    Terror and mystery, guard her shrine, I saw
    Beauty enthroned; and though her gaze struck awe,
I drew it in as simply as my breath.
Hers are the eyes which, over and beneath,
    The sky and sea bend on thee,—which can draw,
    By sea or sky or woman, to one law,
The allotted bondman of her palm and wreath.

This is that Lady Beauty, in whose praise
    Thy voice and hand shake still,—long known to thee
        By flying hair and fluttering hem,—the beat
        Following her daily of thy heart and feet,
    How passionately and irretrievably,
In what fond flight, how many ways and days![103]

Sibylla Palmifera, with her gaze and the agency to "str[ike] awe," assumes the capacity of a commanding artist. She has eyes "which can draw . . . the allotted bondman," which puns on her ability to command his gaze but also to take over the role of artist. As she appears in the painting, the sibyl is poised for action, her authorial command imminent. Meanwhile, the male artist does not "draw" or sketch, but passively takes in her gaze in the mode of inhalation, passively and without resistance: "I drew it in as simply as my breath." The use of the verb "draw" in this sonnet thus undercuts the male poet/painter's authority, since Sibylla Palmifera draws the attention of gazers, especially to the palm frond she holds as if wielding a pen or paintbrush. The male bondman and sonneteer "draws in" and receives the inspiration she expels. Furthermore, when the speaker first introduces the relationship between male viewer and female subject, ("I saw / Beauty enthroned"), the enjambment of lines 3 and 4 subordinates the male viewer/artist at the end of line 2 to the powerfully "enthroned" female "Beauty" at the start of line 3.

The crux of the sonnet is a phrase that embodies the arresting effect of the entire painting, demarcated through monosyllabic emphasis: "her gaze struck awe." This phrase, resonating against De Quincey's articulation of an "awful parenthesis," highlights the sublime power of Sibylla Palmifera and the suspended attention she draws from her artist and viewer. The framed women who figure in Rossetti's paintings thus exert power despite the confinement of their framed or frozen bodies, just as we witnessed in the sonnets of Chapter 2. Here we have the development of a tradition where women do not merely look out of windows or frames and gaze out at picturesque beauty—they command it, embody it, write it, compose it, and subvert it. As Anne McCarthy argues, awful parenthesis is "not the absence of activity that one feels, but the overwhelming sense of interruption and possibility—a form of hovering."[104]

De Quincey's moment of awakening is particularly salient to Rossetti's poem-paintings because none of Rossetti's women appear truly at rest. They each seem poised to jump out of the frame or pen the sonnet at hand, ready to disturb our suspended state of analysis and reflection. In truth, the suspended body at risk of being awakened is not so much the women's, but ours. This dynamic of restlessness capitalizes upon the same affects of uncertainty produced by the framed bodies of a Lady Laurentini or a Matilda/Madonna.

Through their power of framing and gazing, along with gestures alluding to writing or drawing, Rossetti's women are momentarily granted power through framing devices that shock and surprise. Despite their participation in a tradition customarily oppressive of women and women's bodies, they subvert the common patterns of objectification and framing in much the same way that Gothic heroines or imprisoned damsels do. This unsettling feeling of being looked back at by a framed face is the same experience of the Gothic reader that I have traced in some of the most climactic moments of *Udolpho* and *The Monk*. The mirror-window confusion between life and art is a Victorian formal re-envisioning of the Romantic, Radcliffean realist supernatural.

* * *

They "Writhe, Twist, Wriggle, Foam and Slaver"; "My Head Turns Giddy, My Heart Sickens"

It is no coincidence then that Gothic and Pre-Raphaelite works faced comparably antagonistic receptions, their attackers often employing a similar logic and language. Robert Buchanan, writing under the pseudonym Thomas Maitland, objected to the sensuous realism in Rossetti's treatment of characters like Jenny, harshly deeming Rossetti as the head of the "Fleshly School of Poetry." In his infamous attack, Buchanan is unable to reconcile the "wriggling" realism of Rossetti's women and the holy idolatry with which he treats his female subjects:

> We cannot forbear expressing our wonder, by the way, at the kind of women whom it seems the unhappy lot of these gentlemen to encounter. We have lived as long in the world as they have, but never yet came across persons of the other sex who conduct themselves in the manner described. Females who bite, scratch, scream, bubble, munch, sweat, writhe, twist, wriggle, foam, and in a general way slaver over their lovers, must surely possess some extraordinary qualities to counteract their otherwise most offensive mode of conducting themselves. It appears, however, on examination, that their poet-lovers conduct themselves in a similar manner. They, too, bite, scratch, scream, bubble, munch, sweat, writhe, twist, wriggle, foam, and slaver, in a style frightful to hear of . . . We get very weary of this protracted hankering after a person of the other sex; it seems meat, drink, thought, sinew, religion for the fleshly school. There is no limit to the fleshliness . . . Whether he is writing of the holy Damozel, or of the Virgin herself, or of Lilith, or Helen, or of Dante, or of Jenny the street-walker, he is fleshly all over, from the roots of his hair to the tip of his toes . . .[105]

The corporeal realism that so disgusted Rossetti's detractors drew condemnations that directly echo, in language, critics of Gothic terror and horror seventy years prior.[106] Disavowing the inclusion of several of his own Gothic poems in published collections by Mrs. Mary Robinson, Samuel Taylor Coleridge implored that these contributions be removed. In a letter dated 27 December 1802, he writes:

> I understood that an excessively silly copy of Verses, which I had absolutely forgotten the very writing of, disgraced one of the volumes . . . My dear Miss Robinson! . . . I have a wife, I have sons, I have an infant Daughter—what excuse could I offer to my own conscience if by suffering my name to be connected with those of Mr. Lewis . . . I was the

occasion of their reading the Monk, or the wanton poems of Thomas Little Esqre? Should I not be an infamous Pander to the Devil in the seduction of my own offspring? —My head turns giddy, my heart sickens, at the very thought of seeing such books in the hands of a child of mine . . . O dear Miss Robinson! . . . do plant the night violets of your own Genius and Goodness on the Grave of your dear Parent,—not Hensbane, not Hemlock!107

A logic of contagion drives Buchanan and Coleridge's distress: they both purport that these works allegedly create a physical reaction—an inevitable bodily loss of control due to textual stimulation. In Buchanan's critique, there are three parties at risk. First, the "females" slaver over their lovers in lurid fashion. Next, it is the poet-lovers who likewise "wriggle, foam, and slaver, in a style frightful to hear of." While the first two victims are articulated, the third is merely implied. Rossetti's readers—or Buchanan himself—are next in turn to "bite, scratch, scream, bubble, munch, sweat, writhe, twist, wriggle, foam, and slaver." Victorian anxieties surrounding the pornographic potential of these texts leads Buchanan to even yearn, in a ridiculous rhetorical flourish, for pre-evolutionary asexuality: "At times, in reading such books as this, one cannot help wishing that things had remained forever in the asexual state described in Mr. Darwin's great chapter on Palingenesis."108 In Coleridge's account of 1790s Gothic, readers, too, suffered physiological responses to these works: cold sweats, chills down their spines, hair standing on the back of necks. This loss of bodily control and the possibility of arousal—of becoming physically stimulated by a literary work of art—reflects what is at core not just a moralistic problem, but an aesthetic and also corporeal one. Coleridge maligned Horace Walpole's "Mysterious Mother" as "the most disgusting, detestable, vile composition that ever came from the hand of a man," though he himself had penned several spectacular tales exploiting the Gothic's sensational effects. Coleridge's exaggerated rhetoric obviously replicates the clichés of supernatural and incestuous themes, as he risks becoming "Pander to the Devil" and "fears seduction of [his] own offspring." He ironically echoes the very language of the Gothic tales he means to disavow—proving the power of its contagion.109

Though Pre-Raphaelite art is not traditionally viewed as Gothic, despite its overlap of medieval themes, the wriggling and squirming reaction to these works is at core, I argue, Gothic reader response. To answer the question, "How should one be a Gothic reader?" is also to develop a heuristic for appreciating the power of Rossetti's doubled works and picture poems. Coleridge and Buchanan may lack the vocabulary to identify what Sianne Ngai calls, in the context of American film and literature, "ugly feelings," but they describe the same aesthetic discomfort through affects of anxiety, paranoia, enervation, and sterility. The trope of alternating flesh and symbol in the representation of women's faces and bodies not only shocks readers, but renders them frozen and awestruck—leaving them in a state of Thomas De Quincey's "awful parenthesis."[110] A Gothic reading experience thus exemplifies ideas of suspense and suspension in various forms: in terms of the narrative suspense crafted by the author; a reader's suspension of disbelief; the suspension of unanimated bodies, dead or frozen in a frame; and the Burkean rise and fall of sublimity, marked by a moment of climactic exaltation.

* * *

By exploring interpretive misunderstandings surrounding scenes with women's framed bodies—in both Rossetti's doubled works and in the novels of Radcliffe and Lewis—we have seen how these authors stage interactive scenes of suspense and shock, eliciting the reader's participation in a mini-drama of jarring psychological and physiological responses. Pre-Raphaelite and Gothic writers alike manufacture a condition of disorientation on the part of their readers, who, due to meta-artistic turns in the text, also become spectators of art. This is achieved through a distinct formula: (1) extending moments of anticipation and suspense, (2) inverting expectations of the visual object, and (3) inverting expectations yet again, thus denying a return to "normalcy." Through these moves, readers and viewers are subjected to a recurring sequence of surprises and suspensions, always followed by more revelations and yet another reorientation of the truth. Such constant fluctuations in perception create a world with no reliable sense of stability or normalcy and no promise of rest: a Gothic landscape, resisting interpretation, found in the unique collision of painting and poetry.

Reconsidering now Buchanan and Coleridge's frenetic disavowals of the "fleshly" and "terrorist" schools, we can see why scenes of Gothic picturesque so threatened certain (genteel, male) members of the reading public, rendering them, too, vulnerable bodies exposed to shocks and swaps. The seemingly supernatural elements of Rossetti's pictured women reside in the Gothic forms of their positioning, framing, and smaller poetic details of potential shock and swap.

Like the Gothic novel, Rossetti's paintings promote a version of reading and viewing characterized by movement and fluctuation. Encountering the framed women of Rossetti demands us to waver between perceiving Astarte Syriaca as an attractive, fleshly body or a mythologized deity; between interpreting Sibylla Palmifera as a religious Christian figure or as a sensual Venus body. We alternately recognize the sublime mythological figures (Lilith, Prosperina) or the influential models whose faces stare out from the canvas (Jane Morris, Fanny Cornforth, or Alexis Wilding). Confronting the poems, we must consider Lilith and Sibylla Palmifera as subjects of religious lore or as potential artists or writers with the power to create, frame, and compose words and images in their own right. These subversions are possible through the potential framing and reframing present in each painting and poem, which fluctuate between the picturesque and sublime. Our dynamic interpretations, characterized by such a barrage of perceptive oscillations, owe their lineage to a mode of readership theorized in Gothic novel reading, from the Aikins to Radcliffe to De Quincey. The sublime, the picturesque, suspension, and shock—all Romantic aesthetic concepts essential to Gothic readership—cultivate a viewer's capacity for withstanding and interpreting elements of swap and shock inherent to Rossetti's later works.

While this chapter makes but the briefest of gestures towards the considerable digital afterlife of Rossetti, Martin A. Danahay offers an intriguing twentieth-century approach to this question of fleshly and waxen, real and artistic, in his response to *The Rossetti Archive*, Jerome McGann's impressive online archive of Rossetti poetry and artwork. The free images of Rossetti's paintings online elicit for Danahay a provocative juxtaposition with online pornography.[111] While most scholars are wont to dismiss Buchanan's criticisms of Rossetti's work as pornographic, Danahay "take[s] Buchanan's charges against Rossetti seriously [because] in his own clumsy way he was making astute comments about the intersection of the commodification of women's bodies and Rossetti's sexual desires."[112] The question of treating Rossetti's words as if they were actually flesh exemplifies a central dilemma: in digital pornography, are photos "signs of real women representing actual sexual desire" or merely "tagged enactments of sexualized gestures"? Are the sexual images of "Jenny" just words on a page, and brushstrokes of *Lady Lilith* just paint on a canvas? McGann's virtual database of Rossetti's work magnifies this confusion between real and representative because these works are "doubly mediated," simply "digitized copies of photographs" that, when broken down, are fundamentally pixels on a screen or bits of coded computer language. Danahay's negotiation of Rossetti's "virtual bodies" exemplifies the way that Rossetti's artwork and poetry, from the nineteenth century to the twenty-first, derive meaning from this pivotal negotiation between representation that is fleshly or metaphorical, actual or virtual.[113]

The aspect of threat in Rossetti's paintings and other Pre-Raphaelite works is that the victim or object can suddenly spring to life or return a gaze, upsetting the traditional model of female objectification—whether in the 1860s and 1870s, or one hundred and sixty years later on *The Rossetti Archive* online. Framed, lifeless faces of female victims or idols become powerful, gripping forces that control the reader and viewer. Emily may betray a self-consciousness of her role as a Gothic heroine, just as Laurentini, Matilda, and Rossetti's framed women threaten to leap out from their confinement within a frame. Clearly, these fictional women will not actually come to life—but in the vein of Radcliffe's "explained supernatural," we feel as if they might. As trained Gothic viewers and readers, we must tolerate the loss of interpretative control, the discomfort of suspense, and Aikin's painful disgust of terror.

Remarkably, the four paintings discussed in this chapter showcase women who pose as figures of visual power and control, but from a calm, commanding position of rest. They are ostensibly inactive and non-violent; the women do not, as Buchanan accused, "bite, scratch, scream, bubble, munch, sweat, writhe, twist, wriggle [or] foam." Their looks of apathy or disdain, projecting from underneath the heavy eyelids, mute and emasculate the ecstatic sublime. Instead, it is precisely the Gothic readers and viewers of Rossetti's paintings who are forced into becoming these wriggling bodies. Rossetti's double works force readers into an uncomfortable state of fluctuation as the frames before us switch and swap the terms of our viewing authority—forcing us to writhe and twist in the fashion of rapt Gothic readers, waiting for the next surprise.

Notes

1 Elizabeth Prettejohn, *Rossetti and His Circle* (New York: Stewart Tabori & Chang, 1998), 9.
   See also Yael Shapira, *Inventing the Gothic Corpse: The Thrill of Human Remains in the Eighteenth-Century Novel* (Cham: Palgrave Macmillan, 2018). Shapira uses the line "she yields thee life that

vivifies" to liken Siddal's hair to a Frankensteinian electric charge, "as if [Rossetti is] connected to the lover by jump leads . . . Only the great head of pre-Raphaelite hair persists as both art object and bodily remain" (219–20).

Matthew Campbell offers a Gothic reading of "Life-in-Love," which "ends with the body of the loved one. It fixes on the physical, while drawn to an image of the corpse . . . It is impossible not to see Siddal's abundant undecayed hair here, as reported to Rossetti after the rescue of his poetry from her coffin. There is a ghoulish playing through of unbelieved notions of resurrection." Matthew Campbell, "The Victorian Sonnet," in *The Cambridge Companion to the Sonnet*, ed. A. D. Cousins (Cambridge: Cambridge University Press, 2001), 219–30.

2. Walter Crane, *An Artist's Reminiscences*, 2nd edn (London: Macmillian, 1907), quoted in Prettejohn, *Rossetti and His Circle*, 35.
3. Though I refer to these paintings as a part of the Pre-Raphaelite movement, these paintings and poems were composed in the later portion of Rossetti's career, when he associated with a group of artists quite separate from the first-generation Pre-Raphaelites. The "second phase" artists of the later 1850s include William Morris, Edward Burne-Jones, and Algernon Swinburne. Prettejohn (ed.), Introduction to *The Cambridge Companion to the Pre-Raphaelites* (Cambridge: Cambridge University Press, 2012), 10.
4. All passages from D. G. Rossetti are quoted from *Dante Gabriel Rossetti: Collected Poetry and Prose*, ed. Jerome McGann (New Haven: Yale University Press, 2014). Here, pp. 3–6, ll. 1–4. "The Blessed Damozel," pp. 3–6; "Body's Beauty," p. 161; "Soul's Beauty," p. 161; "Astarte Syriaca," p. 194; "Proserpina (For a Picture)" p. 195.
5. Early critical conversations have explored the meaning of symbolic details in Pre-Raphaelite art, from Jerome J. McGann, "Rossetti's Significant Details" *Victorian Poetry* 7, no. 1 (Spring 1969): 41–5 to George P. Landow's *William Holman Hunt and Typological Symbolism* (London: Yale University Press, 1979).
6. John Ruskin, *Modern Painters*, vol. 1, quoted in David Riede, "The Pre-Raphaelite School," in *A Companion to Victorian Poetry*, ed. Richard Cronin, Alison Chapman and Antony H. Harrison (Malden, MA: Blackwell, 2002).
7. From Rossetti's poem, "St. Luke the Painter."
8. This has been noted, for example, of the woodspurge's "cup of three," or the seven stars and three lilies in "The Blessed Damozel."
9. Prettejohn, *Rossetti and His Circle*, 24.
10. The "Songs of the Art Catholic" comprised a series of poems D. G. Rossetti gathered together in 1847 as part of an early project in imaginative historical reconstruction. See D. G. Rossetti, *The Complete Writings and Pictures of Dante Gabriel Rossetti*, ed. Jerome McGann.

Available at <http://www.rossettiarchive.org/docs/11-1847.raw.html> (last accessed 25 February 2022).
11. Riede, "The Pre-Raphaelite School," 307.
12. Ibid. 308.
13. These instances of framed women's figures in *Udolpho* and *The Monk* differ radically from the framed image of men. Towards the end of *The Italian*, for example, Schedoni learns that Ellena has been carrying a locket with his image. This discovery leads to clarification and resolution rather than uncertainty: Schedoni, realizing that Ellena is his long-lost daughter, refrains from killing her.
14. J. A. George offers a thorough study of the "dual nature of the Gothic" in Pre-Raphaelite medievalism and the work of William Morris especially, focusing on portrayals of Jane Morris as a "dark, silent" and "rather sinister figure" lurking in Morris's paintings. J. A. George, "From King Arthur to Sidonia the Sorceress: the Dual Nature of Pre-Raphaelite Mediaevalism," in *Victorian Gothic: Literary and Cultural Manifestations in the Nineteenth Century*, ed. Ruth Robbins and Julian Wolfreys (Basingstoke: Palgrave Macmillan, 2000).
15. Claudia Johnson, *Equivocal Beings: Politics, Gender, and Sentimentality in the 1790s* (Chicago: University of Chicago Press, 1994).
16. Ann Radcliffe, *The Mysteries of Udolpho*, ed. Bonamy Dobrée (New York: Oxford University Press, 2008), 248. For more on the significance of veils, see Chapter 5 of Eve Sedgewick's *The Coherence of Gothic Conventions*, "The Character in the Veil: Imagery of the Surface in the Gothic Novel." Also see Carol Margaret Davison, "Haunted House/ Haunted Heroine: Female Gothic Closets in 'The Yellow Wallpaper'" *Women's Studies* 33, no. 1 (2004): 47–75.
17. Radcliffe, *The Mysteries of Udolpho*, 248–9.
18. Ibid. 662.
19. See also Anne McCarthy's discussion of the speaker's reaction to the "death-white curtain" in Tennyson's *Maud*. McCarthy, *Awful Parenthesis: Suspension and the Sublime in Romantic and Victorian Poetry* (Toronto: University of Toronto Press, 2018).
20. Radcliffe, *The Mysteries of Udolpho*, 255.
21. Ibid. 662–3.
22. Terry Castle, "The Spectralization of the Other in *The Mysteries of Udolpho*," in *The Female Thermometer: Eighteenth-Century Culture and the Invention of the Uncanny* (Oxford: Oxford University Press, 1995), 129.
23. Lewis, *The Monk*, 40–1.
24. Ibid. 79–81.
25. This is yet another example of Gothic overhearing, leading up to both romantic and criminal confession, as discussed in Chapter 1. Lewis, *The Monk*, 81.

26. Lewis, *The Monk*, 81–2. The Venetian painter Martin Galuppi to whom Matilda refers is not to be confused with the Venetian composer Baldassare Galuppi of Browning's "A Toccata of Galuppi's" (1853).
27. Patrick R. O'Malley, *Catholicism, Sexual Deviance, and Victorian Gothic Culture* (Cambridge: Cambridge University Press, 2006), 18.
28. O'Malley points out the religious imagery behind the misleading name and disguise of the monk Rosario—evoking the Catholic rosary and the Virgin's flower, the rose. "The implicitly homoerotic undertones of Ambrosio's relationship with the gender-bending Matilda are transformed into visual spectacle when Matilda conjures up the image of Lucifer in order to seduce Ambrosio into falling more and more into her power . . . That the monk Rosario—named for this symbol of virginity—turns out to be the seductive and sexually voracious Matilda exemplifies once again the way that the notion of clerical and monastic celibacy becomes a mask for the depths of sexual depravity." O'Malley, *Catholicism*, 39–40.
29. Samuel Taylor Coleridge, "The Mysteries of Udolpho, Review," *The Critical Review* (August 1794), 361–2, in *The Critical Response to Ann Radcliffe*, ed. Deborah D. Rogers (Westport, CT: Greenwood, 1994), 17.
30. "How happens it then," said Mr. S—, "that objects of terror sometimes strike us very forcibly, when introduced into scenes of gaiety and splendour, as, for instance, in the Banquet scene in Macbeth . . . Who ever suffered for the ghost of Banquo, the gloomy and sublime kind of terror, which that of Hamlet calls forth? though the appearance of Banquo, at the high festival of Macbeth, not only tells us that he is murdered, but recalls to our minds the fate of the gracious Duncan, laid in silence and death by those who, in this very scene, are revelling in his spoils. There, though deep pity mingles with our surprise and horror, we experience a far less degree of interest, and that interest too of an inferior kind. The union of grandeur and obscurity, which Mr. Burke describes as a sort of tranquillity tinged with terror, and which causes the sublime, is to be found only in Hamlet; or in scenes where circumstances of the same kind prevail." Ann Radcliffe, "On the Supernatural in Poetry," *New Monthly Magazine* 16, no. 1 (1826), 145–52, in *Gothic Documents: A Sourcebook, 1700–1820*, ed. E. J. Clery and Robert Miles (Manchester: Manchester University Press, 2000), 163–72.
31. John Whale, "Romantics, Explorers, and Picturesque Travelers," in *The Politics of the Picturesque: Literature, Landscape, and Aesthetics since 1770*, ed. Stephen Copley and Peter Garside (Cambridge: Cambridge University Press, 1994), 176.
32. Richard Payne Knight, *An Analytical Inquiry Into the Principles of Taste*, 4th edn (London: Payne and White, 1808), 155.

33. James Buzard, "A Continent of Pictures: Reflections of the 'Europe' of Nineteenth-Century Tourists," *PMLA* 108, no. 1 (January 1993): 30–44.
34. See William Gilpin, *Three essays: On picturesque beauty; On picturesque travel; and On sketching landscape: to which is added a poem, On landscape painting* (London: R. Blamire, 1792).
35. Buchanan's attack on Rossetti and his "Fleshly School" uses the term "picturesque" disparagingly to poke fun of the idea of *ut pictura poesis*.
36. It was because of this cult status as a frenzied fad that Gilpin's picturesque drew so much attention and imitation. Soon, hordes of "picturesque hunters" seeking out an idyllic view to pencil down and take home with them came to be ridiculed. Sir Joshua Reynolds wrote in response to Gilpin's *Essays* on the picturesque: "Without opposing any of your sentiments, it has suggested . . . whether the epithet *picturesque* is not applicable to the excellences of the inferior schools, rather than to the higher. The works of Michael Angelo, Raphael, &c, appear to me to have nothing of it; whereas Reubens, and the Venetian painters may almost be said to have nothing else. Perhaps *picturesque* is somewhat synonymous to the word *taste*; which we should think improperly applied to Homer, or Milton, but very well to Pope, or Prior. I suspect that the application of these words are to excellences of an inferior order; and which are incompatible with the grand stile." Joshua Reynolds, Letter to William Gilpin, London, 19 April 1791.
37. The term "picturesque," which comes from the Italian "pittoresco," came to refer to the style of the seventeenth-century landscape painters Salvator Rossa, Claude Lorrain, and the Poussins. Lorrain and Rosa became representative of the two extremes of the picturesque continuum, with Lorrain representing the placid, while Rosa represented the wild. Straddling the beautiful and the sublime, the picturesque might feature mild English landscapes, such as a sheep pasture, while merely alluding to more intensely beautiful or threatening scenes (by depicting banditti or gypsies in the distance, for example). Buzard, "A Continent of Pictures," 45.
38. Scholars have demonstrated the importance of women's travel writing to Radcliffe and Gothic romances. See Jane Stabler, "Taking Liberties: The Italian Picturesque in Women's Travel Writing," *European Romantic Review* 13, no. 1 (2002): 11–22; Benjamin A. Brabon, "Surveying Ann Radcliffe's Gothic Landscapes," *Literature Compass* 3, no. 4 (2006): 840–5, and George Dekker, *The Fictions of Romantic Tourism: Radcliffe, Scott, and Mary Shelley* (Stanford: Stanford University Press, 2005); and Marshall Brown, "In Defense of Cliché: Radcliffe's Landscapes," in *The Gothic Text* (Stanford: Stanford University Press, 2005).

William Hazlitt joked that "as the traveller advances into the country, robbers and rumours of robbers fly before him with the horizon.

He expressed mock-surprise when he did not find 'a thief concealed behind each bush, or a Salvator Rosa face scowling from a ruined hovel, or peeping from a jutting crag at every turn.'" William Hazlitt, "Notes of a Journey through France and Italy," in *The Collected Works of William Hazlitt*, ed. A. R. Waller and Arnold Glover (London: J. M. Dent & Company, 1903), 249, 199. Charlotte Eaton's *Rome in the Nineteenth Century* (1820), like Austen's *Northanger Abbey*, riffed on these conventions. Describing a gloomy travelers' inn, Eaton mocks, "if we had been heroines, what terrors might have agitated, and what adventures might not have befallen us! But we were not heroical . . . We got up . . . the next morning, un-murdered." Charlotte Eaton, *Rome in the Nineteenth Century: containing a complete account of the Ruins of the Ancient City, the Remains of the Middle Ages, and the Monuments of Modern Times* (Edinburgh: Constable, 1820), 62–3.
39. Thematically, the worshipped female image that transforms from saint to seductress appears vice versa as well. This confusion occurs in a scene of *Mysteries of Udolpho*, where Emily witnesses her father St. Aubert grieving over what she thinks is a picture of his mistress. She suspects her father of adultery until the end of the novel, when she learns this image is actually not a mistress or object of lust, but a lost sister, the Marchioness de Villeroi. What she mistakes for proof of adultery is actually one of fraternal devotion and mourning; the painted mistress is in fact a commemorative image of a loving aunt.
40. McCarthy, *Awful Parenthesis*, 13.
41. "Images of bodies in suspended animation, rapt in trance, or caught in the ellipsis of thwarted speech index an aesthetic response to the ontological conditions of contingency and discontinuity in the self as well as in the world." Ibid.
42. Victor Shklovsky, "Art as Technique," *Russian Formalist Criticism: Four Essays*, trans. Lee T. Lemon and Marion J. Rees (Lincoln: University of Nebraska Press, 1965), 22, quoted in McCarthy, *Awful Parenthesis*, 10.
43. Jonathan Crary, *Suspensions of Perception: Attention, Spectacle, and Modern Culture* (Cambridge, MA: MIT Press, 1999), 10, quoted in McCarthy, *Awful Parenthesis*, 10.
44. "The returning sense of sight came upon me, red, as if it swam in blood; suspended hearing rushed back loud, like thunder; consciousness revived in fear: I sat up appalled, wondering into what region, amongst what strange beings I was waking . . ." Charlotte Brontë, *Villette*, ed. Mark Lilly (London: Penguin Classics, 1985), 237, quoted in McCarthy, *Awful Parenthesis*, 15.
45. On the occasion of discovering what she thinks is the corpse of her aunt, she awakens to find herself being kidnapped and transported by a group of ruffians. *The Mysteries of Udolpho*, 348–9.
46. McCarthy, *Awful Parenthesis*, 15–18.

47. Radcliffe, *Udolpho*, 248–9.
48. McCarthy, *Awful Parenthesis*, 26.
49. Thomas De Quincey, *The Works of Thomas De Quincey*, ed. Grevel Lindop, vol. 3 (London: Pickering & Chatto, 2000), 152.
50. John and Anna Letitia Aikin, "On the Pleasure Derived from Objects of Terror; with Sir Bertrand, A Fragment," in *Miscellaneous Pieces, in Prose: by J. and A. L. Aikin* (London: J. Johnson, 1773), 119–37.
51. Sianne Ngai, *Ugly Feelings* (Cambridge, MA: Harvard University Press, 2005).
52. Robin Sheets, "Pornography and Art: The Case of Jenny," *Critical Inquiry* 14, no. 2 (Winter 1988): 315–34. John P. McGowan, "'The Bitterness of Things Occult': D. G. Rossetti's Search for the Real," *Victorian Poetry* 20, no. 3–4 (1982): 51. Harold L. and Harold Weatherby, "Problems of Form and Content in the Poetry of Dante Gabriel Rossetti," *Victorian Poetry* 2, no. 1 (Winter 1964): 11–19.
53. Weatherby and Weatherby, "Problems of Form and Content," 11–19.
54. It has been noted that Rossetti's framed paintings feature women's faces that are often oversized and seemingly ill-proportioned to their frames. Aside from Rossetti's paintings of women that are face portraits, a number of Pre-Raphaelite paintings by Edward Millais, Holman Hunt, and John William Waterhouse also feature this skewed proportion, which gives the woman a looming and imposing look. Jerome McGann notes the especially "grotesque space" in *Lady Lilith*, which gives the work a bizarre spatial effect where flowers and the wall seem flattened and incongruent, mixing "strange juxtapositions of artificial and natural forms." Available at <http://www.rossettiarchive.org/docs/s193.rap.html> (last accessed 22 May 2014).
55. Susan P. Casteras, "The Double Vision in Portraiture," in *Dante Gabriel Rossetti and the Double Work of Art*, ed. Maryan Wynn Ainsworth (New Haven: Yale University Art Gallery, 1976), 16.
56. Casteras, "The Double Vision in Portraiture," 10.
57. Ford Madox Brown, journal entry dated August 1885, quoted in Casteras, "The Double Vision in Portraiture," 14.
58. Prettejohn, *Rossetti and His Circle*, 18–19.
59. Prettejohn offers as evidence of these "phases" three paintings: *Beata Beatrix*, which features Siddal, *The Blue Bower*, which features Cornforth, and *Proserpine*, which features Morris. Ibid.
60. Ibid. 136.
61. Carl A. Peterson, *The Poetry and Painting of Dante Gabriel Rossetti* (Madison: University of Wisconsin Press, 1951), 135.
62. Castle, "The Specialization of the Other," 128.
63. David Riede, *Dante Gabriel Rossetti Revisited*, ed. Herbert Sussman (New York: Twayne Publishers, 1992), 33.
64. Riede, *Dante Gabriel Rossetti Revisited*, 30.
65. Ibid. 26.

66. "Imagine a tall lean woman in a long dress of some dead purple stuff, guiltless of hoops (or of anything else, I should say), with a mass of crisp black hair heaped into great wavy projections on each of her temples, a thin pale face, a pair of strange sad, deep, dark Swinburnish eyes, with great thick black oblique brows, joined in the middle and tucking themselves away under her hair, a mouth like the 'Oriana' in our illustrated Tennyson, a long neck, without any collar, and in lieu thereof some dozen strings of outlandish beads—in fine Complete. On the wall was a large nearly full-length portrait of her by Rossetti, so strange and unreal that if you hadn't seen her, you'd pronounce it a distempered vision, but in fact an extremely good likeness." Henry James, *Selected Letters*, ed. Leon Edel (Cambridge, MA: Belknap, 1974), 23.
67. Casteras, "The Double Vision in Portraiture," 17–18.
68. Ainsworth, *Dante Gabriel Rossetti and the Double Work of Art*, 18.
69. Rossetti, "Lady Lilith," in *Rossetti Archive Doubleworks*, ed. McGann. Available at <http://www.rossettiarchive.org/docs/s205.rap.html> (last accessed 22 May 2014).
70. Lawrence Starzyk, "Rossetti's 'Jenny': Aestheticizing the Whore," *Papers on Language and Literature* 36, no. 3 (2000): 227.
71. See Elizabeth C. Mansfield, *Too Beautiful to Picture: Zeuxis, Myth, And Mimesis* (Minneapolis: University of Minnesota Press, 2007). This kind of interchangeability or anonymity among multiple women is particularly prevalent in Edward Burne-Jones's "Green Summer" (1864). Critics were disturbed by "the undifferentiated characterizations" of the nine female figures who all share the same languorous mood. Prettejohn, *Rossetti and His Circle*, 33.
72. In Victorian paintings, the depiction of women near windows serves as an exit to the Victorian version of the Gothic castle: an indoor parlor room representing enclosed and stifling domesticity. This theme in Pre-Raphaelite painting has been well explored by scholars such as Gerhard Joseph and William Blissett. Blissett's article, "The Pre-Raphaelite Window," enumerates examples of what Max Beerbohm called "fenestralia," works concerned mainly with accounts of people memorably appearing at windows. To paint a woman confined within domestic quarters near a window releases the tension of a suffocating domestic. This is evident in paintings such as Waterhouse's *The Lady of Shalott*, *I am Half Sick of Shadows*, *Mariana in the South*; Sidney Harold Meteyard's *Lady of Shalott*; Rossetti's *Lady Lilith* and *Aurelia*; and Cowper's *Rapunzel*, where a viewer only obtains refuge from the overwhelming clutter of an indoor parlor by the glimpse through an aperture. See Gerhard Joseph, "Victorian Frames: The Windows and Mirrors of Browning, Arnold and Tennyson," *Victorian Poetry* 16, no. 1–2 (1978) and William Blissett, "The Pre-Raphaelite Window," in *The Journal of Pre-Raphaelite Studies* 13 (Fall 2004): 5–16.

73. Brian Donnelly, *Dante Gabriel Rossetti: The Painter as Poet* (Aldershot and Burlington, VT: Ashgate, 2015).
74. Catherine Golden, "Dante Gabriel Rossetti's Two-Sided Art," *Victorian Poetry* 26, no. 4 (Winter 1988): 400.
75. Golden, "Dante Gabriel Rossetti's Two-Sided Art," 399.
76. Rossetti, "Proserpina."
77. Ibid. lines 1–14.
78. Jerome McGann, Introduction to "Proserpina," *Rossetti Archive Doubleworks*. Available at <http://www.rossettiarchive.org/docs/1-1872.s233.raw.html> (last accessed 22 May 2014).
79. Rossetti, "Proserpina," line 9.
80. Prettejohn, *Rossetti and His Circle*, 69.
81. Theodore Watts-Dunton, "The Truth About Rossetti," *Nineteenth Century* 13 (1883): 412–13, quoted in McGann, *The Rossetti Archive*. Available at <http://www.rossettiarchive.org/docs/s249.rap.html> (last accessed 22 May 2014).
82. William Michael Rossetti, *Dante Gabriel Rossetti as Designer and Writer* (London: Cassell, 1889), quoted in Prettejohn, *Rossetti and His Circle*, 69.
83. The model for the left attendant was Mary "May" Morris, daughter of William and Jane Morris.
84. Rossetti, "Astarte Syriaca," p. 361, lines 1–14. Available at <http://www.rossettiarchive.org/docs/s249.rap.html> (last accessed 22 May 2014).
85. Golden, "Dante Gabriel Rossetti's Two-Sided Art," 394–402.
86. Ibid. 396.
87. Prettejohn, *Rossetti and His Circle*, 31.
88. Ponsonby A. Lyons to Dante Gabriel Rossetti, in *Rossetti Papers 1862 to 1870*, ed. W. M. Rossetti and D. G. Rossetti. Letter of 1870, quoted in Prettejohn, *Rossetti and His Circle*, 30.
89. Griselda Pollock, *Vision And Difference: Femininity, Feminism, and Histories of Art* (London: Routledge, 1988).
90. The remarkable use of mirrors, picture frames, and windows is not specific only to these four works, and not only to Rossetti. His *La Donna Della Finestra* (1879), also modeled on Jane Morris, presents the general case of a framed woman before a window who gazes with a challenging, alluring look through the picture frame and across at the viewer. *La Bella Mano* (1875) features Alexa Wilding's likeness with two handmaids before an orbed, convex mirror or painting. Paintings by other artists also feature this woman of the window, a figure at rest whose vision avoids looking out the aperture. These include *Mariana* (1851) by John Everett Millais, *The Lady of Shalott* (1905) by William Holman Hunt, *Rapunzel Sings from the Tower* (1908) by Frank Cadogan Cowper, and *"I am Halfsick of Shadows," said the Lady of Shalott* (1915) by John William Waterhouse. See Gerhard

Joseph, "Victorian Frames," 71: "In both Victorian poetry and painting the image of the window, oscillating between compositional and iconographic feature, hesitates on the border of the thematic figure—sometimes crossing over to reassume its original metaphoricity." See also Martin Meisel, "'Half Sick of Shadows': The Aesthetic Dialogue in Pre-Raphaelite Painting," in *Nature and the Victorian Imagination*, ed. U. C. Knoepflmacher and G. B. Tennyson (Berkeley: University of California Press, 1977).
91. Ultimately, Bentley reads the painting in terms of a commentary on Rossetti's interest in voyeurism. D. M. R. Bentley, "Dante Rossetti's *Lady Lilith, Sibylla Palmifera*, 'Body's Beauty' and 'Soul's Beauty'," *Journal of Pre-Raphaelite Studies* 13, no. 2 (2004): 65.
92. Ibid.
93. Rossetti, "Lady Lilith," p. 216, lines 1–14.
94. For Bentley, Lilith looking in the mirror combing her hair can thematically represent vanity in a Christian context, contemplative life in the tradition of Dante, or an allegory of Beauty contemplating itself in the classical tradition. Ultimately, however, the painting "is centrally and complexly about the activity of looking at a beautiful female form both for the woman who looks at herself and for the 'men' who look at her." Bentley, "Dante Rossetti's *Lady Lilith, Sibylla Palmifera*," 53.
95. Weatherby, "Problems of Form and Content in the Poetry of Dante Gabriel Rossetti," 18.
96. Rossetti, "Lady Lilith," lines 10–11.
97. Ibid. lines 12–13.
98. McGann, in *The Rossetti Archive: Doubleworks*. David Latham also uses the term "literary grotesque" to characterize the disruptive violence and unstable opposites described in William Morris's 1891 "Address on the Collection of Paintings of the English Pre-Raphaelite School." David Latham, "'World of Its Own Creation': Pre-Raphaelite Poetry and the New Paradigm for Art," *Journal of Pre-Raphaelite Studies* 25 (Spring 2016): 11.
99. Mary Bennett, *Artists of the Pre-Raphaelite Circle: The First Generation: Catalogue of Works in the Walker Art Gallery, Lady Lever Art Gallery and Sudley Art Gallery* (London: Published for the National Museums and Galleries on Merseyside by Lund Humphries, 1988), 169–72.
100. D. G. Rossetti, letter to George Rae, 7 December 1865, in *The Correspondence of Dante Gabriel Rossetti*, ed. William Fredeman (Rochester, NY: D. S. Brewer, 2010), 65.
101. Deborah Cherry, "Elizabeth Eleanor Siddal," in *The Cambridge Companion to the Pre-Raphaelites*, ed. Elizabeth Prettejohn (Cambridge: Cambridge University Press, 2012), 183–95.

102. "Soul's Beauty" appears as Sonnet LXXVIII in *The House of Life* (1881). An earlier version of the poem, "Sibylla Palmifera (For a Picture)" was included in the collection *Sonnets for Pictures* (1870).
103. Rossetti, "Proserpina," 215, lines 1–14.
104. McCarthy, *Awful Parenthesis*, 4.
105. Thomas Maitland [Robert Buchanan], "The Fleshly School of Poetry: Mr. D. G. Rossetti," *The Contemporary Review* 18 (October 1871): 334–50.
106. See Weatherby and Weatherby, "Problems of Form and Content in the Poetry of Dante Gabriel Rossetti," and John P. McGowan, "The Bitterness of Things Occult," 51.
107. Samuel T. Coleridge, quoted in Michael Gamer, "Gothic Fictions and Romantic Writing in Britain," in *The Cambridge Companion to Gothic Fiction*, ed. Jerrold E. Hogle (Cambridge: Cambridge University Press, 2002), 90. The poetry collections to which Coleridge alludes were edited by Mary Robinson's mother.
108. See Robin Sheets, "Pornography and Art: The Case of Jenny."
109. In "The Blasphemy of the Monk," written for the *Critical Review*, Coleridge announces: "[W]e declare it to be our opinion, that the Monk is a romance, which if a parent saw in the hands of a son or daughter, he might reasonably turn pale . . . The shameless harlotry of Matilda, and the trembling innocence of Antonia, are seized with equal avidity, as vehicles of the most voluptuous images . . . Nor must it be forgotten that the author is a man of rank and fortune.–Yes! the author of the Monk signs himself a legislator! We stare and tremble." Samuel Taylor Coleridge, "The Blasphemy of *The Monk*," *Critical Review* (February 1797), reprinted in Victor Sage (ed.), *The Gothick Novel: A Casebook* (Basingstoke: Macmillan, 1990), 42–3.
110. McCarthy, *Awful Parenthesis*.
111. Martin A. Danahay, "Dante Gabriel Rossetti's Virtual Bodies," *Victorian Poetry* 36, no. 4 (Winter 1998): 379–8.
112. Ibid. 379.
113. Ibid.

Chapter 4

The Cloistered Cleric: Confessional, Confinement, and Hopkins's Poetics of Wavering

> The faithful waver, the faithless fable and miss.
> G. M. Hopkins, "The Wreck of the Deutschland"[1]

There is perhaps no poet who more beautifully conveys the experience of Victorian doubt than G. M. Hopkins. So doubtful are his psychic grapplings with God, human suffering, and alienation that critics have happily secured his critical place among the modernists, within a world where God seems dead and the destructive nature of humankind reigns supreme. Yet Hopkins's poetry is also restorative and ennobling. The irrepressible beauty of nature exudes from his verses, exemplifying the sheer beauty of dappled things. His homage to alliterative Old English verse heralds back to times more ancient with a reassuring stability. The rhythms of "chestnut-falls" and "finches' wings" counterpoint the force of his sprung rhythm and arresting spondees: "Praise him."[2] The vibrant hues that color his lines create a boundless landscape in God's glory: "descending blue," "glassy peartree leaves and blooms,"[3] "gold-vermillion," "azurous hung hills," "very-violet-sweet."[4] Hopkins's poetry is one of solitude that carries the spirit of reflection, yet it does not necessarily find solace or repose. He revels in God's grandeur but makes us question the heights to which our own fear and weakness can overwhelm and conquer faith. This "poetics of wavering" that I identify in Hopkins's verses offers a recognition of the motion and movement that allow us to travel through the difficulties of life—whether "riding a river" or having the freedom to waver, to "fable and miss."[5]

Among the Victorian poets, Gerard Manley Hopkins would seem the furthest removed from the heavily commercial, xenophobic, and anti-Catholic world of 1790s English Gothic fiction. An English

Jesuit priest who converted to Catholicism largely as a result of the Oxford Movement, Hopkins stands among the Victorians as a devotional poet who wrote serious spiritual verse. After being received into the church by John Henry Newman in October 1866, he resolved to become a priest in May 1868 upon returning to Hampstead. The burning of his early poems and the seven years of silence that followed his Jesuit initiation mark a commitment to his religious office that effectively cut him off from the public literary scene, though he was still engaged in serial and periodical print culture.[6] It might be said that his literary circle consisted solely of a few family members and his friends, Robert Bridges, Coventry Patmore, and Richard Watson Dixon. Hopkins's isolation and the difficulty of reading him among other contemporary prosodists has also contributed to his being widely regarded as a proto-modernist disaffiliated from other Victorian poets. Paul Mariani has observed, for instance, that a poem like "The Wreck of the Deutschland" is an anomaly in Victorian poetry, showing none of the "ironic ambivalence" or the use of a mask or dramatic persona characteristic of poetry in this period.[7]

Of course, there is little reason to believe that Hopkins was immersed in the tradition of Gothic romance, either while an undergraduate at Oxford or later as a Jesuit priest and professor. Yet the Gothic supernatural is hardly incompatible with Hopkins's poetry or his serious Catholic faith. Hopkins was haunted by God's presence—as haunted by this as by the prospect of God's absence. His ideas of inscape and instress can be violent and punitive, and Hopkins's self-punishing marks and erasures in his journals imply masochistic forms of self-policing. And while there is no evidence in his journals or letters that he read Hogg, Wilde, Radcliffe, Lewis, or de Sade, Hopkins's poetry formally incorporates Gothic patterns identified throughout this book—including accusational trials and confession, the exigencies of physical confinement, and symbolic-realistic descriptions of fleshly detail. This chapter means to show the Gothic inheritance of Hopkins's oeuvre by considering his private poetry, in which he literalizes the cloister as a site of trauma, formally enacting overhearing and confession (Chapter 1), the thrall of confinement (Chapter 2), and fluctuating bodies (Chapter 3) through the trappings of Catholic life. Read against the anti-Catholic backdrop of English Gothic novels and their caricatures of the Inquisition, his poems voice the harrowing experience of suffering clerical bodies in confinement, from monks to nuns. At the same time, his sonnets, dramatic lyrics, and confessions have broad appeal and continue to be legible to a popular, non-Catholic readership. As a major Victorian poet who represents the intersection of Englishness, Catholicism, and homosexuality, Hopkins is a missing figure in any study of English or Irish Gothic.[90]

Certainly, the "Terrible Sonnets" are Gothic in theme: insomnia and utter isolation become expressed through the imagery of live burial, imprisonment, and suffocation. Consider the sonnet "Spelt from Sibyl's Leaves":

> Óur évening is over us; óur night ' whélms, whélms, ánd will end us.
>   Only the beak-leaved boughs dragonish ' damask the tool-smooth bleak light; black,
>   Ever so black on it.[10]

We hear the parallelism and echoes of familiar Gothic themes in "womb-of-all, home-of-all, hearse-of-all night" (l. 2). The two "flocks" tell of "a rack / Where, selfwrung, selfstrung, sheathe- and shelter-less, thoughts against thoughts in groans grind" (l. 13). This *dies irae*, "most carefully timed in *tempo rubato*," presents a fearful apocalyptic vision.[11] Replete with "darkness," "dragons," "hearse," and "womb," they establish the presence of Gothic verses in Hopkins's poetic output. Yet our readings of Hopkins become more interesting when we leave the tropes behind for form. Hopkins's life was book-ended by the rise of the Oxford Movement and the 1885 Criminal Law Amendment Act, which outlawed all male homosexual acts as "acts of gross indecency between men." His formal use and transformations of the cell, the room, the stanza, and the coffin reveal poems in which he is harnessing tropes of the Gothic and transforming them into forms useful for his own work creating autobiographical religious and homoerotic verse.

In what follows, I visit the suffering nuns, caged souls, and desperate monologue in Hopkins's poems that register these Gothic undertones and formal transformations. Through each of these poetic techniques, he creates a reading experience that is marked by wavering, by fear and doubt, cultivating a mode of reading that, like Gothic reading, can cope with sudden blows, changes, and shocks. Hopkins thus builds the stamina of his readers by subjecting them to stresses and fluctuations. The confession, confinement, and bodily representation within his poems utilize Gothic models for drawing out doubt and fear from the reader, particularly within the context of English Catholicism, itself a nexus of Gothic anxieties at play on the nineteenth-century literary scene.

To what extent does Hopkins's poetry inherit familiar tropes and innovations of Gothic form, and how does his devotional verse further develop these forms? The Gothic forms of Hopkins's poetry include his innovations of sprung rhythm, inscape, instress, and his curtal and caudated sonnets, which all comprise a definitive part of Hopkins's major verses between 1875 and his death in 1889. Hopkins lives out the experience of spiritual doubt not simply through religious meditation and composition, but through shocking, bodily experiences of faith and revelation, through stress and instress. This is apparent in the horrifying darkness of his so-called "Terrible Sonnets." In this framing, poems such as "Carrion Comfort" and "No Worst, There is None" represent the authentic, personal chronicling of Catholic confessional, presenting a counterpoint to the often-hypocritical confessions of 1790s Gothic characters and Victorian dramatic monologists. These poems also offer Hopkins's sonnets a sense of relishing in confinement with a taste for punishment, assuming the position of the enthralled prisoner. They explore the Gothic valences of fictional drama and romance within psychological territory; Hopkins describes life in the Jesuit community, often portraying it as a box, coffin, or echoing cell. And much like the "fleshly" women depicted by D. G. Rossetti, Hopkins's shipwrecked nuns of the *Deutschland* are represented as suffering bodies. To be sure, a strong Gothic inheritance is obvious in stark physicalizations of clerical Catholic life—its confinements and apocalyptic visions, especially in the coffin-contained despair of the "Terrible Sonnets," particularly the "dragonish" boughs and the "rack" where "selfwrung, selfstrung" and "shelter-less" "thoughts" "grind" in "groans" in "Spelt from Sibyl's Leaves." But we might not expect to discover that Gothic forms are constitutive even in the celebrated violence of his poetic masterpiece, "The Wreck of the Deutschland." Hopkins's poems are predicated upon experiences of sudden change that induce fear in his readers, not necessarily by expressing horrific content but by staging a physiological experience of doubt and shock.

Thus, even in the poetry of Hopkins, which has often been considered in isolation from other poets, Gothic themes are sublimated into new elements of poetic form in a manner similar to that we have seen in other nineteenth-century poets—suggesting that in this respect, Hopkins is more centrally a part of the Victorian poetic tradition than critics have sometimes allowed. Like his Victorian counterparts, he composed poetry that reflects the historical anxieties of nineteenth-century English life through his use of Gothic forms, without being predicated on Gothic themes. If we can detect such structures within Hopkins's oeuvre and recognize them as a constitutive part of his poetics, particularly in his prosodic innovations of inscape and instress, then we will have realized this book's initial charge of extricating Gothic forms from Gothic themes—freeing our understanding of Gothic forms from the "bag of tropes" and recipe list referenced at the introduction of this book. We will have learned to think about Gothic form as wholly separate from ghosts, goblins, Satan, and stock devices, recognizing its function, for instance, in religious verse. Put differently, Hopkins should be read not simply as a Catholic poet but as a post-Gothic Victorian poet. Reading his verses within a Gothic context shows how his poetry forcefully combats the kitschy camp of Gothic's Catholic representations and forcefully de-ironizes those stereotypes in the nineteenth-century canon of English and Irish literature.

Through his poems, Hopkins was a mythologist of his own pain, and he relies upon his unique positioning of the Anglo-Catholic so fantasized and romanticized, as we will see, during the Oxford Movement and its emergence.[12] Such stereotypes emphasized the English-Italian fascination with foreign otherness, capturing Hopkins's Jesuit experience as an isolated outsider. Most centrally, Hopkins serves as a useful test case for the incorporation of Gothic tropes into Victorian poetry because he actualizes the problematic convergence of Catholicism and a majority English Protestant tradition. He embodies the very fears upon which Gothic texts rely, that is, anxieties about an external Catholic threat polluting a Protestant English identity. Yet, as a living, breathing specimen of an English Catholic priest, expressing himself autobiographically through verse, he contradicts and debunks the theatrical, fictitious, and excessive tropes caricatured in Gothic romance. Here, we have an actual Catholic cleric who does not exemplify the villainous Gothic stereotypes found in contemporary nineteenth-century English fiction, but defies, problematizes, naturalizes, and complicates them. G. M. Hopkins was no monk; and he did not live in a monastery. These are crucial distinctions and this chapter does not mean to conflate the English Jesuit experience with fictional stereotypes of Catholic religious orders from abroad. The very fact that Hopkins's poems portray the spatial and psychological confinement he experienced in terms of Catholicism in Gothic Romance instead shows how the poet, through his works, secularized the Gothic—anglicizing, normalizing, and modernizing tired and xenophobic fictional clichés. In other words, Hopkins, the nineteenth-century poet of lyric verse, writes in response to—not only in spite of—these inherited stereotypes from Gothic romance.

* * *

English prejudices against Catholicism were rampant in nineteenth-century religious and political rhetoric, and literary representation alike. According to Patrick O'Malley, novelists such as Radcliffe, Lewis, and Maturin "propagated images of continental Catholic corruption that could become yet more threatening as the Oxford Movement brought what evangelicals saw as crypto-Romanist theologies and practices into England itself."[13] The English identified Catholicism as a threat infiltrating the homeland, moving towards them from continental Europe, in particular France and Italy, by way of Ireland. Radcliffean romance in particular exacerbated this Catholic discrimination: "The insistent Anglicization and Protestantization of *Udolpho*'s protagonists suggest a structure in which the fundamental conflict lies between Protestant rationalism and Catholic superstition, between English domestic ideology and continental perversions."[14]

This threat, presented through the language and aesthetics of Gothic excess, was what Hopkins had to reconcile in his own life, particularly in the wake of the Roman Catholic Relief Act of 1829 which allowed Catholics to practice law, open schools, and practice their religion. The Oxford Movement from 1833 to 1845 saw a sustained Protestant vigilance against a supposed Catholic threat to England. The bleeding of historical realities with the fictional world of Gothic romance was not uncommon, as misconceptions of Catholic practice abounded. As Diane Hoeveler has shown, authors of Gothic romance manufactured images of Catholicism that became the vivid bugbear for a nationalistic English imaginary. Ideas of Catholicism became inculcated in the public, reinforced through the prolific examples of ritualism, supernaturalism, and excess reiterated in Gothic tales and novels.[15] And as the previous chapters have illustrated, these anti-Catholic prejudices were projected not only through insidious Catholic characters, like monks and nuns, but reified through the formal structures of Gothic romance, through tropes of guilt and suspicion embedded in the English consciousness of what it meant to be Catholic. Cloisters, catacombs, and abbeys were natural settings for rape, infanticide, and other sanctimonious behaviors. What is noteworthy, however, is that while having to write within this literary climate, Hopkins still utilized Gothic forms in genuinely spiritual, non-parodic ways, grappling with questions of his faith amid the Oxford Movement and his Catholic conversion.

Indeed, the representations of Catholicism that circulated within Gothic fiction influenced English life from 1790 to 1870 and vice versa through an influence of mutual exchange. Patrick O'Malley's *Catholicism, Sexual Deviance, and Victorian Gothic Culture* establishes two important premises surrounding the cultural significance of Gothic. First is the idea that the fear and threat of English Catholicism is inextricable from Gothic, particularly fears that the Romish Church was infiltrating Oxford. Second is the identification of Victorian religious writing as Gothic texts that utilize the language of ghosts and hauntings, as seen in the tracts of John Henry Newman and Charles Kingsley. The language, prejudices, images, and structures of Catholic behavior spread to novels, tales, and the English public, each feeding the imagination of the others. Even if Hopkins had little to no contact with Lewis and Radcliffe, their writings are linked through a shared Gothic language. As O'Malley writes, "Although it turns out there are no ghosts in Udolpho, the same cannot strictly be claimed of *Udolpho*, for the ghost of Catholicism haunts the work. Behind the black veil, it turns out, is not a body, but ritual Romanism itself."[16] Laurentini's body, and Gothic fiction more broadly, is the site of convergence for a host of Catholic stereotypes: confession, confinement, idolatry, and an inability to distinguish ritual from substance, simulacrum from life. The confusion between real and symbolic, the bleeding over from fiction to reality, as well as fears of superstition and the dislike of aesthetic excess—all encompass fears of Catholicism infiltrating England and English identity. By the 1860s, the Gothic was not just an English caricature of a foreign Catholic threat within fiction, but an important and constitutive form of expression of English Catholic life.

The English Catholic Cleric

The autobiographical impulse behind so many of Hopkins's poems presents a distinctly powerful point of connection between his Victorian poems and 1790s Gothic romance. While Gothic fiction relies on a blurring of historical and fictional xenophobic and religious stereotypes, Hopkins provides a counter-intuitive example against that powerful Gothic thematic, overturning expectations of what Radcliffean romance had dictated the Catholic cleric figure should be to an English audience. As an actual English Jesuit priest, (as opposed to the fictional Italian monk), he contradicts and complicates the fictive character of the villainous monk that dominated Gothic romances and tales. While most examples of Catholic figures in 1790s Gothic and its Victorian afterlives are hyperbolic and parodic—mostly criminal, hypocritical, dangerous, and perverse, like Lewis's Father Schedoni, Tennyson's St. Simeon Stylites, Browning's monk of the Spanish cloister—Hopkins's use of Gothic forms forces us to take seriously the English Gothic experience, and to qualify the Gothic's representations of a supposed Catholic threat.

As seen in Chapter 1, the Italian Catholic monk was a star figure in the works of Radcliffe and Lewis, from Father Schedoni to Ambrosio. This stock villain character was fueled by the trappings of Gothic superstition, unfair Catholic absolution, sacrilegious penitence, idolatry of high clerics, and the conflated lavishness of Catholic cathedrals and Italian castles. As scholars have long noted, Radcliffe's novels attracted the voracious readership of an English public through their blatantly xenophobic, anti-Catholic backdrop. This is reinforced in her settings of 1590s France or Italy, posing a split between English Protestantism and the Catholicism of southern Europe. She in fact relies upon the Englishness and Protestant leanings of her readership to bolster the villainy of such monks. *The Italian* in particular, (subtitled "*Or, the Confessional of the Black Penitents*"), scandalizes Italy as a nation of criminals and deceivers, while mystifying the Catholic religion as a cultish machine with its own inquisitional tribunals and obscure denominational orders. Of course, Hopkins was not a monk, but a Jesuit priest—and his poems portray for readers not the stereotype of exaggerated Gothic fiction, but the lived experience of religious isolation and the psychological battles experienced by a man of this calling. In this sense, Hopkins brings home and normalizes the anxieties of English Catholic life as a priest, an experience that to many English readers had only been represented and portrayed in outlandish, reductive, and exotic Gothic frameworks. Having inherited an entire literary tradition of Gothic thematic stereotypes, Hopkins's writings deserve readers who might acknowledge and recognize this Gothic baggage his texts must work against.

Walter Scott had credited Radcliffe for firmly introducing Catholicism into the Gothic:

> She selected the new and powerful machinery afforded her by the Popish religion, when established in its paramount superiority, and thereby had at her disposal monks, spies, dungeons, the mute obedience of the bigot,

the dark and denominating spirit of the crafty priest,—and all the thunders of the Vatican, and all the terrors of the Inquisition.[17]

In this sense, Radcliffean representations of Catholicism were both a microcosm and a contributor to the wider understanding of a Catholic "threat":

> With its system of saints, rituals, and seemingly supernatural sacramental theology, Roman (and ultimately ritualist) Catholicism, appeared to many English critics to be an eruption of the medieval into the present, an anachronism as dangerous to liberty and prosperity in contemporary England as the fantastic perils of the Gothic novels were to their continental protagonists.[18]

As O'Malley explains, the threat of Catholicism reaching England soon shifted from the realm of fiction to that of English life. "For Radcliffe, the terrors of Catholic violence and violation [we]re, at least for her English readership, sensational in part because they are largely hypothetical."[19] But by the time Maturin's *Melmoth the Wanderer* was composed, the English Protestant public was already primed to fear the growing Catholic threat, from "the liberalization of laws against Irish Catholic practice and political participation, [to] the Oxford Movement and Newman's 1845 conversion to Catholicism, the 'Papal Aggression' of 1850, and the yearly parliamentary debates around the government endowment of the Irish Maynooth seminary during the early 1860s."[20] In a vicious cycle, this growing anxiety then fueled the anti-Catholicism within fiction, which ratcheted up fears to match the climate of paranoia among reading audiences. And while John Wolffe argues that the convulsive violence of the Gordon Riots actually led to comparative sympathy towards Roman Catholics and a disinclination to militant Protestantism, this lasted for only a couple of decades.[21] The waxing and waning of toleration and anti-Catholic sentiment in England, along with its reflection in literature, has been well mapped out by Alison Milbank, Mark Canuel, Amanda Paxton, Denis Paz, and Susan Griffin.[22] To be sure, the overwhelming Protestant prejudice of Gothic texts, confirmed by J. M. S. Tompkins, Diane Hoeveler, James Whitlark, Anne McWhir, and Leslie Fiedler, is not exhaustive. In *The Gothic and Catholicism: Religion, Cultural Exchange and the Popular Novel, 1785–1829*, Maria Purves complicates our understanding of anti-Catholic Gothic by mapping the increased sympathy towards Catholics coinciding with the passing of Catholic Relief Acts in 1791 and 1793, as seen particularly in England's reception of émigré priests who sought

English refuge and sanctuary from France. Focusing on lesser-known texts, Purves argues that attacks on "monkish superstition" did not dominate all Gothic texts, particularly in tales in which figurations of the cloister, nun, and monk are often represented sympathetically and even heroically.[23]

Hopkins, as an Anglican turned Catholic, embodies the convergence of the Englishman and the Catholic priest, bridging a dichotomy much exaggerated in Radcliffe's world of fiction, but one that was still highly controversial in 1850s England. Prevalent still were "old Protestant stories of gluttonous, lascivious, and sadistic monks," while the opening scene of *The Italian, or the Confessional of the Black Penitents* illustrates this point, centralizing the disbelieving Protestant Englishman discussed in Chapter 1.[24] The same anti-Catholic stereotypes that bolstered the popularity of Radcliffe's novels—especially fixations on lavish displays of wealth and the indulgences of sins—were rehashed by sharp critics of the Oxford Movement, including Hopkins's own father, who opposed his son's turn towards the Roman Catholic Church.

Hopkins's father forbade his son from contact with any of his siblings, for fear of his attempts to convert them, too. Charges against High Church services at the time centered around complaints against the fancy and Romish display of their services. Scottish clergyman John Cumming described the problem:

> Prodigious efforts are being made by the Ritualists to enlist converts, or rather I should say perverts. Young men and young women are captivated and charmed by beautiful music, by a gorgeous ceremonial, by rich and variegated dresses, which also, whether at the ball or at the opera, or in a Ritualistic Church, are no doubt very attractive; and by rites and lights, and attitudes and genueflexions, extremely well done . . . .[25]

In heated letters exchanged with his father, Hopkins defends himself from one of the major attacks of Broad Church critics: that the Holy Roman Church services were showy and practiced an ornate "ritualism." Protestants maligned Catholic ritual as gaudy and theatrical, while Hopkins's reply to his father's threats of estrangement sought to delineate the "simple," "common," and unpretentious reasons for his conversion.

> I am surprised you shd. say fancy and aesthetic tastes have led me to my present state of mind: these wd. be better satisfied in the Church of England, for bad taste is always meeting one in the accessories of Catholicism. My conversion is due to the following reasons mainly

> (I have put them down without order)—(i) simple and strictly drawn arguments partly my own, partly others', (ii) common sense, (iii) reading the Bible, especially the Holy Gospels . . . (iv) an increasing knowledge of the Catholic system (at first under the form of Tractarianism, later in its genuine place) . . .[26]

The attacks leveled against the High Church that Hopkins defends against are religious critiques centered on differences in aesthetics and taste. Many of the same anti-Catholic stereotypes rehearsed in the Gothic novel influenced the succeeding reception of Hopkins's verse style by Protestant critics and readers. Hopkins's signature use of compound words and his Anglo-Saxon-style alliteration were regarded as lush and lavish by early scholars. John T. Netland construed Hopkins's choices in diction as "wildly extravagant linguistic liberties," even those that "startle the reader by their ostensible naturalness."[27] Critics of the 1950s placed Hopkins within the school of decadent poets. His poetry would be prone to attacks of luxury and decadence even well into a century after the Oxford Movement. As Donald Davie argued:

> Hopkins wrote in a decadent age, and if he is its greatest poet, he may be so because he cultivates his hysteria and pushes his sickness to the limit. Certainly he displays, along with frantic ingenuity, another decadent symptom most easily recognized, the refinement and manipulation of sensuous appetite . . . It is the Keatsian luxury carried one stage further, luxuriating in the kinetic and muscular as well as the sensuous. Word is piled on word, and stress on stress, to crush the odours and dispense a more exquisite tang, more exquisite than the life.[28]

A poet himself, Davie preferred the "chaste" diction of Goldsmith and Wordsworth and described the "impurity" of Hopkins's syntax in overtly physical terms: He "has no respect for language, but gives it Sandow-exercises until it is a muscle bound monstrosity."[29] Though the setting and content of Hopkins's devotional verses are primarily stark, bare, and ascetic, the richness of his linguistic style is cast within the ornate, decorative tradition of Gothic aesthetics, furthered Protestant representations of the Roman Catholic Church. To read Keatsian excess in Catholic ritual, and to identify this in Hopkins's poetry, already shows the Protestant leanings of reading practices trained and reinforced through Catholic caricatures of Gothic romance and a wider English tradition of alienating the Catholic Other.[30] Furthermore, the sensuousness that Davie detects is a critique of that startling effect particular to Hopkins, in which he uses linguistic richness to contrast the bleak terror that the poet experienced in the last decade of his life. Here, style counters content in a dynamic clash between "luxury" and deprivation that can be seen in Hopkins's "Terrible Sonnets."

Of course, this idea of aesthetic excess was often couched in terms of homophobia, and Hopkins's homosexuality, discussed at length by scholars such as Julia Saville, appears in his notebook with sometimes gothically violent forms of self-castigation.[31] As R. J. C. Watt puts it, Hopkins's "flirtation with Catholicism had 'the crucial Gothic quality of transgression': Anglicans and his family regarded it with horror; 'pervert' was the word for convert."[32] The Catholic threat abroad came to infiltrate English life at home.

> By the latter half of the nineteenth century, figures such as the Roman Catholic Church and the sexual transgressor could no longer be considered separate and other. This represents in many ways an iconic triumph of the Gothic. Writers such as Radcliffe not only relegated religious and erotic deviance to the Continent but also relied upon a recognizable notion of English sectarian and sexual values. Once the controversialists of the mid-century apply those Gothic tropes to domestic figures, they open the possibility that the supposedly foreign vices they are condemning can be native to Britain as well. The true Gothic anxiety by the end of the nineteenth century is that one might wake up to discover that the fantasized foreigner lives right at home, indistinguishable from the rest of the English citizenry.[33]

O'Malley demonstrates how elements of 1790s Gothic persisted throughout the nineteenth century, not only in novels such as *Lady Audley's Secret* and the vampire culture of John Polidori, Sheridan LeFanu, and Bram Stoker, but even in the language of controversialists, who recruit Gothic tropes and narratives to enliven the threat of Catholic immorality. His chapter on "'The Church's Closet': Victorian Catholicism and the crisis of interpretation" reveals that religious debates surrounding English Catholicism—including writings by John Henry Newman, Charles Kingsley, and John Addington Symonds—recruited Gothic imagery in their rhetoric of opprobrium or even to describe visions of their conversion.

Connections to Gothic romance and Radcliffe in particular, cited in *Catholicism, Sexual Deviance, and Victorian Gothic Culture* are worth revisiting in detail. Kingsley, for example, attacked both Newman's religion and sexuality by utilizing the threatening language of Gothic infiltration, describing Newman's oratorical power as a source of seduction for young men. In "What, Then, Does

Dr. Newman Mean?," Kingsley presents Newman and other converts as villains of Gothic romance who "hid[e] their corruptions behind the excuse of Romanism."[34] In O'Malley's words:

> From the private confessional to the public ritual, from scenes of masochism to scenes of seduction, anti-Catholic evangelicals of the later years of the nineteenth century both rely upon the language of the Gothic and create their own Gothic narratives in order to warn their compatriots of the fundamentally deviant—and devious—dangers of Romanism and ritualism.[35]

Newman, in turn, reclaimed this Gothic language to articulate "a new notion of specifically English Catholic subjectivity" in *Apologia Pro Vita Sua*.[36] In this famous defense of his Catholic faith, Newman recounts early signs and calls to the church as ghostly visions, including allusions to a supernatural hand that appears in the Book of Daniel. Newman even cites Radcliffe by name in a memory from his early youth, when he witnessed the image of the Catholic rosary appearing to him: He saw "a set of beads suspended, with a little cross attached. At this time I was not yet ten years old. I suppose I got these ideas from some romance, Mrs. Radcliffe's or Miss Porter's; or from some religious picture."[37] Symonds, on the other hand, has Gothic, nightmarish visions of a corpse on his bed and a young man kissing his forehead as a key component to the narrative of his "inversion."[38]

> Newman's emphasis on medievalising, phantasmal narratives as the root of the movement toward Catholicism continues where his early references to Radcliffe left off, tracing the Romantic poets and novelists [such as Walter Scott, Southey, and Coleridge] who took up the resonances of Radcliffean Gothic for their own purposes; if for Newman "Nature was a parable" and "Scripture was an allegory," Roman Catholicism was, it seems, a Gothic romance. Newman's genealogy of his own conversion—and thus of nineteenth-century English Romanism itself—thus produces its origin as a literary fascination with the Gothic as a genre.[39]

By drawing upon tropes and language from earlier Gothic, O'Malley contends, controversialists of the nineteenth century "ultimately—and ironically—establish those [Catholic] notions as undeniably *English*."[40]

The Gothic trope of a fixated gaze or fascination takes on heightened religious meaning in the nineteenth century. "Fascination" was a mode of hypnotic attraction, marked by an irresistible and sometimes erotic attraction to evil. This trope is most apparent in sensational works of Male Gothic, such as *The Monk* and *Vathek*, which feature deviance and diabolical desire through explicit representation. As we saw in Chapter 3, objects of fascination induce an affective suspension on the part of the viewer, whose attention is gripped and frozen in time, beyond their own physiological control. In religious writings of the nineteenth century, converts to Catholicism were portrayed as victims of fascination, unable to resist the hypnotic attraction of Romanism. As the Church Association wrote in 1880, "None can deny the [Roman Catholic cathedrals] their powers of fascination. They are masterpieces of art, and miracles of beauty. They exercise an almost irresistible charm over the cultivated mind. Yet heathen temples did the very same!"[41] The aesthetic argument against fixations on visual beauty and seductive attractions likens Catholic ritual and idolatry to the otherworldly gazes of Rossetti's framed women, explored in Chapter 3.

The mutual fixation between Gothic viewers and framed women, from Radcliffe to Lewis to Rossetti, finds renewed force in the anti-Catholic language of writers waging against the "Popery of Oxford." Here, the church seductively invites fascination through its decadent and irresistible framing of ritual pleasures:

> Oxford and Cambridge are, as it were, (speaking in the language of metaphor,) the two Eyes of our Church and Nation, which ought to be wide awake to the best interests of the whole body politic as well as ecclesiastic, and not in disunity ... The visual splendor of Catholicism is literally blinding, hypnotizing the "eyes" of Oxford and Cambridge, the protectors of a unified Church and state, into sleep. In some ways this appeal to the visual represents an alternative strategy to the appeal to the linguistic that continued to characterize much anti-Catholic rhetoric of the mid-century.[42]

This language describing the binding influence of the Romish Church has clear insinuations: that to turn away and break the spell or grip of this fascination requires great moral fortitude and an ability to transcend aesthetic, sensual pleasures. To interrupt the grip of the fascinating gaze is to affect a suspension of the senses, in a Hopkinsian triumph in asceticism.

The preceding chapters on Robert Browning, Elizabeth Barrett Browning and Christina Rossetti, and Dante Gabriel Rossetti have each traced the evolution of Gothic tropes into particular poetic forms: (1) the trope of confession and eavesdropping in the dramatic monologue, (2) liberty within confinement in women's sonnets, (3) the reader's visual experience of "shock and swap" in Pre-Raphaelite picture poems. Each of these Gothic forms, imported from Gothic novels into Victorian poems, gains historical import when viewed through nineteenth-century depictions of English Catholicism: the contested practice of auricular confession; confinement and isolation within the confession box, Jesuit cell, or monastery; and the idea of fascination (visual fixation or attraction to an object) and conversion (turning away). These Gothic tropes, when refracted through often-distorted representations of Catholic life, become useful frameworks for approaching Hopkins's poems and understanding his "poetics of wavering."

Confessional and Audience in the "Terrible Sonnets" (1885)

In a letter to Robert Bridges, Hopkins refers to a set of sonnets that reflect his depression in Dublin, most likely comprising "To seem the stranger," "I wake and feel," "No worst, there is none," "Carrion Comfort," "Patience, hard thing," and "My own heart." During this difficult time of adjustment and isolation, Hopkins reported to his friend, "I think that my fits of sadness, though they do not affect my judgment, resemble madness."[43] As he described, their composition seemed almost supernaturally spontaneous: "I shall shortly have some sonnets to send you, five or more. Four of these came like inspirations unbidden against my will."[44] They reach an almost hysterical pitch of despair, counterbalanced with moments of low and quiet respite.

"I wake and feel the fell of dark, not day" is a poem that is tonally stark and bare, with a speaker surrounded by nothing besides darkness and his own cries; no material objects or glimmers of nature surround him. Instead, within the objective poverty of these lines, any richness in texture develops from Hopkins's workings with phonemes and sensory pyrotechnics. The octave reads:

> I wake and feel the fell of dark, not day.
> What hours, O what black hours we have spent
> This night! what sights you, heart, saw; ways you went!
> And more must, in yet longer light's delay.
>
> With witness I speak this. But where I say
> Hours I mean years, mean life. And my lament

> Is cries countless, cries like dead letters sent
> To dearest him that lives alas! away.[45]

Despite charges of decadence or decoration, the setting here is clearly one of overwhelming darkness and deprivation, of asceticism rather than "sensuous appetite."[46] Any richness or texture is created through alliteration and synesthesia. Hopkins layers on repeated consonants in "feel" and "fell," "dark" and "day," "sights" and "saw," "ways" and "went," "more" and "must," "longer" and "light," and "cries countless, cries." The speaker "feels" darkness, since it cannot be seen in the pitch darkness; time is measured with vision or color in "black hours." But the literary techniques Hopkins employs, even if they suggest multiplication or adornment, are a means of expansion from few resources; it is a sign of making do with a paucity of raw elements: alliteration repeats consonants, yielding two words from one phoneme; synesthesia creates complexity by mixing simple elements and crossing senses. Within the poem, any sense of measurement loses focus in this chaos of senses, with "countless cries" and the sudden expansion from "hours" to "years" to "life." Quite literally, the speaker is creating temporal length and distance from nothing; he projects from what is essentially darkness and void.

Though Hopkins's stylistic and linguistic richness creates a sense of "piling on," it is important to remember that this humble richness, created from paucity, means to accentuate the effects of darkness and despair.[47] The poem's sestet depicts spiritual suffering and the discomfort of insomnia:

> I am gall, I am heartburn. God's most deep decree
> Bitter would have me taste: my taste was me;
> Bones built in me, flesh filled, blood brimmed the curse.
>
> Selfyeast of spirit a dull dough sours. I see
> The lost are like this, and their scourge to be
> As I am mine, their sweating selves; but worse.[48]

The Gothic element in Hopkins's "Terrible Sonnets" comes not from any supernatural elements, but rather from the chilling, skeletal sense of bareness: "Bones built in me, flesh filled, blood brimmed the curse." Projecting this harsh physicality, Hopkins composed sonnets that, if read as confessionals, do not sound out the admission of prosecutable crime. Instead, they confess the guilt of despair, his breach of faith, and a punitive self-loathing. His soliloquizing admits of bitterness and sourness as a taste of one's self.

Hopkins, an English priest, is clearly a far cry from the hypocritical "monkish" villains fictionalized in Radcliffe and Lewis or Tennyson and Browning, including Schedoni, Ambrosio, St. Simeon Stylites, the Bishop who orders his tomb, the monk of the Spanish Cloister, and Bishop Blougram. Through unwitting confessions, those characters betray their own sanctimoniousness because their desires to be recognized for piety outweigh their faith in God. Hopkins's confessionals, however, propose a potential model for what Mill may have considered poetry in its purest form. Unstaged and free of "incident," Hopkins's "Terrible Sonnets" address God directly and were not expected to be read by a wide audience. They are intensely private and spontaneous in their address, offered in the mode of holy prayer. In fact, Hopkins's "Terrible Sonnets," not meant to be read by a public audience or overheard by any third-party auditor, can be seen as situating the genre of honest Catholic confessional within a poetic context. To this effect, Hopkins presents the true meditations of a Catholic priest in a way that rehabilitates confession from its negative representations in Gothic fiction, dramatic monologues, and Broad Church propaganda. His intensely private prayer-poems, monodramas directed towards God, seem to offer a version of the confessional that sheds the incriminating, Gothic valences of a criminal cleric confessing his crime. Instead, they restore the Augustinian sense of a believer confessing his love for God and increasingly register the postmodern doubts and fears of modernity.

However, if pure Millian poetry is executed in the mode of confessional, what marks the difference between a prayer and a poem? All manners of soliloquy, whether sung, written or prayed, engage with the presence or absence of a listening audience. Furthermore, Hopkins's careful choices in language and sounds—the overdecoration of "word . . . piled on word, and stress on stress" that Davie disdained—work against the idea of his poetry as spontaneous and unlabored.[49] I argue that Hopkins's "Terrible Sonnets" in fact complicate our previous models of overhearing in the dramatic monologue—because they betray a strong anxiety surrounding the question of whether his confessions are heard or not by God. The question of whether or not "God has . . . heard a word!" resonates against Browning's egomaniacal monologists who represent the other villainous extreme, where the question of lyric overhearing is a sanctimonious challenge rather than an authentic, unegotistical crisis of religious doubt. Hopkins's uncertainty as to whether his confessions are (over)heard by God is a source of guilt for the poet—guilt about his faith having lapsed—and this is the ultimate source for the "terror" embodied by these "terrible" poems.

One of the practices that attracted Hopkins to the Roman Catholic Church was an emphasis on auricular confessional, a departure from Broad Church practice. As Simon Reader has noted, Hopkins was already using his notebooks for confession and experimenting with this even before his conversion to Catholicism, because High Anglican clergy recommended this practice.[50] Even before his conversion, Hopkins had begun making confessions in 1865 to Canon Henry Parry Liddon, a controversial High Church don who was still a member of the Church of England. Auricular confession allowed a clergyman the authority to grant absolution to the guilty. This places pressure on the confessional not only as a religious practice but as a verse form, one that assumes heightened meaning, comprising Hopkins's hybrid poems that are part sonnet, prayer, confession, and soliloquy. Though the "Terrible Sonnets" are highly dramatic, they are not dramatic monologues, and in fact require an indifference about audience in order to function as pure confessional or prayer.

The publication history of Hopkins's notebooks also brings into question the uneasy ethics of auricular confession. The 1937 *Note-Books and Papers of Gerard Manley Hopkins*, followed by the 1959 *Journals and Papers*, excluded the lists of sins in Notebook C.II, with the understanding that the details often connected to salacious rumors were protected by the seal of the confessional. Leslie Higgins qualifies this, however, reminding us that: "One should remember ... that in 1865–6 Hopkins, an Anglican, was confessing to Liddon and Edward Pusey, Anglican clergymen. They were experimenting with auricular confession, as part of a Tractarian commitment to traditional Christian rites, but this form of purification was not a recognized sacrament of the church, as confession was and is for Roman Catholics."[51] Pusey had revived the practice of auricular confession in 1838, to the objection of others such as Bishop Blomfield. Evangelical and Broad Church critics found auricular confession too "papist" for thriving on secrecy, where "salacious stories of the confessional" damned it as a "fountain of filthiness ... teaching, and ... study[ing] filth and obscene literature, to pollute the purity of our wives, daughters, and little children, by questions and suggestions on the most indecent subjects."[52] Without a doubt, these accusations echo the apprehensive attacks against Rossetti's "fleshly school" and the "terrorist" Gothic literature, discussed in Chapter 3.

The practice of auricular confession became a major site of suspected criminality that drove anti-Catholic prejudices. This builds upon already virulent suspicions of the Catholic father and monk figure as the ultimate transgressor of earned trust: the confessional box became a site for undisclosed liberties undertaken in secret under the guise of confidentiality. O'Malley explains:

> The threat that the confessional poses, according to the tract, is not only theological in its ramifications but also sexual and political, imperiling at once the individual and the nation . . . Most fundamentally . . . the practice of auriculuar confession achieves its simultaneously seductive and treasonous goals through the veil of secrecy. The confessional function as a 'closet' in the imaginations of such Protestant polemicists . . . Drawing together national, sexual, and religious ideological concerns, the rhetoric of 'the Church's closet' both looks back toward the conventions of the Radcliffean Gothic romance and reproduces them as anew genre of controversialist literature.[53]

This idea of the "Church's closet," so apt also for an exploration of Hopkins's devotional and confessional verse, comes from an 1871 anti-Catholic controversialist tract entitled *The Oxford and Roman Railway*. This was one of many such tracts published by the Protestant Evangelical Mission and Electoral Union:

> The Priests use the Confessional to obtain the secrets of the *individual*, the household, or the State. They use it to corrupt, pervert, and enslave their victims—to satiate their own lust, avarice, ambition, and malice. It is "the Church's" closet for pry, intrigue, and "ambiguous familiarity."[54]

Of course, this extreme English phobia of the confessional as a site for fantastical, inexplicable criminality was cultivated in the realm of Gothic fiction. Put plainly, "this anxiety around the Catholic threat to national and familiar security through the secretive power of the confessional [is] an anxiety fundamental to the Radcliffean Gothic" that persists in evangelical circles into the 1890s.[55] "The confessional had been—from Radcliffe to the anti-Catholic polemicists of the mid-nineteenth century — the privileged space of Gothic Catholicism, the consolidation of all the fears of confinement that give Gothic literature its narrative drive."[56] As O'Malley shows, Gothic mode of confession and criminalized speech undergoes development across the century, from 1790s fiction to religious writings of the 1890s. It extends across the range of public and private confessional, from the incredibly public spectacle of Oscar Wilde's trials to the intensely private mode of self-confession in Hopkins's devotional verse.

* * *

In his so-called "Terrible Sonnets," Hopkins replaces the space of the Gothic monastery and translates it into the Jesuit community, thereby harnessing Gothic forms in ways useful and relevant to his own experience. With this transformation, he rewrites the trope of the Gothic monk and rewrites, or translates it, into the Jesuit priest through his use of confessional. As we saw in Chapter 1, the rise of the Victorian dramatic monologue solidified auricular confession as a site of highly suspicious or guilty speech acts. Browning's dramatic monologues are marked by a poetics of anxiety and guilt surrounding overheard confession not typically present in a Romantic conversation poem. Porphyria's lover famously taunts God at the end of Browning's dramatic monologue, challenging a response from above but also drawing the reader's attention to the triangulation of speaker, audience, and auditor at play in the poem's form: "God has not said a word!"[57] For Browning's Caliban, the monologist outright apostrophizes: "Setebos, Setebos, and Setebos!"[58] In a poignant departure from this monomania, Hopkins too points to the silence ringing throughout his poem when he addresses God, but in a way that is painfully searching rather than challenging.

The importance of echoes and overhearing in relation to auricular confession are especially important for reading "No worst, there is none," where the sounds of reverberating words accentuate the silence around the poet-speaker. As if writing alone from within a cell, he awaits a return of his sounds and syllables to confirm the presence or absence of an overhearing God.

No worst, there is none. Pitched past pitch of grief,
More pangs will, schooled at forepangs, wilder wring.
Comforter, where, where is your comforting?
Mary, mother of us, where is your relief?
My cries heave, herds-long; huddle in a main, a chief-
Woe, wórld-sorrow; on an áge-old ánvil wínce and síng—
Then lull, then leave off. Fury had shrieked 'No ling-
Ering! Let me be fell: force I must be brief.'

O the mind, mind has mountains; clíffs of fáll
Frightful, sheer, no-man-fathomed. Hold them cheap

> May who ne'er hung there. Nor does long our small
> Durance deal with that steep or deep. Here! creep,
> Wretch, under a comfort serves in a whirlwind: all
> Life earth does end and each day dies with sleep.[59]

Here the monastery is a location for sounding out desperate cries. The barrage of echoes continue on, with "comforter . . . comforting," "where . . . where . . . where," "mind . . . mind." "More pangs" and "forepangs" reverberates throughout the lonely cell, but the inversion of order ("More pangs" preceding "forepangs") offers us a reminiscence of the unnatural, backwards nature in Barrett Browning's neologism "outbear," in place of "bear out," as discussed in Chapter 2. Throughout "No worst, there is none," the internal rhymes within lines ("steep"/"deep"/"creep") add to the reverberation in what sounds like an overwhelmingly compact space, crammed with words where sounds bounce back quickly in repeated consonants. The proliferation of echoes, alliteration, and rhymes may impart a sense of crowdedness, but ultimately it highlights the emptiness of Hopkins's cell, save himself. His rhetorical questions hang unanswered. The words and sounds are almost suffocating to the point that they fill his "coffin of weakness and dejection." Again, what seems like proliferation and plenty actually exposes loneliness and isolation. Hopkins must fill in space and sound himself, with the echoing of his own words to fill the void of any reply, as he cannot be sure that any other being is present.

The internal resonance of "ling-/Ering," dramatically enjambed to increase the distance and time of the trailing echo, again creates a poetic moment loaded with the questionable absence or presence of God. Does God hear his words? Does God hear his unanswered echoes, too? The silences between resounding rhymes leave space for a breach of faith, a moment of spiritual trial. Whereas Browning's monologists challenged the Romantic lyric tradition by immodestly unheeding any overhearers and thus flaunting their wrongs, Hopkins's speaker risks the very most at the moment that he assumes no auditor and no audience: the insinuation that absolutely no one can bear witness or hear his prayer. The formal space of this poem might be a godless world. To offer a confessional to no listener insinuates that one's faith towards God has disappeared. This sonnet conveys a fear that God does not hear Hopkins's call for mercy, a doubt that is staged with each echo that succeeds a question or startling caesura.

"Forepangs" and "wilder wring" resound against another poem, "Sibyl's Leaves," in which the poet feels as if on "a rack / Where, self-wrung, self-strung . . . thoughts against thoughts in groans grind."

Leslie Higgins attributes this to "the Dolben effect," referring to Hopkins's crisis from his attraction to Rome and his attraction to Digby Macworth Dolben, "an unusually charming and humorous young man, who loved to shock both contemporaries and elders by emotional and religious excess; his poetry reflects his flamboyant interests."[60] The grief and guilt of illicit love also parallels that voiced in Christina Rossetti's 1858 "The Convent Threshold." Hopkins's "selfwrung" connotes a self wrong, as he punishes himself with words reminiscent of the rack; he is "strung" and hung as if in a Gothic, inquisitional court of self-trial and self-torture.

In her introduction to Hopkins's *Diaries, Journals, and Notebooks*, Higgins emphasizes the "self-lacerating inventories of the Oxford diaries," as well as the "sometimes torturous self-examination in notebook C.II."[61] She also draws on Hopkins's famous lists in C.II, which "summarized indulgences and transgressions—actual or imagined—in what became a daily rite of self-castigation."[62] These lists of transgressions began as two or three lines in length, but eventually came to take up entire pages of the diary.

> Every few months, they provided evidence of "sinfulness" to be offered up during auricular confession, thus enabling Hopkins to participate in rituals of admission, penance, and expiation. The entries were written in pencil, in an increasingly small hand, then cancelled—but cancelled carefully, with a thin ruled line. They were thick enough to indicate which sins had been purged, but thin enough so that he could revisit his transgressions and indulge in further self-loathing.[63]

Based upon a letter to Baillie from 1885, Hopkins was a "selftormenter."[64] The meticulous self-monitoring apparent in his lists may be construed as the monk acting as confessor to himself.

In this way, Hopkins's "Terrible Sonnets" stand as confessional poems that demand God as their sole auditor. Here, religious confession becomes spiritually insidious not so much if it is overheard, but if it honestly entertains the fear that there is no audience, no overhearers. Indeed, towards the end of Hopkins's life, especially after he was stricken with typhoid fever in 1889, he developed an increasing sense that his prayers did not reach God. His Jesuit duties also led him to an increasing sense of isolation, where his poems had found no audience aside from Bridges, Patmore, and Dixon. In his letters to them, Hopkins refers to his "wretched state of weakness and weariness" and "fits of sadness."[65] The presentiment that God was not hearing his prayers is intensified in the following sonnet, with the ringing ("wringing") echoes of silence from this speaker's cell. This effect of the echo specifically creates the effect of the empty cell.

Hopkins, in his confessional poems, does not "perform" confession to win a cheap absolution, but solemnly works through lapses in doubt. Though surely no fictional works of Gothic romance, his poems, fraught with religious guilt, align then with the same formal preoccupations: he confesses to himself in solitude, in the mode of prayer, but with the hope of being overheard. This does not boast the lyrical glory and self-assuredness of Romantic apostrophe or a conversation poem, but assumes a somber and fearful Gothic mode of failed triangulation instead.[66] Hopkins's speaker does have an audience in mind—that of God—and it is perhaps this awareness, both as a child of God and as a poet attuned to his own formal posturing, that fuels his sense of guilt and doubt. Here, pondering the basic question of any poet, whether or not one's audience is listening, becomes a sign of spiritual doubt. This self-consciousness, seen poetically in the echoes, wringing, and "elegant" choice of his decorative syntax, betrays the "mere eloquence" indicative of any poet, even those aspiring to the ideal of pure poetic confession—just as those ironized in 1790s Gothic romance.

Back in Chapter 1, Radcliffe's comical scenes of overhearing demonstrated that true, unstaged confessional free of incident and manipulation could not be achieved within the context of the novel. Just as we have seen immortalized in the inquisitional contexts of Gothic fiction, Hopkins cannot elude the inextricable formal associations of confession as incrimination. The aspect of performance behind authentic confession and the anxiety of an overhearing audience in his poetry points to the impossibility of achieving "pure" Millian poetry or confession in poetry, even in the starkest and least "decadent" context of religious prayer. This presents an important convergence on the part of our English Catholic poet: Hopkins leverages Gothic tropes in such a way that allow him to unite distinctly English forms of lyric poetry with his Catholic faith. His national and religious identities find overlap through this particular form of confessional verse.

Liberation in Confinement: Inscape in "The Caged Skylark" and Curtal Sonnets

The space of the confessional, though confining, takes on broader ramifications through wider structures in nineteenth-century Gothic.

Chapter 2, which established a Gothic connection between sonnets and putative confinement, returns here in the thematic-formal message of liberty despite restraint. Just as Keats's, Wordsworth's, Barrett Browning's, and Christina Rossetti's sonnets showed that their stanzas and prison cells were "not so small," (or as Susan Paterson Glover comically puts it, "Radcliffe's convent as comfortable hotel"), the confession chamber became more widely construed in the mid-1800s, assigning connotations of criminality and intrigue in the structure of the monastery more broadly. "While the anti-Catholic polemicists viewed the confessional as a site of seduction and sexual deviance of all kinds, it was at least a temporary confinement. The Catholic monastery, however—and especially the convent—provided the fantasy of permanent internment popularized by the Radcliffean Gothic."[67] The convergence of the monastery and the university became apparent—replacing Rome with Oxford—especially following Newman's conversion to the Roman Catholic faith in 1845. As Newman's center of life moved from Oxford to Rome (and he was made a cardinal thirty-four years later by Pope Leo XIII), the public began to understand the Tractarian Movement as a "Romeward Movement" that exchanged the "Popery of Rome" for the "Popery of Oxford."[68]

During his years at University College Dublin, with an impending sense of death and isolation, Hopkins referred to his cell as "that coffin of weakness and dejection in which I live."[69] His description of this physical living space finds familiar expression in the sonnet form as a cage or prison itself. In Chapter 2, Wordsworth and Keats presented the sonnet as a comfortable cage or a pleasant plot of land; Elizabeth Barrett Browning and Christina Rossetti took up the Gothic rhetoric of confinement and created sonnets that enacted self-imprisonment through further formal innovation. Hopkins, too, engaged in technical experimentations with the sonnet form that offer variations on the themes of spiritual liberation and confinement. In familiar Gothic fashion, the replacement of monastic cells and confession chambers with monasteries more generally signals a disingenuous expansion of space. The monastery that is in fact just a metonym for a single monastic cell upholds the Italian count's reassurance that the dungeon or castle turret is far more spacious and safer than a dangerous alternative. Yet at the same time, Gothic victims are masters of spatial ingenuity, able to twist, turn, and contort themselves to transcend a sense of claustrophobia.

The desolation of the "Terrible Sonnets" is no doubt intensified by the sense of self-punishment and self-flagellation, though here, it is exacerbated within a Catholic rather than a female context. Much like the women pent in their chambers and cells, Hopkins takes on the role of the beaten and incarcerated victim, in a religious mode that celebrates suffering and servitude to a patriarchal master. He uses the sonnet form to vindicate intense, even violent confinement where the body is subjugated and tormented, joining the tradition of "Gothic sonnets" previously established.

Crammed with echoes, alliteration, and dense compound formulations, Hopkins's sonnets can be considered Gothic sonnets, for they portray a limited, even stifling sense of space that mirrors the confinement of the imprisoned soul to the body before transfiguration. This confinement is intensified by the threat of darkness, isolation, and insomnia—elements that serve as fuel and punishment for the speaker's doubt. Whereas the poets previously discussed in Chapter 2 capitalize upon the sonnet's thematic connections with imprisonment and punishment, Hopkins offers up a metasonnet that takes up the imagery of animal-like captivity. "The Caged Skylark," an explicit meditation on confinement, rehearses the message of Wordsworth and Keats's sonnets that such a cage actually "no prison" is. Dated 1877 from St. Beuno's, Wales, this poem uses the skylark as an analogy for the lesson taught in the first exercise of St. Ignatius' *Spiritual Exercise*, which states that "my soul is imprisoned in this corruptible body."[70] The sonnet is housed or caged within a clear *abba abba ccd ccd* rhyme scheme:

> As a dare-gale skylark scanted in a dull cage,
>   Man's mounting spirit in his bone-house, mean house, dwells—
>   That bird beyond the remembering his free fells;
> This in drudgery, day-labouring-out life's age.
>
> Though aloft on turf or perch or poor low stage,
>   Both sing sometímes the sweetest, sweetest spells,
>   Yet both droop deadly sómetimes in their cells
> Or wring their barriers in bursts or fear of rage.[71]

In the first half of the octave, Hopkins compares "Man's mounting spirit" with a "dare-gale skylark." Both are vibrant creatures relegated to dwell in "dull," "mean" spaces—the bird's cage or man's skeleton and bodily form. The skylark, "scanted" in his cage, recalls for us Wordsworth's reference to the sonnet's "scanty plot of ground." In lines 3 to 4, Hopkins draws a distinction between "That" bird and "This" man: "That" bird has at least had the memory of freedom and flight, which are now beyond it ("free fells"). Meanwhile, "This" man has no past memory of such freedom, and can only look forward to it. The "drudgery" of "day-labouring" also connotes darkness, recalling Milton's sonnet "On His Blindness," which asks, "Doth God exact day-labour, light denied?"[72]

The following quatrain, in another closed *abba* unit, does not draw any distinction between the plight of the man and the bird, but rather emphasizes their union. Now conflated, the skylark and poet alliteratively "sing sometimes the sweetest, sweetest spells" within their confines, as Wordsworth might argue in "Nuns Fret Not." But for Hopkins, they alternately "droop deadly" in their cells, or rear against their cage in fear and anger to make their "barriers" "burst." This duality is encased in the single verb "wring," which denotes throttling and strangling, but also the echoing of a vibrant sound: Hopkins uses this word again in "Carrion Comfort" and "No Worst, There is None." It is a word that both shuts up, with violence and confinement, and homophonously "rings" out, with productivity and creativity. As we reach line 8, the "wall" of the octave, we are left with the image of a caged animal violently smashing itself against the cage's walls.

Within this poem, is the bird's cage (or the man's skeleton, or the sonnet's form) ultimately a stimulus for sweet singing? Or is it a cell confining enough to tranquilize or terrorize its prisoner into submission? The final sestet is marked by indecisive oscillation, as seen in the alternating conjunction words that begin each line and alter the logic of each clause: "Not," "Why," "But," "But," and "For."

> Not that the sweet-fowl, song-fowl, needs no rest—
> Why, hear him, hear him babble and drop down to his nest,
>   But his own nest, wild nest, no prison.
>
> Man's spirit will be flesh-bound when found at best,
> But úncúmberèd: meadow-dówn is nót distréssed
>   For a ráinbow fóoting it nor hé for his bónes rísen.[73]

If the first octave ends by warning against the more sobering constraints of the skylark's "dull cage," the sestet offers even more in terms of apology. As line 9 insists, the bird requires rest, lest he drop from exhaustion. We hear, from the repetition in "sweet-fowl, song-fowl" and "hear him, hear him," and from the sighing, as if from weariness, that the skylark needs a respite to function within healthy parameters. The echo effect in these quick repetitions again reminds us of how small the space between these walls may be.

Line 11 reiterates Wordsworth's insistence that such a nest or cage "no prison" is. In this line, the almost-repetitive "own nest, wild nest" stealthily expands the actuality of a single birdcage to the wide purview of nature, just as Wordsworth slowly transitions from nuns' cells to wide, open "furness fells." This insistence that the nest is at least his own, and no prison, echoes the Gothics of Keats's sonnet as well: "If by dull rhymes our English must be chain'd . . . She will be bound with garlands of her own."[74]

Though lines 7–8 argue for a conservative, constraining bent, describing a pitiably defeated and mastered bird, lines 9–10 turn the tables yet again. Lines 9–10 justify the bird's frustration and exhaustion over its confinement, because, as the speaker reminds us, it is not as if birds don't need a rest, too. Every two lines, Hopkins designs yet another turn in logic, arguing the opposite of his previous lines and pivoting around the words "Though . . . Yet . . . Not that . . ."[75] A reader of "The Caged Skylark" is subjected to constant reframings and repositionings in the case for and against confinement, and the octave of the poem is thus conflicted in its final argument. The seemingly repetitive sounds of "sweet-fowl" and "song-fowl" only echo the bird's sweetest spells of line 6, now portraying a frustrated and tired creature whose song is mere "babble," his nest both wild and a prison.

The final three lines are the culminating reason for Hopkins's argument that the cage and body "no prison is." Here he describes man in the state of resurrection, where though he is "flesh-bound," (locked within this echoing "f," "b" pattern in "found at best" and "footing . . . for his bones"), his soul remains "uncumbered." Here, the word "unencumbered" has lost a syllable, as if the poem lacks space to house even the required two letters. Allowing no room for waste on unnecessary sounds, this makes the word require three stresses ("úncúmberèd") instead of four (únèncúmberèd). The neologism sheds its usual spelling and worldly body for a sleeker, more compact form, as man would, leaving his body after salvation. In these ending lines, verticality triumphs, with an upward, ascendant motion rebounding against the heavy gravity of things that weigh down: the "meadow-down" (in parallel to "flesh-bound") is not distressed by a rainbow footing it (it is not held down like one side of a rainbow rooted in a meadow); nor is man distressed for his bones having risen. The heavy weight of "footing" acts like an anchor, with "down" in "meadow-down" functioning as a space (downs) and as a direction in verticality. Despite all the gravity and downward pull of these final lines, this is paradoxically all a negative construction to counter-intuitively argue for the upward pull (of a rainbow, or of souls ascending after death). The argument of salvation and ascendance is always couched in the language of heaviness and being bound.

* * *

Although form can seem rigid and taxing in "The Caged Skylark," Hopkins's additional variations on sonnet form opened up a window for both poetic and spiritual liberation. As previously mentioned, it was during the middle of the nineteenth century that the term "pervert" came to signify sexual deviance more so than it denoted religious conversion, or a turning to a new faith. In 1871, *Dr. Pusey's Insane Project Considered* talks about the "English perverts" who "delight to rub their necks against rusty chains." This links the "perversion" of the Catholic converts to a masochistic bondage similar to that in the controversialists' rhetoric of the convents.[76] Panic set in at the sheer number of prominent citizens "perverting" to Rome.[77] The coalescing of the terms "convert," "pervert," and "invert" also introduces a poetic valence with this idea of turning away. Focusing on the shifting placement of the "volta," or turn, in Hopkins's curtal and caudated sonnets, I explore again the Gothic trope of finding freedom and spatial creativity despite confining formal strictures.

A formal innovator, Hopkins re-envisioned a sonnet that both expanded and contracted the poetic form with his "caudated" and "curtal sonnets." "Pied Beauty," "Peace," and "Ash Boughs" are examples of Hopkins's truncated curtal sonnets, comprised of 10.5 lines each, with "curtal" referring to a horse that had its tail bobbed. He explains in his "Author's Preface" to the *Poems*:

> Nos. 13 and 22 are Curtal-Sonnets, that is they are constructed in proportions resembling those of the sonnet proper, namely 6 + 4 instead of 8 + 6, with however a half-line tailpiece (so that the equation is rather $12/2 + 9/2 = 21/2 = 10 ½$).[78]

Hopkins first proposed the curtal sonnet as a means of compensating for a discrepancy in language: Italian syllables trip off the tongue and elide, so that a pentameter line in the Italian sonnet could often house fourteen to fifteen syllables. An English line of pentameter, however, was constrained to a maximum of ten syllables without the help of elisions, which made the line too "short, light, tripping and trifling," an imperfection in Hopkins's eyes.[79] As Lois Pitchford writes,

"According to Hopkins the sonnet in English of fourteen lines was loose and flabby. He wished to tighten it and make the form compact around the idea."[80] Hopkins combated this "flabbiness" by increasing the "pressure" of his sonnets to match the pressure of the Italian sonnet, using the analogy of balloons filled with air. The caudated sonnet, on the other hand, expanded the sonnet form by appending a six-line "tail" to the end, usually with extra enjambment between lines 14 and 15 to increase the effect of elongation. "That Nature is a Heraclitean Fire" was written as a caudated sonnet.

Hopkins's seemingly rigid prosodic techniques are in fact not as exacting as the numbers and fractions in his "Author's Preface" might indicate. Despite his mathematical proportions, the poet's delineation of more rules and more formal distinctions can be read in a more liberating light, when considered within his idea of "inscape," an object's unique form or shape imbued by God. In a sense, Hopkins can be understood as breaking down the sonnet form and celebrating the individuality of its varied reincarnations, moving away from conceiving of the sonnet as a solidly dictated form. Regarding each poetic form as one of God's miraculous creations, he stops to appreciate the instress of each different permutation, as he does in "Pied Beauty." Hopkins creates more technical restraints in the form of his poems in a manner that is not only productive but diversifying. Much in the same way that Christina Rossetti's *bouts-rimés* in *Maude* yield a proliferation of sonnets portraying girls with distinct personalities, Hopkins's curtal and caudated sonnets do the same by delineating different inscapes. In other words, he multiplies the possibilities of a sonnet's inscape, reveling in the glory of God's numerous creations as well as his own. There is not one sonnet form, but myriad variations that collectively comprise that category. Thus the form of "Peace" and "Ash Boughs" are each their own distinct vessels, uniquely different due to the presence of God within them. To apply the idea of inscape to poetic forms themselves helps one to understand that the skylark's cage "no prison" is. The cage or skeleton is not just a shell, but each a distinct, wild, and organic form that represents the individuating work of God.

"The Windhover"

In his consideration of Hopkins's works in relation to the visual arts, George P. Landow observes that the poet "seems to share a great deal with the early Pre-Raphaelites who, following Ruskin, attempted to combine an extreme hard-edge realism with elaborate symbolism derived ultimately from habits of reading scripture common to both Protestants and Catholics."[81] Indeed, in his use of Gothic forms, Hopkins shows commonalities with Rossetti in his use of both fleshly and symbolic objects as loci for meaning and aesthetic value. This double commitment to realism and symbolism is crucial to readings of "The Windhover," which is very conspicuously dedicated "To Christ our Lord." Hopkins perhaps wrote this poem based on Psalm 91:4, literalizing a metaphor to visualize and stage the comfort and safety of Christ in literal terms of nature: "He shall defend thee under his wings, and thou shalt be safe under his feathers."[82]

> I caught this morning morning's minion, king-
>   dom of daylight's dauphin, dapple-dáwn-drawn Falcon, in his riding
>   Of the rólling level ùndernéath him steady áir, and stríding
> High there, how he rung upon the rein of a wimpling wing
> In his ecstasy! then off, off forth on swing,
>   As a skate's heel sweeps smooth on a bow-bend: the hurl and gliding
>   Rebuffed the big wind. My heart in hiding
> Stirred for a bird,—the achieve of, the mastery of the thing!
>
> Brute beauty and valour and act, oh, air, pride, plume, here
> Buckle! AND the fire that breaks from thee then, a billion
> Times told lovelier, more dangerous, O my chevalier!
>
> No wónder of it: shéer plód makes plóugh down síllion
> Shine, and blue-bleak embers, ah my dear,
> Fall, gáll themsélves, and gásh góld-vermílion.[83]

In this well-known poem, readers are meant to read the windhover both as a sign of nature's beauty, a sign of God's creation, and as Jesus Christ ("O my chevalier!"). However, rather than rest on the simultaneity of both readings, I suggest that a sense of wavering, of flickering back and forth between the two understandings of the image, is more fitting to Hopkins's project and better complements his work in the "Wreck." The "sillion / Shine," "blue-bleak embers," and "gold-vermillion" offer the example of flickering and flames which effect the similar flashing of images that can be staged in the reader's mind. The windhover's quick flight erupts like fire in the second stanza in a way that presents movement and change over the rest and fixity of the first stanza. In essence, I propose a reading of Hopkins's symbolic-realist moments in much the same way that viewers of Rossetti's paintings and poems would experience a quick fluctuation of just what they are seeing—momentary uncertainty surrounding the fleshly object or the idealized symbol. Hopkins's verses are trials of perception and revelation, testing readers to make sense of the uncanny embers, at once lifeless and meaningless ash, but in another moment, flaming and lifelike in our eyes as a symbol of Christ. In terms of Hopkins's poetry, this flashing or fluctuation need not indicate doubt or a lack of faith, but, as we will soon see in the "Wreck," it actually proves an understanding of the active process that is instress, presently perceiving the duality of God's work in whatever inscape opens up before us.

The rocky experience of Hopkins's reader is analogous to that of viewers interpreting Rossetti's Pre-Raphaelite paintings, who are made to focus on the "wriggling" and the "fleshly," rather than so easily coming to rest at the implied symbol. It also mirrors the experience of Gothic readers, who turn away, falter, faint, or waver upon encountering scenes of terror and shock. Such a reading supports Hopkins's conception of arriving at God's inscape in tragedy as a difficult process that necessitates work and active participation through the process of instress and stress. To this end, a reader's experience of the rocky ebbs and flows between object and symbol enacts the storm that believers and doubters must undergo. Moreover, this experience of vacillating is a bodily response, living through the physical stresses like the nun or the windhover that mirror the fluctuation of one's progressing faith. And because each reader's experience of the metrical stresses and symbolic fluctuations varies distinctly from person to person, this yields a myriad of individuated instress-experiences for each poem, neither confined nor tied to any single inscape of that verse.

"Riding a River": The Gothics of Stress, Instress, and Inscape in "The Wreck of the Deutschland"

William Wordsworth's defense of the sonnet, which I examined in Chapter 2, insists that "Nuns Fret Not"; while Leigh Hunt, in his note on the poem for *The Book of the Sonnet*, worried on behalf of the "thousands of nuns" who, "no doubt, have fretted horribly, and do fret" in their hermitages.[84] Some sixty-five years later, in an entirely separate historical moment, Hopkins famously questioned the plight of suffering nuns, addressing the five women shipwrecked at the mouth of the River Thames in "The Wreck of the Deutschland." This poem, which broke his seven years of silence, presents a prosodic landscape and a moral world where storm and stress dominate, in which the cruel hand of God is read as a sign of his love and power. As he recounts in an 1878 letter to R. W. Dixon:

> When in the winter of '75 the *Deutschland* was wrecked in the mouth of the Thames and five Franciscan nuns, exiles from Germany by the Falk Laws, aboard of her were drowned I was affected by the account and happening to say so to my rector he said that he wished some one would write a poem on the subject.[85]

The resulting ode preoccupies itself with the physical suffering of the tragic nuns at the same time that it celebrates God's hand in such innocent suffering. Though in a pointedly different context from "Nuns Fret Not," Hopkins's poem resonates with the lesson in Wordsworth's Gothic sonnet that the patient forbearance of pain or death leads to reward—especially female suffering endured under the reassurance of a male master. To read the nuns' deaths as proof of God's presence and power is a matter of faith; but to bear witness to the tragedy as a source of transfiguration or spiritual refreshment ventures into the realm of Gothic thrall and enthrallment we saw in Chapter 2. As Virginia Ellis describes, the poem may seem

> alien to some readers, or actually offensive, and even a sympathetic reader may sense a kind of coldness, though a fiery coldness at its heart: a failure of human sympathy for those who wretchedly, and by lay standards needlessly, suffered and died, which results from the poem's and the poet's passionate commitment to the concept of redemptive suffering.[86]

The poem's subtitle indicates not tragedy, but a "happy" occasion: "The Wreck of the Deutschland: to the happy memory of five Franciscan nuns, exiles by the Falck Laws, drowned between midnight and morning of December 7."[87]

Gothic forms predicated upon death and violence are evident in Hopkins's conceptions of both inscape and instress. The Gothic recognition of beauty in dead things both values and transcends morbidity. We see this in the plight of the nuns and in Hopkins's conception of inscape, celebrating the hand of God in all of nature's living, dead, and dying things. While inscape for Hopkins is an object's form, vessel, or unique, God-imbued shape, instress is the force of being that holds the inscape together. Instress is also the impulse from the inscape that carries its whole into the beholder. It is both the activation energy and the kinetic energy necessary to make an object's beauty show. Usually, the release or realization of instress is seen as a triumphant moment, as in the recognition of God's imprint upon all "dappled things."[88] But there is also a potentially destructive impulse behind instress, which can certainly be seen in "The Wreck." Hopkins's own explanation of these terms famously uses as an exemplar the inscape of a dead tree. Preceding the following passage, he specifies that instress is most usually perceived by a person when they are alone:

> There is one notable dead tree . . . the inscape markedly holding its most simple and beautiful oneness up from the ground through a graceful swerve below (I think) the spring of the branches up to the tops of the timber. I saw the inscape freshly, as if my mind were still growing, though with a companion the eye and the ear are for the most part shut and instress cannot come.[89]

It is notable that Hopkins's example to explain the concept of inscape is a dead object in nature, an otherwise negative or gloomy image that here yields grace, freshness, and spring. The tragedy of the *Deutschland*, then, is loss of human life that can yield positivity for those who can "s[ee] the inscape freshly." We see further Gothic undertones of inscape in a journal entry from 13 July 1871: "It is not that inscape does not govern the behavior of things in slack and decay as one can see even in the pining of the skin in the old and even in a skeleton but that horror prepossesses the mind."[90]

As Hopkins's explanations show, inscape requires active participation to be recognized and perceived. This can be seen in stanzas 5 to 6 of "The Wreck of the Deutschland," where the inscape of the storm is recognized through quite violent stresses. We recognize the contrast between inscape and instress, rest and motion, in the steady water versus wavering storms in Hopkins's imagery. Hopkins's use of stresses (in terms of beatings, flagellation, storm, and metric stress) places particular emphasis on the physical experience of suffering through God's poundings and thrashings in the storm.

> I kiss my hand
> To the stars, lovely-asunder
> Starlight, wafting him out of it; and
> Glow, glory in thunder;
> Kiss my hand to the dappled-with-damson west:
> Since, tho' he is under the world's splendour and wonder,

> His mystery must be instressed, stressed;
> For I greet him the days I meet him, and bless when I understand.
>
> Not out of his bliss
> Springs the stress felt
> Nor first from heaven (and few know this)
> Swings the stroke dealt—
> Stroke and a stress that stars and storms deliver,
> That guilt is hushed by, hearts are flushed by and melt—
> But it rides time like riding a river
> (And here the faithful waver, the faithless fable and miss).[91]

In the passage above, the "dappled-with-damson west" recalls the beauty of dappled things in "Pied Beauty." Yet this recognition of beauty is clearly the calm before the impending storm, as mirrored in the grander structure of Part I and Part II. Part the First, which is ten stanzas long, is mostly autobiographical, meditating on when the author succumbed to the stresses of God in acknowledgment of his mastery. Part the Second is a longer twenty-five stanzas, creating a 2:5 ratio in the poem as a whole. This second part moves outside of the self and narrates the incident of the shipwreck. Specifically, in stanzas 17 to 19, Hopkins recounts the episode when the tall nun is confronted with the stress of God's power. Throughout, the poem's speaker recognizes God's hand and presence in the events of this disaster. My reading of "The Wreck of the Deutschland" thus dwells upon the stress and violence imbedded in "instress" rather than featuring its more celebratory representations, as seen in "Pied Beauty" or even the "The Caged Skylark." In the lines quoted above, the "stress," "stroke," and "swings the stroke dealt" carry the sense of motion and force through which God's "mystery must be instressed, stressed." The "hushed" guilt and melting hearts offer a sense of nature revealing its underlying form and inscape to the attuned viewer.

In this sense, instress delivers, through action, the inscape of both the positive, serene side of nature (stars) and its darker, threatening counterparts (storm): we see this in the "Stroke and a stress that stars and storms deliver." To ride the waves of instress and feel this push and pull is what it means to be faithful, enduring the uncertainty of highs and lows. "The faithful waver, the faithless fable and miss." This line, set off in parentheses, offers a momentary respite through reassuring words of advice: those who are faithless "fable"; they believe in easy, false symbolism with easy, packaged morals.

The faithless learn meanings from stories, without experiencing stress of suffering themselves. Hopkins has transformed the noun "fable" into a verb here. "To fable" sounds active and unstable, perhaps akin "to wobble" or "to waver." "To fable" may also be to lie and fib, to tell fables. This stanza makes clear that to maintain a strong belief in God is not to stand still, unwavering in faith, but in fact to waver and to bend to endure the painful fluctuation. Here we recognize familiar valences of the Gothic reading experience from Chapter 3, where the shocks and swaps of visual perception are akin to the peripeteias of the nun's narrative. Catastrophes in life offer no smooth transitions, but rather sudden reversals that upend world views, between a godly and a godless world. This jolting and elasticity are not the basis of doubt, as one might expect, but the basis of belief. The experience of recognizing God's imprint in nature and on the world is a process and journey, like "riding a river."

"Riding a river" serves as an apt metaphor for a reader journeying through the metric turbulence of Hopkins's verse. The difficulty of the poem is not so much in keeping track of the stresses or "counting" his sprung rhythm, but of violently experiencing the stresses, enduring the poet's recreation of the shocks and turns alongside God's presence.[92] Furthermore, Hopkins's method of counting accentual meter re-enacts the practice of keeping faith, holding one's unfulfilled expectations until the following line is to be satisfied. For even in the leniency and liberality of scansion across lines, things always add up. As Hopkins explains:

> It is natural in Sprung Rhythm for the lines to be *rove over*, that is for the scanning of each line immediately to take up that of the one before . . . and in fact the scanning runs on without break from the beginning, say, of a stanza to the end and all the stanza is one long strain, though written in lines asunder.[93]

Note that the language of "strain" and "asunder" here acknowledges the difficulty of breaking patterns and pushing them to extremes. As R. J. C. Watt argues in "Hopkins and the Gothic Body," sprung rhythm is "nothing more or less than an attempt to liberate feet in verse," emphasizing formal freedom over constraint.[94] The essence of sprung rhythm is that "one stress makes one foot, no matter how many or few the syllables." In effect, then, by seemingly creating more rules and theoretical delineations in his "Author's Preface," Hopkins actually frees meter of the chains of syllabic meter, opting for accentual meter instead. We can hear in his explanation of these prosodic adjustments the innovations of Gothic form we have previously recognized, whether in Keats's "sandals more interwoven / To fit the naked foot of poesy" or in Barrett Browning's and Christina Rossetti's *bouts-rimes*. Hopkins chooses to formulate the experience of "riding a river" within the rubric of restriction and thrall. Such Gothic poetics, featuring formal, innovative pyrotechnics in confinement, allow Victorian poets to choreograph a physical understanding of the poem within a Gothic reader.

The Gothic Poetics of Wavering

In my readings of Hopkins, I spotlight the active verb of the faithful—those who triumphantly "waver"—in order to fully explore the ideas behind a Gothic poetics of wavering, which carries meanings of uncertainty, restlessness, change, and conversion. Unpacking this term yields myriad valences and reflections across Hopkins's poems, from "Pied Beauty" to "The Windhover" to "The Wreck." To be wavering is to be endlessly turning, without the guarantee of rest. It draws on the Old Norse *vafra*, to hover about, and from the Latin *vertere*, meaning to "turn"—an etymological root for the English word "verse" and a relation to the poetically significant Italian "volta." To water implies restlessness linked to the motion of water, waves, and undulations. It is fitting also for sound in the sense of aural frequencies, of soundwaves, cries, and echoes ("ling-ering!"). It relates to the waves and wind necessary to stay buoyant up in the air ("The Windhover"), or to waves of grief and the water of tears or drowning ("The Wreck").

Indeed, all these waves and undulations of sound, air, song, and doubt pervade Hopkins's poems. And the prosodic wavering of his sprung rhythm, accumulating more or fewer syllables per line, also contributes to the ebb and flow driving this poetics. Most centrally, of course, is the experience of wavering in one's faith. As we see in nearly all of Hopkins's poems, it is the wavering that keeps one afloat—not drowning under waves of grief—that maintains a dynamic equilibrium of faith in God. To constantly renew and doubt one's faith in God is exhausting, punishing work, and always wavering ensures a life that is guaranteed no rest but earnestly committed to the labor of renewing this faith, swimming, flying, or pushing head on against resistance. Endlessly turning, with no repose, marks the experience of Hopkins's Catholic faith—with each turn of his poetic lines and each volta of his "Terrible Sonnets." This is Hopkins's poetics of wavering.

That Hopkins's poems invite a Gothic readership and cultivate Gothic forms of reading is evident in his poetics of wavering. While existing readings of "The Wreck of the Deutschland" have conceived of the poem as a practice in enduring or overcoming the stresses that God bestows, the Gothic component resides in the constant and utter doubt of faith—leaving us in restless motion. Hopkins's poetry necessitates that readers put in the work to arrive at a recognition of God's presence, both spiritually and in the technical experience of understanding the language of his poem. This labor relies on the physicality of bodily suffering. We embody the wavering faith and feel, through imagery, the fluctuations of each swell and crest of doubt. Because of Hopkins's sprung rhythm and his difficult, compound neologisms, fully realizing the "inscape" imbedded within a scene of nature or a work of God requires taxing, rigorous participation on behalf of the reader. This pressure, labor, and stress pulls from both sides: as Netland puts it, inscape "can only be perceived by the instressing nature of God and the receptive instress of the reader."[95]

A reader of Hopkins must thus be open to receive the inscape of a poem—both its message and its form—just as a Gothic reader must be open to suffer the shocks and uncertainties of the explained supernatural. As we saw in Chapter 3, Gothic readers must welcome the experience of shock and swap in successive bouts of startling reframings. The difficulty of undergoing suspense and suspension is compounded in Gothic reading because of the successive and repetitive change. In his more harrowing poems, Hopkins emphasizes the physical details and textures of this wavering that challenges readers to a breaking point. In so doing, Hopkins presents the intensity of successive shocks as the challenge of willful submission, echoing the constant, alternating surrenders to God or to fits of doubt, and the masochistic nature of repetitive flagellations. The release and perception of inscape and instress is a two-way street, where a reader must be poised to experience shocks, blows, doubt, and surprise. This is the mode of Gothic readership that accepts the exhausting, endless trials of instability and doubt.

The Symbolic Realism of Suffering Nuns

By now, to uncover Gothic forms of reading in Hopkins's religious verse should no longer seem irreverent with regard to the poet's spiritual convictions. The recognition of Gothic forms does not, for instance, contradict the readings of Martin Dubois in *Gerard Manley Hopkins and the Poetry of Religious Experience,* which emphasizes the varied and fluctuating nature of Hopkins's spiritual awareness over a cohesive, unified vision.[96] To locate the Gothic in Hopkins is not to create sanctimonious connections across common characters or themes, comparing the five Franciscan nuns to fictional nuns from Gothic works, whether Diderot's *The Nun* (1796), English chapbooks like *Anecdotes of a Convent* (1771) and *Atrocities of the Convent* (1808), or the "Tale of the bleeding nun" adapted by Matthew Lewis and other novelists. Rather, we might recognize that reading Hopkins's poems requires adopting familiar modes of Gothic readership—agreeing to be bent under the violence of stresses that embody corporal, visceral forms of spiritual doubt. When a beacon of hope does rise up in "The Wreck," it is no wonder that the six-foot tall nun becomes a locus that is at once symbolic, representative, literal, and metonymical. Identifying the Gothic forms that Hopkins employs in his representation of the nuns, we might focus particularly on the role of fleshly and corporeal representation and the use of symbolic realism in the context of this religious poem.[97]

The famous "tall nun" in "The Wreck of the Deutschland" serves as a symbol of a "Biblical prophetess crying out warnings from her watch-tower."[98] This is not your typical damsel in distress, but at once a towering Christ-like martyr figure and a suffering female body. Stanza 17 heralds the arrival of the nun as a strong "lioness" and "prophetess" who is "towered in the tumult."

>   They fought with God's cold—
>   And they could not and fell to the deck
> (Crushed them) or water (and drowned them) or rolled
>   With the sea-romp over the wreck.
> Night roared, with the heart-break hearing a heart-broke rabble,
> The woman's wailing, the crying of the child without check—
>   Till a lioness arose breasting the babble,
> A prophetess towered in the tumult, a virginal tongue told.
>
>   Ah, touched in your bower of bone,
>   Are you! turned for an exquisite smart,
> Have you! make words break from me here all alone,
>   Do you!—mother of being in me, heart.
> O unteachably after evil, but uttering truth,
> Why, tears! is it? tears; such a melting, a madrigal start!
>   Never-eldering revel and river of youth,
> What can it be, this glee? the good you have there of your own?

> Sister, a sister calling
> A master, her master and mine!—
> And the inboard seas run swirling and hawling;
> The rash smart sloggering brine
> Blinds her; but she that weather sees one thing, one;
> Has one fetch in her: she rears herself to divine
> Ears, and the call of the tall nun
> To the men in the tops and the tackle rode over the storm's brawling.[99]

At the same time that she embodies such powerful symbolism, however, the nun is a fleshly woman, whose suffering was what first brought Hopkins's attention to the composition of this poem. According to *The London Times* on 11 December 1875, "the chief sister, a gaunt woman 6 ft. high call[ed] out loudly and often 'O Christ, come quickly!' till the end came."[100] The verbs in Hopkins's poem, "crushed," "drowned," and "roared," are simultaneously literal indicators of nature and aptly chosen parallel verbs. Hopkins wrote, "What refers to myself in the poem is all strict and literally true and did all occur; nothing is added for poetical padding."[101] Like Rossetti's framed female faces and bodies, Hopkins's tall nun is both a suffering body and a metaphorized symbol of strength and salvation. As Virginia Ellis recognizes, the poem represents "a fusion of physical and spiritual fact, of inner and outer event"; "the literal was recognized by [Hopkins] as metaphorical but 'metaphor' in turn reveals a higher literalness."[102] In the metaphor of the "lioness," which channels pride, bravery, and royalty, her body is also distinctively female (and not just a "lion").

This doubly literal and symbolic technique, or symbolic realism, continues throughout the numerological insistence of the following stanzas:

> She was first of a five and came
> Of a coifèd sisterhood.
> (O Deutschland, double a desperate name!
> O world wide of its good!
> But Gertrude, lily, and Luther, are two of a town,
> Christ's lily and beast of the waste wood:
> From life's dawn it is drawn down,
> Abel is Cain's brother and breasts they have sucked the same.)
>
> Five! the finding and sake
> And cipher of suffering Christ.
> Mark, the mark is of man's make
> And the word of it Sacrificed . . .[103]

Like Rossetti's spurge of three, the number "five" is literal and symbolic, referring to the five wounds of Christ, and continuing on in stanzas 22 and 23. Similarly, the lament for the "Deutschland" invokes both a physical object, the name of the boat, but also works metonymically, as a critique of Germany, the country of Martin Luther, and also Bismark's anti-Catholic Falk Laws. The nun is both a "Sister," her appellation and title in her religious office, but also literally just "a sister calling / A master," an individual sibling in a particular convent and from a particular family. The "gaunt figure" of the nun is not simply spectral, or a sibyl haunting the poem, but a figure of realism, as Meredith Martin draws out in her reading of the poem.

Martin, reading stress and scars in the text of the poem as "the stigma of meter," likewise emphasizes the coinciding of two types of physical marks: symbolic text and the material marks on the page. She reads with attention to the physicality of marks and stresses, both on the nuns' bodies and on the page. She notes, "The Wreck of the Deutschland" was rejected by editors due to the confusing "mess of marks."[104] (Hopkins wrote, in his essay "Rhythm and other Structural Parts of Rhetoric—Verse," that "we may think of words as heavy bodies.")[105] Of the Tall Nun, she writes:

> She is both "nun" and "none," one part of a larger pattern of inscape that marks her for transformation into the divine. The transformation foreshadowed here is one in which Hopkins transforms the nuns, who are martyred by God (the "mártyr-máster," as he is called in line 167), into holy marks ... With Christ watching, the poem narrates the transformation of the nuns' bodies into text: "in thy sight / Storm flakes were scróll-leaved flowers" (167–8). Flakes, for Hopkins, means sea-flints but also flesh. It is the nuns' flesh that is "scróll-leaved," inscribed by their own salvation.[106]

In many ways, Martin's reading of the nun's flesh reinforces the Gothic qualities of these passages in "The Wreck of the Deutschland," in which the nun's corporeality is comparably as important as the fleshliness of Rossetti's women. Realism and symbolism converge in a version of symbolic realism necessary for this affective prosody to take effect on its readers. The poem is a Gothic body: it is a messy overlap of the nuns' image, the nuns' bodies, and the body of the text. The Gothic bodies of the nuns and the Gothic body of the poem suffer the blows and marks of both the poet and of God:

> "The stroke dealt" is not only a blow from the Lord but also the "strike" of stress above the line, particularly noticeable in this primarily monosyllabic stanza . . . The line also refers to the process of marking the "strokes of stress" on a poem about divine transformation, itself a process in which the poet wavers.[107] . . . Over the letters is the whip, the punishing spiritual devotion between Christ and the poet, between the word and its stress . . .[108]

The imprint of scars, cuts, blows, and whips are Gothic in their violence and punishment, not only in a Catholic context but with sadist or masochistic overtones as well. Where I depart from Martin is my turn away from a narrative of single transformation and insistence on the discomfort of continued fluctuation or "wavering," as previously discussed. For Martin, "Hopkins suggests, using stress marks, that the mystery of Christ is potentially readable. By 'meteing' or measuring Christ in verse with the appropriate stress, Hopkins is able to greet Christ."[109] My focus instead on the act of wavering throughout "The Wreck of the Deutschland" takes shape through even more than scansion. Hopkins's poetics further insists that "to waver" or "to fable" emerges with a stronger sense of motion through the idea of a "turn," particularly "turning away from" in the sense of conversion or perversion. As cited earlier in this chapter, Patrick O'Malley discusses the historical use of the terms "pervert," "invert," and "convert," noting the shift from a Catholic context to a homosexual and pejorative one. Hopkins's turn away from the church, or from heteronormative life, might be construed then as a series of many returns and turnings away, rather than a single decision. He is constantly and unrelentingly turning away from and back towards God, wavering in his faith. In this sense, the reader and the poet experience the fluctuations seen in the Gothic swaps and switches of Radcliffe's and Lewis's double swaps or in Rossetti's framed women, where the challenge of confrontation requires not one act of turning away and coming straight again, but rather a series of unnerving upendings, possibly followed by more tests of faith. In Martin's reading, faithful wavering is guaranteed to fall into the right path:

> By performing the process of reckoning with the words as flesh and that flesh as scored and scarred, the poem is riddled with its own anxiety about the necessary wavering that "reading" those marks requires. If we

have wavered, with the marks, into the right understanding, the stigma will be transferred from the page and into our minds and effect a kind of transformation (or a verse-conversion).[110]

In my own reading, Hopkins and the Franciscan nuns reside in a more Gothic world than one might think, one in which the guarantee of transformation is never taken for granted, and never so simple—thus creating the suspense and suspension of rewarded faith that is part and parcel of the Gothic reading experience.

This distinctly Gothic form of physicalized wavering and constant motion is a poetic mode not precluded by Hopkins's religious commitment. From his permutations of nouns into verbs, and the recurrence of words that seem to reappear within his poems, Hopkins's is a poetry of restlessness. The quick-paced vacillation between perceiving an object or seeing it as a symbol is important for the staging of spiritual perception and belief. This "work" and process of uncertainty is truer to faith than a comfortable acceptance of the windhover as both the bird and Christ, at the same time: "the faithless fable and miss."[111] In "The Wreck of the Deutschland," too, the nun is not a figure that simply transformed from a suffering female body into a bodiless representation of holy salvation. The vertical move from physical pain to symbolic transcendence is never meant to be an easy transition for Hopkins; he does not transcend the physical world of pain into the spiritual world of reward to arrive at a state of rest. Instead, he moves "backwards," focusing first on physical suffering and second on spiritual redemption, spending twice as many stanzas on the thrashing "stresses" doled out by God, the fluctuations of his love. The structure of "The Wreck" paves the way for an uncertain wavering between the lows of enduring the literal stresses exacted as punishment, with the highs of perceiving God's inscape. It is this back-and-forth momentum that fuels the poem's tumultuous pace, imitating the deadly storm. Whether riding a river through water and storm—or catching pockets of wind like a bird's wings in the air, whether sounding echoing cries of despairs in loud undulations of sound waves—or the iambic waves of prosodic meter, wavering is a key physical experience behind Hopkins's verses. "The faithful waver, the faithless fable and miss." To waver is the condition the true believer, and the constant restlessness—that denial of rest and safety—a remnant of the Gothic literary experience implicit in Hopkins's poetics of wavering.

Notes

1. All poems by G. M. Hopkins refer to *The Poetical Works of Gerard Manley Hopkins*, ed. Norman H. MacKenzie (Oxford: Oxford University Press, 1990). Here, p. 120, Part I, Stanza 6, line 48.
2. Hopkins, "Pied Beauty," in *The Poetical Works*, p. 145, lines 4, 11.
3. Hopkins, "Spring," p. 142, lines 7, 6.
4. Hopkins, "The Windhover," p. 144, line 14; "Hurrahing in Harvest," p. 148, lines 9, 10.
5. Hopkins, "The Wreck of the Deutschland," pp. 119–28. Here, p. 120, Part I, Stanza 6, lines 47–8.
6. For more on Hopkins's "Very Victorian Reading Habits," see Leslie Higgins's introduction to *The Collected Works of Gerard Manley Hopkins, Volume 3: Diaries, Journals, and Notebooks* (Oxford: Oxford University Press, 2015), 38–44.
7. Paul Mariani, *A Commentary on the Complete Poems of Gerard Manley Hopkins* (Ithaca: Cornell University Press, 1970), 47.
8. Maria LaMonaca's *Masked Atheism* explores the Victorians' fear of Anglo and Roman Catholicism through readings of Charlotte Brontë, George Eliot, Christina Rossetti, Elizabeth Barrett Browning, Michael Field (*Masked Atheism: Catholicism and the Secular Victorian Home* (Athens: Ohio State University Press, 2008)).
9. For the reasons I have mentioned, scholars have not generally recognized Hopkins as a Gothic poet nor read his works as Gothic texts. One exception is R. J. C. Watt, whose "Hopkins and the Gothic Body" provides a survey of the Gothic elements in the writing of Gerard Manley Hopkins. These include the notion of a split self in "The Terrible Sonnets," comparable to the double personalities in James Hogg's *Confessions of a Justified Sinner* and Oscar Wilde's *The Picture of Dorian Gray*; representations of London as a "Gothic labyrinth" rife with "sordidness and sin"; and the Gothic, "fake-authentic" Englishness of Hopkins's invented terminology in "inscape" and "instress." Hopkins also figures briefly in Amanda Paxton's discussion of bridal mysticism in *Willful Submission: Sado-Erotics and Heavenly Marriage in Victorian Poetry* (Charlottesville: University of Virginia Press, 2018). R. J. C. Watt, "Hopkins and the Gothic Body," in *Victorian Gothic: Literary and Cultural Manifestations in the Nineteenth Century,* ed. Ruth Robbins and Julian Wolfreys (Basingstoke: Palgrave Macmillan, 2000), 60–89.
10. Hopkins, "Spelt from Sibyl's Leaves," pp. 190–1, lines 7–9.
11. "This sonnet shd. be almost sung: it is most carefully timed in *tempo rubato*." Hopkins, Letter to Bridges, 11 December 1886, vol. 2, 842.
12. See Chapter 3, "The Oxford Movement" in Mark Knight and Emma Mason (eds), *Nineteenth-Century Religion and Literature* (Oxford: Oxford University Press, 2007).

13. Patrick O'Malley, *Catholicism, Sexual Deviance, and Victorian Gothic Culture* (Oxford: Oxford University Press, 2006), 94.
14. Ibid. 35.
15. Diane Long Hoeveler, *The Gothic Ideology: Religious Hysteria and Anti-Catholicism in British Popular Fiction, 1780–1880* (Cardiff: University of Wales Press, 2014).
16. O'Malley, *Catholicism*, 37.
17. Walter Scott, *The Lives of the Novelists*, 2 vols. (Philadelphia: H. C. Carey and I. Lea, et al., 1825), vol. 1, 198, quoted in Hoeveler, *The Gothic Ideology*, 47.
18. O'Malley, *Catholicism*, 20.
19. Ibid.
20. Ibid.
21. John Wolffe, *The Protestant Crusade in Great Britain 1829–1860* (Oxford: Oxford University Press, 1991), 13–14.
22. Alison Milbank, *God & the Gothic: Religion, Romance and Reality in the English Literary Tradition* (Oxford: Oxford University Press, 2018); Mark Canuel, *Religion, Toleration, and British Writing, 1790–1830* (Cambridge: Cambridge University Press, 2002); Amanda Paxton, *Willful Submission*, especially Chapter 2; Denis G. Paz's *Popular Anti-Catholicism in Mid-Victorian England* (Stanford: Stanford University Press, 1992); Susan Griffin, *Anti-Catholicism and Nineteenth-Century Fiction* (Cambridge: Cambridge University Press, 2004).
23. Maria Purves, *The Gothic and Catholicism* (Cardiff: University of Wales Press, 2009), 2.
24. Paz, *Popular Anti-Catholicism*, 54.
25. John Cumming, "Ritualism—What is it?" in *Ritualism, The Highway to Rome* (London: James Nisbet and Co., 1867) extracted in *Anti-Catholicism in Victorian England*, ed. E. R. Norman (London: George Allen & Unwin, 1968), 194–5. Cumming was a virulent anti-Catholic spokesman who denounced John Henry Newman and won the disfavor of George Eliot. His other books include *The Romish Church a Dumb Church*, 1853.
26. All letters by Hopkins are quoted from *The Collected Works of Gerard Manley Hopkins, Volumes 1 and 2: Correspondence 1852–1881, 1882–1889*, ed. R. K. R. Thornton and Catherine Phillips (Oxford: Oxford University Press, 2015). Here, Letter to his father, 16–17 October 1866, vol. 1, p. 116.
27. John T. Netland, "Linguistic Limitation and the Instress of Grace in *The Wreck of the Deutschland*," *Victorian Poetry* 27, no. 2 (Summer 1989): 191.
28. Donald Davie, *Purity of Diction in English Verse* (London: Routledge & Kegan Paul, 1967), 171–5.
29. A reference to bodybuilder and showman Eugen Sandow. Donald Davie, *Purity of Diction in English Verse* (London: Routledge, 1967), 175.

30. Touching on Hopkins but briefly, Martin Lockerd recognizes the lasting legacy of "decadent Catholicism" in the age of high modernism in his book *Decadent Catholicism and the Making of Modernism* (London: Bloomsbury, 2020).
31. Julia F. Saville, *A Queer Chivalry: The Homoerotic Asceticism of Gerard Manley Hopkins*, (Charlottesville: University of Virginia Press, 2000).
32. Watt, "Hopkins and the Gothic Body," 68.
33. O'Malley, *Catholicism*, 93.
34. Ibid. 86.
35. Ibid. 73–4.
36. Ibid. 74.
37. John Henry Newman, *Apologia Pro Vita Sua, being a reply to a pamphlet entitled "What, Then, Does Dr. Newman Mean?"* (London: Longman, Green, Longman, Roberts, and Green, 1864), 58, quoted in O'Malley, *Catholicism*, 84.
38. O'Malley, *Catholicism*, 96.
39. Ibid. 85.
40. Ibid. 74.
41. James Bateman, *The Church Association: Its Policy and Prospects*, 3rd edn (London: William Ridgway, 1880), 56, quoted in O'Malley, *Catholicism*, 92.
42. Peter Maurice, *Postscript to the Popery of Oxford: The Number of the Name of the Beast* (London: Seeleys, 1851), 6, quoted in O'Malley, *Catholicism*, 93.
43. Hopkins, Letter to Robert Bridges, 17–29 May 1885, vol. 2, p. 734.
44. Hopkins, Letter to Bridges, 1–8 September 1885, vol. 2, p. 743.
45. Hopkins, ("I wake and feel the fell of dark, not day . . ."), p. 181, lines 1–8.
46. Davie, *Purity of Diction*, 171.
47. "Piling on" refers to Donald Davie's reading, quoted earlier in this chapter: "Word is piled on word, and stress on stress, to crush the odours and dispense a more exquisite tang, more exquisite than the life." Davie, *Purity of Diction*, 171–5.
48. Hopkins, ("I wake and feel the fell of dark, not day . . ."), lines 9–14.
49. Davie, *Purity of Diction*, 175.
50. Simon Reader, *Notework: Victorian Literature and Nonlinear Style* (Stanford: Stanford University Press, 2021).
51. Higgins, introduction to *The Collected Works*, 15.
52. John Shelton Reed, *Glorious Battle: The Cultural Politics of Victorian Anglo-Catholicism* (Nashville: Vanderbilt University Press, 2000), 196.
53. Ibid. 73.
54. Ibid. 72
55. Ibid. 76.
56. Ibid. 174.

57. Browning, "Porphyria's Lover," in *The Poetical Works of Robert Browning. Volume 3: Bells and Pomegranates I–VI*, ed. Ian Jack and Rowena Fowler (Oxford: Clarendon Press, 1988), lines 99–101.
58. Browning, "Caliban upon Setebos," l. 24.
59. Hopkins, "No worst, there is none", p. 182, ll. 1–14.
60. Robert Bernard Martin, "Dolben, Digby Augustus Stewart Mackworth (1848–1867)," *Oxford Dictionary of National Biography*, quoted in Higgins, introduction to *The Collected Works*, 18.
61. Higgins, introduction to *The Collected Works*, 10, 18.
62. Ibid. 17.
63. Ibid. 17–18.
64. Hopkins, Letter to Baillie, 24 April – 17 May 1885, vol. 2, p. 729, quoted in Higgins, introduction to *The Collected Works*, 16.
65. Hopkins, Letter to Bridges, 4–5 January 1883, vol. 2, p. 559; Hopkins, Letter to Bridges, 17 May 1885, p. 734.
66. See discussions of apostrophe by Jonathan Culler, J. Douglas Kneale, and Brian McGrath. Jonathan Culler, "Apostrophe" *Diacritics* 7, no. 4 (Winter 1977): 59; Jonathan Culler, *Theory of the Lyric* (Cambridge, MA: Harvard University Press, 2017); J. Douglas Kneale, "Romantic Aversions: Apostrophe Reconsidered" *ELH* 58, no. 1 (Spring 1991): 141–65; Brian McGrath, *The Poetics of Unremembered Acts: Reading, Lyric, Pedagogy* (Evanston, IL: Northwestern University Press, 2012).
67. O'Malley, *Catholicism*, 78.
68. Ibid. 157.
69. Hopkins, Letter to Bridges, 1–2 April 1885, vol. 2, p. 722.
70. *The Spiritual Exercises of St. Ignatius Loyola*, trans. Elisabeth Tetlow (Lanham, MD: University Press of America, 1987). For Hopkins's own notes on "The Spiritual Exercises," see *The Collected Works*, ed. Catherine Phillips, 281–2.
71. Hopkins, "The Caged Skylark," p. 148, lines 1–8.
72. John Milton, "Sonnet XIX: On His Blindness," in *The Poetical Works of John Milton* (London: Macmillan, 1905), 551.
73. Hopkins, "The Caged Skylark," lines 9–14.
74. John Keats, "If By Dull Rhymes," in *The Poetical Works of John Keats* (London: Moxon, Son and Co., 1871), 346, line 14.
75. Hopkins, "The Caged Skylark," lines 5, 7, 9.
76. O'Malley, *Catholicism*, 91.
77. Ibid. 92.
78. Hopkins, "Author's Preface," *The Collected Works*, 49.
79. Quoted in Lois Pitchford, "The Curtal Sonnets of Gerard Manley Hopkins" *Modern Language Notes* 67, no. 3 (March 1952), 166.
80. Pitchford, "The Curtal Sonnets," 169.
81. George P. Landow, "Gerard Manley Hopkins and the Visual Arts," *The Victorian Web*. Available at <http://www.victorianweb.org/authors/hopkins/artov.html> (last accessed 22 May 2014).

82. Norman H. MacKenzie, *A Reader's Guide to Gerard Manley Hopkins* (Philadelphia: St. Joseph's University Press, 2008), 25.
83. Hopkins, "The Windhover," 144.
84. Leigh Hunt, *The Book of the Sonnet*, ed. S. Adams Lee (Stanford: Stanford University Press, 1989), 431, quoted in Phelan, *The Nineteenth-Century Sonnet* (New York: Palgrave Macmillan, 2005), 18.
85. Hopkins, Letter to R. W. Dixon, 5 October 1878, vol. 1, p. 317.
86. Virginia Ridley Ellis, *Gerard Manley Hopkins and the Language of Mystery* (Columbia: University of Missouri Press, 1991), 66.
87. Hopkins, "The Wreck of the Deutschland," stanzas 5–6.
88. Hopkins, "Pied Beauty," line 1.
89. Hopkins, Journal from 15 September 1871, in *The Collected Works, Volume 3*, 505.
90. Hopkins, Journal from 13 June 1871, in *The Collected Works, Volume 3*, 513.
91. Hopkins, "The Wreck of the Deutschland," stanzas 5–6.
92. Sprung Rhythm was a crucial element to the poem, for after "The Wreck of the Deutschland" was initially rejected from *The Month* in July 1875, Hopkins would only allow for it to be published if the stress marks were included.
93. Hopkins, "Author's Preface," *The Collected Works*, 115.
94. R. J. C. Watt, "Hopkins and the Gothic Body," 68.
95. Netland, 'Linguistic Limitation,' 198.
96. Martin Dubois, *Gerard Manley Hopkins and the Poetry of Religious Experience* (Cambridge: Cambridge University Press, 2017).
97. See Amanda Paxton's treatment of the "The Tall Nun" and "Queering the Bride" in Chapter 4, "Catholicism and the Metaphysics of Longing," of *Willful Submission*. Diane Hoeveler presents a comprehensive overview of the role of the nun in Gothic narratives in "The Construction of the Gothic Nun: Fantasies and the Religious Imaginary," Marquette University. Available at <http://epublications.marquette.edu/cgi/viewcontent.cgi?article=1008&context=cah> (last accessed 15 January 2018).
98. MacKenzie, *A Reader's Guide*, 22.
99. Hopkins, "The Wreck of the Deutschland," stanzas 17–19.
100. "The bodies of the four German nuns," *London Times*, 11 December 1875, 12, quoted in Mariani, *Gerard Manley Hopkins: A Life* (New York: Viking Penguin, 2008), 143.
101. Mariani, *Commentary on the Complete Poems*, 49.
102. Ellis, *Gerard Manley Hopkins*, 67.
103. Hopkins, "The Wreck of the Deutschland," stanzas 20–1.
104. Meredith Martin, "Gerard Manley Hopkins and the Stigma of Meter and the Stigma of Meter" *Victorian Studies* 50, no. 2 (Winter 2008): 243–54 (247).

105. Hopkins, *The Journals and Papers of Gerard Manley Hopkins*, ed. Humphrey House (London: Oxford University Press, 1959), 269, quoted in Martin, "Gerard Manley Hopkins," 245.
106. Martin, "Gerard Manley Hopkins the Stigma of Meter," 250.
107. Ibid. 249.
108. Ibid. 251.
109. Meredith Martin, *The Rise and Fall of Meter: Poetry and English National Culture 1860–1930* (Princeton: Princeton University Press, 2012), 62.
110. Ibid. 251–2.
111. Hopkins, "The Wreck of the Deutschland," line 48.

Conclusion. Emily Brontë's Udolphics: The Gondal and Non-Gondal Poems

In this book, I have proposed, and hopefully shown, that reading 1790s Gothic novels helps to make us better readers of Victorian poetry. The claim is a challenging one because it demands reading long, eight-hundred-page Gothic novels seriously—reading them closely, and formally—without necessarily reverting to familiar patterns of paranoid reading or suspicious hermeneutics. Nor does it lean on statistical reading from a distance, counting off the number of Minerva titles published or tallying the salaries of women writers in a single decade. The crux of this study, in suggesting we read these baggy containers for their formal value, undercuts the prominence of Gothic themes to focus instead on Gothic forms and structures. Such a formal approach unifies disparate shapes across seemingly noncomplementary units and containers. Moving from novels to poems, crossing from Romantic to Victorian, Gothic forms travel and transform as they do their work. Those Gothic forms—of confinement, guilty overhearing, shock and swap, and wavering, as discussed in each of the preceding chapters—embody constructs of restraint and excess. As we have seen, the machinery of confinement and liberation are often bound together in tangible, embodied ways: Where the characters stand, hidden from view, enact triangulation. How a poem's lines wrap around the page can seem to stifle a poem's speaker. The physical experience of close reading Gothic form becomes inextricable from its content, where the stuff that fills unwieldy "lyric buckets" and "well-wrought urns" asks readers to undergo contortions. The speaker, poet, and reader, all parties involved, might twist, writhe, and waver. That Gothic reading experience prevails in readings of even the most canonical Victorian poems.

 The argument of this book has progressed chronologically across the nineteenth century, chapter by chapter, to explore the Gothic forms hidden in plain sight, often within poems where Gothic themes may not be detectable at all: in Browning's early dramatic monologues (contemporaneous with Tennyson's) from the 1830s; in meta-sonnets by Elizabeth Barrett and Christina Georgina Rossetti from the 1840s; in picture poems and doubled works from Dante Gabriel Rossetti's 1860s second phase; and in the poetry of Gerard Manley Hopkins in the 1870s and 1880s. For this concluding chapter, I break the chronology to visit an earlier moment, turning our attention to the poetry of Emily Brontë.

A consideration of the Gothic forms in Victorian poetry would not be complete without the Brontës, whose novels are seminal to the scholarship of Victorian Gothic. Their major novels, including *Jane Eyre*, *Villette*, and *Wuthering Heights*, fueled the landmark criticism of Ellen Moers, Diane Hoeveler, Julian Fleenor, Devendra Varma, and Gilbert and Gubar, scholars who first theorized the Female Gothic tradition. As a component of the Brontë siblings' "play," "Gothic provided basic material . . . a set of conventions that could be used first as raw material, then as the chief ingredient of parody, and finally—though gradually—as a means to explore the riddles of our thought and feeling."[1] But as so many Brontë scholars have remarked, criticism on the poetry of the Brontë sisters is sparse, particularly for that of Emily. Critics from Janet Gezari to Christine Alexander continue to express surprise that an author as canonical as Emily Brontë is excluded to the extent that she is from anthologies of poetry, even collections featuring Victorian women writers.[2] Reasons for such omissions range from the difficulty of placing Brontë's poems among other women poets and feminist criticism, to the enduring debate among scholars of whether to treat her oeuvre as separate corpuses of Gondal or non-Gondal poems.[3]

In 1970, Robert Heilman declared Emily Brontë's *Wuthering Heights* a vanguard text of the "New Gothic," indicating that the novel invokes themes from first-generation Gothic texts, only to resist them and embrace anti-Gothic themes instead.[4] I locate the critical neglect of Emily Brontë's poetry as a problem of genre and categorization. Put simply, Emily Brontë's novels have been cast as Victorian New Gothic, whereas her poems appear comparatively retrograde in their adherence to Romantic or first-generation Gothic. The poems seem stuck in the past, juvenile in their imitation of 1790s Gothic, repetitive rather than rebellious. The stark divide in the critical reception of Emily Brontë's poetic corpus and that of her prose works rests on a central question: Why does her poetry seem to perpetuate tired Gothic clichés, while her novels resist and upend them in innovative ways?

An initial survey of Emily Brontë's poems reveal a majority of verses deeply entrenched in Gothic themes and language. Modeled directly from Gothic romance, they smack of "old" Gothic, as stanzas mostly tied to her Gondal saga recount the tragedies, betrayals, love affairs, imprisonments, and murders of characters such as Augusta Geraldine Almeda, Alexandra Elbe, Rosina Alcona, and Julius Brenzaida.

> A sudden chasm of ghastly light . . .
> The shrieking wind sank mute and mild . . .
> In plundered churches piled with dead . . .
> My couch lay in a ruined hall . . .
> An undefined an awful dream . . .
> A sound unutterably drear . . .[5]

These lines, extracted from a fragment in the T2 manuscript dated 14 October 1837, which was published only in 1910, are representative of Emily Brontë's "Gondal poems." They comprise a romantic world, recounting intrigue, adultery, and incest among royalty, enslavement, and decaying dynasties. The backdrop is familiar Gothic territory: ruined castles, churches littered with dead bodies, night terrors, rocks and crags. In these poems, Brontë continuously draws from that familiar bag of tropes. Among the diction reused in her poems, we see most commonly "drear," "ghastly," "dream of horror," "chill," "gloomy," "groaning," "dongeons," "fetters chains," "shadows," "phantom horrors," "spectral dream," "flesh," and "chain." Certainly, Brontë's poetry from the 1830s to 1850s models familiar Gothic elements of excess and sameness. But was she reusing these mechanics in tired ways—or did she conscientiously recruit these tropes in order to write experimentally "against" a preceding tradition of first-generation 1790s Gothic?

Surely, this divide between New and Old Gothic in critical reception is a disingenuous one, and the question as to whether Emily Brontë, like Radcliffe, was "far too enlightened to ever see a ghost" is more than just a circumstance of timeline and historical context. While Joseph Wiesenfarth argues that Jane Austen had officially "knocked" the old Gothic formula "out of style" by 1818, the Brontë siblings, having lived relatively isolated lives in Haworth, England, had often belated access to periodicals and books.[6] Their library consisted of texts gifted from their father or from his parsonage, and the periodicals were often received at several months' delay. Due to this temporal remove, it is conceivable their readings and writings were clearly still steeped in the traditional Gothic. Still, to operate as if Brontë were a Victorian New-Gothic novelist but a Romantic Old-Gothic poet plays into familiar arguments relegating Gothic influence to juvenilia, treating Gothic as a phase to grow out of—as if, for an author-heroine, the Gothic influence is something to triumph over as she reaches literary maturity.

To pose Emily Brontë's poetic reception as a problem of genre, and to question how the Gothic functions in nineteenth-century poetry versus prose, is to shine a light on problematic critical expectations of what we consider typical Gothic forms. We successfully identify Victorian Gothic in the shape of long Victorian novels (read: *Villette*), tales and short stories (Poe), and in so much of the juvenilia (tales of Angria and Glass Town). Within poetry—especially Romantic poetry—we primarily recognize Gothic texts in the form of long Gothic narrative romances, à la Byron, and in Keats's *The Eve of St. Agnes* or *Isabella and the Pot of Basil*. But this again exposes a critical lacuna, surrounding that nagging discomfort of how to approach the territory of Gothic lyrics and shorter poems, if they are not dramatic monologues or dramatic lyrics such as "La Belle Dame sans Merci." How might a Victorian poet compose a short Gothic poem while not playing a role?

Compounding this difficulty is the fact that so much of Emily Brontë's poetic corpus is presented in the form of fragments. Far more familiar to us is the generic hybrid of Gothic romance: the long novel "interspersed with pieces of poetry" in the tradition of Ann Radcliffe or Charlotte Smith. As readers, we often crave a framed narrative in which to situate the dramatic lyrics we read: the verses provide a respite from the heavy prose, while the framed narrative allows the poem to breathe. In such romances, the poetic speaker is assumed to be the Gothic heroine, as seen in Chapter 2. But since Emily and Anne Brontë's prose writings from their Gondal saga have been lost, only their poems and fragments survive, leaving a far less complete vision of their oeuvre than of Charlotte and Branwell's Glass Town and Angria. This only adds to the difficulty of Emily Brontë's reception as a poet straddling the Romantic and Victorian eras.

One convenient narrative driving the critical wedge that distinguishes the Brontë sisters' novels from their poetic productions has been the idea that overt, superficial Gothic trappings become concealed as psychological terror in a more "mature work" like *Wuthering Heights*. Gondal, Angria, and Glass Town, clearly modeled after historical and Gothic romance, were "continents filled with African princes, slave trading, wars, and all manner of Gothic devices and tropes."[7] Unsurprisingly, these Gothic elements are often discounted as signs of the young writers' developmental phase. As Diane Hoeveler writes:

> Their mature novels retain these marks, but the Gothic undergoes a sea change in their later works. In addition to the familiar plot devices (disputed inheritances, orphaned heroines, bifurcated characters, traces of incest, and triangulated love affairs), the Gothic has also become internalized as a series of psychological states, like hypochondria, melancholia, and obsessive-compulsive traits.[8]

What kind of readings might reconcile Emily Brontë's prose writing with her Gothic poetry? Might this help recuperate the critical marginalization of Emily Brontë as poet?

To answer the questions posed in this section, I read Emily Brontë's poetry alongside that of Elizabeth Barrett Browning, Christina Georgina Rossetti, and Gerard Manley Hopkins, inviting comparisons to those poets' uses of Gothic forms discussed earlier in this book. Spotlighting parallel echoes, confessionals, cries, and confinement within Brontë's sonnets and verses helps to showcase her poetry in a new framework: through these readings, Brontë emerges as a Victorian Gothic poet among her counterparts in the nineteenth century, rather than a remote writer cast in solitude and belatedness, stuck in a past of 1790s old Gothic romance. This establishes Emily Brontë's connection to nineteenth-century Gothic forms in three ways, each by means of a distinctly Radcliffean afterlife: (1) by tracing the Gothic's transmission through Victorian print culture; (2) by showcasing the Radcliffean merging of foreign and English landscapes in Brontë's poems; and finally, (3) by highlighting the similarity of Brontë's verses to other Victorian poets who successfully incorporated Gothic forms into their poetry. Simply put, this coda to *The Gothic Forms of Victorian Poetry* confirms Emily Brontë's role as a Gothic poet and not just as a Gothic novelist, drawing out relevant Radcliffean connections and the "Udolphics" behind many of her verses (and not just the ostensibly Gondal poems). The influence of the Romantic Gothic novel on Victorian lyric poetry is a valuable line to trace. And as this book has consistently argued, 1790s Gothic did not disappear after 1800 and re-emerge, newly anti-Gothic, ninety years later. Until Emily Brontë's death in 1848, Gothic forms remained a consistent force in British poetry. Individually and collectively, those forms construct a Radcliffean world that is infused with the ghostly and Gothics of the everyday.

Periodicals and Annuals in the Brontë Household

It is well known that Patrick Brontë raised four voracious young readers by indulging their desires for new stories, shared through periodicals and magazines. They savored copies of *Blackwoods* and imitated them through their miniature experiments in publication, editorship, and authorship with their own hand-sewn magazines, some just two inches in height. Their chief influences of Gothic and romance were, of course, Walter Scott and Lord Byron. Each of the four children chose one author as a literary patron saint after which to model their writings. But the Brontë children were also exposed to the Gothic through numerous Romantic writers who influenced their play, reading not only Wollstonecraft and Mary Shelley, or Ann Radcliffe's *The Italian* and Jane Austen's *Northanger Abbey*, but also the "down-market garish works typified by authors such as Thomas Isaac Horsley Curties, George Walker, and W. H. Ireland."[9] The preface in Charlotte's own little newspaper declares "her very Gothic intent" to "unveil a scene of murders, thefts, hypocrisy, perjury and so forth which can scarcely be paralleled in the annals of another city."[10]

Periodicals were also a major influence in the Brontë household, especially printed tales and fragments. (Emily Brontë would later differentiate between "tales" and "fragments" in the subtitles in her own notebooks.)[11] Tracing the rich afterlife of Radcliffe's novels in periodical and annual illustrations by artists such as John Martin, Christine Alexander has shown how the Brontës received a Radcliffean education and were immersed in a Victorian strain of Udolphics, through the medium of Victorian print culture. As Robert Mayo reports, monthly magazines continued to "fe[e]d the imaginations of generations of leisured middle-class readers long after the Gothic novel itself seemed to have lost its appeal." In particular, *Blackwood's Magazine*, *Fraser's Magazine*, and *Lady's Magazine* made their way into the Brontë household. For the *Lady's Magazine*, which had a circulation of sixteen thousand, terror was a regular ingredient. Between 1791 and 1812, it printed twenty-one Gothic romances in serialized form, including ones titled "The Monk" and "The Robbers." When she was still alive, the Brontës' mother Maria Branwell would bring home copies of the magazine, as did their aunt in later years.[12]

Annuals represent another key but oft-neglected medium for transmitting a Radcliffean afterlife into the Brontë household in the decades following the 1790s. These gift books, containing poetry and prose fiction with engraved plates for illustrations, were introduced to the English market in 1822. They included Gothic tales and fragments and continued to be printed well into the 1850s. Annuals that the Bronte family owned include *Friendship's Offering*, *The Literary Souvenir*, and the *Forget Me Not*. The circulation of these annuals was considerable: *Friendship's Offering* sold over thirty-five thousand copies in its first few weeks of publication. The titles included in such annuals reveal an obvious glut of Gothic content: "The Haunted Chamber," "The Night of the Necker," "The Convent of Chaillot," "The Curate-Confessor of Virofloy, a real Ghost Story," "A Tale of the Forest," and "A Tale of Disobedience; Or, the Mysterious Chamber."[13] For Alexander:

> the Gothic frees [Emily Brontë] to achieve two apparently contradictory ends: on the one hand to imitate the Annuals and indulge in her love of the exotic, the licentious, and the mysterious, and increasingly to indulge in her fascination with the darker recesses of the mind and its relationship to natural phenomena; and on the other hand to assume the anti-Gothic stance that Heilman noted was so characteristic in the novels. Here her revisionist methodology is not far removed from Jane Austen's parody, and, again, we can find clear models in the periodical literature and in the Annuals Bronte read.

In this reading by Alexander, Brontë's commitments to "old" Gothic or New Gothic are not mutually exclusive.

Radcliffean Landscape and Time-Space in Haworth, England

This robust afterlife of 1790s Gothic, transmitted through 1830s magazines and annuals, allowed Emily Brontë to inherit a distinctly Radcliffian mode of framing her stories: she adopted the timescale and landscape that overlapped stormy, antique Gothic settings upon a contemporary English backdrop. The Gondal stories are meant to take place from 1825 to 1830, though, as Derek Roper comments, they reflect more a romantic, fifteenth-century backdrop of noble intrigue, in the vein of Byron's romances and Scott's historical romances. Of course, romances like *The Mysteries of Udolpho* were well known for creating a setting of fifteenth-century France or Italy that felt inexplicably similar to eighteenth-century England, this strange overlapping creating a distinct chronotope for Radcliffean

Gothic. As Alexander has noted, this same time-space continued to be overlaid onto the Brontës' new fiction:

> The pages of the Bronte juvenilia have all the classic machinery of Mrs. Radcliffe's landscapes, largely filtered through Scott, Hogg, and Byron, and reinforced by their many other imitators contributing to the Annuals. Her early romances were set in the Glass Town equivalents of Scotland, Ireland, and even the fertile home counties of England; and her earliest ghost stories and Tales of the Islanders were set solidly in the British Isles. The 'classic scenery' of Verdopolis, as Glass Town is later called, is essentially Radcliffean; transposed from Europe not to Africa but to England, an England that is echoed in the many Claudian landscapes by Turner and others in the Annuals. In "High Life in Verdopolis" we behold "the landscape in perfection."[14]

Thanks to this remarkably useful Radcliffean chronotope, "groaning trees," "dungeon crypts," "chill chains," and "churches with dead bodies" do not inhabit only a fictional world in fifteenth-century-like Gondal, but hold a place in Brontë's own Yorkshire.

There are thus two important elements to Emily Brontë's locating her own identity within the Gothic. (1) First, the Gothic influence was coming to her not from a foreign world, but through the medium of domestic, familiar genres such as Victorian periodicals and annuals. (2) Second, Brontë's oeuvre, in mirroring the Radcliffean collapsing of timescales and landscapes—the ancient foreign and contemporary domestic—shows that Brontë conceived of her own home and daily life in Gothic terms, even within her local northern English countryside. This understanding helps to weaken the distinction between the Gondal/Non-Gondal poems and encourage a unified reading of the two notebooks.

The Gondal and Non-Gondal Debate

The separation of Emily Brontë's "Gondal" and "non-Gondal" writings have fueled a long-standing rift in critical assessments of Emily Brontë's poetic oeuvre. Emily began transcribing poems in two new notebooks in February 1844, which have become her most important manuscripts (MS A and B). The first MS A, nicknamed the Hornesfeld Manuscript, was a 7- by 4.25-inch notebook labeled with her initials and the date ("E J B. Transcribed February 1844"), with poems arranged approximately by theme. The other notebook (MS B), referred to as the Gondal Notebook, was sixty-eight lined pages 6 by 4 inches with a red cover, labeled with the poet's full name and the words "Gondal Poems," followed by forty-five poems.

Brontë's maintenance of two simultaneous notebooks suggests a separation between two modes of poetry writing, one personal and realistic, one fictive and fantastical. Taking seriously the separation between Gondal and non-Gondal poems, earlier scholars have tended to discredit the juvenilia of Emily and Anne. Derek Stanford and Muriel Spark, for instance, found their younger works overly derivative of Byron and too far in the vein of melodrama.[15] In some harsher assessments, scholars labeled poems like "The Prisoner" as "second-rate," "facile metrical scribbling" of "no genius" to which "Emily was particularly prone when inspiration did not move."[16] This signals a biographical assessment that divorces the masterful author of *Wuthering Heights* from the poet Emily Brontë, and one that champions the later poems over her early ones, in turn advocating a treatment of the Gondal and non-Gondal works as separate entities.

Other scholars consider all of Brontë's poems as comprising a single epic work centered around the Gondal fantasy. Fannie E. Ratchford, in her preface to the Hatfield edition of the poems, assesses that the majority of the poems and fragments, or at least one half of the 193 poems and fragments, are Gondal poems. According to biographer John Hewish, when all three sisters decided to each submit novels for publication and Emily began work on *Wuthering Heights*, she still declared her loyalty to the Gondal characters, writing in 1845 that "we intend sticking firmly by the rascals." But Stanford argues that reading Brontë's poems through a Gondal framework weakens their literary worth: "Besides providing a structure of theatrically sham material—a structure totally inadequate to bear the intense verbal beauty and profound and feeling thought which emerges from it in many superb detachable poems—it encouraged the writing of much bad verse."[17]

Still more scholars regard all of Emily's oeuvre as a consistent whole mapping an intuitive progression.[18] According to Alexander, Emily "moves seamlessly in her poetry between Gondal and the real world," and her younger writings within an imaginative world had a positive effect on her mature writing, providing "sustenance, security, and inspiration for her intensely secretive and self-contained personality."[19] Alexander reads the majority of Brontë's two hundred poems, half of which were composed for Gondal, as dramatic lyrics, noting that any of the works classified as Emily's "personal" poems may well have originated as Gondal poems, such as "Alone I sat" and "I'll come when thou art saddest": "Gondal allows Emily a lyric impersonality: she can participate in different scenarios, write with abandon and yet write intensely out of her own experience."[20] Denis Donoghue provides a most thorough consideration by identifying Gondal-personal poems of Emily Brontë as something between dramatic monologue, soliloquy, and mask poetry, comparing her lyric voice to Shakespearean, Browningesque, and Yeatsian, Eliotian, and even Proustian models.[21]

Brontë's Prisoner Poems

The fluid possibilities of reading Brontë's poems as dramatic lyrics, fantastic poems of Gothic romance, personal poems, or verses embedded within a wider prose frame can be found in her various "prisoner poems." "O God of heaven," reproduced below, is among the forty-six slips (designated manuscripts D and T) that were sold by Arthur Nicholls. (The original orthography of Emily's poems has been preserved below as they appear in Derek Roper's edition of *The Poems of Emily Brontë*, rather than presented with regularized spelling):

August 7 1837

O God of heaven! the dream of horror
The frightful dream is over now
The sickened heart The blasting sorrow
The ghastly night the ghastlier morrow
The aching sense of utter woe

The burning tears that would keep welling
The groans that mocked at every tear
That burst from out their dreary dwelling
As if each gasp were life expelling
But life was nourished by dispair

The tossing and the anguished pineing
The grinding teeth and stareing eye
The agony of still repineing
When not a spark of hope was shineing
From gloomy fate's relentless sky

The impatient rage the useless shrinking
From thoughts that yet could not be borne

The soul that was forever thinking
Till nature maddened tortured sinking
At last refused to mourn—

—Its over now—and I am free
And the ocean wind is caressing me
The wild wind from that wavey main
I never thought to see again
Bless thee Bright Sea—and glorious dome

And my own world my spirits home
Bless thee Bless all—I can not speak
My voice is chocked but not with greif
And salt drops from my haggard cheek
Descend like rain upon the heath

How long they've wet a dongoen floor—
Falling on flag-stones damp and grey
I used to weep even in my sleep
The night was dreadful like the day

I used to weep when winters-snow
Whirled through the grateing stormily
But then it was a calmer woe
For every thing was drear as me

The bitterest time the worst of all
Was that in which the summer sheen
Cast a green luster on the wall
That told of fields of lovelier green

Often I've sat down on the ground
Gazing up to that flush scearce seen
Till heedless of the darkness round
My soul has sought a land serene

It sought the arch of heaven devine
The pure blue heaven with clouds of gold
It sought my Fathers home and mine
As I remembered it of old

O even now too horribly
Come back the feelings that would swell
When with my face hid on my knee
I strove the bursting groans to quell

I flung myself upon the stone
I howled and tore my tangled hair
And then when the first gush had flown
Lay in unspeakable dispair

Sometimes a curse some times a prayer
Would quiver on my parched tongue
But both without a murmer there
Died in the breast from whence they sprung

And so the day would fade on high
And darkness quench that lonely beam
And slumber mold my misery
Into some strange and spectral dream
Whose phantom horrors made me know
The worst extent of human woe—

But this is past and why return
O'er such a past to brood and mourn?
Shake off the fetters Break the chain
And live and love and smile again.

The waste of youth the waste of years
Departed in that dongoens thrawl
The gnawing greif the hopeless tears
Forget them—O forget them all—[22]

In addition to this prisoner poem stand many others, among them "Written in the Gaaldine prison caves," "Silent is the House—," and "The Prisoner." Still another poem worth exploring that is certainly a Gondal poem is "Written in the Gaaldine prison caves, To A.G.A.," dated 6 January 1840, which comes from the "Gondal Notebook," numbered Poem 72 in the Roper edition. Emily was angered when Charlotte came upon her notebook of Gondal poems in the autumn of 1845 and read her entries. But after overcoming this violation of privacy, she allowed Charlotte to persuade her to contribute poems for printing, offering twenty-one verses in all, all from the Hornesfeld manuscript of Gondal poems.[23]

Yet more poems were appended to the 1850 edition of *Wuthering Heights* and *Agnes Grey* and published, resulting in versions that Jane Gezari believes were "aggressively edited" by Charlotte. Of these revisions prepared for publication was "The Prisoner," drawn from "Silent is the House," both poems of which are in the Gondal

Notebook. Due to limitations of space, I do not quote both poems in their entirety here but discuss key changes made. The core of the original poem, lines 13–96 remain the same, with the poem beginning, "In the dungeon crypts idly did I stray / Reckless of the lives wasteing there away; / 'Draw the ponderous bars, open Warder stern!' / He dare not say me nay—the hinges harshly turn—."[24] We learn that the protagonist is a beautiful, mild, statuesque heroine of the Radcliffean type, held captive in the dungeon: "The captive raised her face; it was as soft and mild / As sculptured marble saint or slumbering, unweaned child / It was so soft and mild, it was so sweet and fair / Pain could not trace, a line nor greif a shadow there!"[25] Lord Julian witnesses the suffering of A. G. Rochelle and the jailor's treatment of her, and, fearing for her languishment and imminent death, hopes to free her: "'Rochelle, the dungeons teem with foes to groge our hate— / 'Thou art too young to die by such a bitter fate!' / With hurried blow on blow I struck the fetters through / Regardless how that deed my after hours might rue." (ll. 123–6). In the revised version for publication, titled "The Prisoner. Fragment," the names of Rochelle and Julian are eliminated. Lines 13–96 of the Gondal version are kept, while the opening three stanzas and closing fourteen stanzas are cut to eliminate some of the narrative framing and description of the castle: "Silent is the House—all are laid asleep; / One, alone, looks out o'er the snow-wreaths deep; / Watching every cloud, dreading every breeze / That whirls the wildering drifts and bends the groaning trees—."

If we consider individual lines from the four prison poems mentioned above (labeled #7, 123, 124, and 72 in Roper's edition), without troubling about the presence or absence of a Gondal frame, these prisoner poems begin to sound distinctly similar to the sonnets of Elizabeth Barrett: "I count the dismal time by months and years / Since last I felt the green sward under foot . . . Nature's lute / Sounds on, behind his door so closely shut, / A strange wild music to the prisoner's ears."[26] Compare this to a stanza from Brontë's "The Prisoner":

> Oh, dreadful is the check—intense the agony—
>   When the eye begins to hear, and the eye begins to see
>   When the pulse begins to throb, the brain to think again,
>   The soul to feel the flesh, and the flesh to feel the chain.[27]

Due to what we know of her oeuvre, one is less inclined to read EBB's "The Prisoner" as a fictional scene of Gothic romance, or as a short poem to be framed within a longer prose novel. Indeed, given the context of Barrett Browning's 1844 *Poems*, this would indicate some misreading on our part. Yet approaching Brontë's prisoner poems as excerpts or as fragments allows the personal reading of dramatic lyric to come through. As a narrative whole, the poems are a bit too awash in repetition and excess, their repeated mention of "dungeons" perhaps too heavy-handed to be considered short biographical lyrics. But selected lines, excerpted from the poem above, might also not sound too different form Christina Rossetti's second poem in "The Thread of Life," also explored in Chapter 2: "Thus am I mine own prison. Everything / around me free and sunny and at ease: / Or if in shadow, in a shade of trees."[28] We might have an easier time situating Emily Brontë among fellow Victorian women poets when we allow for her personal lyrics and dramatic lyrics to coincide. Derek Stanford gets it right when he insists that the poems need not be categorized as Gondal pieces *or* non-Gondal works: "Emily and a Gondal character could speak together in the same poem; that Emily could speak through a Gondal mouthpiece; and that this mouthpiece could offer her what she sometimes might have needed—a mask."[29]

Violence in Nature: Yorkshire Inscape and Instress

Emily Brontë's potential as a Gothic poetess comes not from confinement or imprisonment, but rather a Gothic vision of her environment and landscape, marked very fundamentally by violence and death. At heart, Brontë does not transplant a Gothic setting onto Victorian life, but acknowledges that the Yorkshire moors are Gothic, with death a constitutive part of daily life. Carol Margaret Davison has explained how the Brontës led a "life-in-death" existence, where death played a central role in their psychological and artistic development. Citing the early death of Emily's two eldest sisters and her mother—in an era when 41 per cent of children died before the age of six, with high mortality rates among Haworth's parishioners especially—Davison argues that early death was a ubiquity for Emily, while death-in-life was her reality.[30] To be near close ones was often to imagine them in spectral capacities. And as we will see, her perception of nature's violence was an essential element to a Radcliffean remapping of a phantasmic English countryside. "The spectralization of the other," which Terry Castle identifies as characteristic of the world of *Udolpho*, appears to have been a useful tool for Brontë's survival. Distinctions between death and life, Gothic and non-Gothic, Gondal and non-Gondal begin to fade in her poems.[31]

The overlaying of a fantastic Gondal backdrop upon the rough Yorkshire landscape yields connections between the poems of Emily Brontë and G. M. Hopkins. Just as Hopkins lived within a monastery in which he did not need to manufacture terror of the "convent threshold," so too did Brontë locate the Gothic in her own backyard. The moors behind Haworth Parsonage are violent and unforgiving: this is a Gothic landscape that is not fantastic fiction, but Brontë's reality. Put differently, the inscape of Brontë's nature in Yorkshire is intrinsically violent. She feels the stresses and beatings of the natural world around her, where, within a Gothic framework, the default language is the language of violence. Brontë and Hopkins share an understanding of the inscape of their environments as a Gothic force. The natural world around them is imbued with the violence instressed in the environment by God, placed there by him and planted, as seeds ready to explode or germinate. We can thus recognize the strong resemblance between the punitive violence of Hopkins's God in a passage from "The Wreck of the Deutschland" as similar in spirit, swiftness, and motion to Brontë's verses:

> Not out of his bliss
> Springs the stress felt
> Nor first from heaven (and few know this)
> Swings the stroke dealt—
> Stroke and a stress that stars and storms deliver,
> That guilt is hushed by, hearts are flushed by and melt—
> But it rides time like riding a river
> (And here the faithful waver, the faithless fable and miss).

From Hopkins's poem sounds the punishing violence of nature through "riding a river," "the stroke dealt," and hearts that are "flushed by and melt." We see the same awareness of the "stroke and a stress," of "the stroke dealt," through active verbs like "springs" and "swings" in Emily Brontë's poetry as well. "High waving heather, 'neath stormy blasts bending" is a poem that showcases violence in nature that is "immediate in time, explosive and spectacular in space, . . . erupting into instant sensational visibility."[32] Written on 13 December 1836, the poem comprises three six-line stanzas of a resounding dactylic meter, depicting a climate that might represent harsh winters in Haworth, the cruel landscape of a fictive Gondalian world, or both:

> High waveing heather 'neath storming blasts bending
> Midnight and moon light and bright shineing stars

Darkness and glory rejoiceingly blending
Earth riseing to heaven and heaven descending
Mans spirit away from its drear dongoen sending
Bursting the fetters and breaking the bars

All down the mountain sides wild forests lending
One mighty voice to the life giveing wind
Rivers their bank in the jubilee rending
Fast through the vallys a reckless course wending
Wild and deeper their waters extending
Leaving a desolate desert behind

Shining and lowering and swelling and dieing
Changing for ever from midnight to noon
Roaring like thunder like soft music sighing
Shadows on shadows advanceing and flying
Lightening bright flashes the deep gloom defying
Comeing as swifly and fadeing as soon[33]

Reading the poetry of G. M. Hopkins helps one understand the violence that critics have had difficulty reckoning with in Emily Brontë's poetry. Brontë's poem features blasts from a storm that celebrate the glory—"rejoiceingly"—of nature's physical power. Almost relentless in their poetic density, these lines seem designed to overwhelm the reader with alliteration, parallelism, and rhyme so tightly condensed as to pack a powerful sonic punch. In the first stanza alone, the alliteration feels unrelenting, as seen in "high heather," "blasts bending," "midnight and moonlight," "shining stars," "heaven and heaven," "drear dungeon," and "bursting . . . breaking . . . bars." The quickly successive consonance leaves no respite for a reader experiencing such visual and aural "bursts" or "blasts." Further still, yet more complex examples of parallelism or consonance within the lines create a feeling of yet deeper storminess: we hear this in the assonance of the o and y sounds in "glory rejoiceingly" and through the internal rhyme and consonance in the paired words "midnight and moonlight." The reader is pushed in different directions through a quick succession of opposing vertical movements in "earth rising to heaven" and "heaven descending." This assault of patterns and repetitions, waged upon the reader's senses, creates an experience of battering and endurance in just the first six lines; twelve more are to follow. Brontë's verb choices are no less impactful, with a barrage of strong active verbs in "bending," "bursting," and "breaking" that present a vision of nature that is physically forceful and even menacing. Nature here is majestic in spirit, yet pathetic fallacy vivifies a world that seems to mirror a speaker who is angry, imprisoned, and yearning to break free. The *abaaab* rhyme scheme conjures an overpowering intensity with ending *a* sounds that monopolize the middle of each stanza, as in "bending," "blending" "descending" "sending"—all forceful verbs that indicate movement and direction of one in the thrall of nature's violent glory.

Brontë's choice in meter further reinforces the pace of quick blows throughout her stanzas. Written in a brisk dactylic tetrameter, the poem assumes a fast tempo that belies both vivacity and a certain restlessness. The gerunds arrive at the end of each line as if each successive line of eleven syllables is rushing ahead, unable to pause for a moment of rest but urgently pushing already to the next line, hurried forward by the "life giving wind" of line 8. Here, the participial forms ("bending," "blending," "descending," "sending") obviate any need for enjambment to convey a sense of anticipation movement, with independent clauses that never land but always drive forward.

Amidst the busy horizontal movement of dactyls beating across the page, Brontë creates an interesting matrix of vertical directions as well, with natural figures pointing upwards in the "high waving heather," "bright shining stars," "earth rising to heaven," and the "spirit away . . . sending." These upward motions are all contrasted by the sense of the high waving heather low down on earth, grounded, "[be]neath stormy blasts." The downwards movement continues in the very motion of "bending" or folding, "heaven descending," and "all down the mountain sides," which begins the following stanza. As in the poetry of Hopkins, nature's power is shown to be alternately ennobling and ascending, or bending and breaking. Throughout, the synergistic horizontal and vertical activity renders the poem a tour de force of dizzying motion in nature's harsh impact.

Gothic Endings: The Spectralization of Everyday Life

While it is a luxury to close read an Emily Brontë poem in its entirety, so many of her existing verses survive only as fragments written on strips of paper. Even in fragments of only four lines, the opening words immediately identify them as Gothic, in but so short a space. We see this in "In dungeons dark I cannot sing," or "I knew not 'twas so dire a crime," or "I am the only being whose doom." Indeed, the archival history of Emily Brontë's poetry itself rings with a bit of the

Gothic. Due to the loss of Emily and Anne's Gondal prose, scholars have had to unearth remnants of their saga through the poetry notebooks, in contrast to the tales of Glass Town and Angria of Charlotte and Branwell, which have been preserved. Thanks to the fragmentary nature of her poems and the missing prose, scholars have been left to piece them together and bring them back to life, reconstructing it from remnants and remains. The Gondal reconstructions by Laura Hinkley, Fannie Ratchford, and W. D. Paden exemplify this work of re-erecting a collapsed oeuvre.[34] Missing the complete corpus, we are left to study the ruins of those juvenilian empires, in Gothic fashion, as if they are sunken churches or deserted castles.

But great readers of Radcliffe can help us to make sense of Emily Brontë's poetic corpus. To apply Terry Castle's pivotal recognition of "the supernaturalization of everyday life," for instance, helps solve or even negate the problem of Gondal/non-Gondal distinctions:

> Old-fashioned ghosts, it is true, have disappeared from the fictional world, but a new kind of apparition takes their place. To be a Radcliffean hero or heroine in one sense means just this: to be "haunted," to find oneself obsessed by spectral images of those one loves. One sees in the mind's eye those who are absent; one is befriended and consoled by phantoms of the beloved. Radcliffe makes it clear how such phantasmata arise. They are the products of refined sentiment, the characteristic projections of a feeling heart. To be haunted, according to the novel's romantic myth, is to display one's powers of sympathetic imagination; the cruel and the dull have no such hallucinations. Those who love, by definition, are open to the spirit of the other.
>
> Already, given what we might call Radcliffe's persistently spectralized language, one cannot merely say with aplomb that the supernatural is "explained" in *The Mysteries of Udolpho*. To speak only of the rationalization of the Gothic mode is to miss one of Radcliffe's most provocative rhetorical gestures. The supernatural is not so much explained in *Udolpho* as it is displaced. It is diverted—rerouted, so to speak, into the realm of the everyday. Even as the old-time spirit world is demystified, the supposedly ordinary secular world is metaphorically suffused with a new spiritual aura.[35]

As we saw earlier, Emily Brontë's poems—in dramatizing and describing a speaker's relationship with nature or romance—consistently employ spectralized language. In this sense, it does not matter whether or not we insist upon reading a poetic fragment by Emily Brontë as a dramatic lyric, Gondalian excerpt, or biographical verses. They are all Gothic in ways that are not mutually exclusive.

To recognize them as Gothic is to recognize the doubled and manifold possibility of Gothic forms, particularly by embracing a mode of Gothic reading that embraces spectralized language as necessarily omnipresent and pervasive, in our nineteenth-century canon and in everyday life.

Castle's memorable reading of the ending to *Udolpho* and its haunting beauty trains us to become better readers of Victorian poetry—specifically, better readers of Gothic closure or goodbyes. I end with a non-Gondal poem, its text dated from 1850, which expresses a kind of renunciation of the world of romance and Gothic. While Edward Chitham has attributed this poem to Emily, the authorship of this poem has been questioned by Derek Roper and Christine Alexander, who suggest the true author was Charlotte Brontë. The feminine rhymes and iambic meter, they argue, are more akin to Charlotte's style. For me, the speaker's choice between two paths, one of romance and one of reality, anticipates the divide of the reception that Emily Brontë's poems would later go on to face from scholars. But regardless of the stanzas' authorship, we hear Charlotte's "rebuke" lingering more than anything from the first line. Here, Charlotte rebukes Emily for her inability to turn away from Gothic romance, "always back returning."

Stanzas

Often rebuked, yet always back returning
    To those first feelings that were born with me,
And leaving busy chase of wealth and learning
    For idle dreams of things which cannot be:

To-day, I will seek not the shadowy region,
    Its unsustaining vastness waxes drear;
And visions rising, legion after legion,
    Bring the unreal world too strangely near.

I'll walk, but not in old heroic traces,
    And not in paths of high morality,
And not among the half-distinguished faces,
    The clouded forms of long-past history.

I'll walk where my own nature would be leading:
    It vexes me to choose another guide:
Where the grey flocks in ferny glens are feeding;
    Where the wild wind blows on the mountain side.

> What have those lonely mountains worth revealing?
> More glory and more grief than I can tell:
> The earth that wakes *one* human heart to feeling
> Can centre both the worlds of Heaven and Hell.

As we see in this poem, even Brontë's non-Gondal poems are still Gothic, borrowing a page from *The Mysteries of Udolpho* and encompassing the explained supernatural of everyday life. Her Gondal and non-Gondal poems are equally Gothic as she locates—in Radcliffean fashion—the Gothics of the everyday. Exemplifying Terry Castle's "spectralization of everyday life" through her "persistently spectralized language," Emily's workings and reworkings of Gondal and non-Gondal poems, her revisions of poems like "Silent is the House—" into "The Prisoner," and her various fragments on slips of paper are all equally suffused with displaced Gothic energies.[36] It is through such Udolphics that her poetry does not lack the sophistication of *Wuthering Heights*, but mirrors it.

Notes

1. Christine Alexander, "'That Kingdom of Gloom': Charlotte Brontë, the annuals, and the Gothic," *Nineteenth-Century Literature* 47, no. 4 (March 1993): 409–36.
2. Gezari cites Virginia Blain's 2001 anthology as "representative, not eccentric, in excluding [Emily] Brontë." Jane Gezari, *Last Things* (Oxford: Oxford University Press, 2007), 3.
3. Gezari links this to Charlotte's comment that her sister's poems were not "at all like the poetry women generally write." She also cites in criticism the "recurrently expressed difficulty contending with an inspirational force whose powers are awful and insidious as a specifically feminine difficulty" and the problem of fitting Emily Brontë's poems within the framework of Angela Leighton or Isobel Armstrong's models. Gezari, *Last Things*, 11–12.
4. Robert B. Heilman, "Charlotte Brontë's 'New Gothic,'" in *The Brontës: A Collection*, ed. Ian Gregor (Englewood Cliffs, 1970).
5. All poems by Emily Brontë are cited from *The Poems of Emily Brontë*, ed. Derek Roper with Edward Chitham (Oxford: Clarendon Press, 1995). Here, "A sudden chasm of ghastly light," pp. 42–3, lines 1, 5, 13, 25, 41, 45.
6. Joseph Wiesenfarth, *Gothic Manners and the Classic English Novel* (Madison: Wisconsin University Press, 1988), 3, quoted in Alexander, "That Kingdom of Gloom," 409–10.

7. Diane Hoeveler, "The Brontës and the Gothic Tradition," in Diane Hoeveler and Deborah Denenholz Morse (eds), *A Companion to The Brontës* (Oxford: Wiley Blackwell, 2016), 34.
8. Ibid.
9. Ibid. 31–2.
10. Though Charlotte Brontë later went out of her way to dismiss the influence that these magazines and downmarket Gothic had on her later writing, parts of *The Professor* can be likened to Matthew Lewis's *The Monk*, while "Villette pursues the anti-Catholic aspects of the Gothic, the whiggish and militantly Protestant fear of all things European and Roman Catholic . . . Lucy's fascination, attraction, and repulsion towards Catholicism and all things European will not be so easily rejected; instead, they emerge symbolically in the repeated episodes of the spectral nun . . . [Lucy] very self-consciously places herself in a Gothic ambiance reminiscent of Radcliffe's Ellena or Emily reading by a flickering candle . . ." The echoing of those themes include the likeness of Zamorna to a ghostly monk haunting the ruins of a monastery (from Glass Town/Verdopolis); doppelgängers of Zamorna; and the theme of body-snatching in stories with Charles Wellesley and Captain Tree. Hoeveler, "The Brontës and the Gothic Tradition," 31–5, 41.
11. Alexander, "That Kingdom of Gloom," 411.
12. Ibid.
13. These appeared in annuals such as *The Keepsake, The Gem, The Amulet, The Literary Souvenir, Friendship's Offering, The Continental Annual and Romantic Cabinet*, and *Heath's Book of Beauty*. Alexander, "That Kingdom of Gloom," 413–4.
14. Alexander recognizes an important bridging figure in John Martin, the painter who illustrated annuals between the years 1826 and 1839. "In the years in which Bronte wrote her juvenilia, Martin supplied over twenty-seven designs for Annuals and journals from his now famous paintings. Descriptions of the early Glass Town, the geographical focus of the juvenilia, can only be described as fantastic, drawing on a variety of Gothic romantic sources ranging from Coleridge's subterranean caverns 'measureless to man' to Martin's rendering of Milton's vast bridge spanning Chaos, both images that Charlotte Bronte knew well . . . 'An Adventure in Italy' evokes all the hallmarks of Salvator Rosa. Here we encounter bloodthirsty banditti, violence, and rapine under cover of night. But more significant for our purposes is the undercutting of Gothic expectations in the telling of the story. After coloring our imagination with images of the picturesque sublime-figures poised on precipitous rocks and silhouetted against the twilight sky—the narrator debunks our expectation of the romantic villain . . . Meanwhile, Marian [Hume] assumes all the attributes and talents of the virginal Gothic heroine: she has lost one parent, she plays the harp, her drawing shows exquisite taste, she reads the best French and Italian works,

indulges in a little light needle-work, and rivals the flowers of the forest in loveliness." Alexander, "That Kingdom of Gloom," 417–19, 426.
15. Christine Alexander (ed.), Introduction to *The Brontës: The Tales of Glass Town, Angria, and Gondal* (New York: Oxford University Press, 2010), xxxviii.
16. Muriel Spark and Derek Stanford, *Emily Brontë: Her Life and Work* (New York: Coward-McCann, 1966), 128.
17. Ibid.
18. Scholars who ascribe to a holistic approach to Brontë's oeuvre have created a sequential chronology of Brontë's works that helps them understand Gondal as a "*Wuthering Heights* in the making." Fannie Ratchford, *Gondal's Queen: Novel in Verse by Emily Jane Brontë* (Austin: University of Texas Press, 1955), 27. Mary Visick, in *The Genesis of Wuthering Heights*, looks to the Gondal poems specifically as original models for the characters of Catherine, Heathcliff, and Edgar. The appendix to her book includes a meticulous chart mapping out Brontë's own Gondal attributions to speakers of her poems as seen in the Hatfield collection with possible parallels in specific chapters of *Wuthering Heights*. Mary Visick, *The Genesis of Wuthering Heights* (Hong Kong: Hong Kong University Press), 1967.
19. Alexander, Introduction to *The Brontës*, xxvi.
20. Ibid. xxxix.
21. Denis Donoghue, "Emily Brontë: The Latitude of Interpretation," in Thomas John Winnifrith (ed.), *Critical Essays on Emily Brontë* (New York: Macmillan, 1997), 89.
22. "O God of heaven!," in *The Poems of Emily Brontë*, 38–40.
23. Gezari, *Last Things*, 5.
24. "The Prisoner. A Fragment," in *The Poems of Emily Brontë*, 181–3. Here, lines 1–4.
25. "Silent is the House," in *The Poems of Emily Brontë*, pp. 176–81, lines 25–8. Also lines 13–16 in "The Prisoner."
26. Elizabeth Barrett Browning, "The Prisoner," ll. 1–2, 6–8.
27. Brontë, "The Prisoner," ll. 53–6
28. Christina Rossetti, "The Thread of Life," *The Complete Poems of Christina Rossetti*, vol. 2, ed. R. W. Crump (Baton Rouge: Louisiana State University Press, 1986), 1–3.
29. Muriel Spark and Derek Stanford, *Emily Brontë: Her Life and Work* (New York: Coward-McCann, 1966), 123.
30. B. E. Torgerson, *Reading the Brontë Body: Disease, Desire, and the Constraints of Culture* (Basingstoke: Palgrave Macmillan, 2007), 1, quoted in Carol Davison, "The Brontës and the Death Question," in *A Companion to the Brontës*, 385.
31. Gaskell's 1857 biography of Charlotte Brontë conflates Haworth Parsonage and its graveyard, which "rises above the church, and is terribly full of uptight tombstones." Numerous critics have identified

Emily's obsession with death and the grave, which combined "a type of pathological morbidity and death drive ... expressed in both Christian and Romantic terms," as seen in her elegies, which "maneuver between Enlightenment consolatory moralizing and Gothic sensationalism." Given their father's duties as the village parson, the children also contemplated death "in the context of divine judgment and as a form of Christian duty." Davison reads many of the juvenilia poems as constituting "a type of Graveyard Poetry in that they render poetic visions of the beyond/next world while exploring the interrelated Christian themes of faith, doubt, and divine judgment." Davison, "The Brontës and the Death Question," 385–7.

32. Rob Nixon, *Slow Violence and the Environmentalism of the Poor* (Cambridge, MA: Harvard University Press, 2011), 3.
33. Brontë, "High waveing heather," in *The Poems of Emily Brontë*, pp. 31–2, ll. 1–18.
34. See "Gondal Reconstructions" in Appendix VII of *The Poems of Emily Brontë*, 305–7.
35. Terry Castle, "The Spectralization of the Other in *The Mysteries of Udolpho*," in *The Female Thermometer: Eighteenth-Century Culture and the Invention of the Uncanny* (Oxford: Oxford University Press, 1995), 123–4.
36. Ibid. 124.

Bibliography

Aikin, John and Anna Letitia. "On the Pleasure Derived from Objects of Terror; with Sir Bertrand, A Fragment." In *Miscellaneous Pieces, in Prose: by J. and A. L. Aikin*. London: J. Johnson, 1773, 119–137.

Ainsworth, Maryan Wynn, ed. *Dante Gabriel Rossetti and the Double Work of Art*. New Haven: Yale University Art Gallery, 1976.

Alexander, Christine. "'That Kingdom of Gloom': Charlotte Brontë, the annuals, and the Gothic." *Nineteenth-Century Literature* 47, no. 4 (March 1993): 409–36.

Alexander, Christine, ed. *The Brontës: The Tales of Glass Town, Angria, and Gondal*. Edited by and with an introduction by Christine Alexander. New York: Oxford University Press, 2010.

Armstrong, Isobel. "Browning's *Mr. Sludge,'The Medium.'*" *Victorian Poetry* 2, no. 1 (Winter 1964): 1–9.

Armstrong, Isobel. *Victorian Poetry: Poetry, Poetics and Politics*. New York: Routledge, 1993.

Barrett Browning, Elizabeth. *Aurora Leigh*. Edited by Margaret Reynolds. New York: Norton, 1996.

Barrett Browning, Elizabeth: *The Complete Works of Elizabeth Browning*, vol. 2. Edited by Charlotte Porter and Helen A. Clarke. New York: Thomas Y. Crowell, 1900.

Battaglia, Beatrice. "The 'Pieces of Poetry' in Ann Radcliffe's *The Mysteries of Udolpho*." *DQR Studies in Literature* 39, no. 1 (2007): 137–51.

Bennett, Mary. *Artists of the Pre-Raphaelite Circle: The First Generation: Catalogue of Works in the Walker Art Gallery, Lady Lever Art Gallery and Sudley Art Gallery*. London: Published for the National Museums and Galleries on Merseyside by Lund Humphries, 1988.

Bentley, D. M. R. "Dante Rossetti's *Lady Lilith, Sibylla Palmifera*, 'Body's Beauty' and 'Soul's Beauty.'" *The Journal of Pre-Raphaelite Studies* 13, no. 2 (2004): 63–74.

Billone, Amy. *Little Songs: Women, Silence, and the Nineteenth-Century Sonnet*. Columbus: Ohio University Press, 2007.

Blair, Kirstie. *Form and Faith in Victorian Poetry and Religion*. Oxford: Oxford University Press, 2012.

Blakey, Dorothy. *The Minerva Press 1790–1820*. London: The Bibliographic Society of Oxford University Press, 1939.

Blissett, William. "The Pre-Raphaelite Window." *The Journal of Pre-Raphaelite Studies* 13 (Fall 2004): 5–16.

Bloom, Harold. "The Breaking of Form." In *The Lyric Theory Reader: A Critical Anthology*, ed. Virginia Jackson and Yopie Prins (Baltimore: Johns Hopkins University Press, 2014), 276.

Botting, Fred. *Gothic: The New Critical Idiom*. London: Routledge, 1996.

Brabon, Benjamin A. "Surveying Ann Radcliffe's Gothic Landscapes." *Literature Compass* 3, no. 4 (2006): 840–5.

Bracken, James K. and Joel Silver, eds. *The British Literary Book Trade, 1700–1820*. Detroit: Gale Research, 1995.

Brontë, Anne, Branford, Charlotte, and Emily. *The Brontës: The Tales of Glass Town, Angria, and Gondal*. Edited by and with an introduction by Christine Alexander. New York: Oxford University Press, 2010.

Brontë, Charlotte. *Villette*. Edited by Mark Lilly. London: Penguin Classics, 1985.

Brontë, Emily. *The Poems of Emily Brontë*. Edited by Derek Roper with Edward Chitham. Oxford: Clarendon Press, 1995.

Brown, Ford Madox. Journal entry, August 1885. Quoted in Susan P. Casteras, "The Double Vision in Portraiture." In *Dante Gabriel Rossetti and the Double Work of Art*, ed. Maryan Wynn Ainsworth, 9–35. New Haven: Yale University Art Gallery, 1976.

Brown, Marshall. *The Gothic Text*. Stanford: Stanford University Press, 2005.

Brown, Nicola, Carolyn Burdett, and Pamela Thurschwell, eds. *The Victorian Supernatural*. Cambridge: Cambridge University Press, 2004, 109–27.

Brown, Susan. "The Victorian Poetess." In *The Cambridge Companion to Victorian Poetry*, ed. Joseph Bristow, 180–202. Cambridge: Cambridge University Press, 2000.

Browning, Robert. *Robert Browning's Poetry: A Norton Critical Edition*. 2nd edn. Edited by James F. Loucks and Andrew M. Stauffer. New York: Norton, 2007.

Browning, Robert. *The Complete Works of Robert Browning*, vol. 6. Edited by John C. Berkey, Allan C. Dooley and Susan E. Dooley. Athens: Ohio University Press, 1996.

Browning, Robert. *The Poetical Works of Robert Browning*, vol. 3, *Bells and Pomegranates, I–VI*. Edited by Ian Jack, Margaret Smith, and Rowena Fowler. Oxford: Clarendon Press, 1988.

Browning, Robert. *The Poetical Works of Robert Browning*, vol. 4, *Bells and Pomegranates VII–VIII*. Edited by Ian Jack, Rowena Fowler, and Margaret Smith. Oxford: Clarendon Press, 1991.

Browning, Robert. *The Poetical Works of Robert Browning*, vol. 5, *Men and Women*. Edited by Ian Jack and Robert Inglesfield. Oxford: Clarendon Press, 1995.

Browning, Elizabeth Barrett and Robert. *The Letters of Elizabeth Barrett Browning*. Edited by Frederic G. Kenyon. New York: Macmillan, 1898.

Browning, Robert and Elizabeth Barrett Browning. *The Brownings' Correspondence*, vol. 23. Edited by Philip Kelley, Scott Lewis, Edward Hagan, Joseph Phelan, and Rhian Williams. Winfield, KS: Wedgestone Press, 2016.

Browning, Robert and Elizabeth Barrett Browning. *The Brownings' Correspondence*, vol. 24. Edited by Philip Kelley, Edward Hagan, and Linda M. Lewis. Winfield, KS: Wedgestone Press, 2016.

Buzard, James. "A Continent of Pictures: Reflections of the 'Europe' of Nineteenth-Century Tourists." *PMLA* 108, no. 1 (January 1993): 30–44.

Byron, Glennis. *Dramatic Monologue*. London: Routledge, 2003.

Campbell, Matthew. "The Victorian Sonnet." In *The Cambridge Companion to the Sonnet*, ed. A. D. Cousins. Cambridge: Cambridge University Press, 2001, 219–30.

Canuel, Mark. *Religion, Toleration, and British Writing, 1790–1830*. Cambridge: Cambridge University Press, 2002.

Casteras, Susan P. "The Double Vision in Portraiture." In *Dante Gabriel Rossetti and the Double Work of Art*, ed. Maryan Wynn Ainsworth. New Haven: Yale University Art Gallery, 1976, 9–35.

Castle, Terry. *The Female Thermometer: Eighteenth-Century Culture and the Invention of the Uncanny*. Oxford: Oxford University Press, 1995.

Chapman, Alison. "Mesmerism and Agency in the Courtship of Elizabeth Barrett and Robert Browning." *Victorian Literature and Culture* 26, no. 2 (1998): 303–19.

Chapman, Alison. "Sonnet and Sonnet Sequence." In *A Companion to Victorian Poetry*, ed. Richard Cronin, Alison Chapman and Antony H. Harrison. Malden: Blackwell, 2002, 99–114.

Chapman, Alison. *The Afterlife of Christina Rossetti*. New York: St Martin's Press, 2000.

Clery, Emma J. *The Rise of Supernatural Fiction, 1762–1800*. Cambridge: Cambridge University Press, 1995.

Clery, Emma J. *Women's Gothic: From Clara Reeve to Mary Shelley*. Tavistock: Northcote House, 2000.

Clune, Michael. "Formalism as the Fear of Ideas." *PMLA* 132, no. 5 (Oct. 2017): 1195–9.

Coleridge, Samuel Taylor. *Biographia Literaria: or, Biographical Sketches of my Literary Life and Opinions*. London: G. Bell, 1817.

Coleridge, Samuel Taylor. *Coleridge: The Early Family Letters*. Edited by James Engell. Oxford: Clarendon Press, 1994.

Coleridge, Samuel Taylor. *Lyrical Ballads 1798 and 1800*. Edited by Michael Gamer and Dahlia Porter. Toronto: Broadview, 2008.

Coleridge, Samuel Taylor. Review of *Hubert de Sevrac*. *Critical Review* 23 (August 1798): 472.

Coleridge, Samuel Taylor. "Review of Matthew G. Lewis, *The Monk.*" *Critical Review* (February 1797): 194–200.
Coleridge, Samuel Taylor. *The Complete Poetical Works of Samuel Taylor Coleridge. Volume 1: Poems.* Edited by Ernest Hartley Coleridge. Oxford: Oxford University Press, 1912.
Coleridge, Samuel Taylor. *The Collected Works of Samuel Taylor Coleridge.* Vol. 14, *Table Talk I.* Edited by Carl Woodring. Princeton: Princeton University Press, 1990.
Coleridge, Samuel Taylor. "*The Mysteries of Udolpho,* Review." *The Critical Review* (August 1794): 361–72.
Cook, Eleanor. *Browning's Lyrics: An Exploration.* Toronto: University of Toronto Press, 1974.
Cottom, Daniel. *The Civilized Imagination: A Study of Ann Radcliffe, Jane Austen, and Sir Walter Scott.* Cambridge: Cambridge University Press, 1985/2009.
Crane, R. S. *Critical and Historical Principles of Literary History.* Chicago: University of Chicago Press, 1971.
Crane, Walter. *An Artist's Reminiscences.* 2nd edn. London: Macmillan, 1907.
Crary, Jonathan. *Suspensions of Perception: Attention, Spectacle, and Modern Culture.* Cambridge, MA: MIT Press, 1999.
Culler, A. Dwight. "Monodrama and the Dramatic Monologue." *PMLA* 90 (1975): 368–74.
Culler, Jonathan. "Apostrophe." *Diacritics* 7, no. 4 (Winter 1977): 59.
Culler, Jonathan. *Theory of the Lyric.* Cambridge: Harvard University Press, 2017.
Cumming, John. "Ritualism—What is it?" In *Ritualism, The Highway to Rome.* London: James Nisbet and Co., 1867.
Danahay, Martin A. "Dante Gabriel Rossetti's Virtual Bodies." *Victorian Poetry* 36, no. 4 (Winter 1998): 379–98.
Davie, Donald. *Purity of Diction in English Verse.* London: Routledge & Kegan Paul, 1967.
Davison, Carol. "The Brontës and the Death Question." In *A Companion to the Brontës*, ed. Diane Hoeveler and Deborah Denenholz Morse. Oxford: Wiley Blackwell, 2016.
Davison, Carol Margaret. "Haunted House/Haunted Heroine: Female Gothic Closets in 'The Yellow Wallpaper.'" *Women's Studies* 33, no. 1 (2004): 47–75.
London: Pickering & Chatto, 2000.
Dekker, George. *The Fictions of Romantic Tourism: Radcliffe, Scott, and Mary Shelley.* Stanford: Stanford University Press, 2005.
De Quincey, Thomas. *The Works of Thomas De Quincey*, vol. 3. Edited by Grevel Lindop.
Dickerson, Vanessa. *Victorian Ghosts in the Noontide: Women Writers and the Supernatural.* Columbia: University of Missouri, 1996.

Donnelly, Brian. *Dante Gabriel Rossetti: The Painter as Poet*. Aldershot and Burlington, VT: Ashgate, 2015.

Donoghue, Denis. "Emily Brontë: The Latitude of Interpretation." In Thomas John Winnifrith, ed. *Critical Essays on Emily Brontë*. New York: Macmillan, 1997.

Doyle, Arthur Conan. *The History of Spiritualism*, vol. 1. New York: George H. Doran Company, 1926.

Dubois, Martin. *Gerard Manley Hopkins and the Poetry of Religious Experience*. Cambridge: Cambridge University Press, 2017.

Dubrow, Heather. *Echoes of Desire: English Petrarchism and its Counterdiscourses*. Ithaca, NY: Cornell University Press, 1995.

Dubrow, Heather. "Guess Who's Coming to Dinner? Reinterpreting Formalism and the Country House Poem." *Modern Language Quarterly* 61 (2000): 65.

Eaton, Charlotte. *Rome in the Nineteenth Century: Containing a complete account of the Ruins of the Ancient City, the Remains of the Middle Ages, and the Monuments of Modern Times*. Edinburgh: Constable, 1820.

Ellis, Virginia Ridley. *Gerard Manley Hopkins and the Language of Mystery*. Columbia: University of Missouri Press, 1991.

Enfield, William. Review of *Mysteries of Udolpho*. *Monthly Review* 15 (November 1794): 278–83.

Erickson, Lee. "The Self and Others in Browning's 'Men and Women.'" *Victorian Poetry* 21, no. 1 (1983): 53.

Feldman, Paula R. and Daniel Robinson, eds. *A Century of Sonnets: The Romantic-Era Revival 1750–1850*. Oxford: Oxford University Press, 1999.

Felluga, Dino Franco. "Novel Poetry: Transgressing the Law of Genre." *Victorian Poetry* 41, no. 4 (Winter 2003): 490–9.

Ferguson, Frances. *Pornography, the Theory: What Utilitarianism Did to Action*. Chicago: University of Chicago Press, 2004.

Fleenor, Juliann E., ed. *The Female Gothic*. Fountain Valley, CA: Eden Press, 1983.

Flint, Kate. "'. . . As a Rule, I Does Not Mean I': Personal Identity and the Victorian Woman Poet." In *Rewriting the Self: Histories from the Renaissance to the Present*, ed. Roy Porter, 156–66. London: Routledge, 1997.

Gamer, Michael. "Gothic Fictions and Romantic Writing in Britain." In *The Cambridge Companion to Gothic Fiction*, ed. Jerrold E. Hogle. Cambridge: Cambridge University Press, 2002, 86–102.

Gamer, Michael. *Romanticism and the Gothic: Genre, Reception, and Canon Formation*. Cambridge: Cambridge University Press, 2000.

Garrett, Marvin P. "Language and Design in 'Pippa Passes.'" *Victorian Poetry* 13, no. 1 (1975): 47–60.

Gaylin, Ann. *Eavesdropping in the Novel from Austen to Proust*. Cambridge: Cambridge University Press, 2002.

Gazzaniga, Andrea. "'This Close Room': Elizabeth Barrett Browning's Proximal Poetics in Sonnets from the Portuguese." *Victorian Poetry* 54, no. 1 (2016): 67–92.

George, J. A. "From King Arthur to Sidonia the Sorceress: the Dual Nature of Pre-Raphaelite Mediaevalism." In *Victorian Gothic: Literary and Cultural Manifestations in the Nineteenth Century*, ed. Ruth Robbins and Julian Wolfreys. Basingstoke: Palgrave Macmillan, 2000, 90–108.

Gezari, Jane. *Last Things*. Oxford: Oxford University Press, 2007.

Gilbert, Sandra M. and Susan Gubar. *The Madwoman in the Attic: The Woman Writer and the Nineteenth-Century Literary Imagination*. New Haven: Yale University Press, 1979.

Gilpin, William. *Three essays: On picturesque beauty; On picturesque travel; and On sketching landscape: to which is added a poem, On landscape painting*. London: R. Blamire, 1792.

Godwin, William. *Caleb Williams* (1795). Edited by David McCracken. New York: W. W. Norton, 1977.

Going, William T. "The Term Sonnet Sequence." *Modern Language Notes* 62 (1947): 400–2.

Going, William T. *Scanty Plot of Ground: Studies in the Victorian Sonnet*. The Hague: Mouton, 1976.

Golden, Catherine. "Dante Gabriel Rossetti's Two-Sided Art." *Victorian Poetry* 26, no. 4 (Winter, 1988): 394–402.

Grass, Sean. *The Self in the Cell: Narrating the Victorian Prisoner*. New York: Routledge, 2003.

Gray, Erik. "Andrea del Sarto's Modesty." In *Robert Browning's Poetry: A Norton Critical Edition*. 2nd edn. Edited by James F. Loucks and Andrew M. Stauffer. New York: W.W. Norton, 2007, 643–650.

Griffin, Susan. *Anti-Catholicism and Nineteenth-Century Fiction*. Cambridge: Cambridge University Press, 2004.

Griffiths, Eric. "The Disappointment of Christina G. Rossetti." *Essays in Criticism* 47, no. 2 (April 1997): 107–42.

Grimes, Hilary. *The Late Victorian Gothic: Mental Science, the Uncanny, and Scenes of Writing*. Aldershot: Ashgate, 2011.

Haefele-Thomas, Ardel. *Queer Others in Victorian Gothic*. Cardiff: University of Wales Press, 2012.

Haggerty, George. *Gothic Fiction/Gothic Form*. University Park: The Pennsylvania State University Press, 1989.

Hallam, Arthur Henry. *The Writings of Arthur Hallam*. Edited by T.H. Vail Motter. London: Oxford University Press, 1943.

Hammer, Langdon. "Fantastic Forms." *PMLA* 132, no. 5 (October 2017): 1200–5.

Hansard's Parliamentary Debates. Third series. London: Cornelius Buck, 1856.

Harrington, Emily, *Second Person Singular: Late Victorian Women Poets and the Bonds of Verse*. Charlottesville: University of Virginia Press, 2014.

Hassett, Constance. *Christina Rossetti: The Patience of Style*. Charlottesville: University of Virginia Press, 2005.

Hazlitt, William, "Notes of a Journey through France and Italy." In *The Collected Works of William Hazlitt*, ed. A. R. Waller and Arnold Glover. London: J. M. Dent & Company, 1903, 85–304.

Heilman, Robert B. "Charlotte Bronte's 'New Gothic.'" In *From Jane Austen to Joseph Conrad: Essays Collected in Memory of James T. Hillhouse*, ed. Robert Rathburn and Martin Steinmann Jr. Minneapolis: University of Minnesota Press, 1958, 118–32.

Heilman, Robert B. "Charlotte Brontë's 'New Gothic.'" In *The Brontës: A Collection*, ed. Ian Gregor. Englewood Cliffs, 1970.

Helsinger, Elizabeth. *Poetry and the Thought of Song in Nineteenth-Century Britain*. Charlottesville: Virginia University Press, 2015.

Hensley, Nathan. "After Death: Christina Rossetti's Timescales of Catastrophe." *Nineteenth-Century Contexts* 38, no. 5 (2016): 399–415.

Hill, Marylu. "'Eat Me, Drink Me, Love Me': Eucharist and the Erotic Body in Christina Rossetti's Goblin Market." *Victorian Poetry* 43 (2005): 455–72.

Hoeveler, Diane Long. *Gothic Feminism: The Professionalization of Gender from Charlotte Smith to the Brontës*. Pennsylvania: Pennsylvania State University Press, 1998.

Hoeveler, Diane Long. *The Gothic Ideology: Religious Hysteria and Anti-Catholicism in British Popular Fiction, 1780–1880*. Cardiff: University of Wales Press, 2014.

Hoeveler, Diane Long. "The Construction of the Gothic Nun: Fantasies and the Religious Imaginary," Marquette University, Milwaukee, WI, <http://epublications.marquette.edu/cgi/viewcontent.cgi?article=1008&context=cah> (last accessed 15 January 2018).

Hoeveler, Diane and Deborah Denenholz Morse, eds. *A Companion to The Brontës*. Oxford: Wiley Blackwell, 2016.

Hogle, Jerrold E., ed. *The Cambridge Companion to Gothic Fiction*. Cambridge: Cambridge University Press, 2002.

Hollander, John. *The Work of Poetry*. New York: Columbia University Press, 1997.

Hopkins, Gerard Manley. *The Collected Works of Gerard Manley Hopkins, Volumes 1 and 2: Correspondence 1852–1881, 1882–1889*. Edited by R. K. R. Thornton and Catherine Phillips. Oxford: Oxford University Press, 2015.

Hopkins, Gerard Manley. *The Collected Works of Gerard Manley Hopkins, Volume 3: Diaries, Journals, and Notebooks*. Edited by Leslie Higgins. Oxford: Oxford University Press, 2015.

Hopkins, Gerard Manley. *The Journals and Papers of Gerard Manley Hopkins*. Edited by Humphrey House. London: Oxford University Press, 1959.

Hopkins, Gerard Manley. *The Poetical Works of Gerard Manley Hopkins*. Edited by Norman H. MacKenzie. Oxford: Oxford University Press, 1990.

Horricks, Ingrid. "'Her Ideas Arranged Themselves': Re-Membering Poetry in Radcliffe." *Studies in Romanticism* 47, no. 4 (2008): 507–27.

Houston, Gail Turley. *From Dickens to Dracula: Gothic, Economics and Victorian Fiction*. Cambridge: Cambridge University Press, 2005.

Hume, Robert D. "Gothic Versus Romantic: A Revaluation of the Gothic Novel." *PMLA* 84, no. 2 (March 1969): 282–90.

Hunt, Leigh. *The Book of the Sonnet*. Edited by S. Adams Lee. Stanford: Stanford University Press, 1989.

Hurley, Kelly. *The Gothic Body: Sexuality, Materialism, and Degeneration at the Fin de Siècle*. Cambridge: Cambridge University Press, 1996.

Ignatius, of Loyola, Saint. *The Spiritual Exercises of St. Ignatius Loyola*. Translated by Elisabeth Tetlow. Lanham, MD: University Press of America, 1987.

Jackson, Virginia. "The Poet as Poetess." In *The Cambridge Companion to Nineteenth-Century American Poetry*, ed. Kerry Larson. Cambridge: Cambridge University Press, 2011, 54–75.

Jackson, Virginia and Yopie Prins, eds. *The Lyric Theory Reader: A Critical Anthology*. Baltimore: Johns Hopkins University Press, 2014.

James, Henry. *Selected Letters*. Edited by Leon Edel. Cambridge, MA: Belknap, 1974.

Johnson, Claudia. *Equivocal Beings: Politics, Gender, and Sentimentality in the 1790s*. Chicago: University of Chicago Press, 1994.

Joseph, Gerhard. "Victorian Frames: The Windows and Mirrors of Browning, Arnold and Tennyson." *Victorian Poetry* 16, no. 1–2 (1978): 71–3.

Kaczorowski, Robert J. "The Common-Law Background of Nineteenth-Century Tort Law." *Ohio State Law Journal* 51, no. 5 (1990): 1127–99.

Karlin, Daniel. *The Figure of the Singer*. Oxford: Oxford University Press, 2013.

Keats, John. *The Letters of John Keats: Volume 1, 1814–1821*. Edited by Hyder E. Rollins. Cambridge, MA: Harvard University Press, 1980.

Keats, John. *The Letters of John Keats: Volume 2, 1814–1821*. Edited by Hyder Edward Rollins. Cambridge, MA: Harvard University Press, 1958.

Keats, John. *The Poetical Works of John Keats*. London: Moxon, Son and Co., 1871.

Kelly, Gary. *English Fiction of the Romantic Period 1789–1830*. New York: Routledge, 1989.

Keown, John. *Abortion, Doctors and the Law: Some Aspects of the Legal Regulation of Abortion in England from 1803 to 1982*. Cambridge Studies in the History of Medicine. Cambridge: Cambridge University Press, 1988.

Kiely, Robert. *The Romantic Novel in England*. Cambridge, MA: Harvard University Press, 1972.

Kneale, J. Douglas. "Romantic Aversions: Apostrophe Reconsidered." *ELH* 58, no. 1 (Spring 1991): 141–65.

Knight, Mark and Emma Mason, eds. *Nineteenth-Century Religion and Literature*. Oxford: Oxford University Press, 2007.

Knight, Richard Payne. *An Analytical Inquiry Into the Principles of Taste*. 4th edn. London: Payne and White, 1808.

Knoepflmacher, Ulrich C. "Projection and the Female Other: Romanticism, Browning, and the Victorian Dramatic Monologue." *Victorian Poetry* 22, no. 2 (1984): 139–59.

Knoepflmacher, Ulrich C. and Logan D. Browning, eds. *Victorian Hybridities: Cultural Anxiety and Formal Innovation*. Baltimore: Johns Hopkins University Press, 2010.

Knowles, Archibald C. *The Practice of Religion: A Short Manual of Instructions and Devotions*. New York: Edwin S. Gorham, 1918.

Kramer, Dale. "Character and Theme in *Pippa Passes*." *Victorian Poetry* 2 (1964): 241–9.

Kramnick, Jonathan and Anahid Nersessian. "Form and Explanation." *Critical Inquiry* 43 (Spring 2017): 650–69.

Laird, Holly. "The Death of the Author by Suicide: Fin-de-Siecle Poets and the Construction of Identity." In *The Fin de Siecle Poem: English Literary Culture and 1890s*, ed. Joseph Bristow. Athens: The Ohio University Press, 2005, 116–51.

LaMonaca, Maria. *Masked Atheism: Catholicism and the Secular Victorian Home*. Athens: Ohio State University Press, 2008.

Landow, George P. "Gerard Manley Hopkins and the Visual Arts." *The Victorian Web*, <http://www.victorianweb.org/authors/hopkins/artov.html> (last accessed 22 May 2014).

Landow, George P. *William Holman Hunt and Typological Symbolism*. London: Yale University Press, 1979.

Langbaum, Robert. *The Poetry of Experience: The Dramatic Monologue in Modern Literary Tradition*. New York: Random House, 1957.

Latham, David "'World of Its Own Creation': Pre-Raphaelite Poetry and the New Paradigm for Art." *Journal of Pre-Raphaelite Studies* 25 (Spring 2016), 11.

Law, Graham. "Minerva Press." In *The Oxford Companion to the Book*, ed. Michael F. Suarez and H. R. Woudhuysen. Oxford: Oxford University Press, 2010.

Leighton, Angela. *Hearing Things: The Work of Sound in Literature*. Cambridge, MA: Harvard University Press, 2018.

Leighton, Angela. "On the 'hearing ear': Some Sonnets of the Rossettis." *Victorian Poetry* 47, no. 3 (Fall 2009): 505–16.

Leighton, Angela. *Victorian Women Poets: Writing Against the Heart*. Charlottesville: University of Virginia Press, 1992.

Levine, Naomi. "Elizabeth Barrett Browning's Historiographical Poetics." *Modern Language Quarterly* 77, no. 1 (March 2016): 81–104.
Levinson, Marjorie. "What is New Formalism?" *PMLA* 122, no. 2 (March 2007): 558–69.
Lewis, Matthew. *The Monk: A Romance* (1796). Edited by Howard Anderson. New York: Oxford University Press, 2008.
Lipski, Jakub and Jacek Mydla, eds. *The Enchantress of Words, Sounds and Images: Anniversary Essays on Ann Radcliffe, 1764–1823*. Washington DC: Academica Press, 2015.
Lockerd, Martin. *Decadent Catholicism and the Making of Modernism*. London: Bloomsbury, 2020.
Lootens, Tricia. *Lost Saints: Silence, Gender, and Victorian Literary Canonization*. Charlottesville: University of Virginia Press, 1996.
Lootens, Tricia. *The Political Poetess: Victorian Femininity, Race, and the Legacy of Separate Spheres*. Princeton: Princeton University Press, 2017.
Loudon, Irvine. *Death in Childbirth*. Oxford: Clarendon Press, 1992.
Luu, Helen. "A Matter of Life and Death: The Auditor-Function of the Dramatic Monologue." *Victorian Poetry* 54, no. 1 (Spring 2016): 19–38.
MacKenzie, Norman H. *A Reader's Guide to Gerard Manley Hopkins*. Philadelphia: St. Joseph's University Press, 2008.
McCarthy, Anne. *Awful Parenthesis: Suspension and the Sublime in Romantic and Victorian Poetry*. Toronto: University of Toronto Press, 2018.
McGann, Jerome. *Dante Gabriel Rossetti and the Game That Must Be Lost*. New Haven: Yale University Press, 2000.
McGann, Jerome J. "Rossetti's Significant Details." *Victorian Poetry* 7, no. 1 (Spring 1969): 41–54.
McGann, Jerome, ed. "The Complete Writings and Pictures of Dante Gabriel Rossetti." *The Rossetti Archive*. Available at <http://www.rossettiarchive.org/racs/doubleworks.rac.html> (last accessed 22 May 2014).
McGowan, John P. "'The Bitterness of Things Occult': D. G. Rossetti's Search for the Real." *Victorian Poetry* 20, no. 3–4 (1982): 45–60.
McGrath, Brian. *The Poetics of Unremembered Acts: Reading, Lyric, Pedagogy*. Evanston: Northwestern University Press, 2012.
McKnight, Natalie J. *Suffering Mothers in Mid-Victorian Novels*. New York: St. Martin's Press, 1997.
Mahawatte, Royce. *George Eliot and the Gothic Novel*. Cardiff: University of Wales Press, 2013.
Maitland, Thomas. [Robert Buchanan]. "The Fleshly School of Poetry: Mr. D. G. Rossetti." *The Contemporary Review* 18 (October 1871): 334–50.
Makala, Melissa. *Women's Ghost Literature in Nineteenth-Century Britain*. Cardiff: University of Wales Press, 2013.
Mansfield, Elizabeth C. *Too Beautiful to Picture: Zeuxis, Myth, And Mimesis*. Minneapolis: University of Minnesota Press, 2007.

Mariani, Paul L. *A Commentary on the Complete Poems of Gerard Manley Hopkins*. Ithaca, NY: Cornell University Press, 1970.
Mariani, Paul L. *Gerard Manley Hopkins: A Life*. New York: Viking Penguin, 2008.
Martin, Meredith. "Gerard Manley Hopkins and the Stigma of Meter." *Victorian Studies* 50, no. 2 (Winter 2008): 243–54.
Martin, Meredith. "Hopkins' Prosody." *Hopkins Quarterly* 38, no. 1–2 (Winter/Spring 2011): 1–30.
Martin, Meredith, *The Rise and Fall of Meter: Poetry and English National Culture 1860–1930*. Princeton: Princeton University Press, 2012, 62.
Mason, Emma. *Christina Rossetti: Poetry, Ecology, Faith*. Oxford: Oxford University Press, 2018.
Massé, Michelle A., *In the Name of Love: Women, Masochism and the Gothic*. Ithaca, NY: Cornell University Press, 1992.
Maturin, Charles. *Melmoth the Wanderer* (1820). Edited by Douglas Grant. New York: Oxford University Press, 2008.
Matus, Jill. *Unstable Bodies: Victorian Representations of Sexuality and Maternity*. Manchester: Manchester University Press, 1995.
Mazel, Adam. "'You, Guess': The Enigmas of Christina Rossetti." *Victorian Literature and Culture* 44 (2016): 511–33.
Meisel, Martin. "'Half Sick of Shadows:' The Aesthetic Dialogue in Pre-Raphaelite Painting." In *Nature and the Victorian Imagination*, ed. Ulrich C. Knoepflmacher and G. B. Tennyson. Berkeley: University of California Press, 1977, 309–40.
Mellor, Anne. *Romanticism and Gender*. New York: Routledge, 1993.
Mermin, Dorothy. *Elizabeth Barrett Browning: The Origins of a New Poetry*. Chicago: University of Chicago Press, 1989.
Mermin, Dorothy. *The Audience in the Poem: Five Victorian Poets*. New Brunswick: Rutgers University Press, 1983.
Mermin, Dorothy. "The Damsel, the Knight, and the Victorian Woman Poet." *Critical Inquiry* 13, no. 1 (Autumn 1986): 64–80.
Milbank, Alison. *God & the Gothic: Religion, Romance and Reality in the English Literary Tradition*. Oxford: Oxford University Press, 2018.
Miles, Robert. "Ann Radcliffe and Matthew Lewis." In *A Companion to the Gothic*, ed. David Punter. Malden: Blackwell, 2000, 41–57.
Miles, Robert. *Ann Radcliffe: The Great Enchantress*. Manchester: Manchester University Press, 1995.
Mill, John Stuart. *The Collected Works of John Stuart Mill*, vol. 1: *Autobiography and Literary Essays*. Edited by John M. Robson and Jack Stillinger. Toronto: University of Toronto Press, 1981.
Millward, Robert and Frances Bell. "Infant Mortality in Victorian Britain: The Mother as Medium." *The Economic History Review* 54, no. 4 (November 2001): 699–733.
Milton, John. *The Poetical Works of John Milton*. London: Macmillan, 1905.

Moers, Ellen. *Literary Women: The Great Writers*. New York: Doubleday, 1976.
Morgan, Monique. *Narrative Means, Lyric Ends: Temporality in the Nineteenth-Century British Long Poem*. Columbus: The Ohio State University Press, 2009.
Morrison, Paul. "Enclosed in Openness: *Northanger Abbey* and the Domestic Carceral." *Texas Studies in Literature and Language* 33, no. 1 (Spring 1991): 1–23.
Murphy, Patricia. *The New Woman Gothic: Reconfigurations of Distress*. Columbia: University of Missouri Press, 2016.
Napier, Elizabeth R. *The Failure of Gothic: Problems of Disjunction in an Eighteenth-Century Literary Form*. Oxford: Oxford University Press, 1987.
Neiman, Elizabeth and Tina Morin, eds. "The Minerva Press and the Romantic-Era Literary Marketplace." *Romantic Textualities: Literature and Print Culture, 1780–1840*, no. 23 (Summer 2020), <http://www.romtext.org.uk/issues/issue-23/> (last accessed 1 November 2021).
Netland, John T. "Linguistic Limitation and the Instress of Grace in *The Wreck of the Deutschland*." *Victorian Poetry* 27, no. 2 (Summer 1989): 187–99.
Ngai, Sianne. *Ugly Feelings*. Cambridge, MA: Harvard University Press, 2005.
Nixon, Rob. *Slow Violence and the Environmentalism of the Poor*. Cambridge, MA: Harvard University Press, 2011.
Norman, E. R. *Anti-Catholicism in Victorian England*. London: George Allen & Unwin, 1968.
Norton, Rictor. *Mistress of Udolpho: The Life of Ann Radcliffe*. London: Leicester University Press, 1999.
O'Malley, Patrick. *Catholicism, Sexual Deviance, and Victorian Gothic Culture*. Oxford: Oxford University Press, 2006.
Otto, Peter. "Radcliffe and her Imitators." Gothic Fiction: Rare Printed Works from the Sadleir-Black Collection of Gothic Fiction at the Alderman Library, University of Virginia, <http://www.ampltd.co.uk/digital_guides/gothic_fiction/Contents.aspx> (last accessed 15 December 2019.
Pattison, Robert. *Tennyson and Tradition*. Cambridge, MA: Harvard University Press, 1979.
Paxton, Amanda. *Willful Submission: Sado-Erotics and Heavenly Marriage in Victorian Poetry*. Charlottesville: University of Virginia Press, 2018.
Paz, Denis G. *Popular Anti-Catholicism in Mid-Victorian England*. Stanford: Stanford University Press, 1992.
Pearsall, Cornelia. *Tennyson's Rapture: Transformation in the Victorian Dramatic Monologue*. Oxford: Oxford University Press, 2008.
Perloff, Marjorie. "Can(n)on to the Right of Us, Can(n)on to the Left of Us: A Plea for Difference." In *The Lyric Theory Reader*, ed. Jackson and Prins.
Peterson, Carl A., *The Poetry and Painting of Dante Gabriel Rossetti*. Madison: University of Wisconsin Press, 1951.

Phelan, Joseph. *The Nineteenth-Century Sonnet*. New York: Palgrave Macmillan, 2005.
Pitchford, Lois S. "The Curtal Sonnets of Gerard Manley Hopkins." *Modern Language Notes* 67, no. 3 (March 1952): 165–9.
Pollock, Griselda. *Vision And Difference: Femininity, Feminism, and Histories of Art*. London: Routledge, 1988.
Potter, Franz J. *The History of Gothic Publishing, 1800–1835: Exhuming the Trade*. New York: Palgrave, 2005.
Prettejohn, Elizabeth. *Rossetti and His Circle*. New York: Stewart Tabori & Chang, 1998.
Prettejohn, Elizabeth, ed. *The Cambridge Companion to the Pre-Raphaelites*. Cambridge: Cambridge University Press, 2012.
Prins, Yopie. *Victorian Sappho*. Princeton: Princeton University Press, 1999.
Punter, David. *The Literature of Terror: A History of Gothic Fictions from 1765 to the Present Day*. London: Longman, 1980.
Punter, David and Elisabeth Bronfen. "Gothic: Violence, Trauma and the Ethical." In *The Gothic: Essays and Studies*, ed. Fred Botting. London: Routledge, 1996, 7–21.
Punter, David and Glennis Byron, *The Gothic*. Malden: Blackwell Publishing, 2004.
Purves, Maria. *The Gothic and Catholicism: Religion, Cultural Exchange and the Popular Novel, 1785–1829*. Cardiff: University of Wales Press, 2009.
Quint, David. *Epic and Empire: Politics and Generic Form from Virgil to Milton*. Princeton: Princeton University Press, 1993.
Radcliffe, Ann. "On the Supernatural in Poetry." *New Monthly Magazine* 16, no. 1 (1826). In *Gothic Documents: A Sourcebook, 1700-1820*, ed. E. J. Clery and Robert Miles. Manchester: Manchester University Press, 2000, 163–72.
Radcliffe, Ann. *The Castles of Athlin and Dunbayne*, 1821 edn. Reprint, New York: Arno Press, 1972.
Radcliffe, Ann. *The Italian, or the Confessional of the Black Penitents: A Romance* (1797). Edited by Frederick Garber. New York: Oxford University Press, 1998.
Radcliffe, Ann. *The Mysteries of Udolpho* (1794). Oxford World's Classics. Edited by Bonamy Dobrée. New York: Oxford University Press, 2008.
Radcliffe, Ann. *The Poems of Mrs. Ann Radcliffe*. London: J. Smith, 1816.
Radcliffe, Ann. *The Romance of the Forest* (1791). Oxford World's Classics. Edited by Chloe Chard. New York: Oxford University Press, 2009.
Ratchford, Fannie. *Gondal's Queen: Novel in Verse by Emily Jane Brontë*. Austin: University of Texas Press, 1955.
Raven, James and Antonia Forster, eds. *The English Novel 1770–1829: A Bibliographical Survey of Prose Fiction in the British Isles*, Volume 1: 1770–1799. Oxford: Oxford University Press.
Raymond, Mark. "The Romantic Sonnet Revival: Opening the Sonnet's Crypt." *Literature Compass* 4, no. 3 (2007): 721–36.

Reader, Simon. *Notework: Victorian Literature and Nonlinear Style*. Stanford: Stanford University Press, 2021.

Reed, John Shelton. *Glorious Battle: The Cultural Politics of Victorian Anglo-Catholicism*. Nashville: Vanderbilt University Press, 2000.

Reynolds, Joshua. Letter to William Gilpin. London: 19 April 1791. Cited in William Gilpin, *Three Essays: On Picturesque Beauty; on Picturesque Travel; and on Sketching Landscape: to which is added a Poem, on Landscape Painting*. London: Blamire, 1974.

Richter, David H. *The Progress of Romance: Literary Historiography and the Gothic Novel*. Columbus: The Ohio State University Press, 1996.

Ridenhour, Jamieson. *In Darkest London: The Gothic Cityscape in Victorian Literature*. Washington DC: Rowman & Littlefield, 2013.

Riede, David G. *Allegories of One's Own Mind: Melancholy in Victorian Poetry*. Columbus: Ohio State University Press, 2005.

Riede, David G. *Dante Gabriel Rossetti and the Limits of Victorian Vision*. Ithaca, NY: Cornell University Press, 1983.

Riede, David G. *Dante Gabriel Rossetti Revisited*. Edited by Herbert Sussmann. New York: Twayne Publishers, 1992.

Riede, David G. "Genre and Poetic Authority in Pippa Passes." *Victorian Poetry* 27, no. 3–4 (1989): 49–64.

Riede, David G. "The Pre-Raphaelite School." In *A Companion to Victorian Poetry*, ed. Richard Cronin, Alison Chapman, and Anthony H. Harrison. Malden: Blackwell, 2002.

Roberts, Adam. "Browning, the Dramatic Monologue and the Resurrection of the Dead. In *The Victorian* Supernatural, ed. Nicola Brown, Carolyn Burdett, and Pamela Thurschwell. Cambridge: Cambridge University Press, 2004, 109–27.

Robbins, Ruth and Julian Wolfreys, eds. *Victorian Gothic: Literary and Cultural Manifestations in the Nineteenth Century*. Basingstoke: Palgrave, 2000.

Rogers, Deborah D., ed. *The Critical Response to Ann Radcliffe*. Westport, CT: Greenwood Press, 1994.

Rogers, Deborah D. *The Matrophobic Gothic and Its Legacy: Sacrificing Mothers in the Novel and in Popular Culture*. New York: Peter Lang, 2007.

Ross, Shawna. *Charlotte Brontë at the Anthropocene*. Albany: SUNY Press, 2020.

Rossetti, Christina. *A Pageant and Other Poems*. London: Macmillan, 1881.

Rossetti, Christina. *Christina Rossetti: Poems and Prose*. Edited by Simon Humphries. New York: Oxford University Press, 2008.

Rossetti, Christina. *Maude: A Story for Girls*. With an Introduction by William Michael Rossetti. London: James Bowden, 1897.

Rossetti, Christina. *The Complete Poems of Christina Rossetti*, vol. 2. Edited by R. W. Crump. Baton Rouge: Louisiana State University Press, 1986.

Rossetti, Dante Gabriel. *Dante Gabriel Rossetti: Collected Poetry and Prose*. Edited by Jerome McGann. New Haven: Yale University Press, 2014.
Rossetti, Dante Gabriel. *The Collected Works of Dante Gabriel Rossetti*, vol. 1. Edited by William M. Rossetti. London: Ellis and Elvey, 1897.
Rossetti, Dante Gabriel. *The Complete Writings and Pictures of Dante Gabriel Rossetti*. Edited by Jerome McGann, <http://www.rossettiarchive.org> (last accessed 22 May 2014).
Rossetti, Dante Gabriel. *The Correspondence of Dante Gabriel Rossetti*. Edited by William Fredeman. Rochester, NY: D. S. Brewer, 2010.
Rossetti, William Michael. *Dante Gabriel Rossetti as Designer and Writer*. London: Cassell, 1889.
Ryals, Clyde de L. *The Poems and Plays of Robert Browning, 1833–1846*. Columbus: The Ohio State University Press, 1983.
Sage, Victor, ed. *The Gothick Novel: A Casebook*. Basingstoke: Macmillan, 1990.
Sandler, Stephanie. "Rhythms, Networks: Caroline Levine Meets Susan Howe and Marina Tsvetaeva." *PMLA* 132, no. 5 (October 2017): 1229.
Saville, Julia F. *A Queer Chivalry: The Homoerotic Asceticism of Gerard Manley Hopkins*. Charlottesville: University of Virginia Press, 2000.
Scarry, Elaine. *The Body in Pain: The Making and Unmaking of the World*. New York: Oxford University Press, 1985.
Schaffer, Talia and Kathy A. Psomiades, eds. *Women and British Aestheticism*. Charlottesville: University Press of Virginia, 1999.
Scheinberg, Cynthia. "Recasting 'Sympathy and Judgment': Amy Levy, Women Poets, and the Victorian Dramatic Monologue." *Victorian Poetry* 35, no. 2 (1997): 173–91.
Scott, Walter. *The Lives of the Novelists*. Philadelphia: H. C. Carey and I. Lea, et al., 1825.
Sedgwick, Eve Kosofsky. *The Coherence of Gothic Conventions*. New York: Arno Press, 1980.
Sessions, Ina Beth. "The Dramatic Monologue." *PMLA* 62 (1947): 503–16.
Seward, Anna. *Original Sonnets on Various Subjects; and Odes Paraphrased from Horace*. London: G. Sael, 1799.
Seward, Anna. "Sonnet XLIII: To May, in the Year 1783." In *Romanticism: An Anthology*, 3rd edn, ed. Duncan Wu. Cambridge, MA: Blackwell, 1995, 92.
Shapira, Yael. *Inventing the Gothic Corpse: The Thrill of Human Remains in the Eighteenth-Century Novel*. Cham: Palgrave Macmillan, 2018.
Shaw, David W. "Lyric Displacement in the Victorian Monologue: Naturalizing the Vocative." *Nineteenth-Century Literature* 52, no. 3 (1997): 302–25.
Shaw, David W. *Origins of the Monologue: The Hidden God*. Toronto: University of Toronto Press, 1999.
Sheets, Robin. "Pornography and Art: The Case of Jenny." *Critical Inquiry* 14, no. 2 (Winter 1988): 315–34.

Shelley, Percy Bysshe. *Shelley's Poetry and Prose*. Edited by Donald H. Reiman and Sharon B. Powers. New York: W. W. Norton & Company, 1977.
Shelley, Percy Bysshe. *Shelley's Poetry and Prose*, 2nd edn. Edited by Donald H. Reiman and Neil Fraistat. New York: W. W. Norton & Company, 2002.
Shires, Linda M. "Browning's Grafts." *Studies in English Literature, 1500-1900* 48, no. 4 (Autumn 2008): 769–78.
Shires, Linda M., "The Dramatic 'I' Poem." *Victorian Poetry* 22, no. 2 (1984): 97–101.
Shklovsky, Victor. *Russian Formalist Criticism: Four Essays*. Translated by Lee T. Lemon and Marion J. Rees. Lincoln: University of Nebraska Press, 1965.
Sinfield, Alan. *Dramatic Monologue*. London: Methuen, 1977.
Slinn, Warwick E. *The Disclosure of Self in Victorian Poetry*. London: Macmillan, 1991.
Smart, Carol, ed. *Regulating Womanhood: Historical Essays on Marriage, Motherhood and Sexuality*. London: Routledge, 1992.
Smith, Andrew and Mark Bennett, eds. *Locating Ann Radcliffe*. London: Routledge, 2019.
Smith, Andrew and William Hughes, eds. *The Victorian Gothic: An Edinburgh Companion*. Edinburgh: Edinburgh University Press, 2012.
Smith, Barbara Herrnstein. *On the Margins of Discourse: The Relation of Literature to Language*. Chicago, University of Chicago Press, 1978.
Smith, Charlotte. *Celestina: A Novel in Four Volumes*. London: T. Cadell, 1791.
Smith, Charlotte. *Elegiac Sonnets*, 3rd edn. London: Dodsley, Gardner and Bew, 1786.
Smith, Charlotte. *Emmeline: the Orphan of the Castle*. London: T. Cadell, 1789.
Spacks, Patricia Meyer. *Desire and Truth: Functions of Plot in Eighteenth-Century English Novels*. Chicago: Chicago University Press, 1990.
Spark, Muriel and Derek Stanford. *Emily Brontë: Her Life and Work*. New York: Coward-McCann, 1966.
Stabler, Jane. "Ann Radcliffe's Poetry: The Poetics of Refrain and Inventory." In *Ann Radcliffe, Romanticism and the Gothic*, ed. Townshend and Wright, 185–202
Stabler, Jane. "Taking Liberties: The Italian Picturesque in Women's Travel Writing." *European Romantic Review* 13, no. 1 (2002): 11–22.
Starzyk, Lawrence. "Rossetti's 'Jenny': Aestheticizing the Whore." *Papers on Language and Literature* 36, no. 3 (2000): 227.
Stein, Richard L. *Victoria's Year: English Literature and Culture, 1837-1838*. New York: Oxford University Press, 1987.
Stone, Marjorie. *Elizabeth Barrett Browning*. New York: St. Martin's Press, 1995.

Symonds, John Addington. "A Comparison of Elizabethan with Victorian Poetry." *Fortnightly Review* 45, no. 265 (January 1889): 55–79.
Taylor, Beverly. "Guide to the Year's Work: Elizabeth Barrett Browning." *Victorian Poetry* 55, no. 3 (Fall 2017): 337–48.
"Terrorist Novel Writing." *The Spirit of the Public Journals for 1797*, 2nd edn. London: James Ridgway, 1799.
Thain, Marion, ed. *The Lyric Poem: Formations and Transformations*. Cambridge: Cambridge University Press, 2013.
"The bodies of the four German nuns." *London Times*, 11 December 1875, 12.
Torgerson, B. E. *Reading the Brontë Body: Disease, Desire, and the Constraints of Culture*. Basingstoke: Palgrave Macmillan, 2007.
Townshend, Dale and Angela Wright, eds. *Ann Radcliffe, Romanticism and the Gothic*. Cambridge: Cambridge University Press, 2014.
Tucker, Herbert F. *Browning's Beginnings: The Art of Disclosure*. Minneapolis: University of Minnesota Press, 1980.
Tucker, Herbert F. "Dramatic Monologue and the Overhearing of Lyric." In *Lyric Poetry: Beyond New Criticism*, ed. Chaviva Hosek and Patricia Parker. Ithaca, NY: Cornell University Press, 1985, 226–43.
Tucker, Herbert F. "From Monomania to Monologue: 'St. Simeon Stylites' and the Rise of the Victorian Dramatic Monologue." *Victorian Poetry* 22, no. 2 (1984): 121–37.
Visick, Mary. *The Genesis of Wuthering Heights*. Hong Kong: Hong Kong University Press, 1967.
Wagner, Corinna, ed. *Gothic Evolutions: Poetry, Tales, Context, Theory*. Toronto: Broadview, 2014.
Wagner, Jennifer Ann. *A Moment's Monument: Revisionary Poetics and the Nineteenth-Century English Sonnet*. London: Associated University Presses, 1996.
Wagner-Lawlor, Jennifer A. "The Pragmatics of Silence, and the Figuration of the Reader in Browning's Dramatic Monologues." *Victorian Poetry* 35 (1997): 287–302.
Waldman, Suzanne. *The Demon and the Damozel: Dynamics of Desire in the Works of Christina Rossetti and Dante Gabriel Rossetti*. Athens: Ohio University Press, 2008.
Walpole, Horace. *The Castle of Otranto, a Gothic Story*, 5th edn. London: J. Dodsley, 1786.
Watt, James. *Contesting the Gothic: Fiction, Genre, and Cultural Conflict, 1764–1832*. Cambridge: Cambridge University Press, 2004.
Watt, R. J. C. "Hopkins and the Gothic Body." In *Victorian Gothic: Literary and Cultural Manifestations in the Nineteenth Century*, ed. Robbins, Ruth and Julian Wolfreys. London: Palgrave Macmillan, 2000, 60–89.
Weatherby, Harold L. and Harold Weatherby. "Problems of Form and Content in the Poetry of Dante Gabriel Rossteti." *Victorian Poetry* 2, no. 1 (Winter 1964): 11–19.

Webster, Augusta. *Augusta Webster: Portraits and Other Poems*. Edited by Christine Sutphin. Peterborough, ON: Broadview, 1999.

Whale, John. *The Politics of the Picturesque: Literature, Landscape, and Aesthetics since 1770*. Edited by Stephen Copley and Peter Garside. Cambridge: Cambridge University Press, 1994.

Wiesenfarth, Joseph. *Gothic Manners and the Classic Manners*. Madison: Wisconsin University Press, 1988.

Wilt, Judith. *Ghosts of the Gothic: Austen, Eliot, and Lawrence*. Princeton: Princeton University Press, 1980.

Wolffe, John. *The Protestant Crusade in Great Britain 1829–1860*. Oxford: Oxford University Press, 1991.

Wolfreys, Julian. *Victorian Hauntings: Spectrality, Gothic, the Uncanny and Literature*. New York: Palgrave, 2002.

Wolfson, Susan. *Romantic Shades and Shadows*. Baltimore: Johns Hopkins University Press, 2018.

Wollstonecraft, Mary. *A Vindication of the Rights of Men, in a Letter to the Honourable Edmund Burke, occasioned by his Reflections on the Revolution in France*, 2nd edn. London: J. Johnson, 1790.

Wollstonecraft, Mary. *A Vindication of the Rights of Woman*, 2nd edn. Edited by Carol H. Poston. New York: Norton, 1988.

Wollstonecraft, Mary. *A Vindication of the Rights of Woman; and, The Wrongs of Woman, or, Maria*. New York: Pearson Longman, 2007.

Wordsworth, William. "Preface to the Lyrical Ballads," 2nd edn [1800)]. In *Lyrical Ballads 1798 and 1800: William Wordsworth and Samuel Coleridge*. Edited by Michael Gamer and Dahlia Porter. Toronto: Broadview, 2008.

Wordsworth, William. *The Complete Poetical Works of William Wordsworth*. London: E. Moxon, 1869.

Wordsworth, William. *The Poetical Works of William Wordsworth*, 2nd edn. Edited by Ernest de Selincourt. Oxford: Clarendon, 1959.

Wordsworth, William. *The Poetical Works of William Wordsworth*, vol. 3: *Miscellaneous Sonnets*. London: E. Moxon, 1841.

Wright, Angela. *Britain, France and the Gothic, 1764–1820: The Import of Terror*. Cambridge: Cambridge University Press, 2013.

Wright, Angela. *Gothic Fiction: A Reader's Guide to Essential Criticism*. Basingstoke: Palgrave Macmillan, 2007.

Wu, Duncan, ed. *Romanticism: An Anthology*, 4th edn. Oxford: Blackwell, 2006.

Index

Adorno, Theodor, 22
Aikin, Anna Laetitia and John, 105, 165–67, 198–9
Alexander, Christine, 259, 263, 276–77, 279
Alighieri, Dante, 149, 169
Allen, Emily, 16
Armstrong, Isobel, 10, 73, 80, 277
Austen, Jane, 4, 10, 17, 106, 135, 204, 260, 263–4
  Northanger Abbey, 4, 264

Barbauld, Anna Laetitia *see* Aikin, Anna Laetitia
Barrett, Elizabeth *see* Browning, Elizabeth Barrett
Beardsley, Aubrey, 186
Beckford, William, 17, 65, 94, 107–8
Bentham, Jeremy, 54
Billone, Amy, 26n, 105
Bloom, Harold, 9, 22
Botting, Fred, 10
bouts-rimés, 21, 94, 119, 122–7, 130–2, 238, 245
Bowles, Samuel, 105
Bridges, Robert, 211, 224, 231
Brontë, Anne, 261, 266, 275
  Agnes Grey, 269
Brontë, Branwell, 261, 275
Brontë, Charlotte, 261, 263, 276–6, 278–9n
  Jane Eyre, 11, 259
  Tales of Angria and Glass Town, 261, 275; *see also* Gondal
  Villette, 11, 22, 163, 204n, 259, 261, 278n
Brontë, Emily, 20, 22, 258–77, 280n
  "High waving heather," 272–4
  "The Prisoner," 269–70, 277
  "Silent is the House—," 269–70, 277
  Wuthering Heights, 11, 22, 259, 261, 266, 269, 277, 279n
Brontë, Patrick, 260, 263, 280n

Browning, Elizabeth Barrett, 10, 20–2, 72, 94, 108–19, 123, 129, 135–9n, 223, 230, 233, 245, 259, 262, 271
  Aurora Leigh, 94, 109, 114, 118–19
  Poems (1844), 94, 109, 111, 117, 271
  "The Prisoner," 109–11
  "The Runaway Slave at Pilgrim's Point," 114
  Sonnets from the Portuguese, 109, 139n
  "The Soul's Expression," 109, 112–19, 129
Browning, Robert, 1, 10, 20, 33, 36, 38, 78, 79–80n, 223, 259
  "Andrea del Sarto," 38, 67–71, 78
  Bells and Pomegranates, 48
  "Caliban Upon Setebos," 71, 73–4, 86n, 229
  "The Confessional," 38, 59–62
  "Dis Aliter Visum," 71
  Dramatic Lyrics, 33, 59, 67
  Dramatis Personae, 46, 71–2, 79n
  "James Lee's Wife," 71
  "The Last Ride Together," 71
  "Madhouse Cells," 20, 35, 37, 46
  Men and Women, 46, 67, 71
  Mister Sludge, "The Medium," 38, 71–8
  "My Last Duchess," 1, 33–4, 36, 74
  Pauline, 10, 34
  Pippa Passes, 20, 38, 48–57, 63, 76, 78, 82n, 84n
  "Porphyria's Lover," 33–4, 39, 47, 53, 57, 64, 74, 79n, 188–9, 229
  The Ring and the Book, 3, 63
  "The Soliloquy of Spanish Cloister," 20, 38, 57, 62–7, 70, 78, 89n, 115, 217, 226
  "The Statue and the Bust," 71
  "Two in the Campagna," 71
Buchanan, Robert, 159–60, 195–9, 203
Burke, Edmund, 19, 152, 158–9, 161, 167, 197, 202n; *see also* sublime

Buzard, James, 159, 203n
Byron, Glennis, 26n, 36, 80n
Byron, Lord, George Gordon, 5, 16, 159, 261, 263–6
   Childe Harold's Pilgrimage, 5
   The Corsair, 5
   The Giaour, 5

Castle, Terry, 13, 15, 155, 167, 169, 271, 275–7
Catholic Relief Acts (1791, 1793), 218
caudated sonnets, 213, 237–8
Chitham, Edward, 276
Clery, Emma, 11, 17, 88n
Clough, Arthur, 7
Coleridge, Samuel Taylor, 3, 16, 28–9n, 76–7, 90, 104–5, 134n, 158–62, 195–7, 222, 278n
   Christabel, 86n, 154, 163
   Lyrical Ballads, 3, 99, 102, 104, 115
   Rime of the Ancient Mariner, 62, 79n, 86n
Collins, Wilkie, 2
confession, confessional, 6, 22, 38, 44, 57–63, 210–33, 262; *see also* Browning, "The Confessional"
confinement, self-confinement, *or* imprisonment, 1–8, 14, 20–3, 34–5, 68, 85, 90–103, 109–22, 130–2, 133n, 1362n, 144, 160, 172, 194, 199, 210–6, 228, 232–6, 258, 262; *see also* enclosure
Contagious Disease Act (1864), 21, 113
Cook, Eliza, 92
Cornforth, Fanny, 146, 169–71, 188, 198, 205
Crane, Walter, 144
Crary, Jonathan, 162
Criminal Law Amendment Act (1885), 6
curtal sonnets, 213, 232, 237–8

Danahay, Martin A., 198–9
Darwin, Charles, 196
Davie, Donald, 220, 226
Davison, Carol Margaret, 85n, 201n, 271, 280n
De La Cruz, Sor Juana Inés, 132
De Quincey, Thomas, 163–7, 181, 183, 194, 197–8
De Sade, Marquis, 16, 211
   Justine, 55
De Staël, Madame, 92, 159
Derrida, Jacques, 13
Dickinson, Emily, 10, 92

Dixon, Richard Watson, 211, 231, 241
double works, 2, 9, 21, 70, 144–99; *see also* picture poems; Rossetti, Dante Gabriel
Doyle, Arthur Conan, 72
Drake, Nathan, 16
dramatic monologue, 1, 5–9, 15–16, 20, 26n, 28n, 34–78, 79–88n, 117, 127, 177–8, 226–9, 261, 267
Dubois, Martin, 247
Dubrow, Heather, 8, 133n

eavesdropping, 1, 6, 20, 35, 37, 40, 52, 56–7, 75, 81n, 83n, 223; *see also* overhearing; Gothic overhearing
Eliot, George, 7, 27, 252, 253
Ellis, Virginia, 241, 248
enclosure, poetics of, *or* Gothic enclosure, 14, 21, 34, 91, 95, 100, 119, 121, 131; *see also* confinement
explained supernatural, 17–18, 72, 77, 146, 154, 162, 168, 199, 246, 275; *see also* realist supernatural

Feldman, Paula, 105
Felluga, Dino Franco, 16
Female Gothic, 11, 12, 17–19, 31n, 94, 108, 146; *see also* Male Gothic
Ferguson, Frances, 54–5, 167
fin de siècle, 2, 11, 129, 140n
Fleenor, Julian, 17, 259
Fleshly School of Poetry, 21, 160, 203n, 227
French Revolution, 2, 4, 19

Gamer, Michael, 10, 31n
Gaylin, Ann, 52, 81n, 83n
Gazzaniga, Andrea, 115, 138–9n
Gezari, Janet, 259, 269, 277n
Gilbert, Sandra and Sara Gubar, 10, 259
Gilpin, William, 159
Godwin, William, 7, 20, 28, 64, 95, 111, 116
   Caleb Williams, 20, 64, 95, 111
Golden, Catherine, 175, 181–2
Goldsmith, Oliver, 220
Gondal, non-Gondal, 258–62, 264–75
Gothic
   heroine, 2–3, 13–20, 25n, 40–3, 50, 90–132, 153–5, 194, 199, 261–2, 275; *see also* Gothic poetess
   motherhood, 2, 6, 21, 94, 108–9, 114–15
   overhearing, 2, 6–8, 20, 22–3, 33, 35–6, 38, 40, 56–7, 67, 78, 201n, 258

Index   301

picturesque, *or* picturesque scenes of terror, 158, 160–6, 180, 197
poetess; *see also* Gothic heroine; poetess; sonneteer, figure of the (female)
reader response, 24n, 36, 104, 155, 162, 166, 172, 182–3, 196–8, 240
shock and swap, 6–7, 21, 144, 150–1, 154–5, 161–2, 166–7, 170–2, 181, 183, 197–9, 224, 244–6, 258
sonnets, 23, 91, 96, 241; *see also* metasonnets; poetics of enclosure
tropes and forms, 1–8, 12, 20–1, 49, 94–6, 102–6, 131, 150–4, 197, 212–15, 221–32, 260–2
Grass, Sean, 110
Griffith, Eric, 121

Hardy, Thomas, 7
Harper, Frances, 92
H. D. (Hilda Doolittle), 92
Heilman, Robert, 24n, 259, 264
Helsinger, Elizabeth, 111, 140n
Hemans, Felicia, 15, 92, 117
Higgins, Leslie, 227, 231, 252n
Hoeveler, Diane Long, 11, 17, 215, 218, 19, 259, 262
Hogg, James, 211, 252, 265
Hogle, Jerrold, 10
Hollander, John, 111, 134n
Home, Douglas, 77
Hopkins, Gerard Manley, 3, 9–10, 15, 20–2, 132, 210–51, 259, 262, 272–4
    "Ash Boughs," 237, 238
    Author's Preface, 237, 238, 244
    "The Caged Skylark," 232–7, 243
    "Carrion Comfort," 213, 224, 235
    curtal and caudated sonnets, 213, 232, 237–8
    "No Worst, There is None," 213, 224, 229–30, 235
    "Peace," 237–8
    "Pied Beauty," 237–8, 243, 245
    "Terrible Sonnets," 21, 212–13, 221, 224–33, 245
    "The Windhover," 238–40, 245, 251
    "The Wreck of the Deutschland," 3, 9, 210–11, 213, 239–51, 272
Hornesfeld Manuscript, 265, 269
horror, 17, 155, 161, 167, 195, 202n; *see also* terror; Male Gothic
Hulme, Robert, 10
Hunt, Leigh, 99, 240
Hurley, Kelly, 26n, 61

imprisonment, *see* confinement; self-confinement; enclosure
Inquisition, Spanish, 7, 20, 22, 35, 38–9, 56–62, 64–72, 78, 85n, 88n, 99, 115, 211, 217–18, 231–2
inscape, 211–14, 232, 238–43, 246, 249, 251, 252n, 271–2
instress, 21, 211–14, 238, 240–6, 252n, 271–2

Jackson, Virginia, 15, 78–9, 93
James, Henry, 170, 206n
Johnson, Claudia, 151, 167

Keats, John, 5, 10, 11, 13, 16, 28n, 47, 79n, 91, 94, 98, 111, 117, 119–20, 135n, 220, 233–4, 236
    The Eve of Saint Agnes, 5, 16, 105, 135n, 261
    "If By Dull Rhymes Our English Must Be Chain'd," 94–5, 100–3, 117, 119–20, 236, 245
    Isabella, or the Pot of Basil, 5, 16, 105, 135n, 261
    "La Belle Dame Sans Merci," 5, 261
    Lamia, 5
    "Ode to a Nightingale," 44, 67
Kingsley, Charles, 86, 216, 221–22
Knight, Richard Payne, 159
Knoepflmacher, Ulrich, 16, 28, 47, 82
Kramnick, Jonathan, 8, 25n

Landon, Letitia Elizabeth, 92, 103, 127, 129
Lane, William 3, 17, 28, 31, 135
Langbaum, Robert, 36, 57, 66, 78
Le Fanu, Sheridan, 16, 221
Lee, Sophia, 17
Leighton, Angela, 26, 37, 93, 111, 140, 277
Levine, Caroline, 12, 15, 25
Levine, Naomi, 118
Levinson, Marjorie, 8
Levy, Amy, 15, 80, 127, 129
    "To a Minor Poet" 114
    "To a Dead Poet," 127
Lewis, Matthew, 1–3, 5, 7, 9, 11, 16–20, 23, 25n, 34, 40, 46–9, 59, 62, 70, 92, 95, 100, 104, 108, 115, 155, 161–2, 175, 183, 187, 195, 197, 211, 215–17, 223, 226, 247, 250
    The Monk, 1, 9, 17, 20, 25n, 34–5, 46, 56–8, 60, 62, 87n, 95–6, 100, 104, 115, 151, 155–61, 166, 186, 189, 194, 196, 201–2n, 209n, 226, 278n

Lootens, Tricia A., 92–3, 106, 126–7, 129, 142–3
Lorrain, Claude, 160, 203n

McCarthy, Anne, 16, 162–4, 167, 194, 201
McGann, Jerome, 149, 170, 177, 191, 198, 205
Maitland, Thomas *see* Buchanan, Robert
Male Gothic, 12, 17, 31n, 94, 108, 167, 223; *see also* Female Gothic
Mariani, Paul, 211
Married Women's Property Act (1870), 6, 94
Martin, John, 263, 278
Martin, Meredith, 10, 249–50
Matrimonial Causes Act (1857), 94
Maturin, Charles, 85n, 215, 218
  Melmoth the Wanderer, 85n, 218
Meeke, Mary, 17
Meredith, George, 7
Mermin, Dorothy, 26, 36, 80, 93, 136
metasonnets, 1, 5, 20, 91–7, 109, 111, 118–19, 122–3, 234
Milbank, Alison, 218
Miles, Robert, 10, 17, 31n
Mill, John Stuart, 23, 33, 39–48, 55–6, 63–5, 70, 79n, 81n, 6, 232
Milton, John, 159, 186, 203, 235, 278
  Paradise Lost, 159
Moers, Ellen, 17, 31n, 259
More, Hannah, 93, 117
Morgan, Monique, 16
Morris, Jane, 144, 146, 169–70, 175–8, 180, 182, 186, 198, 201n, 207n
Morris, Mary "May," 207n
Morris, William, 144, 179, 200–1n, 207–8n

Netland, John T., 220, 246
Nersessian, Anahid, 8, 25n
New Critics, 11–12, 23, 258
New Formalism, 8, 12, 15
Newman, John Henry, 211, 216, 218, 221–2, 233, 253n
Ngai, Sianne 166, 197
Nicholls, Arthur, 267

O'Malley, Patrick, 13, 157, 215–18, 221–2, 228, 250
overhearing *see* Gothic overhearing; eavesdropping
Oxford Movement, 5, 13, 131, 211–12, 214–20, 233

Patmore, Coventry, 140, 211, 231
Paxton, Amanda, 219

Paz, Denis, 219
Pearsall, Cornelia, 10, 37, 78
Perloff, Marjorie, 12
Phelan, John, 122, 133n
physical close reading, 8–9, 19, 91–2, 100, 183, 196, 240, 245–51, 258; *see also* Gothic reader response
picture poems, 1, 5, 9, 146–9, 167, 171–97, 224, 259; *see also* double works
picturesque, 151, 158–66; *see also* picturesque scenes of terror; Gothic picturesque
Pitchrod, Lois, 237
Plath, Sylvia, 92, 129
Platzner, Robert, 10
Poe, Edgar Allan, 11, 16, 170, 261
poetess, 19–20, 90–132, 138n, 142–3n, 271; *see also* Gothic poetess; sonneteer, figure of the
Polidori, John, 221
Pre-Raphaelite Brotherhood, 5, 21, 144, 8
  The Germ, 148
Prettejohn, Elizabeth, 149, 183
Price, Uvedale, 159
Prins, Yopie, 15, 78–9, 93, 117, 129
Proctor, Adelaide Anne, 92
Punter, David, 10, 32n
Purves, Maria, 218–19
Pusey, Edward, 227, 237

Radcliffe, Ann, 1–23, 34, 40–50, 56, 59, 62–3, 90–109, 70–7, 90–109, 122–3, 132, 135–6n, 144, 144–99, 203n, 211–33, 250, 260–77
  The Castles of Athlin and Dunbayne, 16, 132n
  A Sicilian Romance, 16, 132n; "The Bat," 90, 106
  Gaston de Blondeville, 16
  "Go, Pencil!," 90, 106–7
  The Italian, 15–16, 20, 35, 41, 45–8, 56–8, 62–3, 70, 85n, 87n, 90, 96, 100–1, 219, 263
  The Mysteries of Udolpho, 1–3, 16–20, 34–5, 43–5, 50, 56–7, 70, 90, 95–7, 100, 104–7, 144, 146, 150–8, 161–6, 171, 180, 194, 201n, 204n, 215–16, 264, 271, 275–7
  The Romance of the Forest, 16, 20, 29n, 56, 95–6, 101, 109, 136n
  "Shipwreck," 90
Ratchford, Fannie, 266, 275, 279n
Reader, Simon, 227

realist supernatural, 2, 10, 13, 17–18, 21, 146–50, 154, 162–7, 194; *see also* explained supernatural
Reeve, Clara, 17
Richter, David, 11
Riede, David, 26n, 49, 54–5, 79n, 82n, 149, 69
Robinson, Daniel, 105
Robinson, Mary, 29n, 79n, 92–3, 103–5, 117, 195, 209n
Roche, Regina Maria, 17, 29n
Rogers, Deborah, 18, 114
Roman Catholic Relief Act (1829), 5–6, 215
Roper, Derek, 264, 267, 269–70, 276
Rosa, Salvatore, 160
Rossetti, Christina Georgina, 10, 20–2, 90, 93–4, 103, 117, 119, 122, 126, 140–3n, 223, 231, 233, 238, 245, 252n, 259, 262, 271
  "The Convent Threshold," 231
  Later Life, 122
  Maude, 94, 119, 122–31, 238
  Monna Innominata, 122
  A Pageant and Other Poems, 119
  "The Prisoner," 266, 269–70, 277
  "The Thread of Life," 90, 94, 103, 119–22, 126, 131
Rossetti, Dante Gabriel, 2, 9–10, 20–2, 79n, 132, 144–99, 200n, 205n, 213, 223, 227, 239–40, 248–50, 259
  Astarte Syriaca, 145–6, 161, 169, 171, 178–83, 191–2, 198
  "The Blessed Damozel," 147–9, 168
  Lady Lilith, 145–6, 157, 161, 170–1, 179, 183–91, 195, 198, 205–6n
  Proserpine, or *Proserpina*, 146, 161, 171–8, 183, 191–2, 200
  Sibylla Palmifera, 145–6, 161, 171, 179, 183, 189–94, 198
Rossetti, William Michael, 126, 179–80
Ruskin, John, 34, 140n, 148, 159, 238

Sandler, Stephanie, 9
Sappho, 92, 117, 129
Scott, Sir Walter, 16, 217, 222, 263–5
Sedgwick, Eve, 14–15, 37
self-confinement, *see* confinement; enclosure
Sessions, Ina Beth, 36, 38, 49
Seward, Anna, 91–4, 103–5, 135n
Shaw, David, 16, 28n, 37
Sheets, Robin, 168
Shelley, Mary, 11, 117, 263
  Frankenstein, 11, 117
Shelley, Percy Bysshe, 55
Shklovksy, Victor, 162

Siddal, Elizabeth, 144, 168–9, 200n, 205n
Sigourney, Lydia Huntley, 92
Sinfield, Alan, 70, 80n, 88n
sister arts, poetry and painting, 9, 144–9; *see also* Pre-Raphaelite Brotherhood; double works
Smith, Andrew, 17
Smith, Charlotte, 91–8, 102, 104–7, 113, 117, 126–8, 141n, 261
  Elegiac Sonnets, 96, 98, 102, 106
Solomon, Simeon, 186
sonneteer, figure of the (female), 21, 90–4, 102–32, 133–4n; *see also* poetess
Spark, Muriel, 266
Stanford, Derek, 266, 271
Starzyk, Lawrence, 171
Stevenson, Robert Louis, 2
  The Strange Case of Dr. Jekyll and Mr. Hyde, 2
Stoker, Bram, 2, 221
  Dracula, 2
sublime, 18, 32n, 36, 113, 151–2, 157–63, 167–7, 171–7, 182–3, 194–9, 202–3n, 278n; *see also* Burke, Edmund
suspension, suspense, 128, 150–4, 162–7, 171–2, 176–80, 197–9, 223, 246, 251
Swinburne, Algernon Charles, 11, 79n, 200n
Symonds, John Addington, 79n, 221–2

Tennyson, Lord Alfred, 1–3, 10, 15, 28n, 33, 36, 40, 47, 60, 79–80n, 82n, 88n, 133n, 206n, 217, 226, 259
  "Mariana," 1–2
  Maud, 10, 79n, 201n, 239
  "St. Simeon Stylites," 2, 15, 33, 133n, 217, 226
terror, "terrorist School," 3–4, 17–18, 21, 31n, 104, 134n, 155, 158–9, 161–3, 165–7, 197, 199, 202n, 227; *see also* horror; Female Gothic
picturesque scenes of terror, 158–66, 180–2; *see also* Gothic picturesque
Thain, Marion, 39, 47, 79n, 81n
tort law, 38, 54–5
Townshend, Dale, 17
Tucker, Herbert, 10, 16, 28n, 35–8, 44, 46–7, 56, 82n, 86n

Varma, Devendra, 259

Wagner-Lawlor, Jennifer, 36, 74, 103, 134n
Walpole, Horace, 11, 16–17, 196
  The Castle of Otranto, 16, 24n

Watt, R. J. C., 221, 244, 252n
wavering, poetics of, 188, 210, 212, 224, 239, 242–6, 250–1, 258
Weatherby, Harold, 168, 188
Weber, Augusta, 15, 66, 88n
Whistler, James McNeil, 169, 186
Wilde, Oscar, 142n, 186, 211, 228, 252n
 The Picture of Dorian Gray, 11, 154, 252n
Wilding, Alexa, 146, 168, 170–1, 188, 198, 207n
Wolfson, Susan, 13–15
Wollstonecraft, Mary, 5, 7, 19–20, 92, 94–6, 111, 115–17, 263
 Maria, 20, 94–6, 111, 115–17
Wordsworth, William, 3, 9–10, 31, 36, 44, 79, 82n, 91, 94–5, 98–106, 111, 128, 132, 137, 140n, 220, 233–6, 240–1
 Goody Blake and Harry Gill, 31n, 104, 135n
 Lyrical Ballads, 3, 99, 102, 104, 115
 "Nuns Fret Not," 94–5, 98–102, 128, 132, 235, 240–1
 "The Thorn," 99, 104, 115
Wright, Angela, 11, 17
Wu, Duncan, 113

Yeats, William Butler, 13, 267

EU representative:
Easy Access System Europe
Mustamäe tee 50, 10621 Tallinn, Estonia
Gpsr.requests@easproject.com

www.ingramcontent.com/pod-product-compliance
Lightning Source LLC
Chambersburg PA
CBHW051110230426
43667CB00014B/2513